Instant Pot Cookbook:

Mouth-Watering Meat Recipes

David Maxwell

Contents

About this Book 24
Introduction to the Instant Pot 25
How to use the Instant Pot 28
   3 Most Important Function Keys I Use 28
      Manual 28
      Keep Warm/Cancel 29
      Sautée' 29
   Pressure Release Methods 30
      Quick Release 30
      Natural Release 30
      10 Minute Release 31
Red Meat Recipes 31
   Apple Cider Pork Ribs 31
   Bacon and Braised Cabbage 32
   Bacon Fillets 33
   Balsamic Chops with Onions 34
   Balsamic Fried Beef Roast 36
   Baracoa Chuck 37
   Barbacoa 38
   Beef Brisket with Thyme Sauce 39
   Beef Cremini 40
   Beef Egg Casserole 42
   Beef Mushrooms with Vegetables 43
   Beef Neck with Fire-Roasted Tomatoes 45
   Beef Patties with Cabbage 46

Beef Ragout	48
Beef Ribs with Mashed Cauliflower	49
Beef Roast Curry	50
Beef Steak in Balsamic Sauce	52
Beef Stroganoff	53
Beef Stuffed Peppers	54
Beef with Cabbage	55
Beef with Greens	57
Black Pepper Venison	58
Braised Brisket	59
Braised Short Ribs	60
Braised Venison	62
Butter Beef Roast	62
Butter Lamb Shoulder	64
Button Mushroom and Pepper Pork	65
Caribbean Beef	67
Cauliflower Lamb Curry	68
Cheesy Cajun Beef	69
Chili Lamb Leg	70
Chili Meatballs	71
Chili Mushroom Beef Shank	72
Chili Shoulder Roast	73
Chinese Pork Strips	75
Chinese Pulled Pork	76
Citrus Lamb	77
Classic Ginger Curry	79

Classic Meatloaf 80
Corned Beef and Cabbage 82
Corned Beef with Cabbage 83
Creamy Beef Chili 84
Creamy Garlic Pork Sausage 85
Creamy Kashmir Lamb 86
Creamy Onion Pork Chops 88
Creamy Shiitake Beef Sirloin 88
Creamy Sour Pork Chops 90
Crispy Garlic Lamb Chops 91
Cuban Pork 93
Curried Lamb with Zucchini and Tomatoes 94
Curry Ginger Pork 95
Dijon Pork with Turmeric 96
Easy Butter Chops 97
Easy Lamb Kebab 99
Easy Pork Ribs 100
Eggplant and Lamb Curry 101
Feta Lamb Meatballs in a Tomato Sauce 103
Five Spice Short Ribs 104
Fragrant Lamb Riblets 105
Garlic Lamb Meatballs 106
Garlic Pork Chops 107
Garlic Venison Shoulder 109
Ginger Lamb Shoulder 110
Ginger Pork 111

Gingery Lamb with Apples 113

Goat Meat Stew 114

Goat Shank in Garlic Sauce................................. 115

Greek Feta Meatballs 117

Greek Lamb Skewers... 118

Grilled Beef Tenderloin 120

Ground Beef Shawarma 121

Ground Pork with Eggs....................................... 122

Hawaiian Pork 123

Heavy Balsamic Lamb Shoulder 124

Heavy Mushroom Pork 125

Herb-Packed Meatloaf 126

Hot Lamb Rack with Almonds 127

Hot Tomatillo Pork 129

Hungarian Goulash... 130

Hungarian Porkolt 131

Instant Beef Stew 132

Instant Bolognese Sauce 133

Italian Beef Chuck Roast..................................... 134

Italian Beef Dish 135

Italian Lamb Shanks 136

Italian Roast 137

Jamaican Jerk Pork 139

Jerk Pork... 140

Juicy Pot Roast 141

Kaccha Meatballs 141

Keto Sambar 143

Knorr Demi-Glace Beef 144

Lamb Chops with Vegetables.................................... 146

Lamb Neck with Broccoli.. 147

Lamb Riblets with Herbs 148

Lamb Ribs with Garlic Gravy 149

Lamb Shoulder Hash 151

Lamb with Port Wine and Garlic Gravy................ 152

Lasagne 153

Machaca... 155

Marinated Beef Shank 156

Marinated Pork... 157

Meatballs in Enchilada Sauce................................... 159

Meatballs in Tomato Sauce....................................... 160

Mediterranean Beef Meatballs................................ 161

Mediterranean Pork.. 163

Mediterranean Tenderloin 164

Mexican Pork Carnitas 165

Milk Braised Pork Loin 167

Minty Lamb and Spinach Salad 168

Mustard Cheese Meatballs 169

Parsi Veal with Eggs 170

Pepper Curry... 172

Pepper Short Ribs 173

Pepperoncini Pot Roast.. 174

Picadillo... 175

Pork and Brussel Sprouts 176
Pork Butt Chops in Creamy Gravy 177
Pork Butt in Garlic Gravy 178
Pork Carnitas 180
Pork Chops 181
Pork Chops with Cheese and Prosciutto 182
Pork Chops with Sautéed Peppers 183
Pork Cutlets with Avocado Sauce 185
Pork Cutlets with Mushrooms 186
Pork in Tomato Sauce 187
Pork Keto Risotto with Eggs 188
Pork Leg Roast 190
Pork Loin with Leeks 191
Pork Neck with Jalapeno Peppers 192
Pork Neck with Sesame Seeds and Soy Sauce 194
Pork Shoulder with Sweet Potatoes 195
Pork Steak in Mushroom Sauce 196
Portobello Pork Butt 197
Pressure Cooked Pastrami 199
Puerto Rican Pork 200
Pulled BBQ Pork 201
Quick Cheddar Beef Hash 202
Ribs and Kielbasa with Sauerkraut 203
Rosemary Beef Roast 204
Rosemary Pork Shoulder 205
Saffron Cauliflower Rice with Pork 206

Sage and Marjoram Lamb 208
Savory Cauliflower Beef Roast 209
Seasoned Apple Cider Vinegar Beef.................... 210
Shredded Beef with Pepper Rings....................... 211
Simple Beef and Broccoli Dish 212
Simple Butter Lamb 213
Simple Holiday Roast 214
Simple Tomato Pork Chops................................... 215
Slowly Cooked Lamb Shoulder Kebab.................. 217
Slowly Cooked Pork with Leeks............................ 218
Spicy and Smokey Pork 219
Spicy Burgers... 220
Spicy Garam Masala Beef Roast........................... 221
Spicy Goulash 223
Spicy Lamb 224
Spicy Lamb Coriander Curry................................. 226
Spicy Lamb Patties 227
Spicy Pork Butt 228
Spicy Pork with Celery... 229
Spinach Beef with Bell Peppers............................ 231
Spring Lamb Neck with Greens 232
Spring Onion Pork 234
Spring Vegetable Pork... 235
Steamed Pork Neck.. 236
Sweet and Balsamic Glazed Pork Loin................. 237
Sweet and Sour Pork Ribs 239

Sweet Coconut Lamb Shoulder 240
Sweet Coconut Pork 241
Sweet Dijon Pork Chops 243
Sweet Garlic Pork 244
Sweet Pork with Cauliflower 245
Sweet Ribs 247
Tender Venison 248
Thai Pork with White Pepper Gravy 249
Tomato Lamb Shanks with Thyme 250
Tomato Lamb with Brussels Sprouts 252
Tomato Pork Roast 253
Tomato Rasam 254
Tomato Ribs 256
Veal Masala Curry 257
Veal with Garlic 259
Venison with Béarnaise Sauce 260
Vinegary Lamb Shanks 261
White Wine Pork Belly 262
Wontons 263
Zucchini Noodles with Sesame Seeds 264
Zucchini Pork 266
Zucchini Stew 268

Seafood Recipes 270
5-Minute Mussels Soup 270
5-Minute Shrimp Soup 271
Adobo Shrimps 272

Almond and Dijon Tilapia	273
Bacon Shrimps	274
Black Cauliflower Pasta	275
Caramelized Tilapia	277
Catfish with Soy Sauce and Dill	278
Cheesy Tuna and Noodles	279
Chili Anchovy	279
Chili Hake Fillets	280
Chili Lime Salmon	282
Chili Mahi-Mahi	283
Clams in a White Wine Sauce	284
Classic Fish Stew	285
Classic Lobster Tomato Stew	286
Coconut Milk Cod	287
Cod Chowder with Bacon	288
Cod with Coriander	290
Creamy Crabmeat	291
Creamy Mussel Soup	292
Creamy Shrimp Stew	293
Crunchy Almond Tuna	294
Easy Catfish Stew	295
Easy Shrimp Cauliflower Risotto	296
Fish Korma	297
Fish Pho	299
Fish Sauce Squid	300
Fish Soup	301

- Fish Stock 302
- Garlic Butter Crab Legs.. 303
- Ginger Salmon with Vegetables 304
- Ginger Tilapia Fillets 305
- Green Pesto Tuna Steak 307
- Gruyere Lobster Keto Pasta 308
- Haddock and Cheddar... 309
- Herbed Catfish 310
- Hot and Lemony Salmon 311
- Indian Broccoli Shrimp 312
- Instant Lobster Tails 313
- Instant Steamed Salmon 314
- King Prawn Stew with Avocado.............................. 315
- Lemon Mussels with Asparagus 317
- Lemon Pepper Wild Alaskan Cod 318
- Lemony and Garlicky Prawns 319
- Lime and Garlic Flavored Octopus 320
- Lobster Tails in Butter Sauce.................................. 321
- Mackerel Salad... 322
- Mackerel with Cherry Tomatoes............................. 323
- Mayo Haddock 324
- Mediterranean Salmon 325
- Mussel Chowder 326
- Orange Glazed Salmon Fillets................................. 327
- Parmesan-Crusted Salmon...................................... 329
- Party Oysters.. 330

- Prawn Curry 330
- Quick and Easy Dijon Halibut 332
- Salmon Fillet with Dill 332
- Salmon in Lime Sauce 334
- Salmon Keto Macaroni 335
- Salmon on a Veggie Bed 336
- Salmon Steaks with Cheese 337
- Salmon with Broccoli 338
- Saucy Trout with Chives 339
- Sea Bass in a Tomato Feta Sauce 340
- Seafood Paella 341
- Seafood Stew 342
- Shrimp and Tomato Casserole 344
- Shrimp Casserole 345
- Shrimp Scampi 347
- Shrimp with Asparagus and Cajun Seasoning 347
- Shrimps with Tomatoes and Feta 348
- Shrimpy Zoodles 349
- Simple Squid Stew 350
- Sockeye Salmon 352
- Sour King Scallops 353
- Spaghetti Squash with Shrimp and Asparagus 354
- Spiced Jamaican Jerk Fish 355
- Spicy Pepper Salmon 356
- Spicy Shrimp Keto Pasta 358
- Spicy Trout with Broccoli 359

Spring Fish Stew 361
Spring Onion Prawn Stew.. 362
Squid Rings with Potato and Spinach 364
Steamed Mussels with Thyme 365
Stewed Scallops and Mussels............................. 367
Sweet and Spicy Trout.. 367
Sweet Broccoli Fish Stew.................................... 369
Sweet Rosemary Cod Fillet................................. 370
Sweet Teriyaki Shrimps 372
Thai Seafood Cauliflower Rice............................ 373
Tiger Prawn Paella.. 374
Tilapia Bites 376
Tilapia Curry 377
Tomato Shrimp Stew... 378
Tomato Tuna Pasta 380
Trout Casserole 381
Tuna Steak with Mushrooms 382
White Fish in Ginger Orange Sauce..................... 383
White Fish Stew 384
Wild Alaskan Cod with Cherry Tomatoes............ 385
Wild Alaskan Salmon.. 387
Wrapped Zesty and Herbed Fish 388

Poultry Recipes 390
Aromatic Turkey... 390
Asian Chicken Thighs... 391
Baby Spinach Chicken Wings.............................. 392

Balsamic Chicken Breast with Basil 393

Barbecue Chicken 395

Buffalo Chicken Meatballs 396

Buffalo Chicken Stew 397

Butter Chicken Legs 398

Cajun Chicken Breast 399

Cajun Rotisserie Chicken 400

Cajun Turkey in Marsala Sauce 401

Cauliflower Turkey Risotto 402

Cheesy Chicken with Jalapenos 404

Cheesy Turkey 405

Chicken Alfredo Pasta 406

Chicken and Portabella Mushrooms 407

Chicken and Spinach Salad 408

Chicken Biryani 409

Chicken Breast with Spinach 410

Chicken Cacciatore 412

Chicken Casserole 413

Chicken Curry 414

Chicken Drumsticks with Mushrooms 415

Chicken Fajitas 416

Chicken Legs the Hungarian Way 418

Chicken Lettuce Wraps 419

Chicken Liver Pate 420

Chicken Makhani 421

Chicken Paprikash 422

Chicken Pot Roast	423
Chicken Ranch Immerse	425
Chicken Sausage and Kale Soup	426
Chicken Tagine	427
Chicken Teriyaki	428
Chicken Thighs in a Balsamic Sauce	430
Chicken Tikka Masala	431
Chicken Tostadas	432
Chicken with Capers and Parsley	433
Chicken with Spaghetti Squash	434
Chili Turkey Casserole	436
Chinese Simmered Chicken	437
Cider Partridge with Apples	439
Citrus Chicken Thighs	440
Clear Chicken and Spinach Soup	441
Coconut Turkey Curry	442
Confit Duck Legs with Thyme	443
Cream Cheese Chicken with Bacon	444
Creamy Cauliflower Chicken	445
Creamy Chicken Wings with Peppers	447
Creamy Turkey with Broccoli	449
Curried Chicken with Tomatoes, Spinach and Yogurt	451
Duck Breast with Prosciutto	452
Duck Breast with Prosciutto	454
Duck Breasts with Mushrooms	455

Easy Chicken Thighs 456

Easy Poussin.. 457

Easy Turkey Roast 458

Fall-Off-Bone Chicken Drumsticks...................... 459

Garam Masala Chicken 460

Garlic and Paprika Whole Chicken 462

Garlic Meatballs 463

Garlicky and Lemony Turkey............................... 464

Ginger Chicken with Vegetables 466

Glazed Duck Breast 467

Habanero Chicken... 468

Hearty Duck Stew.. 469

Herb Marinated Chicken Fillets........................... 470

Hot Artichoke Stew 472

Hot Chicken Wings.. 473

Italian Chicken Thighs 474

Italian Duck with Spinach..................................... 475

Jalapeno Chicken 477

Keto Piccata 478

Leftover Chicken with Broccoli and Parmesan.... 479

Lemon Herb Wings 480

Lemongrass and Spinach Turkey Soup................ 481

Lime and Salsa Chicken with Cauliflower Rice 482

Marinara and Cheese Stewed Chicken 483

Masala Chicken Curry 484

Mexican Chicken Soup 485

Moroccan Risotto	486
Mozzarella and Tomato Chicken	487
Mughlai Almond Chicken	488
Orange-Flavored Duck	490
Parmesan Chicken Wings	491
Pina Colada Chicken	492
Pollo en Salsa Roja	493
Roast Goose	494
Roasted Chicken	495
Rosemary Chicken with Bacon	496
Salsa Verde Chicken	498
Savory Turkey Breast	498
Sesame Ginger Chicken	500
Shredded Chicken Breasts	501
Shredded Chicken with Shiitake	502
Simple Chicken Vindaloo	503
Simple Frozen Chicken Breasts	505
Simple Turkey Stew	505
Smoked Slow-Cooked Turkey	506
Soft and Juicy Chicken	507
Spiced Turkey	508
Spicy Chicken Stew	509
Spicy Chicken with Lime	511
Spicy Keto Pasta	513
Spicy Shredded Chicken with Asparagus	515
Summer Chicken Cacciatore	516

Sweet Chicken Leg Stew 517

Sweet Chicken Salad with Cheese....................... 519

Sweet Chicken Thighs 520

Sweet Chicken Wings....................................... 521

Sweet Chili Thighs with Cloves.......................... 522

Sweet Orange Turkey Legs................................ 524

Sweet Turkey Drumsticks.................................. 526

Taco Chicken 527

Tandoori Chicken 528

Tarragon Chicken with Mushrooms.................... 530

Teriyaki Chicken Thighs with Peppers................ 531

Thai Basil Goose Cubes 532

Thyme Roasted Chicken with Dill...................... 533

Tikka Masala 535

Turkey and Cauliflower Enchilada Casserole 536

Turkey and Mushrooms in a Creamy Wine Sauce 538

Turkey Breast with Cranberries 539

Turkey Breast with Garlic Gravy........................ 541

Turkey Breast with Gorgonzola Sauce 542

Turkey Breast with Salsa Verde 543

Turkey Burgers.. 545

Turkey Cauliflower Curry 546

Turkey Keto Lasagna 547

Turkey Leg with Garlic..................................... 550

Turkey Meatballs in Sweet Sauce 551

Turkey Meatballs in Tomato Sauce 552

Turkey Roast 553

Turkey with Mushrooms 554

Turmeric Chicken 556

White Chicken with Cauliflower............................ 558

Worcestershire Belizean Chicken......................... 559

BONUS: Breakfast Recipes 561

Almond Bread in a Mug 561

Almond Flour Breakfast Bread 562

Almond Porridge 563

Asparagus with Cottage Cheese........................... 565

Avo Bacon Muffins 566

Avocado Chicken with Spinach 567

Avocado Eggs Stir-Fry... 569

Baby Spinach Egg Cups... 570

Bacon and Cheese Egg Bake.................................. 571

Bacon Brussels Sprouts 572

Bacon Cheese Rolls 573

Baked Avocado with Eggs 575

Beef Kale Patties 576

Beef Shiitake Bowl 577

Blackberry Cobbler.. 578

Blueberry Cinnamon Scones 579

Boiled Eggs with Spinach....................................... 581

Breakfast Biscuit.. 583

Breakfast Brownie Muffins..................................... 584

Breakfast Caulicheese 585

Breakfast Cauliflower Tots 586

Breakfast Cinnamon Bars 587

Breakfast Frittata 588

Breakfast Plum Cake 590

Broccoli Ham and Pepper Frittata 591

Carrot and Pecan Muffins 592

Cauliflower and Sausage Egg Pie 593

Cauliflower Fritters 594

Cauliflower Mash 596

Cauliflower-Crusted Sausage and Avocado Breakfast Pizza 597

Cheesy Bacon and Chive Omelet 598

Cheesy Breakfast Bagels 599

Cheesy Chili Mexican Frittata 600

Cheesy Egg Muffins 602

Cheesy Eggs de Provence 603

Cheesy Quesadillas 604

Cheesy Tomato Frittata 606

Cherry Clafoutis 607

Chia Rum Pancakes 608

Chicken and Greens Frittata 609

Chorizo Shakshuka 612

Cinnamon Pancakes 613

Coconut Cherry Pancakes 614

Cottage Cheese and Pine Nut Egg Pie 615

Cream Cheese Pancakes	616
Creamy Avocado Muffins	617
Creamy Mushrooms with Thyme	619
Creamy Raspberry Mug Cake	620
Creamy Smoked Salmon	621
Creamy Vanilla Chia Seeds	623
Crustless Meat-Loaded Quiche	624
Crustless Quiche	625
Delicious Pumpkin Bread	626
Easy Deviled Eggs	628
Eggs and Cream	629
Eggs with Spicy Marinara Sauce	630
Giant Ricotta and Blueberry Pancake	632
Green Beans with Bacon	633
Ground Beef with Steamed Cauliflower	634
Ham and Dill Pressure-Cooked Eggs	635
Hollandaise Eggs and Ham	637
Indian Zucchini Kheer	637
Italian Omelet with Herbs	638
Jalapeno Egg Poppers	639
Jalapeno Popper Keto Frittata	640
Kale Cheddar Cheese Omelet	643
Leek Stir-Fry	644
Mushroom and Spinach Omelet Pie	645
Mustard Pork with Mushrooms	646
No-Crust Tomato & Spinach Quiche	647

Onion and Spinach Omelet with Goat Cheese 649
Pizza Frittata 650
Poached Eggs with Garlic Spinach........................ 651
Poached Eggs with Mushrooms 652
Poached Eggs with Tomatoes 654
Poppy Seed Lemony Muffins 654
Pumpkin Hemp Spread 656
Quick and Easy Paprika Eggs 657
Raspberry Mousse 658
Rich Plantain Bread 659
Ricotta and Sausage-Crusted Pie 660
Salted Thyme Biscuits 661
Sausage and Bacon Omelet 663
Sausage and Cheddar Frittata............................... 664
Sausage and Eggs Casserole................................. 665
Scotch Eggs 666
Scrambled Eggs with Cranberries 667
Scrambled Eggs with Ground Beef...................... 669
Scrambled Eggs with Tomato and Green Onions 670
Simple Hardboiled Eggs 671
Simple Spicy Scrambled Eggs 672
Slow-Cooked Good-Morning Casserole 673
Smoked Salmon Baked Eggs 674
Spicy Mushroom Chicken with Eggs................... 675
Spinach Bacon Frittata 676
Spinach Omelet... 677

Steamed Eggs with Scallions 678

Steamed Eggs with Scallions 679

Sunrise Almond and Coconut Cake 681

Sweet Chia Pudding 682

Thyme Prosciutto Eggs 683

Veggie Egg Cups 684

Zucchini Walnut Bread 685

Endnote 687

About this Book

My name is David Maxwell, and I am a nutritionist and fitness enthusiast based in New York. As a nutritionist, I am helping out people with their diet plans all the time.

In order to have full control over what you eat, you will need to cook your own food. However, if you work full time or have a hectic schedule, you will hardly ever have the time to cook using conventional means. This is where the Instant Pot comes in. The instant pot is easily one of the most popular and fastest growing cooking appliances of today's time and rightly so. Using the instant pot, you can cook all your favourite dishes lightning fast and with minimal effort!

Introduction to the Instant Pot

The instant pot is one of the most popular kitchen gadgets at present. The instant pot is gaining popularity today because it is easy to use, and does EVERYTHING!

It can slow cook a recipe over several hours, or prepare the same recipe in less than ten minutes! Vegetables, poultry, breakfast food, or any other food that comes to your mind, can be cooked with the instant pot, and in multiple ways.

Before we get started with the recipes, I would like to introduce the Instant pot to you, in case you're a beginner, or don't even have an instant pot yet. It is totally worth it to invest in an instant pot.

On a personal note, I absolutely LOVE my instant pot. I am currently using the IP-DUO60, which is one of the most popular instant pot models in America. If you have a different model, or wish to buy a different model, don't worry. All instant pot models have similar functions and all recipes in this book will turn out beautifully, no matter which instant pot you are using.

Go ahead and browse the different instant pot models on amazon.com if you don't own one yet>>

Why the Instant Pot?

Simply put, the Instant pot is an electric pressure cooker + slow cooker. If you're a busy person who likes to come home to delicious hot food, or simply a lazy person who likes to fix and forget, the Instant Pot will sail your boat in either case.

Like all pressure cookers, the instant pot can cook food under high temperature and pressure, greatly reducing the cooking time and energy needed. Although pressure cooking is fast and energy efficient, this does not give the food enough time to the ingredients to achieve the epitome of flavour. Although pressure cooking is great in a rush, chicken is best cooked slowly.

Another great thing about the instant pot is that you do not require any skill to cook delicious meals. If your ingredients are fresh, every recipe will turn out great, no matter how bad a cook you are.

Accessory Recommendations

In this section I will the list the Items that I personally like to use, and if you're using the kindle version of this book, you will also find plenty of useful links to amazon.

As I said before, I use the IP-DUO60. A great accessory to use with that is the inner pot.

Make sure the inner pot you buy is the right size for your instant pot.

Go ahead and browse all the available instant pots on amazon>>

Another invaluable accessory is the instant pot tempered glass lid. There are many sizes available, one for every available size of the instant pot. Make sure that the one you get is the right size for your particular instant pot. These are great for storing leftovers in the fridge.

Go ahead and browse the instant pot Lids on amazon>>

How to use the Instant Pot

Make sure you thoroughly read the user guide that comes with the Instant Pot. That is the best guide you will find out there. It contains important safety instructions and also lists functions of all buttons. It is not in the scope of this book to get too deep into it.

So, once you've read the manual of the Instant Pot thoroughly, let us move on to some of the functions I find most useful.

3 Most Important Function Keys I Use

Manual

One button you will be pressing a lot on your instant pot is the 'Manual' button. When you push it, the number 30 is displayed (meaning 30 minutes) then you adjust the time with the + and - buttons.

In case you missed this little detail in the manual, this time displayed means the amount of time it will cook for ONCE THE INSTANT POT ACHIEVES THE COOKING PRESSURE. In other words, the food will cook for a few minutes longer than the number displayed. These few minutes will vary in accordance with the amount of water inside the cooker, and other factors.

So, if you wish to cook rice, the pot will take approximately 5-8 minutes to come to pressure, then cook for approximately 4 minutes, followed by approximately 10 minutes of pressure release. In total, this comes to approximately 20 minutes. So, although potentially you only put the number 4 on the minute counter, it still took you approximately 20 minutes to prepare the rice. So, keep this in mind while you cooking.

Keep Warm/Cancel

This is another button you'll be pressing a lot. After your cooking is done, the instant pot automatically switches to the "Keep Warm" mode. This button witches between the "keep warm" and "standby" mode.

Sautée'

A few of the recipes in this book require you to sauté onions and stuff. You can use this button to do the open lid sauté'. The sauté mode comes in three modes: low, medium, and normal. By default, it is set on normal.

Pressure Release Methods

There is a steam release handle on top of the Instant Pot. If you wish to cook under high pressure, this should be turned to "Sealing". Turning it to "Venting" allows the pressure to gradually release.

The Instant pot cannot be opened until you completely release the pressure.
There are three most common ways of doing that.

Quick Release

If you like livin on the edge, you may use this method to release the steam. When your recipe is cooked, push the cancel button, ensuring the Instant pot is not applying any heat to the food, and then switch the handle to 'venting'.

It goes without saying that you should keep your skin away from the outlet. Also, if your food contains a lot of liquid, some of that liquid might also squirt out with the steam, so be careful.

Use this release method only when you're in a rush. This method wastes energy and could get a little ugly if you're not careful.

Natural Release

This is the most energy efficient way of releasing steam. However, it is also the longest. Depending on the amount of food in the pot, this process could take ten to thirty minutes. While the steam releases, your food is also gradually steam cooked further. So, if you wish to use this method of releasing steam, you might have to heat the food for less time as compared to the quick release method.

10 Minute Release

This is my favourite method of releasing steam. It is a hybrid of both the methods above. Basically, you Allow the pressure to release naturally for ten minutes, and then you turn the valve to 'venting'. This is much safer, as the pressure and temperature are not dangerously high in there anymore.

Red Meat Recipes

Apple Cider Pork Ribs

Aggregate Time to Prepare: **55 Minutes**

Yield: 5 Servings

Ingredients:

- 1 cup beef broth
- 1 onion, thinly sliced
- 2 celery stalks, chopped
- 2 eggs, whole
- 2 green bell peppers, sliced
- 2 lbs pork ribs, chop into smaller pieces
- 3 tbsp apple cider vinegar
- ¼ cup canned tomatoes, sugar-free
- ¼ cup celery leaves, chopped
- ¼ cup light soy sauce

Spices:

- 1 tsp chili powder
- 2 tsp salt
- ¼ cup swerve

How to Cook:

1. Put ribs in the pot and pour in enough water to cover. Shut and secure the lid and set the steam release handle to the "Sealing" position. Push the "Meat" button and turn the timer to 20 minutes on high pressure
2. When finished, release the pressure using the quick release method and open the lid. Move the ribs to a deep container and chill for some time.
3. Remove the water Switch your Instant Pot to "'Sauté" mode.
4. After that, whisk together eggs, apple cider, soy sauce, swerve, salt, and chili powder. Rub the meat with this mixture and let it sit for some time.
5. Put in celery stalks, onions, and peppers to the pot and cook for 8-10 minutes, stirring continuously. Sprinkle with some more salt and put in tomatoes. Pour in the broth and continue to cook until most of the liquid has evaporated.
6. After that put in the readied pork and coat thoroughly with vegetables.
7. Push the "Cancel" button and drizzle with fresh celery leaves. Allow it to sit for some time prior to serving.

Nutritional Info: (Calories 321| Total Fats: 8.6g | Net Carbs: 6.1g | Protein: 51.7g |Fiber: 1.3g)

Bacon and Braised Cabbage

Aggregate Time to Prepare: **20 Minutes**

Yield: **4 Servings**

Ingredients:

- 1 ½ cups Beef Broth
- 1 pound Cabbage, shredded
- 2 tbsp. Butter
- 4 large Bacon Slices, diced
- ½ tsp Black Pepper
- ½ tsp Salt

How to Cook:

1. Switch your Instant Pot to "Sauté" mode and put in bacon.
2. Cook until crunchy and put in the butter to melt.
3. Stir in the cabbage, salt, and pepper.
4. Pour the broth over and shut and secure the lid.
5. Switch the Instant Pot to "High" and cook for 10 minutes.
6. Release the pressure using the quick release method.
7. Your dish is ready! Have fun!

Nutritional Info: (Calories 220 | Total Fats 9g | Net Carbs 5g | Protein 8g | Fiber: 1.2g)

Bacon Fillets

Aggregate Time to Prepare: 30 Minutes

Yield: 4 Servings

Ingredients:

- 1 green bell pepper, thinly sliced
- 1 lb pork fillet, central chop
- 1 pickle, sliced
- 1 small chili pepper

- 2 boiled eggs
- 2 oz prosciutto
- 2 small onions, thinly sliced
- 2 tbsp balsamic vinegar
- 3 bacon slices, chopped
- 3 tbsp butter
- ¼ cup fresh parsley, thinly sliced

Spices:

- 1 tsp smoked pepper

How to Cook:

1. Turn on your Instant Pot and Switch your Instant Pot to "'Sauté" mode. Heat the butter and put in onions, bacon, prosciutto, bell pepper, and chili pepper.
2. Cook for 3-4 minutes, stirring continuously and then put in pickle and season with smoked pepper. Drizzle with balsamic vinegar and continue to cook for one minute.
3. After that put in the fillets and pour in ½ cup of water. Simmer for 10-15 minutes, turning a couple of times.
4. When finished, push the "Cancel" button. Move the fillets to serving plates and spread on top sliced eggs. Serve with the sauce from the pot.

Nutritional Info: (Calories 396 | Total Fats: 21.7g | Net Carbs: 5.4g | Protein: 41.7g | Fiber: 1.5g)

Balsamic Chops with Onions

Aggregate Time to Prepare: **55 Minutes**

Yield: 4 Servings

Ingredients:

- 2 large onions, chopped
- 2 tbsp olive oil
- 3 tbsp balsamic vinegar
- 3 tbsp butter
- 4 garlic cloves, whole
- 4 pork chops, approximately 1-inch thick

Spices:

- 1 tsp dried thyme
- 1 tsp salt

How to Cook:

1. Rub the meat with spices and save for later.
2. Oil-coat a fitting baking pan with oil and place chops along with onions and whole garlic cloves. Drizzle with some more oil and tightly cover with aluminium foil.
3. Turn on your Instant Pot and pour in two cups of water. Set the trivet at the bottom of the inner pot and place the pan on top.
4. Shut and secure the lid and set the steam release handle. Switch your Instant Pot to "Manual" mode and cook for 35 minutes on high pressure.
5. When finished, depressurize using the quick release method. Cautiously open the lid and remve the baking pan with pork.
6. Remove the trivet and the rest of the water from the pot and Switch your Instant Pot to "'Sauté" mode.
7. Oil-coat the inner pot with butter and heat up. Put in balsamic vinegar and briefly cook – for 1 minute.

8. After that put in onions from the baking pan and stir thoroughly. Cook for another minute and finally put in the meat.
9. Brown for 2-3 minute on each side.
10. When finished, take out of the pot and serve instantly.

Nutritional Info:(Calories 429 | Total Fats: 35.6g | Net Carbs: 6.4g | Protein: 19.1g |Fiber: 1.7g)

Balsamic Fried Beef Roast

Aggregate Time to Prepare: **25 Minutes**

Yield: **8 Servings**

Ingredients:

- 1 tbsp olive oil
- 2 lbs beef chuck roast, chop into bite-sized pieces
- 3 garlic cloves, crushed
- ¼ cup balsamic vinegar
- ½ cup heavy cream
- ½ cup shallots, chopped

Spices:

- 1 tbsp dried parsley, thinly sliced
- 1 tsp black pepper, ground
- 1 tsp dried oregano, ground
- 1 tsp salt
- ¼ tsp dried marjoram, ground

How to Cook:

1. Thoroughly wash the meat under cold running water and pat dry with a kitchen towel. Move to a large

cutting board and chop into bite-sized pieces. Rub with salt and pepper and save for later.
2. Oil-coat the stainless steel insert of your instant pot with olive oil. Put in shallots and garlic. Stir-fry for 2-3 minutes, stirring continuously.
3. After that, put in meat chops and cook for 10 minutes.
4. Pour in the heavy cream and balsamic vinegar. Drizzle with the rest of the spices and stir thoroughly. Bring it to a boil and cook for 10-15 additional minutes, or until the sauce thickens.
5. Move to a serving dish and if you want, drizzle with some lemon juice prior to serving.
6. Have fun!

Nutritional Info: (Calories 464 | Total Fats 36.1g | Net Carbs: 2.5g | Protein 30.2g |Fiber: 0.2g)

Baracoa Chuck

Aggregate Time to Prepare: **75 Minutes**

Yield: **4 Servings**

Ingredients:

- 1 Onion, sliced
- 1 tbsp. Cumin
- 1 tbsp. Oregano
- 2 pounds Chuck Roast
- 4 Garlic Cloves, minced
- 8 ounces canned Green Chilies, chopped
- ½ cup Water
- ½ tsp Pepper
- Juice of 2 Lemons

How to Cook:

1. Mix everything in the Instant Pot.
2. Shut and secure the lid and set it to MANUAL.
3. Switch the Instant Pot to "High" and cook for 60 minutes.
4. Push CANCEL and release the pressure quickly.
5. Shred the meat with 2 forks inside the pot.
6. Switch your Instant Pot to "Sauté" mode and cook for 5 additional minutes.
7. Your dish is ready! Have fun!

Nutritional Info: (Calories 640| Total Fats 44g | Net Carbs 4.5g | Protein 63g |Fiber: 1.5g)

Barbacoa

Aggregate Time to Prepare: **485 Minutes**

Yield: **9 Servings**

Ingredients:

- 1 tbsp. Dried Oregano
- 1 tsp Ground Black Pepper
- 2 Chipotle Chiles in Adobo Sauce
- 2 tbsp. Adobo Sauce
- 2 tbsp. Apple Cider Vinegar
- 2 tbsp. Lime Juice
- 2 tsp Cumin
- 2 tsp Sea Salt
- 2 whole Bay Leaves
- 3 lbs. Beef Brisket (trimmed and chop into 1½ inch cubes)
- 5 cloves Garlic (minced)

- ½ cup Beef Broth
- ½ tsp Ground Cloves

How to Cook:

1. Put the broth, chipotle chilies in adobo sauce, garlic, apple cider vinegar, lime juice, dried oregano, cumin, sea salt, black pepper, and ground cloves using a food processor and blend until smooth.
2. Put beef in a container and pour over it mixed spices. Toss thoroughly to mix.
3. Move into the Instant Pot and put in bay leaves.
4. Set the Instant Pot to "Slow Cook" and adjust to low pressure, and manually turn the timer and cook for 8 hours.
5. Allow for the Instant Pot to naturally release the pressure. Remove the lid and shred the meat using a fork.
6. Stir thoroughly so that meat would reabsorb the juices and serve.

Nutritional Info: (Calories: 242 | Total Fats: 11g | Net Carbs: 1g | Proteins: 32g |Fibers: 1g)

Beef Brisket with Thyme Sauce

Aggregate Time to Prepare: 45 Minutes

Yield: 5 Servings

Ingredients:

- 1 cup beef stock
- 1 cup heavy cream
- 1 medium-sized onion, chopped
- 2 lbs beef brisket

- 3 garlic cloves, thinly sliced

Spices:

- 1 tsp sea salt
- 2 tsp fresh thyme, chopped
- ½ tsp black pepper, ground
- ½ tsp red pepper flakes

How to Cook:

1. Thoroughly wash the meat under cold running water and pat dry with a kitchen paper. Liberally rub with salt and pepper and save for later.
2. Turn on the Instant Pot and put in onions and garlic, Switch your Instant Pot to "'Sauté" mode and cook for 3 minutes.
3. After that, put in meat and pour in the beef stock and 1 cup of water. Shut and secure the lid and close the steam release handle. Switch your Instant Pot to "Manual" mode and turn the timer to 25 minutes. Cook on "High" pressure.
4. When finished, depressurize using the quick release method and open the pot.
5. Stir in the heavy cream and the rest of the spices. Simmer for 10 additional minutes.
6. Have fun!

Nutritional Info: (Calories 437 | Total Fats 29.4g | Net Carbs: 3g | Protein 56.5g | Fiber: 0.8g)

Beef Cremini

Aggregate Time to Prepare: **40 Minutes**

Yield: 4 Servings

Ingredients:

- 1 cup Cremini mushrooms, thinly sliced
- 1 lb beef shoulder roast, chop into bite-sized pieces
- 1 small red onion, diced
- 1 tbsp butter
- 2 cups beef broth
- ½ cup heavy cream

Spices:

- 1 tsp dried thyme, ground
- 1 tsp garlic powder
- 1 tsp salt
- ½ tsp white pepper, ground

How to Cook:

1. Turn on your Instant Pot and Switch your Instant Pot to "'Sauté" mode. Melt the butter in the stainless steel insert and put in mushrooms. Drizzle with salt and thyme. Cook for 10 minutes and then pour in the heavy cream. Bring it to a boil and simmer for 5 minutes, stirring intermittently.
2. When finished, move the mushrooms along with liquid to a food processor. Pulse until creamy and smooth. Save for later.
3. Put in the meat chops to the pot and drizzle with white pepper, garlic powder, and a pinch of salt. Pour in the broth and securely lock the lid by moving the valve to the "Sealing" position. Turn the timer to 15 minutes and cook on "High" pressure.
4. When finished, depressurize using the quick release method and open the pot.

5. Move the meat to a serving plate and drizzle with creamy sauce.
6. Serve instantly.

Nutritional Info: (Calories 283 | Total Fats 17.2g | Net Carbs: 3.4g | Protein 26.7g | Fiber: 0.7g)

Beef Egg Casserole

Aggregate Time to Prepare: **15 Minutes**

Yield: 3 Servings

Ingredients:

- 1 lb ground beef
- 1 tbsp fresh parsley, thinly sliced
- 1 tbsp olive oil
- 6 large eggs
- ¼ cup milk, full-fat
- ¼ cup mozzarella, crumbled

Spices:

- 1 tsp salt
- ¼ tsp chili powder
- ¼ tsp dried rosemary, ground
- ½ tsp black pepper, ground

How to Cook:

1. In a large mixing container, mix ground beef, mozzarella, milk, and parsley. Combine until thoroughly blended.
2. In a separate container, mix eggs and all the spices. Mix until fluffy and pour over the meat mixture. Stir all thoroughly with a wooden spatula.

3. Oil-coat a fitting oven-safe container with olive oil and put in meat mixture. Tenderly push with your palm to flatten the surface and save for later.
4. Turn on the Instant Pot and pour 1 cup of water in the stainless steel insert. Place your trivet in the bottom of your instant pot and place the container on top.
5. Shut and secure the lid and close the steam release handle. Switch your Instant Pot to "Manual" mode and turn the timer to 7 minutes. Cook on "High" pressure.
6. When your instant pot sounds the end signal. Perform a quick pressure release and open the lid.
7. Cautiously remove the container from the pot and serve instantly.
8. If you want, you can also spread on top sour cream or Greek yogurt.

Nutritional Info: (Calories 483 | Total Fats 25g | Net Carbs: 2g | Protein 59.9g | Fiber: 0.3g)

Beef Mushrooms with Vegetables

Aggregate Time to Prepare: 35 Minutes

Yield: 8 Servings

Ingredients:

- 1 cup broccoli, chopped
- 1 cup button mushrooms, chopped
- 1 cup cauliflower, chopped
- 1 medium-sized red bell pepper, chopped

- 1 medium-sized red onion, chopped
- 2 garlic cloves, thinly sliced
- 2 lbs beef tenderloin, chop into bite-sized pieces
- 4 cups beef stock

Spices:

- 1 tsp black pepper, ground
- 1 tsp sea salt
- ¼ tsp dried marjoram, ground
- ¼ tsp dried sage, ground

How to Cook:

1. Thoroughly wash the meat under cold running water and pat dry with a kitchen paper. Move to a cutting board and chop into bite-sized pieces. Drizzle with salt, pepper, sage, and marjoram. Combine with your hands to allow spices to penetrate into the meat.
2. Turn on your Instant Pot and place the meat in the stainless steel insert. Spread on top mushrooms and vegetables. Slowly pour in the broth and shut and secure the lid.
3. Set the steam release handle by moving the valve to the "Sealing" position. Switch your Instant Pot to "Manual" mode and turn the timer to 25 minutes. Cook on "High" pressure.
4. When your instant pot sounds the end signal, depressurize using the quick release method and open the pot.
5. Move all to a serving container and if you want, garnish with some thinly sliced chives or green onions.

Nutritional Info: (Calories 263 | Total Fats 10.8g | Net Carbs: 3.3g | Protein 35.4g | Fiber: 1.3g)

Beef Neck with Fire-Roasted Tomatoes

Aggregate Time to Prepare: **30 Minutes**

Yield: **4 Servings**

Ingredients:

- 1 cup beef broth
- 1 cup onions, thinly sliced
- 1 small zucchini, cubed
- 12 oz beef neck, chopped into bite-sized pieces
- 2 cups fire-roasted tomatoes, diced
- 2 tbsp black sesame seeds
- 3 tbsp butter
- ½ cup Parmesan cheese, grated

Spices:

- 1 tbsp cayenne pepper
- ½ tsp chili pepper
- ½ tsp cumin powder
- ½ tsp salt

How to Cook:

1. Turn on your Instant Pot and heat up the butter on the "Sauté" mode. Put in onions and cook until translucent.
2. After that put in tomatoes and sesame seeds. Pour in approximately 3 tablespoons of water and continue to cook for 5 minutes.

3. Lastly, put in the meat and zucchini. Drizzle with salt, chili, cayenne, and cumin powder. Stir thoroughly and pour in the broth.
4. Shut and secure the lid and set the steam release handle to the "Sealing" position. Switch your Instant Pot to "Manual" mode and turn the timer to 15 minutes.
5. When done, depressurize using the quick release method and open the lid.
6. Drizzle with grated Parmesan and serve.

Nutritional Info: (Calories 310 | Total Fats: 17.4g | Net Carbs: 5.1g | Protein: 30.2g |Fiber: 17.4g)

Beef Patties with Cabbage

Aggregate Time to Prepare: **25 Minutes**

Yield: 8 Servings

Ingredients:

- 1 lb purple cabbage, shredded
- 1 tbsp fresh parsley
- 1 tbsp olive oil
- 2 eggs
- 2 garlic cloves, minced
- 2 oz cottage cheese
- 3 lbs lean ground beef
- ½ cup heavy cream
- ½ cup tomatoes, diced

Spices:

- 1 tsp salt
- ¼ tsp dried rosemary, ground

- ½ tsp black pepper, ground
- ½ tsp dried oregano, ground

How to Cook:

1. Mix ground beef, cottage cheese, eggs, garlic, and parsley in a large mixing container. Drizzle with some salt and pepper and mix until thoroughly mixed. Make the 1 1/2 –inch balls and tenderly push with your palm to form patties. Save for later.
2. Oil-coat the stainless steel insert of your instant pot with olive oil. Switch your Instant Pot to "Sauté' mode and put in the patties. Cook for 2-3 minutes on each side and then put in tomatoes. Bring it to a boil and cook for 5 additional minutes. Remove the patties from the pot and move to a container. Cover with a lid and save for later.
3. After that, put in shredded cabbage, heavy cream, and cottage cheese. Drizzle with oregano and rosemary and shut and secure the lid. Close the steam release handle and switch to "Manual' mode. Turn the timer to 5 minutes and cook on "High" pressure.
4. When finished, depressurize using the quick release method and open the pot. Allow it to chill for some time.
5. Move patties to serving dish and serve with creamy cabbage.
6. Have fun!

Nutritional Info: (Calories 397 | Total Fats 16.5g | Net Carbs: 3g | Protein 55g | Fiber: 1.7g)

Beef Ragout

Aggregate Time to Prepare: **40 Minutes**

Yield: 6 Servings

Ingredients:

- 1 cup tomatoes, diced
- 1 small celery stalk, chopped
- 1 small onion, thinly sliced
- 1 small red chili pepper, diced
- 1 tbsp olive oil
- 2 cups beef stock
- 2 lbs beef steak, chop into bite-sized pieces
- 4 garlic cloves, crushed

Spices:

- 1 bay leaf
- 1 tsp black pepper, ground
- 1 tsp dried oregano, ground
- 1 tsp salt

How to Cook:

1. Turn on your Instant Pot and coat the stainless steel insert with olive oil. Switch your Instant Pot to "Sauté' mode and onions, celery, garlic, and chili pepper. Stir-fry for 4-5 minutes, or until the onions translucent.
2. Put in meat chops and drizzle with salt, oregano, and pepper. Pour in the beef stock and throw in the bay leaf. Shut and secure the lid and close the steam release handle. Switch your Instant Pot to "Manual" mode and turn the timer to 20 minutes. Cook on "High" pressure. When your instant pot sounds the

end signal, release the pressure using the quick release method and open the lid.
3. Stir in the tomatoes and Switch your Instant Pot to "'Sauté" mode. Bring it to a boil and cook for 10 additional minutes, stirring intermittently. Remove the bay leaf and move all to a serving dish. If you want, you can also garnish with some thinly sliced parsley or spread on top sour cream.

Nutritional Info: (Calories 322 | Total Fats 12.1g | Net Carbs: 2.6g | Protein 47.4g |Fiber: 1g)

Beef Ribs with Mashed Cauliflower

Aggregate Time to Prepare: 50 Minutes

Yield: 6 Servings

Ingredients:

- 1 cup cauliflower
- 1 tbsp butter
- 1 tbsp olive oil
- 2 lbs beef ribs
- 2 tbsp green onions, chopped
- 3 cups beef broth
- ¼ cup milk

Spices:

- 1 tbsp fresh mint, chopped
- 1 tsp cayenne pepper, ground
- 1 tsp dried thyme, ground
- 1 tsp garlic powder
- 1 tsp sea salt

How to Cook:

1. Turn on your Instant Pot and grease the stainless steel with olive oil. Put in the beef ribs and drizzle with salt, thyme, and cayenne pepper. Cook for 5 minutes on each side, or until browned.
2. Pour in 2 cups of broth and shut and secure the lid. Close the steam release handle and switch to "Manual' mode. Turn the timer to 10 minutes and cook on "High" pressure.
3. When finished release the pressure using the quick release method and open the pot. Allow it to chill for some time.
4. Remove the meat along with liquid from the pot and pat dry the insert with a kitchen paper.
5. Switch your Instant Pot to "Sauté' mode and melt the butter in the insert. Put in cauliflower and drizzle with some salt and mint to taste. Cook for 2-3 minutes, stirring intermittently.
6. Pour in the rest of the broth and milk. Shut and secure the lid. Set the steam release handle and switch to "Manual' mode. Turn the timer to 7 minutes and cook on "High" pressure.
7. When finished, depressurize using the quick release method and open the pot. Move all to a large container and mash with a potato masher. Stir in the garlic powder and serve with beef ribs.

Nutritional Info: (Calories 350 | Total Fats 14.7g | Net Carbs: 2g | Protein 49.2g |Fiber: 0.7g)

Beef Roast Curry

Aggregate Time to Prepare: **45 Minutes**

Yield: 6 Servings

Ingredients:

- 1 cup cauliflower, chopped
- 1 cup cherry tomatoes, diced
- 1 medium-sized onion, chopped
- 2 cups unsweetened coconut milk, full-fat
- 2 lbs beef roast, chop into bite-sized pieces
- 2 tbsp coconut oil
- 2 tbsp fresh parsley, thinly sliced

Spices:

- 1 tsp garlic powder
- 1 tsp sea salt
- 2 tsp curry powder
- ½ tsp black pepper, ground

How to Cook:

1. Turn on the Instant Pot and push the "Sauté" button. Melt the coconut oil in the stainless steel insert and put in meat. Cook for 5 minutes, or until lightly browned. Take the meat out of the pot and save for later.
2. Put in onions and stir-fry for 3-4 minutes, or until the onions translucent. After that, put in diced tomatoes and drizzle with salt, pepper, curry powder, garlic powder, and parsley. If you want, you can also put in some dried oregano or thyme. Bring it to a simmer and cook for 5 minutes.
3. Pour in the coconut milk and put in cauliflower. Return the meat to the pot and stir thoroughly. Scurely lock the lid and close the steam release handle.

4. Push the "Manual" button and turn the timer to 25 minutes. Cook on "High" pressure.
5. When finished, depressurize using the natural release method.
6. Open the pot and move the curry to a serving pot.
7. Serve warm.

Nutritional Info:(Calories 526 | Total Fats 33.2g | Net Carbs: 8.8g | Protein: 48.7g |Fiber: 3.3g)

Beef Steak in Balsamic Sauce

Aggregate Time to Prepare: 30 Minutes

Yield: 6 Servings

Ingredients:

- 1 cup balsamic vinegar
- 1 cup bone broth
- 1 small red onion, thinly sliced
- 2 tbsp olive oil
- 4 garlic cloves, thinly sliced
- 4 lbs beef steak
- ½ cup button mushrooms, sliced
- ½ cup heavy cream

Spices:

- 1 tsp black peppercorns, whole
- 1 tsp fresh rosemary, thinly sliced
- 2 tsp fresh thyme, thinly sliced
- 2 tsp sea salt

How to Cook:

1. Thoroughly wash the meat under cold running water and move to a large container. Put in balsamic vinegar, salt, thyme, peppercorns, and rosemary. Combine to mix and cover with an aluminium foil. Refrigerate for at least 30 minutes.
2. Plug in your in instant pot and coat the stainless steel insert with olive oil. Switch your Instant Pot to "Sauté' mode and put in mushrooms, garlic, and onions. Cook for 5 minutes, stirring intermittently. Put in meat along with marinade and pour in the broth.
3. Shut and secure the lid and switch to "Manual' mode. Turn the timer to 15 minutes and cook on "High" pressure. When finished, depressurize using the quick release method and Switch your Instant Pot to "'Sauté" mode again. Stir in the heavy cream and cook for 5 additional minutes.
4. Move the meat to a serving platter and spoon over the balsamic sauce. If you want, you can also drizzle with some thinly sliced green onions or fresh parsley.

Nutritional Info: (Calories 670 | Total Fats 27.3g | Net Carbs: 2.5g | Protein 95.8g | Fiber: 0.7g)

Beef Stroganoff

Aggregate Time to Prepare: 20 Minutes

Yield: 4 Servings

Ingredients:

- 1 cup Beef Broth

- 1 lbs. Beef Sirloin Steak (chop into ½ inch strips)
- 1 small Onion (diced)
- 1 tsp Smoked Paprika
- 2 cloves Garlic (crushed)
- 2 rashers Bacon (diced)
- 3 tbsp. tomato paste
- ½ cup Sour Cream
- ½ lbs. Mushrooms (quartered)

How to Cook:

1. Put all ingredients, except sour cream, in the Instant Pot and stir to mix.
2. Shut and secure the lid and turn the timer and cook for 20 minutes at high pressure.
3. Depressurize using the natural release method and then mix in the sour cream.
4. Serve warm.

Nutritional Info: (Calories: 260 | Total Fats: 14g | Net Carbs: 4.8g | Proteins: 26.5g |Fibers: 1.2g)

Beef Stuffed Peppers

Aggregate Time to Prepare: **35 Minutes**

Yield: **4 Servings**

Ingredients:

- 1 cup Tomato Sauce
- 1 Egg. Beaten
- 1 pound ground Beef
- 1 Tomato, diced
- 1 tsp Italian Seasoning
- 2/3 cup Water

- 4 Bell Peppers
- 5 tbsp. Coconut Flour
- ½ Onion, diced

How to Cook:

1. In a large container, place the beef, diced tomatoes, egg, seasoning, and flour.
2. Combine to mix until thoroughly blended.
3. Cut off the tops of the bell peppers. Remove the seeds.
4. Separate the meat mixture among the hollowed peppers.
5. Mix the water and half of the tomato sauce in the Instant Pot.
6. Put the peppers and pour the rest of the tomato sauce over.
7. Close peppers with the cut-off tops.
8. Switch the Instant Pot to "High" and cook for 15 minutes.
9. Depressurize using the natural release method.
10. Your dish is ready! Have fun!

Nutritional Info: (Calories 443 | Total Fats 32g | Net Carbs 9g | Protein 23g |Fiber: 5g)

Beef with Cabbage

Aggregate Time to Prepare: **40 Minutes**

Yield: **4 Servings**

Ingredients:

- 1 cup cabbage, shredded
- 1 lb ground beef

- 1 red bell pepper, thinly sliced
- 2 cups beef broth
- 2 green chili peppers
- 2 small onions, thinly sliced
- 4 garlic cloves, crushed
- 4 tbsp butter

Spices:

- 1 tbsp peppercorn
- 1 tbsp yellow mustard seeds
- 2 tsp coriander seeds
- 2 tsp turmeric powder
- 4 cloves, whole
- ½ tsp ginger powder

How to Cook:

1. Turn on your Instant Pot and put in meat, onions, garlic, peppercorn, coriander seeds, mustard seeds, and turmeric powder. Stir thoroughly and Switch your Instant Pot to "'Sauté'' mode.
2. Cook for 4-5 minutes, stirring continuously.
3. After that put in cabbage and stir thoroughly. Carry on cooking for an additional 2-3 minutes.
4. Pour in the broth and put in the rest of the ingredients. Stir thoroughly and shut and secure the lid. Set the steam release handle and switch to ''Manual' mode. Turn the timer to 10 minutes on high pressure.
5. When finished, depressurize using the natural release method and open the lid. Serve instantly.

Nutritional Info: (Calories 365 | Total Fats: 19.4g | Net Carbs: 6.5g | Protein: 38.1g | Fiber: 1.7g)

Beef with Greens

Aggregate Time to Prepare: 50 Minutes

Yield: 8 Servings

Ingredients:

- 1 cup fresh kale, chopped
- 1 cup fresh spinach, chopped
- 1 small onion, chopped
- 2 cups beef broth
- 2 lbs beef chuck roast, chop into bite-sized pieces
- 2 tbsp butter
- 4 garlic cloves, thinly sliced

Spices:

- 1 tsp sea salt
- ¼ tsp dried thyme, ground
- ½ tsp black pepper, ground

How to Cook:

1. Mix spinach and kale in a large colander. Thoroughly wash thoroughly under cold running water and drain. Chop into small pieces and save for later.
2. Turn on your Instant Pot and Switch your Instant Pot to "'Sauté" mode. Melt 1 tablespoon of the butter in the stainless steel insert and put in garlic and onions. Cook for 3-4minutes, stirring intermittently.
3. Put in meat and drizzle with salt and pepper. Pour in the broth and lock the lid. Set the steam release handle and switch to "Manual' mode. Turn the timer to 20 minutes and cook on "High" pressure.
4. When finished, depressurize using the quick release method by moving the valve to the "Venting"

position. Open the pot and put in spinach, kale and the rest of the butter. Cook for 5 additional minutes, or until the greens are wilted.
5. Turn off your Instant pot and move all to a serving container.
6. If you want, you can also spread on top sour cream or cream cheese and have fun!

Nutritional Info: (Calories 458 | Total Fats 34.8g | Net Carbs: 2.2g | Protein 31.5g |Fiber: 0.5g)

Black Pepper Venison

Aggregate Time to Prepare: **50 Minutes**

Yield: 6 Servings

Ingredients:

- 1 cup cherry tomatoes, sliced
- 1 tbsp. butter
- 2 large onions, thinly sliced
- 2 lbs. leg of venison, chopped into bite-size pieces
- 2 tbsp. olive oil

Spices:

- 1 tsp salt
- 2 tbsp. fresh parsley, thinly sliced
- ½ tsp black pepper

How to Cook:

1. Thoroughly wash the meat under cold running water and pat dry with a kitchen paper. Cut into bite-sized pieces and save for later.

2. Turn on the Instant Pot and grease the bottom of the stainless steel insert with some oil. About 2 tablespoons will be enough.
3. Make the first layer with chopped meat. Put in onions, tomatoes, parsley, salt, and pepper. Stir thoroughly and put in approximately 2 cups of water.
4. Closet he lid and set the steam release handle. Push the 'Meat' button and cook for 30 minutes.
5. When finished, depressurize using the natural release method and open the lid. Stir in one tablespoon of butter and serve instantly.

Nutritional Info: (Calories 246 | Total Fats 8.2g | Net Carbs: 4.4g | Protein 34.1g |Fiber: 1.4g)

Braised Brisket

Aggregate Time to Prepare: 80 Minutes

Yield: 8 Servings

Ingredients:

- 1 tbsp. Mustard
- 2 cups Onions (chop to ribs)
- 2 lbs. Beef Brisket (chop into four pieces)
- 2 tbsp. Tomato Puree
- 2 tbsp. Worcester Sauce
- 2 tsp Ground Black Pepper
- 2 tsp Liquid Smoke
- 2 tsp Salt
- ½ cup Water
- ½ tsp Xanthan Gum

How to Cook:

1. Sprinkle the brisket with salt and pepper and save for later.
2. In a container mix together the water, tomato puree, Worcester and liquid smoke. Save for later.
3. Spread the onions in the Instant Pot, place the brisket on top and pour over with mixed sauce.
4. Shut and secure the lid, and turn the timer and cook for 70 minutes at high pressure.
5. When finished depressurize using the quick release method.
6. Remove the brisket with tongs, and using a hand blender blend together onions and cooking juices.
7. Switch your Instant Pot to "Sauté" mode and put in xanthan gum. Stir thoroughly and reduce to favoured consistency.
8. Allow the brisket to rest for 10 minutes before slicing and serving with the reduced sauce.

Nutritional Info: (Calories: 200 | Total Fats: 8g | Net Carbs: 4g | Proteins: 24g | Fibers: 1g)

Braised Short Ribs

Aggregate Time to Prepare: **60 Minutes**

Yield: **8 Servings**

Ingredients:

- 1 can Diced Tomatoes
- 1 large Onion (diced)
- 2 stalks Celery (diced)
- 2 tbsp. Coconut Sugar
- 2 tbsp. Olive Oil
- 2 tsp Garlic (minced)

- 2 tsp Ground Black Pepper
- 2 tsp Sea Salt
- 3 tbsp. Coconut Aminos
- 4 lbs. Boneless Beef Short Ribs
- ¼ cup Balsamic Vinegar
- ½ cup Red Wine
- ⅔ cup Paleo Balsamic Ketchup

How to Cook:

1. Pat dry the ribs with a kitchen towel and season them with salt and pepper.
2. Set the Instant pot to "Sauté" and put in one tablespoon olive oil to it. Brown the ribs on both sides, two minutes on each side. Brown them in 2-3 batches to prevent overcrowding them. Save for later browned ribs.
3. Put in another tablespoon of olive oil to the pot, and put in the onions, celery and garlic. Sauté them for 2-3 minutes while intermittently stirring, until they are softened.
4. Put in all rest of the ingredients and stir to mix. Then put in the short ribs and stir to coat them.
5. Shut and secure the lid and turn the timer and cook for 45 minutes at high pressure.
6. When finished allow the pressure to be released naturally for 15 minutes and then quick release it.
7. Serve with mashed or riced cauliflower.

Nutritional Info: (Calories: 387 | Total Fats: 43g | Net Carbs: 8g | Proteins: 38g |Fibers: 3g)

Braised Venison

Aggregate Time to Prepare: **12 Hours**

Yield: **4 Servings**

Ingredients:

- 1 large onion, thinly sliced
- 2 garlic cloves, whole
- 2 lbs. leg of venison
- 2 tbsp. butter
- 3 cups beef stock

Spices:

- 1 bay leaf
- 1 tbsp. fresh thyme
- 1 tsp salt
- ¼ cup celery leaves, chopped

How to Cook:

1. Put the ingredients in your instant pot and set the 'Slow Cooker' mode. Set the steam release handle and adjust to 12 hours.
2. When finished, depressurize using the natural release method and open the lid. Move to a deep pot and bring it to a boil. Decrease the heat to medium and cook until all the liquid evaporates.

Nutritional Info: (Calories 326 | Total Fats 8.5g | Net Carbs: 3.3g | Protein 52.5g | Fiber: 0.8g)

Butter Beef Roast

Aggregate Time to Prepare: **55 Minutes**

Yield: 8 Servings

Ingredients:

- 1 medium-sized onion, chopped
- 1 medium-sized red bell pepper, chopped
- 2 cups bone broth
- 4 lbs beef roast
- 4 tbsp butter, separated
- ½ cup fresh cilantro, chopped

Spices:

- 1 tsp black pepper, ground
- 1 tsp dried oregano, ground
- 1 tsp dried rosemary, ground
- 1 tsp sea salt
- 1 tsp smoked paprika, ground

How to Cook:

1. Turn on your Instant Pot and put in 1 tablespoon of butter in the stainless steel insert. Tenderly stir until melt and put in meat. Drizzle with oregano, rosemary, paprika, salt, and pepper. Cook for 5-7 minutes on each side. Remove the meat to a large container and cover with a lid.
2. After that, put in 1 more tablespoon of the butter to the pot. Put in onions and red bell pepper and cook for 2-3 minutes.
3. Return the meat to the pot and gradually pour in the broth. Shut and secure the lid and close the steam release handle.
4. Switch your Instant Pot to "Manual" mode and turn the timer to 20 minutes. Cook on "High" pressure.
5. When finished, depressurize using the natural release method and open the pot. Switch your Instant Pot to

"Sauté' mode and mix in the rest of the butter and cilantro. Simmer for 10-15 minutes more.
6. Push the "Cancel" button and turn off the pot. Move the meat to serving plate and gradually drizzle with the liquid from the pot.
7. Have fun!

Nutritional Info: (Calories 506 | Total Fats 20g | Net Carbs: 2.2g | Protein 74.3g |Fiber: 0.8g)

Butter Lamb Shoulder

Aggregate Time to Prepare: **50 Minutes**

Yield: 5 Servings

Ingredients:

- 1 tomato, chopped
- 2 cups beef broth
- 2 lbs lamb shoulder, chopped
- 3 tbsp butter
- 4 garlic cloves, crushed
- ½ eggplant, cubed

Spices:

- 1 ½ tsp salt
- 1 cinnamon stick
- 1 tbsp ginger, freshly grated
- 1 tsp black pepper, ground
- 1 tsp onion powder
- 2 tsp coriander powder
- 2 tsp cumin powder

How to Cook:

1. In a small container, mix salt, black pepper, cumin powder, coriander powder, and grated ginger. Save for later.
2. Wash thoroughly the meat and rub with spices. Save for later.
3. Turn on your Instant Pot and Switch your Instant Pot to "'Sauté" mode. Oil-coat the inner pot with butter and heat up. Put in meat, in several batches, and cook for 4-5 minutes, turning once. Take out of the pot and save for later.
4. After that put in eggplant and garlic. Sprinkle with some salt and cook for 5 minutes, stirring continuously. Put in tomatoes and stir thoroughly. Carry on cooking for an additional minute.
5. After that put in the meat and pour in the broth. Shut and secure the lid.
6. Make sure the steam release handle is on the "Sealing" position and switch to "Manual' mode. Cook for 25 minutes on high pressure.
7. When finished, depressurize using the natural release method and open the lid. Serve instantly.
8. If you want, you can also use the "Slow Cooker" mode and cook for 8 hours on low.

Nutritional Info:(Calories 431 | Total Fats: 20.9g | Net Carbs: 2.5g | Protein: 53.7g | Fiber: 1.8g)

Button Mushroom and Pepper Pork

Aggregate Time to Prepare: **40 Minutes**

Yield: **4 Servings**

Ingredients:

- 1 cup button mushrooms, sliced
- 1 garlic clove, crushed
- 1 lb pork loin, chop into bite-sized pieces
- 2 cups beef broth
- 2 red bell peppers, sliced
- 3 tbsp olive oil
- ½ cup sun-dried tomatoes

Spices:

- ¼ tsp black pepper, freshly ground
- ½ tsp dried oregano
- ½ tsp salt

How to Cook:

1. Thoroughly wash the meat and place on a cutting board. Chop into bite-sized pieces and save for later.
2. Turn on your Instant Pot and Switch your Instant Pot to "'Sauté" mode. Oil-coat the inner pot with oil and heat up. Put in peppers and garlic. Cook for 4-5 minutes and then put in the pork.
3. Brown on all sides for about 2 minutes, stirring continuously.
4. After that season with salt, pepper, and oregano. Put in mushrooms, tomatoes, and pour in the broth. Stir thoroughly and shut and secure the lid.
5. Make sure the steam release handle is on the "Sealing" position and switch to "Manual' mode.
6. Turn the timer to 15 minutes on high pressure.
7. When finished, depressurize using the natural release method for 15-20 minutes prior to serving.

Nutritional Info: (Calories 299| Total Fats: 15.4g | Net Carbs: 5.4g | Protein: 33.5g |Fiber: 1.3g)

Caribbean Beef

Aggregate Time to Prepare: 60 Minutes

Yield: 4 Servings

Ingredients:

- 1 cup Water
- 1 tsp Garlic Powder
- 1 tsp grated Ginger
- 1 tsp Thyme
- 2 pounds Beef Roast
- 4 Whole Cloves
- ¼ tsp Pepper
- ½ tsp Salt

How to Cook:

1. Mix all of the spices and rub into the meat.
2. Stick the cloves into the beef.
3. Put the beef inside the Instant Pot.
4. Pour the water around it.
5. Shut and secure the lid and set it to MANUAL.
6. Switch the Instant Pot to "High" and cook for 45 minutes.
7. Release the pressure using the quick release method.
8. Move the beef to a cutting board and shred it with two forks.
9. Serve as favoured.
10. Have fun!

Nutritional Info: (Calories 710| Total Fats 1.1g | Net Carbs 1.1 g | Protein 55g |Fiber: 0.2g)

Cauliflower Lamb Curry

Aggregate Time to Prepare: **45 Minutes**

Yield: **4 Servings**

Ingredients:

- 1 cup coconut milk, full-fat
- 1 cup zucchini chunks
- 1 lb lamb stew meat, cubed
- 2 cups cauliflower florets
- 2 tbsp apple cider vinegar
- 3 tbsp ghee
- 4 garlic cloves, minced

Spices:

- 1 tsp black pepper, freshly ground
- 2 tbsp fresh ginger, grated
- 2 tbsp garam masala
- 2 tsp turmeric powder
- ¼ cup chopped cilantro

How to Cook:

1. Thoroughly wash the meat and place in a container with a tight lid. Sprinkle with garlic, ginger, salt, and pepper. Pour in the coconut milk and apple cider. Combine thoroughly and shut and secure the lid. Refrigerate for 30 minutes.
2. Take the meat out of the fridge and place in the pot along with the cauliflower, ghee, garam masala, and turmeric powder.
3. Stir thoroughly and shut and secure the lid. Make sure the steam release handle is on the "Sealing" position and switch to "Manual' mode.

4. Turn the timer to 20 minutes on high pressure. When finished, release the pressure by moving the pressure valve to the "Venting" position.
5. Open the lid and mix in zucchini. Shut and secure the lid again and continue to cook for an additional 5 minutes on the "Manual" mode.
6. When finished, release the pressure using the quick release method and open the lid.
7. Stir in cilantro and serve instantly.

Nutritional Info:(Calories 457| Total Fats 32.3g | Net Carbs: 5.1g | Protein: 34.8g |Fiber: 3g)

Cheesy Cajun Beef

Aggregate Time to Prepare: **20 Minutes**

Yield: **4 Servings**

Ingredients:

- 1 cup Beef Broth
- 1 pound Ground Beef
- 1 tbsp. Cajun Seasoning
- 1 tbsp. Olive Oil
- 12 ounces Mexican Cheese Blend
- 2 tbsp. Tomato Paste

How to Cook:

1. Switch the Instant Pot to "Sauté" mode and heat the oil.
2. Put in beef and cook until browned.
3. Stir in the tomato paste and Cajun seasoning.

4. Pour the broth over and shut and secure the lid.
5. Switch the Instant Pot to "High" and cook for 7 minutes.
6. Depressurize quickly.
7. Stir in the cheese and cook on HIGH for 5 additional minutes.
8. Release the pressure using the quick release method.
9. Your dish is ready! Have fun!

Nutritional Info: (Calories 400| Total Fats 16g | Net Carbs 4g | Protein 33 g |Fiber: 0.2g)

Chili Lamb Leg

Aggregate Time to Prepare: 60 Minutes

Yield: 4 Servings

Ingredients:

- 2 cups beef stock
- 2 lbs lamb leg, boneless and chopped
- 2 red chili peppers, chopped
- 3 garlic cloves, crushed
- 3 tbsp olive oil

Spices:

- 1 thyme sprig
- 1 tsp salt
- 2 tsp chili powder
- ½ tsp black pepper, ground

How to Cook:

1. Thoroughly wash the meat thoroughly under cold running water and pat dry with a kitchen towel.

2. Rub thoroughly with oil and garlic. Drizzle with salt, pepper, and chili powder. Tightly cover with aluminium foil and refrigerate for 30 minutes.
3. After that plug in the instant pot and remove the meat from the fridge. Put in the pot and put in beef stock. Put in thyme sprig and chopped chili peppers.
4. Shut and secure the lid and set the steam release handle to the "Sealing" position. Switch your Instant Pot to "Manual" mode and turn the timer to 20 minutes on high pressure.
5. When finished, depressurize using the natural release method and open the lid.
6. Serve instantly.

Nutritional Info: (Calories 524 | Total Fats: 27.4g | Net Carbs: 0.9g | Protein: 65.2g | Fiber: 0.1g)

Chili Meatballs

Aggregate Time to Prepare: 40 Minutes

Yield: 4 Servings

Ingredients:

- 1 Egg
- 1 pound ground Beef
- 2/3 Salsa
- ¼ cup Arrowroot
- ¼ tsp Garlic Powder
- ¼ tsp Pepper
- ¼ tsp Salt
- ½ cup Tomato Sauce
- ½ tsp Chili Powder

How to Cook:

1. Mix the meat, egg, arrowroot, salt, pepper, and chili powder, in a container.
2. Make meatballs out of the mixture.
3. Mix everything else in the Instant Pot.
4. Put the meatballs inside and shut and secure the lid.
5. Choose MANUAL.
6. Cook on LOW for 30 minutes.
7. Depressurize quickly.
8. Your dish is ready! Have fun!

Nutritional Info: (Calories 498| Total Fats 19 | Net Carbs 4g | Protein 45g |Fiber: 0.5g)

Chili Mushroom Beef Shank

Aggregate Time to Prepare: **40 Minutes**

Yield: **4 Servings**

Ingredients:

- 1 cup button mushrooms, sliced
- 1 cup tomatoes, diced
- 1 small green chili pepper, chopped
- 1 tbsp olive oil
- 2 cups beef broth
- 2 lbs beef shank
- 3 garlic cloves, minced

Spices:

- 1 tbsp fresh ginger, grated
- 1 tsp dried thyme, ground
- 1 tsp salt

- ¼ tsp red chili flakes

How to Cook:

1. Thoroughly wash the meat under running water and pat dry with a kitchen towel. Rub with salt and pepper and save for later.
2. Turn on the Instant Pot and Switch your Instant Pot to "'Sauté" mode. Oil-coat the stainless steel with olive oil and put in green chili and garlic. Cook for 2 minutes, stirring continuously.
3. Put in mushrooms and cook for 5 minutes.
4. After that, put in meat and drizzle all with thyme, chili, and ginger. Stir thoroughly and pour in the broth. Shut and secure the lid and close the steam release handle.
5. Switch your Instant Pot to "Manual" mode and turn the timer to 25 minutes. Cook on "High" pressure.
6. When your instant pot sounds the end signal, depressurize using the quick release method and open the pot. Switch your Instant Pot to "Sauté' mode and mix in the diced tomatoes. Cook for 5 minutes, stirring intermittently. Turn off your Instant pot and move all to serving containers.

Nutritional Info: (Calories 492 | Total Fats 18.8g | Net Carbs: 3.6g | Protein 72.5g | Fiber: 1.1g)

Chili Shoulder Roast

Aggregate Time to Prepare: **45 Minutes**

Yield: **4 Servings**

Ingredients:

- 1 cup tomatoes, diced
- 1 medium-sized yellow bell pepper, chopped
- 1 small red onion, thinly sliced
- 1 tbsp olive oil
- 2 cups beef broth
- 3 garlic cloves, crushed
- 3 lbs beef shoulder roast

Spices:

- 1 tsp dried basil, ground
- 1 tsp dried oregano, ground
- 1 tsp fresh rosemary, thinly sliced
- 1 tsp red chili powder
- 1 tsp smoked paprika, ground
- 2 tsp sea salt

How to Cook:

1. Put the rinsed meat in a large container and liberally rub with salt, chili powder, paprika, oregano, and basil. Save for later.
2. Turn on your Instant Pot and coat the stainless steel insert with olive oil. Switch your Instant Pot to "Sauté' mode and put in onions and bell peppers. Stir-fry for 3-4 minutes and put in meat.
3. Cook for 5 minutes on each side, or until golden brown.
4. Put in diced tomatoes and pour in the broth. Shut and secure the lid and set the steam release handle. Switch your Instant Pot to "Manual" mode and turn the timer to 20 minutes. Cook on "High" pressure.
5. When your instant pot sounds the end signal, depressurize using the quick release method and open the pot. Cautiously move the meat to a cutting

board. Using two forks, shred and return the meat to the pot.
6. Switch your Instant Pot to "Sauté' mode and cook until sauce thickens. Turn off your Instant pot and mix in the fresh rosemary.
7. Serve warm.

Nutritional Info: (Calories 595 | Total Fats 28.7g | Net Carbs: 5.8g | Protein 72.9g |Fiber: 2.1g)

Chinese Pork Strips

Aggregate Time to Prepare: **55 Minutes**

Yield: **4 Servings**

Ingredients:

- 1 egg
- 1 lb pork neck, chop into 2-inch long strips
- 1 spring onion, thinly sliced
- 1 tbsp rice vinegar
- 2 red bell peppers, sliced into strips
- 2 tbsp dark soy sauce
- 2 tbsp light soy sauce
- 3 tbsp vegetable oil
- ½ cup canned bamboo, chopped

Spices:

- ½ tsp salt
- ½ tsp stevia powder

How to Cook:

1. Thoroughly wash the meat and place on a large cutting board. Using a sharp knife, chop into strips

and place in a deep container. Put in one egg, salt, and soy sauce. Cover with a lid and set it sit for 10-15 minutes.
2. Turn on your Instant Pot and Switch your Instant Pot to "'Sauté" mode. Put in half of the meat and cook for 6-7 minutes, stirring continuously. Repeat with the rest of the meat and take out of the pot. Save for later.
3. After that, coat the inner pot with oil and heat up. Put in bamboo and sliced bell peppers. Cook for 7-8 minutes, stirring continuously.
4. Drizzle with stevia and rice vinegar and put in the meat. Stir thoroughly and put in onions.
5. Carry on cooking for an additional 2-3 minutes.
6. Push the "Cancel" button and serve instantly.

Nutritional Info: (Calories 302 | Total Fats: 15.5g | Net Carbs: 5.3g | Protein: 33g | Fiber: 1.3g)

Chinese Pulled Pork

Aggregate Time to Prepare: 60-65 Minutes

Yield: 6 Servings

Ingredients:

- 1 cup Chicken Broth
- 1 tbsp. Tomato Paste
- 1 tsp Smoked Paprika
- 2 lbs. Pork Shoulder
- 2 tbsp. Garlic Paste
- 2 tsp Ginger (grated)
- 4 tbsp. Soy Sauce
- 4 tbsp. Sugar-Free Tomato Sauce

- 5 drops Liquid Sweetener

How to Cook:

1. Put all ingredients, except pork, in a container and mix thoroughly.
2. Put in pork to the container and toss thoroughly to coat.
3. Move the pork to the Instant Pot and pour over the rest of the sauce.
4. Shut and secure the lid, and set the Instant Pot manually to 60 minutes cooking time at high pressure.
5. Let naturally release the pressure.
6. Shred the pork using a fork and mix thoroughly to soak the sauce.
7. If a thicker sauce is favoured set the Instant Pot to "Sauté" and reduce to favoured consistency.

Nutritional Info: (Calories: 459 | Total Fats: 35g | Net Carbs: 3g | Proteins: 30g | Fibers: 0g)

Citrus Lamb

Aggregate Time to Prepare: 50 Minutes

Yield: 4 Servings

Ingredients:

- 1 cup cherry tomatoes, chopped
- 1 cup cilantro, thinly sliced
- 1 cup coconut milk, full-fat
- 1 lb lamb tenderloin, chopped into bite-sized pieces
- 2 cups chicken broth
- 2 large onions, thinly sliced

- 2 tbsp apple cider
- 2 tbsp lemon juice
- 3 tbsp butter

Spices:

- 1 tbsp cumin powder
- 1 tsp salt
- 2 tsp garam masala
- 2 tsp turmeric powder
- 3 tbsp chili powder

How to Cook:

1. Thoroughly wash the meat under cold running water and pat dry with some kitchen paper. Liberally drizzle with salt and pepper and place in the instant pot.
2. Switch your Instant Pot to "Sauté' mode and cook for 4-5 minutes, stirring intermittently.
3. After that put in the rest of the ingredients and season with spices. Stir thoroughly and shut and secure the lid.
4. Make sure the steam release handle is on the "Sealing" position and switch to "Manual' mode.
5. Turn the timer to 15 minutes on high pressure.
6. When your instant pot sounds the end signal, push the "Cancel" button and depressurize using the natural release method. Cautiously open the lid and chill for some time prior to serving.

Nutritional Info:(Calories 224| Total Fats: 7.4g | Net Carbs: 6.6g | Protein: 28.8g |Fiber: 2.5g)

Classic Ginger Curry

Aggregate Time to Prepare: **35 Minutes**

Yield: **6 Servings**

Ingredients:

- 1 onion, thinly sliced
- 2 cups tomatoes, chopped
- 2 lbs leg of lamb, chopped into bite-sized pieces
- 3 garlic cloves, minced
- 3 tbsp ghee
- 4 cups vegetable broth
- 5 chili peppers, whole

Spices:

- 1 tsp cardamom powder
- 1 tsp cumin powder
- 2 tbsp cayenne pepper
- 2 tsp fennel powder
- 2 tsp salt
- 2 tsp turmeric powder
- 3 tbsp fresh ginger, grated
- 5 cloves
- ½ black pepper, freshly ground
- ½ tsp cinnamon powder
- ½ tsp coriander powder
- ½ tsp nutmeg powder

How to Cook:

1. Turn on your Instant Pot and Switch your Instant Pot to "'Sauté" mode. Oil-coat the inner pot with ghee and put in the meat. Cook for 4-5 minutes or until

lightly browned. Take out of the pot and move to a large platter.
2. After that put in onions, garlic, chilies, and ginger. Carry on cooking for an additional 3-4 minutes, or until the onions are translucent and chilies soft. Stir thoroughly and put in tomatoes.
3. Cook for 3-4 minutes, stirring continuously and then drizzle with the rest of the spices. Pour in the broth and stir thoroughly.
4. Shut and secure the lid and set the steam release handle to the "Sealing" position. Push the "Stew" button.
5. When finished, depressurize using the natural release method and open the lid. Stir thoroughly again and serve instantly.

Nutritional Info: (Calories 385| Total Fats 18.5g | Net Carbs: 4.1g | Protein: 46.6g |Fiber: 1.3g)

Classic Meatloaf

Aggregate Time to Prepare: **70 Minutes**

Yield: **6 Servings**

Ingredients:

- 1 cup almond flour
- 1 cup cherry tomatoes, chopped
- 2 lbs ground pork
- 2 small onions, thinly sliced
- 2 spring onions, thinly sliced
- 2 tbsp butter
- 3 garlic cloves, crushed
- 3 tbsp olive oil

- ½ cup celery stalk, thinly sliced

Spices:

- 1 tsp salt
- 2 tsp dried celery
- ½ tsp white pepper, ground

How to Cook:

1. In a large container, mix the ground pork with onions, spring onions, celery stalk, and garlic. Drizzle with salt, celery, and pepper.
2. After that put in approximately one cup of almond flour and mix thoroughly agan. If you want, you can also put in a handful of thinly sliced almonds for a crunchy taste.
3. Move the mixture to a large piece of plastic foil and cover tightly. Refrigerate for 30 minutes.
4. In the mean time, place cherry tomatoes using a food processor and process until smooth. Put in olive oil and mix thoroughly. Set aside.
5. Take the meat out of the fridge and place back in the mixing container. Put in tomatoes and butter. Combine thoroughly again and shape the meatloaf using a large piece of plastic foil. Put in a baking dish and loosely cover with aluminium foil.
6. Turn on your Instant Pot and set the trivet at the bottom of the inner pot. Pour in one cup of water and place the baking dish on top.
7. Shut and secure the lid and set the steam release handle to the "Sealing" position. Switch your Instant Pot to "Manual" mode and turn the timer to 20 minutes on high pressure.

8. When finished, depressurize using the quick release method and open the lid. Take the pan out of the instant pot and chill for some time.
9. Your dish is ready! Have fun!

Nutritional Info:(Calories 358 | Total Fats: 18.5g | Net Carbs: 3.8g | Protein: 41.4g |Fiber: 1.7g)

Corned Beef and Cabbage

Aggregate Time to Prepare: 20-25 Minutes

Yield: 12 Servings

Ingredients:

- 10-15 Black Peppercorns
- 2 tsp Ground Mustard
- 30 oz. Cabbage (chop into wedges)
- 4 cloves Garlic
- 4 lbs. Corned Beef Brisket
- 4 oz. Carrots (chop into inch chunks)
- 4 stalks Celery (chop into inch chunks)
- 8 oz. Onions (chop into ribs)
- Water, as needed

How to Cook:

1. Put the beef brisket in Instant Pot and pour enough water to just cover it.
2. Put and lock the lit, and set the Instant Pot to "Meat/Stew" and set the timer to 60 minutes at high pressure.
3. When finished allow the pressure to be released naturally and remove the brisket from pot and save for later.

4. Put in all other ingredients to pot, place and lock the lid, and set the Instant Pot to "Soup" and set the timer to 15 minutes.
5. While the vegetables are cooking chop the brisket into half-inch slices and save for later.
6. When vegetables are done depressurize using the quick release method and place the brisket in it to warm up.
7. Serve warm.

Nutritional Info: (Calories: 334 | Total Fats: 22.8g | Net Carbs: 5.5g | Proteins: 23.7g | Fibers: 2.6g)

Corned Beef with Cabbage

Aggregate Time to Prepare: 60 Minutes

Yield: 6 Servings

Ingredients:

- 1 Celery Stalk, chopped
- 1 large Carrot, sliced
- 1 Onion, chopped
- 1 tbsp. Butter
- 1 tsp Garlic Powder
- ½ tsp Cumin
- 2 Bacon Slices, diced
- 3 cups Veggie Broth
- 3 pounds Corned Beef, chopped
- 3 pounds Red Cabbage, chopped
- ½ tsp Salt

How to Cook:

1. Melt the butter in the Instant Pot using the "Sauté" mode.
2. Put in bacon and cook until crunchy.
3. Put in beef and cook until browned on all sides.
4. Stir in the rest of the ingredients.
5. Switch the Instant Pot to "High" and cook for 35 minutes.
6. Your dish is ready! Have fun!

Nutritional Info: (Calories 320| Total Fats 30g | Net Carbs 6g | Protein 30g |Fiber: 1g)

Creamy Beef Chili

Aggregate Time to Prepare: 30 Minutes

Yield: 4 Servings

Ingredients:

- 1 cup heavy cream
- 1 lb ground beef
- 1 medium-sized red bell pepper, chopped
- 1 small red onion, chopped
- 1 tbsp olive oil
- 2 cups tomatoes, diced
- 3 garlic cloves, minced
- ½ cup beef broth

Spices:

- 1 tsp garlic powder
- 1 tsp kosher salt
- ½ tsp chili powder
- ½ tsp dried rosemary, ground
- ½ tsp smoked paprika

How to Cook:

1. Turn on your Instant Pot and Switch your Instant Pot to "'Sauté" mode. Oil-coat the stainless steel insert with olive oil and put in ground beef, onion, and bell pepper. Drizzle with salt and garlic powder. Using a wooden spatula, stir thoroughly and cook for 5 minutes.
2. Put in tomatoes and pour in the broth. Shut and secure the lid and set the steam release handle. Switch your Instant Pot to "Manual" mode and turn the timer to 5 minutes. Cook on "High" pressure.
3. When finished, depressurize using the quick release method and open the pot. Stir in the heavy cream and drizzle with chili powder, salt, paprika, and rosemary.
4. Switch your Instant Pot to "Sauté' mode and cook for 10 additional minutes.
5. Move all to a serving dish and have fun!

Nutritional Info: (Calories 390 | Total Fats 22.3g | Net Carbs: 7.7g | Protein 37.3g | Fiber: 2.3g)

Creamy Garlic Pork Sausage

Aggregate Time to Prepare: 35 Minutes

Yield: 4 Servings

Ingredients:

- ¼ cup Arrowroot
- ¼ tsp Pepper
- ½ tbsp. Olive Oil
- ½ tsp Salt

- 1 pound Pork Sausage
- 1 tsp Thyme
- 2 cups Milk
- 4 Garlic Cloves, minced

How to Cook:

1. Switch the Instant Pot to "Sauté" mode and heat the oil.
2. Put in the garlic and thyme and cook for one minute.
3. Put in sausage and cook it until it becomes brown. Make sure to break the sausage as cooking.
4. Pour 1 ½ cups of the milk over it.
5. Shut and secure the lid. Cook on HIGH for 5 minutes.
6. In the mean time, whisk together the arrowroot, rest of the milk, salt, and pepper.
7. Release the pressure using the quick release method and whisk in the arrowroot mixture.
8. Switch your Instant Pot to "Sauté" mode and cook for 5 minutes, or until thickened.
9. Your dish is ready! Have fun!

Nutritional Info: (Calories 410| Total Fats 30 | Net Carbs 5g | Protein 25g |Fiber: 0.6g)

Creamy Kashmir Lamb

Aggregate Time to Prepare: 50 Minutes

Yield: 4 Servings

Ingredients:

- 1 cup plain yogurt, full-fat
- 1 tbsp fresh parsley, thinly sliced
- 1 tbsp lime juice, freshly squeezed

- 2 lbs lamb shoulder, boneless and chopped into bite-sized pieces
- 2 tbsp olive oil

Spices:

- 1 tsp Kashmir red chili powder
- 1 tbsp fresh ginger, grated
- ¼ tsp saffron
- 1 tsp salt

How to Cook:

1. In a large container, mix yogurt, chili powder, ginger, saffron, and salt. Combine until thoroughly blended and save for later.
2. Thoroughly wash the meat under running water and pat dry with a kitchen paper. Discard any bones and chop into bite-sized pieces.
3. Put the meat in the container with yogurt mixture and stir thoroughly to coat all and blend together. Cover the container with aluminium foil and refrigerate for at least 30 minutes.
4. Turn on the Instant Pot and grease the stainless steel with olive oil. Push the "Sauté" button and put in meat with marinade. Pour in 1 cup of water and securely lock the lid.
5. Close the steam release handle and push the "Manual" button. Turn the timer to 30 minutes and cook on "High" pressure.
6. When finished, release the pressure using the quick release method and open the pot.
7. Push the "Sauté" button and cook for 10 additional minutes, or until the sauce thickens.
8. Move to a serving dish and drizzle with parsley and lime juice prior to serving.

Nutritional Info: (Calories 533 | Total Fats 24.5g | Net Carbs: 6g | Protein: 67.4g | Fiber: 0.3g)

Creamy Onion Pork Chops

Aggregate Time to Prepare: 30 Minutes

Yield: 4 Servings

Ingredients:

- 10 ounces Chicken Broth
- 10 ounces French Onion Soup
- 4 Pork Chops
- ½ cup Sour Cream

How to Cook:

1. Mix the broth and pork in the Instant Pot and shut and secure the lid.
2. switch your instant pot to "Manual" mode.
3. Cook for 12 minutes on HIGH.
4. Depressurize using the natural release method.
5. Stir in the rest of the ingredients.
6. Switch your Instant Pot to "Sauté" mode and cook for 7 minutes.
7. Your dish is ready! Have fun!

Nutritional Info: (Calories 480 | Total Fats 28g | Net Carbs 9g | Protein 37g | Fiber: 1.9g)

Creamy Shiitake Beef Sirloin

Aggregate Time to Prepare: 50 Minutes

Yield: 6 Servings

Ingredients:

- 1 cup heavy cream
- 1 cup pearl onions, chopped
- 1 cup Shiitake mushrooms, chopped
- 1 tbsp butter
- 2 lbs beef sirloin, chop into bite-sized pieces
- 3 cups beef broth
- 5 bacon slices, chopped

Spices:

- 1 tsp black pepper, freshly ground
- 1 tsp fresh sage, chopped
- 1 tsp fresh thyme, chopped
- 1 tsp salt

How to Cook:

1. Turn on the Instant Pot and Switch your Instant Pot to "'Sauté" mode. Put in chopped bacon and stir-fry for 2-3 minutes. Remove the bacon from the pot and save for later.
2. Put in butter and tenderly melt, stirring continuously. Put in mushrooms and onions. Cook for 5-7 minutes and take out of the pot.
3. Put in meat and drizzle with salt and pepper. Cook for 5 minutes and then pour in the broth. Shut and secure the lid and close the steam release handle. Push "Manual" button and turn the timer to 25 minutes. Cook on "High pressure.
4. When finished, depressurize using the quick release method by moving the valve to the "Venting" position.

5. Open the pot and put in mushroom mixture, bacon, and heavy cream. Switch your Instant Pot to "Sauté' mode and bring it to a boil. Stir in the sage and thyme. Simmer for 10 additional minutes.Turn off your Instant pot and move all to a serving dish.

Nutritional Info:(Calories 431 | Total Fats 18.8g | Net Carbs: 5.9g | Protein 55.1g |Fiber: 1.5g)

Creamy Sour Pork Chops

Aggregate Time to Prepare: **45 Minutes**

Yield: **6 Servings**

Ingredients:

- 1 celery stalk, chopped
- 1 cup button mushrooms
- 1 cup cream cheese
- 1 cup sour cream
- 2 tbsp butter
- 2 tbsp Parmesan cheese
- 3 tbsp fresh parsley, thinly sliced
- 3 tbsp gorgonzola cheese
- 4 pork chops, boneless
- ¼ cup heavy cream
- ¼ cup vegetable stock
- ½ cup milk

Spices:

- 1 tsp dried rosemary
- ¼ tsp dried oregano
- ½ tsp white pepper

How to Cook:

1. Put the meat in the pot and pour in enough water to cover. Shut and secure the lid and set the steam release handle to the "Sealing" position. Push the "Meat" button and cook for 9 minutes on high pressure.
2. When finished, depressurize using the quick release method and open the lid. Remove the meat and the water from the pot and Switch your Instant Pot to "'Sauté" mode.
3. Oil-coat the inner pot with one tablespoon of butter and heat up. Put in mushrooms and cook for 5-6 minutes, stirring continuously. After that put in cheese, heavy cream, sour cream, and pour in the milk and the stock. Drizzle with pepper, rosemary, and oregano.
4. Tenderly simmer for 5-6 minutes, stirring continuously. Take out of the pot and chill for some time. Move to a blender and pulse until completely smooth. Save for later.
5. After that put in the rest of the butte rin the pot and put in chopped celery stalk. Cook for 4-5 minutes, stirring continuously.
6. Lastly, put in the meat and brown for 3-4 minutes on each side.
7. Serve with the cheese mixture.

Nutritional Info: (Calories 482 | Total Fats: 34.3g | Net Carbs: 4.5g | Protein: 38.6g | Fiber: 0.4g)

Crispy Garlic Lamb Chops

Aggregate Time to Prepare: 30 Minutes

Yield: 4 Servings

Ingredients:

- 1 cup button mushrooms, sliced
- 2 cups vegetable stock
- 3 garlic cloves, crushed
- 4 lamb chops, approximately 1 lb
- 4 tbsp butter
- ¼ cup soy sauce

Spices:

- 1 tsp black pepper, ground
- 1 tsp salt
- ½ tsp garlic powder
- ½ tsp mustard, ground
- ½ tsp smoked paprika

How to Cook:

1. Put the meat in the pot and pour in the stock. Shut and secure the lid and set the steam release handle to the "Sealing" position. Switch your Instant Pot to "Manual" mode and cook for 15 minutes on high pressure.
2. When finished, depressurize using the quick release method and open the lid. Remove the chops from the pot and save for later.
3. Remove the liquid and Switch your Instant Pot to "'Sauté" mode. Heat up the inner pot and then put in butter. Put in chops and brown for 3-4 minutes on one side. Turn over and continue to cook for an additional 2-3 minutes. Remove from the pot.
4. After that put in mushrooms and cook until the liquid evaporates. Put in garlic and pour in the soy sauce.

Sprinkle with spices and cook for an additional 4-5 minutes, stirring continuously.
5. Push the "Cancel" button and put in browned chops. Coat thoroughly with the sauce and serve.

Nutritional Info: (Calories 331 | Total Fats: 20g | Net Carbs: 2.4g | Protein: 33.9g | Fiber: 0.6g)

Cuban Pork

Aggregate Time to Prepare: **35 Minutes**

Yield: **10 Servings**

Ingredients:

- 1 Bay Leaf
- 1 tbsp. Salt
- 3 lbs. Pork Shoulder (all fat removed)
- 6 cloves Garlic
- ⅓ cup Lime Juice
- ½ tbsp. Cumin
- ½ tbsp. Fresh Oregano
- ⅔ cup Grapefruit Juice

How to Cook:

1. Put all ingredients, except pork and bay leaf, using a food processor and blend until smooth.
2. Cut the pork in four pieces and place in a container with the marinade. Refrigerate overnight.
3. Move the pork and marinade into the Instant Pot and put in a bay leaf. Shut and secure the lid and manually set it to 80 minutes at high pressure.
4. When finished allow the pressure to be released naturally.

5. Remove the pork from pot, preserving one cup of cooking liquids, and shred it using a fork.
6. Return the shredded pork in the Instant Pot and put into it preserved cooking liquids. Stir thoroughly to mix.
7. Serve warm with cauliflower rice.

Nutritional Info: (Calories: 213 | Total Fats: 9.5g | Net Carbs: 2g | Proteins: 26.5g | Fibers: 0.5g)

Curried Lamb with Zucchini and Tomatoes

Aggregate Time to Prepare: 3 hours and 40 Minutes

Yield: 4 Servings

Ingredients:

- 1 ½ tbsp. Curry Powder
- 1 Carrot, thinly sliced
- 1 cup diced Tomatoes
- 1 Onion, diced
- 1 pound Lab, chop into cubes
- 1 tbsp. Ghee
- 1 tsp grated Ginger
- 1 Zucchini, diced
- 2 tsp minced Garlic
- ½ cup Coconut Milk

How to Cook:

1. Put the lamb, ginger, garlic, and coconut milk, in a container.
2. Cover and place in the fridge to marinate for 3 hours.

3. Move the lamb, along with the juices, to the Instant Pot.
4. Put in the carrot, onion, tomatoes, and ghee.
5. Shut and secure the lid and cook for 20 minutes on HIGH.
6. Depressurize using the natural release method.
7. Stir in the zucchini and cook using the "Sauté" mode for 5-6 additional minutes.
8. Your dish is ready! Have fun!

Nutritional Info: (Calories 338| Total Fats 21g | Net Carbs 7.5g | Protein 23g |Fiber: 3g)

Curry Ginger Pork

Aggregate Time to Prepare: 25 Minutes

Yield: 4 Servings

Ingredients:

- 1 garlic clove, crushed
- 1 lb pork neck, chop into thin strips
- 1 spring onion, chopped
- 1 tbsp rice vinegar
- 2 small onions, sliced
- 2 tsp sesame oil
- ¼ cup olive oil

Spices:

- 1 tsp fresh ginger, grated
- 2 tsp curry powder
- ½ tsp salt

How to Cook:

1. Turn on your Instant Pot and heat up the oil. Put in the meat and cook for 4-5 minutes. Take out of the pot and save for later.
2. After that put in onions, garlic, and spring onions. Sauté for 3-4 minuts, stirring continuously.
3. Stir in ginger and garlic powder. Put in the emat and season with salt. Cook for 2 additional minutes.
4. Push the "Cancel" button. Remove the meat with the curry sauce from the pot and drizzle with sesame oil prior to serving.

Nutritional Info: (Calories 540 | Total Fats: 34.8g | Net Carbs: 4.1g | Protein: 48.7g |Fiber: 4.1g)

Dijon Pork with Turmeric

Aggregate Time to Prepare: 30 Minutes

Yield: 4 Servings

Ingredients:

- 1 cup heavy cream
- 1 large onion, sliced
- 1 lb pork neck, chopped into bite-sized pieces
- 2 tbsp Dijon mustard
- 3 cups beef broth
- 4 tbsp olive oil

Spices:

- 1 tsp salt
- 2 tsp dried celery
- ½ tsp red pepper, freshly ground

How to Cook:

1. Turn on your Instant Pot and Switch your Instant Pot to "'Sauté" mode. Oil-coat the inner pot with some oil and put in onions. Sauté for 3-4 minutes and then put in the meat. Carry on cooking for an additional 5-6 minutes, stirring intermittently.
2. Sprinkle with salt, pepper, and celery and take out of the pot. Move to a deep container.
3. In a separate container, mix together heavy cream, Dijon mustard, and the rest of the olive oil. Stir thoroughly and pour over the meat.
4. Put back to the pot and pour in the broth. Stir thoroughly and shut and secure the lid.
5. Make sure the steam release handle is on the "Sealing" position and switch to "Manual' mode. Turn the timer to 15 minutes on high pressure.
6. When finished, depressurize using the natural release method and open the lid. Serve instantly.

Nutritional Info: (Calories 435 | Total Fats: 30.5g | Net Carbs: 4.3g | Protein: 34.7g | Fiber: 1.1g)

Easy Butter Chops

Aggregate Time to Prepare: 35 Minutes

Yield: 4 Servings

Ingredients:

- 1 cup vegetable stock
- 1 small onion, chopped
- 1 tbsp tomato paste
- 2 tbsp Dijon mustard
- 3 garlic cloves, crushed
- 3 tbsp almond flour

- 4 pork chops, with bones
- 4 tbsp butter

Spices:

- 1 tsp salt
- 2 tsp smoked paprika
- ½ tsp black pepper, freshly ground

How to Cook:

1. Turn on your Instant Pot and Switch your Instant Pot to "'Sauté" mode. Oil-coat the inner pot with butter and put in onions. Sauté until translucent.
2. After that put in garlic and continue to cook for an additional 1-2 minutes.
3. Lastly, put in chops, two at the time, and cook for 2-3 minutes on each side. Take out of the pot and place on a large platter. Slightly coat each piece with Dijon mustard and drizzle liberally with salt, pepper, and paprika.
4. Put the meat back in the pot and pour in the stock. Stir in tomato paste and shut and secure the lid.
5. Make sure the steam release handle is on the "Sealing" position and switch to "Manual' mode.
6. Cook for 22 minutes on high pressure.
7. When finished, depressurize using the natural release method and open the lid. Stir in the almond flour and let it sit, covered, for 10 minutes prior to serving.

Nutritional Info:(Calories 383 | Total Fats: 18.9g | Net Carbs: 3g | Protein: 47.2g |Fiber: 1.2g)

Easy Lamb Kebab

Aggregate Time to Prepare: 25 Minutes

Yield: 5 Servings

Ingredients:

- 1 lb ground lamb tenderloin
- 3 garlic cloves, crushed
- 3 tbsp butter, softened
- 3 tbsp olive oil
- ½ cup diced canned tomatoes, sugar-free
- ½ cup onions, thinly sliced
- ½ large eggplant, peeled
- oz ground beef

Spices:

- 1 tbsp cayenne pepper
- 1 tsp chili powder
- 1 tsp cumin powder
- 1 tsp dried oregano
- 1 tsp salt

How to Cook:

1. In a medium-sized container, mix together ground lamb, ground beef, onions, garlic, olive oil, salt, cumin oregano, cayenne, and chili powder. Combine thoroughly and shape bite-sized balls. Save for later.
2. Position balls and eggplant slices on soaked skewers and drizzle with some more olive oil.
3. Turn on your Instant Pot and Switch your Instant Pot to "'Sauté" mode. Oil-coat the inner pot with butter and heat up.

4. Put in skewers, in two batches, and cook for 4-5 minutes on one side. Turn over and continue to cook until lightly golden brown.
5. Remove the skewers from the pot and put in diced tomatoes. Sprinkle with some salt, pepper, and oregano. Stir thoroughly and cook for about 2 minutes.
6. Turn off the Instant Pot by pressing the "Cancel" button.
7. Put skewers on a serving platter and drizzle with the tomato sauce.

Nutritional Info: (Calories 419 | Total Fats: 25.3g | Net Carbs: 3g | Protein: 41.9g |Fiber: 2.1g)

Easy Pork Ribs

Aggregate Time to Prepare: 30 Minutes

Yield: 5 Servings

Ingredients:

- 1 cup cauliflower, chopped into florets
- 1 cup portobello mushrooms, chopped
- 1 cup tomatoes, diced
- 1 tsp apple cider vinegar
- 2 celery stalks, chopped
- 2 garlic cloves, whole
- 2 lbs pork ribs
- 2 red bell peppers, chopped
- 2 tbsp hot chili sauce, sugar-free
- 3 tbsp butter
- 5 cups beef broth
- ½ cup onions, thinly sliced

Spices:

- 1 tsp dried celery
- 2 tsp onion powder
- 2 tsp salt
- ½ tsp black pepper, freshly ground

How to Cook:

1. Put the ribs in the pot and pour in enough water to cover. Put in celery stalks and shut and secure the lid. Make sure the steam release handle is on the "Sealing" position and push the "Meat" button.
2. Turn the timer to 15 minutes on high pressure.
3. When finished, depressurize using the quick release method and open the lid.
4. After that mix in the rest of the ingredients and drizzle with salt, pepper, celery, and onion powder. Stir all thoroughly and shut and secure the lid again.
5. Make sure the steam release handle is on the "Sealing" position and continue to cook for an additional 7 minutes.
6. When finished, depressurize using the quick release method and open the lid.
7. Serve instantly.

Nutritional Info: (Calories 633| Total Fats: 40.7g | Net Carbs: 7.1g | Protein: 54.9g |Fiber: 2.1g)

Eggplant and Lamb Curry

Aggregate Time to Prepare: **50 Minutes**

Yield: **4 Servings**

Ingredients:

- 2 green chili peppers, whole
- 2 lamb shanks
- 4 cups beef broth
- 4 garlic cloves, whole
- 4 tbsp ghee
- 4 tbsp yogurt
- ½ eggplant, cubed

Spices:

- 1 tbsp oregano
- 1 tbsp smoked paprika
- 2 bay leaves
- 2 cinnamon sticks
- 2 tbsp cumin seeds
- 2 tsp salt

How to Cook:

1. Put the meat in a large container. Liberally drizzle with salt, pepper, garlic, paprika, oregano, and cumin seeds.
2. Turn on your Instant Pot and Switch your Instant Pot to "'Sauté" mode. Oil-coat the inner pot with ghee and put in the meat. Cook for 3-4 minutes, stirring continuously.
3. When the meat is nicely browned on all sides, drizzle with some more spices and put in eggplants. Cook for 5 minutes.
4. Pour in the broth and put in yogurt and chili peppers. Stir thoroughly and shut and secure the lid. Make sure the steam release handle is on the "Sealing" position and switch to "Manual' mode.
5. Turn the timer to 30 minutes on high pressure.

6. When finished, depressurize using the natural release method and open the lid. Chill for some time and serve.

Nutritional Info:(Calories 392| Total Fats 22.7g | Net Carbs: 4.3g | Protein: 38.4g |Fiber: 2.2g)

Feta Lamb Meatballs in a Tomato Sauce

Aggregate Time to Prepare: 25 Minutes

Yield: 6 Servings

Ingredients:

- 1 ½ pounds ground Lamb
- 1 Bell Pepper, diced
- 1 Egg
- 1 Onion, chopped
- 1 tbsp. chopped Mint
- 1 tbsp. Water
- 1 tsp Oregano
- 2 tbsp. chopped Parsley
- 2 tbsp. Olive Oil
- 2 tsp minced Garlic
- 24 ounces canned diced Tomatoes
- ½ cup Almond Flour
- ½ cup crumbled Feta Cheese

How to Cook:

1. In a container, mix the egg, lamb, half of the garlic, almond flour, water, mint, parsley, and feta.
2. Make meatballs out of the mixture.

3. Switch the Instant Pot to "Sauté" mode and heat the oil.
4. Put in the onion and pepper and cook for 3 minutes.
5. Put in the rest of the ingredients and stir to mix.
6. Put the meatballs inside.
7. Shut and secure the lid and cook on HIGH for 8 minutes.
8. Your dish is ready! Have fun!

Nutritional Info: (Calories 345| Total Fats 17g | Net Carbs 8g | Protein 35g |Fiber: 1.3g)

Five Spice Short Ribs

Aggregate Time to Prepare: 40 Minutes

Yield: 4 Servings

Ingredients:

- 1 tbsp. grated Ginger
- 1 tsp Five Spice Powder
- 1/3 cup Coconut Aminos
- 2 pounds Beef Short Ribs
- 3 tsp minced Garlic
- ¼ cup Sweetener
- ½ cup Bone Broth

How to Cook:

1. Mix together the broth, coconut aminos, sweetener, garlic, five-spice powder, and ginger.
2. Put in the short ribs and shut and secure the lid.
3. Switch your Instant Pot to MEAT/STEW and cook for 35 minutes.
4. Depressurize using the natural release method,

5. Your dish is ready! Have fun!

Nutritional Info: (Calories 420| Total Fats 41g | Net Carbs 6g | Protein 39g |Fiber: 0.1g)

Fragrant Lamb Riblets

Aggregate Time to Prepare: **45 Minutes**

Yield: **4 Servings**

Ingredients:

- 1 tbsp lemon juice
- 3 garlic cloves, crushed
- 4 slabs of lamb riblets, approximately 2 lbs
- 4 tbsp ghee
- 5 cups beef broth

Spices:

- 1 tsp salt
- 2 cloves, whole
- 2 tsp chili powder
- ¼ cup fresh coriander, chopped

How to Cook:

1. Wash thoroughly the meat and place in the pot. season with salt and chili pepper and pour in the broth.
2. Put in lemon juice and cloves. Shut and secure the lid and set the steam release handle to the "Sealing" position.
3. Switch your Instant Pot to "Manual" mode and cook for 40 minutes on high pressure. If you want, you can also slow cook for 6-8 hours.

4. When finished, depressurize using the natural release method and open the lid. Remove the cloves and mix in ghee. Drizzle with coriander and serve instantly with some cauliflower puree or fresh vegetable salad.

Nutritional Info: (Calories 375| Total Fats: 22.8g | Net Carbs: 1.9g | Protein: 38.1g |Fiber: 0.1g)

Garlic Lamb Meatballs

Aggregate Time to Prepare: 25 Minutes

Yield: 4 Servings

Ingredients:

- 1 cup cauliflower, chopped into small florets
- 1 lb ground lamb, tender parts like neck or loin
- 2 tbsp almond flour
- 2 tbsp olive oil
- 3 tbsp butter, softened
- 4 garlic cloves, crushed
- 4 large eggs

Spices:

- 1 tsp marjoram
- 1 tsp salt
- ½ tsp white pepper, freshly ground

How to Cook:

1. In a large container, mix together ground lamb, crushed garlic, almond flour, eggs, olive oil, salt, pepper, and marjoram.
2. Combine thoroughly and shape bite-sized balls. Save for later.

3. Oil-coat a small round cake pan with some more oil and make the bottom layer with cauliflower. Position the meatballs on top and tightly cover with aluminium foil
4. Turn on your Instant Pot and set the trivet at the bottom of the inner pot. Pour in one cup of water and place the pan on the trivet.
5. Shut and secure the lid and set the steam release handle to the "Sealing" position.
6. Switch your Instant Pot to "Manual" mode and turn the timer to 12 minutes on high pressure.
7. When finished, depressurize using the quick release method and open the lid. Take the pan out of the instant pot and chill for some time.
8. In the mean time, melt the butter in a microwave and optionally drizzle with some salt. You can put in some fresh or dried herbs of choice and drizzle over the meatballs.
9. Serve instantly with tzatziki dip or Greek yogurt.

Nutritional Info: (Calories 435 | Total Fats: 29.4g | Net Carbs: 2.1g | Protein: 39.1g | Fiber: 0.8g)

Garlic Pork Chops

Aggregate Time to Prepare: 25 Minutes

Yield: 4 Servings

Ingredients:

- 1 cup onions, thinly sliced
- 2 pork chops, 1-inch thick
- 2 tbsp oil
- 3 garlic cloves, crushed

- 4 bacon slices, chopped

Spices:

- 1 tsp black pepper, ground
- 1 tsp salt
- ¼ tsp garlic powder
- ½ tsp dried thyme

How to Cook:

1. Turn on your Instant Pot and Switch your Instant Pot to "'Sauté" mode. Oil-coat the inner pot with oil and heat up.
2. Rub the meat with salt, pepper, garlic and thyme. Save for later.
3. Put in onions and garlic to the pot. Sauté for 2-3 minutes and then put in the bacon. Carry on cooking for an additional 2 minutes, stirring continuously.
4. After that put in the seasoned meat and briefly brown for 2 minutes on each side.
5. Push the "Cancel" button and pour in one cup of water. Shut and secure the lid and set the steam release handle to the "Sealing" position.
6. Switch your Instant Pot to "Manual" mode and turn the timer to 13 minutes.
7. When finished, depressurize using the natural release method and open the lid.
8. If you want, you can also brown the meat in a large non-stick skillet over medium-high heat prior to serving.

Nutritional Info:(Calories 340 | Total Fats: 18.8g | Net Carbs: 3g | Protein: 37.2g | Fiber: 0.7g)

Garlic Venison Shoulder

Aggregate Time to Prepare: 90 Minutes

Yield: 2 Servings

Ingredients:

- 1 tbsp. butter
- 2 lbs. venison shoulder
- 2 tbsp. apple cider vinegar
- 3 garlic cloves

Spices:

- 1 tsp garlic powder
- 1 tsp salt
- 2 tsp ginger, grated
- ½ tsp red pepper flakes
- ½ tsp white pepper

How to Cook:

1. In a small container, mix apple cider, garlic powder, and ginger. Slightly coat the meat with this mixture and save for later. If possible, refrigerate for one hour before cooking.
2. Turn on the Instant Pot and set the 'Sauté' mode. Put in the meat in batches and brown uniformly on all sides. After that put in 1 cup of water and garlic. Shut and secure the lid and set the steam release handle. Push the 'Manual' button and turn the timer to 35 minutes.
3. When finished, depressurize using the quick release method and open the lid. Switch your Instant Pot to "Sauté" mode again. Drizzle the meat with salt,

pepper, and pepper flakes. And butter and cook until the liquid evaporates.

Nutritional Info: (Calories 551 | Total Fats 10.3g | Net Carbs: 1.5g | Protein 100.1g | Fiber: 0.1g)

Ginger Lamb Shoulder

Aggregate Time to Prepare: 35 Minutes

Yield: 4 Servings

Ingredients:

- 1 cup bone broth
- 1 lbs lamb shoulder, chop into bite-sized pieces
- 1 tbsp coconut oil, melted
- 1 tbsp fresh parsley, thinly sliced
- 1 tbsp tomato paste
- 1 medium-sized onion, roughly chopped
- 4 garlic cloves, minced

Spices:

- 1 cinnamon stick
- 1 tbsp fresh ginger, ground
- 1 tsp cumin powder
- 2 tsp coriander, ground
- ¼ tsp black pepper, freshly ground
- ½ tsp salt

How to Cook:

1. In a small container, mix salt, pepper, cumin, and coriander. Combine until mixed and save for later.
2. Thoroughly wash the meat under running water and pat dry with a kitchen paper. Move to a cutting board

and chop into bite-sized pieces using sharp knife. Drizzle with spice mixture and tenderly rub with your hands. Save for later.
3. Turn on the Instant Pot and heat up the oil in the stainless steel insert over the "Sauté" button. Put in onions and garlic. Stir-fry for 3-4 minutes, or until onions translucent.
4. Put in meat and stir thoroughly. Cook for 5 minutes, stirring with a wooden spoon.
5. After that, put in freshly grated ginger, tomato paste, and cilantro. Pour in the broth and stir thoroughly. throw in the cinnamon stick and securely lock the lid.
6. Close the steam release handle and push the "Manual" button. Turn the timer to 25 minutes and cook on "High" pressure.
7. When you hear the cooker's end signal, release the pressure using the quick release method by moving the valve to the "Venting" position.
8. Open the pot and move to serving containers. Drizzle with some fresh parsley and have fun!

Nutritional Info:(Calories 289 | Total Fats 12g | Net Carbs: 5.7g | Protein: 37.8g |Fiber: 1.4g)

Ginger Pork

Aggregate Time to Prepare: **60 Minutes**

Yield: **3 Servings**

Ingredients:

- 1 cup eggplant, chopped
- 1 spring onion, thinly sliced
- 1 tbsp anka sauce

- 1 tbsp balsamic vinegar
- 2 lbs pork loin, chopped into bite-sized pieces
- 2 tbsp light soy sauce
- 3 cups beef stock
- 3 garlic cloves
- 3 tbsp ghee

Spices:

- 1 anise star
- 2 tsp ginger powder
- 2 tsp sea salt
- 3 cloves

How to Cook:

1. Put the meat at the bottom of the instant pot and pour in enough water to cover. Switch your Instant Pot to "Sauté' mode and tenderly bring it to a boil. Cook for 5 minutes, stirring intermittently. Take out of the pot and drain. Save for later.
2. After that coat the inner pot with ghee and heat up. Put in spring onions, ginger powder, anise, and cloves. Simmer for 1 minute, stirring continuously.
3. Pour in the anka sauce and continue to cook for an additional minute. Put in the meat and mix thoroughly.
4. Lastly, put in the rest of the ingredients and shut and secure the lid. Set the steam release handle and switch to "Manual' mode. Turn the timer to 35 minutes on high pressure.
5. When finished, depressurize using the quick release method and open the lid.
6. Serve instantly.

Nutritional Info: (Calories 576| Total Fats 24g | Net Carbs: 2.9g | Protein: 82.7g |Fiber: 1.2g)

Gingery Lamb with Apples

Aggregate Time to Prepare: **50 Minutes**

Yield: **4 Servings**

Ingredients:

- 1 ½ cups Bone Broth
- 1 Large Apple, sliced
- 1 pound boneless Lamb, cubed
- 1 tbsp. Balsamic Vinegar
- 1 tsp Rosemary
- 2 tbsp. Coconut Aminos
- 2 tbsp. Ghee
- 2 tbsp. grated Ginger
- 2 tsp minced Garlic
- ½ Onion, sliced

How to Cook:

1. Melt half of the ghee in the Instant Pot using the "Sauté" mode.
2. Put in the lamb in the Instant Pot and cook until browned on all sides. Move to a plate.
3. Melt the rest of the oil and put in the onion.
4. After 3 minutes of sautéing, put in the ginger and garlic and cook for one additional minute.
5. Stir in the vinegar, broth, and coconut aminos.
6. Put in the apples and place the lamb shanks on top.
7. Shut and secure the lid and cook for 10 minutes on HIGH.

8. Depressurize naturally.
9. Your dish is ready! Have fun!

Nutritional Info: (Calories 300 | Total Fats 12g | Net Carbs 6g | Protein 28g |Fiber: 1.7g)

Goat Meat Stew

Aggregate Time to Prepare: **60 Minutes**

Yield: **4 Servings**

Ingredients:

- 1 cup tomatoes, diced
- 1 medium-sized onion, chopped
- 1 small green chili pepper, chopped
- 1 tbsp balsamic vinegar
- 1 tbsp butter
- 2 lbs goat meat, chop into bite-sized pieces
- 4 garlic cloves, crushed
- ½ cup lemon juice, freshly squeezed
- ½ cup olive oil

Spices:

- 1 tbsp fresh ginger, grated
- 1 tsp coriander powder
- 1 tsp cumin powder
- 1 tsp garam masala powder
- 1 tsp salt
- 2 tsp fresh rosemary, thinly sliced
- ½ tsp black pepper, ground

How to Cook:

1. In a large container, mix olive oil, garlic, lemon juice, vinegar, ginger, cumin powder, garam masala powder, coriander powder, salt, and pepper. Combine until thoroughly blended. Save for later.
2. Thoroughly wash the meat under running water and pat dry with a kitchen paper. Cut into bite-sized pieces and put in it to the container with marinade. Stir thoroughly to coat all the meat and cover with a plastic foil. Refrigerate for 30 minutes, stirring halfway trough.
3. Turn on the Instant Pot and push the "Sauté" button. Put in the onions and green chili pepper. Drizzle with some salt to taste and stir-fry for 3-4 minutes, or until the onions translucent.
4. Put in marinated meat and tomatoes. Put in approximately 3-4 tablespoons of the marinade and pour in 2 cups of water. Stir all thoroughly and securely lock the lid.
5. Close the steam release handle and switch to "Manual' mode. Turn the timer to 45 minutes and cook on "High" pressure.
6. When finished, depressurize using the natural release method.
7. Open the pot and move to a serving pot. If you want, you can also drizzle with some thinly sliced green onions prior to serving and garnish with lime wedges.
8. Have fun!

Nutritional Info:(Calories 530 | Total Fats 34g | Net Carbs: 5.9g | Protein: 39.3g |Fiber: 1.5g)

Goat Shank in Garlic Sauce

Aggregate Time to Prepare: 50 Minutes

Yield: **4 Servings**

Ingredients:

- 1 medium-sized onion, chopped
- 2 tbsp lemon juice, freshly squeezed
- 2 tbsp olive oil
- 3 lbs goat shanks, chop into large pieces
- 6 garlic cloves
- ¼ cup fresh cilantro, chopped
- ½ cup plain yogurt, full-fat

Spices:

- 1 tsp salt
- 1 tsp sesame seeds
- 2-3 cardamom pods
- ¼ tsp cloves, ground

How to Cook:

1. In a food processor, mix yogurt, garlic, cilantro, lemon juice, sesame seeds, cardamom, cloves, and salt. Pulse until smooth and creamy. Save for later.
2. Turn on the Instant Pot and coat the stainless steel insert with olive oil. Put in onions and stir-fry for 3-4 minutes, stirring continuously.
3. Put in meat and drizzle with some salt. Pour enough water to cover and securely lock the lid. Close the steam release handle and push the "Manual" button. Turn the timer to 30 minutes and cook on "High" pressure.
4. When you hear the cooker's end signal, release the pressure using the quick release method and open the pot.

5. Push the "Sauté" button and put in previously readied garlic sauce. Cook for 10 minutes, or the mixture thickens, turning the shank once.
6. Turn off your Instant pot and cautiously move the shank to a serving platter. Drizzle with the rest of the garlic sauce and garnish with some fresh cilantro.
7. Have fun!

Nutritional Info:(Calories 480 | Total Fats 15.8g | Net Carbs: 6.2g | Protein: 74.1g |Fiber: 1.2g)

Greek Feta Meatballs

Aggregate Time to Prepare: **25 Minutes**

Yield: **4 Servings**

Ingredients:

- 1 cup diced canned tomatoes, sugar-free
- 1 green bell pepper, thinly sliced
- 1 lb ground lamb
- 1 onion, thinly sliced
- 2 garlic cloves, crushed
- 2 large eggs, beaten
- 3 tbsp olive oil
- ¼ cup almond flour
- ½ cup feta cheese, crumbled

Spices:

- 1 tbsp fresh mint
- 1 tsp dried oregano
- 2 tbsp fresh parsley
- ½ tsp pepper
- ½ tsp salt

How to Cook:

1. In a large container, mix together ground lamb, eggs, feta, garlic, almond flour, chopped onions, salt, pepper, oregano, mint, and parsley.
2. Combine until completely mixed. With somewhat wet hands, shape the mixture into 12 balls and place in a round oven-safe dish.
3. Pour in the canned tomatoes and put in bell peppers. Drizzle with olive oil and tightly cover with aluminium foil.
4. Turn on your Instant Pot and set the trivet at the bottom of the stainless steel insert. Pour in 1 cup of water and place the container on the trivet.
5. Shut and secure the lid and set the steam release handle to the "Sealing" position.
6. Switch your Instant Pot to "Manual" mode and cook for 12 minutes.
7. When finished, depressurize using the natural release method and open the lid.
8. Remove the container from the pot using oven mitts and chill for some time.
9. If you want, you can also spread on top some Greek yogurt prior to serving.

Nutritional Info: (Calories 428 | Total Fats: 26.3g | Net Carbs: 6.6g | Protein: 39.1g | Fiber: 1.8g)

Greek Lamb Skewers

Aggregate Time to Prepare: 25 Minutes

Yield: 4 Servings

Ingredients:

- 1 cup beef broth
- 1 cup cherry tomatoes, whole
- 1 lb lamb loin, chopped into bite-sized pieces
- 1 onion, chop into wedges
- 1 tbsp butter
- ½ cup fresh parsley, thinly sliced

Spices:

- 1 tsp cumin powder
- ¼ tsp garlic powder
- ½ tsp dried rosemary
- ½ tsp salt

How to Cook:

1. Turn on your Instant Pot and put in chopped lamb. Pour in the broth and shut and secure the lid.
2. Set the steam release handle and switch to "Manual' mode. Turn the timer to 7 minutes on high pressure.
3. When finished, depressurize using the quick release method and open the lid. Remove the meat along with the broth and drain.
4. After that place the meat in a deep container and drizzle with salt, rosemary, cumin, and garlic powder. Coat thoroughly with spices and save for later.
5. Take 12 wooden skewers and soak them in water. Position the meat and vegetables and save for later.
6. Switch your Instant Pot to "Sauté' mode and put in butter. Heat up and tenderly place each skewer in the pot. Cook for 3 minutes and then tenderly turn over and continue to cook for an additional 2-3 minutes.
7. Take out of the pot and serve.

Nutritional Info: (Calories 268 | Total Fats: 11.7g | Net Carbs: 3.6g | Protein: 34g | Fiber: 1.4g)

Grilled Beef Tenderloin

Aggregate Time to Prepare: **35 Minutes**

Yield: **6 Servings**

Ingredients:

- 1 tbsp butter
- 1 tbsp olive oil
- 2 lbs beef tenderloin, chop into bite-sized pieces
- 3 cups beef broth
- 4 garlic cloves, thinly sliced

Spices:

- 1 tsp black pepper, ground
- 1 tsp dried oregano, ground
- 1 tsp dried rosemary, ground
- 1 tsp onion powder
- 1 tsp sea salt

How to Cook:

1. Thoroughly wash the meat under running water and pat dry with a kitchen paper. Move to a cutting board and chop into bite-sized pieces. Put the meat chops in a large container and put in all the spices. Liberally rub with your hands to allow spice to penetrate into the meat. Save for later.
2. Plug in your instant and coat the stainless steel insert with olive oil. Switch your Instant Pot to "Sauté" mode and put in meat chops and garlic. Cook for 5 minutes, or until golden brown.
3. After that, pour in the beef broth and securely lock the lid. Close the steam release handle and switch to

"Manual' mode. Turn the timer to 20 minutes and cook on "High" pressure.
4. When your instant pot sounds the end signal, release the pressure using the quick release method and open the pot. Move the meat to a serving platter and garnish with some thinly sliced chives and fresh thyme prior to serving.

Nutritional Info: (Calories 562 | Total Fats 28.3g | Net Carbs: 2.4g | Protein 69.7g |Fiber: 0.5g)

Ground Beef Shawarma

Aggregate Time to Prepare: **10 Minutes**

Yield: **4 Servings**

Ingredients:

- 1 cup Onions (chop to rubs)
- 1 cup Red Bell Peppers (chop into ¼ inch slices)
- 1 lbs. Lean Ground Beef
- 1 tsp Dried Oregano
- 1 tsp Salt
- 2 cups Cabbage (chop into ½ inch strips)
- ¼ tsp Cayenne Pepper
- ¼ tsp Ground Allspice
- ½ tsp Cinnamon
- ½ tsp Cumin
- ½ tsp Ground Coriander Seeds

How to Cook:

1. Switch your Instant Pot to "Sauté" mode and put in in it the ground beef. Lightly brown it while breaking down into smaller chunks, for around 2 minutes.

2. Put in all other ingredients and stir to mix.
3. Shut and secure the lid, and turn the timer and cook for 2 minutes at high pressure.
4. Let naturally release the pressure for 5 minutes and then quick release it.
5. Serve with tzatziki sauce.

Nutritional Info: (Calories: 191 | Total Fats: 5g | Net Carbs: 6g | Proteins: 25g |Fibers: 2g)

Ground Pork with Eggs

Aggregate Time to Prepare: 20 Minutes

Yield: 4 Servings

Ingredients:

- 1 garlic clove, crushed
- 1 onion, thinly sliced
- 2 bacon slices, chopped
- 3 tbsp butter
- 4 large eggs
- 7 oz ground pork

Spices:

- ½ tsp pepper, freshly ground
- ½ tsp salt

How to Cook:

1. Oil-coat the bottom of the pot with butter and Switch your Instant Pot to "'Sauté'' mode. Put in onions and briefly cook – for 2-3 minutes.
2. After that put in pork, bacon, and garlic. Sprinkle with salt and pepper.

3. Carry on cooking for 5 minutes.
4. Lastly, crack the eggs and cook for 2-3 minutes. Push the "Cancel" button and serve instantly.

Nutritional Info: (Calories 282| Total Fats 19.4g | Net Carbs: 2.8g | Protein: 23.2g |Fiber: 0.6g)

Hawaiian Pork

Aggregate Time to Prepare: 95 Minutes

Yield: 4 Servings

Ingredients:

- 1 tbsp. Olive Oil
- 1/2 cup Water
- 2 pounds Pork Roast
- 2 tbsp. Coconut Aminos
- 2 tbsp. Liquid Smoke
- 2 tbsp. Sweetener

How to Cook:

1. Heat the oil in the Instant Pot using the "Sauté" mode.
2. Put in the pork and cook for approximately 3 minutes on each side. Move to a plate.
3. Mix together the rest of the ingredients in the Instant Pot.
4. Put in the meat and shut and secure the lid.
5. Select MANUAL and cook on HIGH for 60 minutes.
6. Depressurize naturally, approximately 20 minutes.
7. Shred using two forks inside the pot.
8. Serve as favoured.
9. Have fun!

Nutritional Info: (Calories 450 | Total Fats 24g | Net Carbs 1g | Protein 55g | Fiber: 0g)

Heavy Balsamic Lamb Shoulder

Aggregate Time to Prepare: 45 Minutes

Yield: 5 Servings

Ingredients:

- 1 cup vegetable stock
- 1 tbsp Dijon mustard
- 2 lbs lamb shoulder
- 2 tbsp butter
- 2 tbsp soy sauce
- 3 garlic cloves, crushed
- ¼ cup balsamic vinegar
- ¼ cup swerve

Spices:

- 1 tsp dried sage
- 1 tsp salt
- ½ tsp black pepper, freshly ground

How to Cook:

1. Turn on your Instant Pot and Switch your Instant Pot to "'Sauté" mode. Oil-coat the inner pot with butter and heat up.
2. Put in garlic and briefly cook – for 1 minute. After that pour in the soy sauce and balsamic vinegar, Dijon, and swerve. Stir vigorously and cook for 2-3 minutes.
3. Push the "Cancel" button and save for later.

4. Thoroughly wash the meat under cold running water and rub with salt, pepper, and sage. Move to the pot and pour in the stock.
5. Shut and secure the lid and set the steam release handle to the "Sealing" position.
6. Switch your Instant Pot to "Manual" mode and turn the timer to 35 minutes on high pressure.
7. When finished, depressurize using the natural release method and open the lid. Move the meat to a large platter and drizzle with the sauce from the pot.
8. Serve instantly.

Nutritional Info:(Calories 425 | Total Fats: 19.4g | Net Carbs: 1.3g | Protein: 56.9g |Fiber: 0.3g)

Heavy Mushroom Pork

Aggregate Time to Prepare: **40 Minutes**

Yield: **4 Servings**

Ingredients:

- 1 cup mushrooms, sliced
- 1 cup tomato sauce, sugar-free
- 1 lb pork fillet, sliced into half-inch thick slices
- 1 small chili pepper, chopped
- 1 small onion, thinly sliced
- 2 garlic cloves, crushed
- 3 tbsp balsamic vinegar
- 3 tbsp oil

Spices:

- 1 tsp smoked paprika
- 2 tsp dried celery

- ¼ tsp black pepper, freshly ground
- ½ tsp red pepper flakes
- ½ tsp salt

How to Cook:

1. Remove the fillets from the fridge approximately 20 minutes before cooking. Drizzle with salt and pepper and save for later.
2. Turn on your Instant Pot and heat up the oil. Put in fillets and briefly brown on both sides, for 2-3 minutes.
3. Take out of the pot and save for later.
4. After that put in onions and mushrooms. Drizzle with salt, pepper, and celery. Cook for 5-6 minutes and then put in balsamic vinegar, chili, tomato, and garlic. Drizzle with red pepper flakes and smoked paprika. Carry on cooking for 1-2 minutes and put in the meat.
5. Line the meat with the sauce and continue to cook for an additional 10-12 minutes.
6. When finished, push the "Cancel" button and remove form the pot. If you want, you can also drizzle with some grated Parmesan cheese and serve instantly.

Nutritional Info: (Calories 385 | Total Fats: 24.8g | Net Carbs: 4.6g | Protein: 33.2g |Fiber: 1.6g)

Herb-Packed Meatloaf

Aggregate Time to Prepare: **55 Minutes**

Yield: **6 Servings**

Ingredients:

- 1 ½ cups Water
- 1 ½ tsp Parsley
- 1 tsp Garlic Salt
- 1 tsp Oregano
- 1 tsp Rosemary
- 2 tsp Thyme
- 2 Eggs
- 2 pounds ground Beef
- 3 tbsp. Olive Oil
- ¼ tsp Pepper
- ½ tsp Sage

How to Cook:

1. Pour the water into the Instant Pot. Lower the trivet.
2. Oil-coat a loaf pan with the olive oil.
3. Put all of the ingredients in a container and mix with your hand to mix thoroughly.
4. Push the mixture into the pan.
5. Put the loaf pan inside the Instant Pot and shut and secure the lid.
6. Switch your Instant Pot to "Manual" mode and cook on HIGH for 30-35 minutes.
7. Depressurize for 10 minutes.
8. Your dish is ready! Have fun!

Nutritional Info: (Calories 280| Total Fats 13.8g | Net Carbs 1.5g | Protein 25g |Fiber: 0.4g)

Hot Lamb Rack with Almonds

Aggregate Time to Prepare: 35 Minutes

Yield: 4 Servings

Ingredients:

- 1 cup vegetable stock
- 1 tbsp hot chili sauce, sugar-free
- 2 pieces of 4-bone racks, trimmed
- 2 tbsp Dijon mustard
- 4 tbsp olive oil
- ¼ cup almonds, thinly sliced
- ¼ cup apple cider vinegar

Spices:

- 1 tsp salt
- ¼ tsp chili powder
- ½ tsp dried basil

How to Cook:

1. Wash thoroughly the meat and place in the pot. Pour in the stock and shut and secure the lid. Set the steam release handle and switch to "Manual' mode.
2. Turn the timer to 10 minutes on high pressure.
3. In the mean time, in a small container, whisk together apple cider, Dijon mustard, hot chili sauce, olive oil, salt, basil, and chili. Save for later.
4. When your instant pot sounds the end signal, depressurize using the quick release method and open the lid.
5. Take the meat out of the pot and chill for some time.
6. Preheat the oven to 350 degrees F. Line some parchment paper over a baking sheet and save for later.
7. Liberally brush each piece of lamb with the mustard mixture and drizzle with almonds.
8. Bake for 10-15 minutes or until lightly golden brown.

Nutritional Info: (Calories 351 | Total Fats: 24.7g | Net Carbs: 1g | Protein: 29.8g |Fiber: 1.1g)

Hot Tomatillo Pork

Aggregate Time to Prepare: 55 Minutes

Yield: 4 Servings

Ingredients:

- 1 tbsp. Olive Oil
- 16 ounces Keto Tomatillo Salsa
- 2 pounds Pork Sirloin, sliced
- 2 tsp Cumin
- 2 tsp garlic Powder
- ¼ tsp Salt

How to Cook:

1. Heat the oil in the Instant Pot using the "Sauté" mode.
2. In the mean time, season the pork with the spices.
3. Put in to the pot and cook until browned on all sides.
4. Pour the salsa over and shut and secure the lid.
5. Switch the Instant Pot to "High" and cook for 45 minutes.
6. Release the pressure using the quick release method.
7. Your dish is ready! Have fun!

Nutritional Info: (Calories 400| Total Fats 7g | Net Carbs 4g | Protein 14g |Fiber: 5g)

Hungarian Goulash

Aggregate Time to Prepare: 4 hours and 20 Minutes

Yield: 8 Servings

Ingredients:

- 1 ½ cups Beef Broth
- 1 Bell Pepper, diced
- 1 cup chopped Onion
- 15 ounces canned and diced Tomatoes
- 2 Celery Stalks, chopped
- 2 cups cubed Daikon Radish
- 2 pounds Beef, cubed
- 2 tbsp. Butter
- 2 tbsp. Paprika
- 2 tsp minced Garlic
- ½ tsp Caraway Seeds
- ½ tsp Caraway Seeds
- ½ tsp Salt

How to Cook:

1. Melt the butter in the Instant Pot using the "Sauté" mode.
2. Put in the onions and cook for 2 minutes.
3. Stir in garlic and paprika and cook for 1 minute.
4. Put in beef and cook until browned.
5. Put in caraway seeds, pepper, and salt.
6. Stir in the rest of the ingredients and shut and secure the lid.
7. Switch your Instant Pot to SLOW COOK and cook on HIGH for 4 hours.
8. Depressurize and serve.
9. Have fun!

Nutritional Info: (Calories 345| Total Fats 24g | Net Carbs 5.8g | Protein 24g |Fiber: 2.8g)

Hungarian Porkolt

Aggregate Time to Prepare: **40 Minutes**

Yield: **8 Servings**

Ingredients:

- 1 large Onion (diced)
- 1 medium Red Bell Pepper (diced)
- 1 tbsp. Vegetable Oil
- 1 tsp Ground Black Pepper
- 1 tsp Salt
- 14 oz. Diced Tomatoes (canned)
- 2 cups Beef Broth
- 2 lbs. Beef Chuck Steak (chop into 1-2 inch chunks)
- 3 tbsp. Sweet Paprika
- 4 cloves Garlic (minced)
- ½ tbsp. Cornstarch (dissolved in ½ tbsp. Water)

How to Cook:

1. Put the beef in a container and put in salt and pepper, and toss to mix.
2. Switch your Instant Pot to "Sauté" mode and put into it the oil. Put in beef and brown it while intermittently stirring for 5 minutes. Remove the beef from pot and save for later.
3. Put in to pot onions and bell pepper and cook for 5 minutes while regularly stirring.
4. Put in garlic and stir thoroughly.

5. Put in the tomatoes, beef broth, paprika and browned beef, and stir thoroughly to mix.
6. Shut and secure the lid, and set the Instant Pot to "Meat/Stew" and decrease the time to 25 minutes.
7. When finished allow the pressure to be released naturally for 10 minutes and then quick release.
8. Switch your Instant Pot to "Sauté" mode and put in the dissolved cornstarch. Stir thoroughly and cook for 5 minutes to thicken.
9. Serve warm.

Nutritional Info: (Calories: 273 | Total Fats: 15g | Net Carbs: 7g | Proteins: 23g | Fibers: 2g)

Instant Beef Stew

Aggregate Time to Prepare: **50 Minutes**

Yield: **4 Servings**

Ingredients:

- 1 Bell Pepper, diced
- 1 Carrot, sliced
- 1 cup Cauliflower Rice
- 1 Onion, sliced
- 1 pound Beef, chop into cubes
- 1 tbsp. Olive Oil
- 2 cups Beef Broth
- 2 tsp minced Garlic
- 4 Bacon Slices, cubed
- ¼ cup Red Wine
- ¼ tsp Pepper
- ½ cup Green Beans, chopped
- 1 tbsp. Thyme

- 1 Bay Leaf
- ½ tsp Salt

How to Cook:

1. Heat the oil in the Instant Pot using the "Sauté" mode.
2. Put in the beef cubes and cook until browned. Move to a plate.
3. Put in the bacon and cook until it begins to crisp.
4. Put in onions and pepper and cook for 3 minutes.
5. Put in the carrots and garlic and cook for 1 minute.
6. Return the beef to the pot.
7. Pour the broth and wine over.
8. Put in thyme, seasonings, and bay leaf.
9. Shut and secure the lid and cook for 20 minutes on HIGH.
10. Depressurize and mix in the green beans and cauliflower.
11. Switch the Instant Pot to "High" and cook for 10 additional minutes.
12. Your dish is ready! Have fun!

Nutritional Info: (Calories 380| Total Fats 16g | Net Carbs 8.5g | Protein 40g |Fiber: 2.3g)

Instant Bolognese Sauce

Aggregate Time to Prepare: 15 Minutes

Yield: 4 Servings

Ingredients:

- 1 can low-carb Pasta Sauce
- 1 pound ground Beef

- 2 tsp minced Garlic
- ¼ cup chopped Parsley

How to Cook:

1. Mix everything in the Instant Pot.
2. Shut and secure the lid and set the Instant Pot to MANUAL.
3. Switch the Instant Pot to "High" and cook for 8 minutes.
4. Release the pressure using the quick release method.
5. Serve or store in mason jars.
6. Have fun!

Nutritional Info: (Calories 340| Total Fats 11g | Net Carbs 5g | Protein 35g |Fiber: 0.5g)

Italian Beef Chuck Roast

Aggregate Time to Prepare: **45 Minutes**

Yield: **6 Servings**

Ingredients:

- 1 cup tomatoes, diced
- 1 small onion, chopped
- 1 tbsp butter
- 2 cups beef broth
- 3 lbs beef chuck roast, boneless
- 5 garlic cloves, minced

Spices:

- 1 tsp fresh oregano, thinly sliced
- 1 tsp sea salt
- ½ tsp black pepper, ground

- ½ tsp dried basil, ground

How to Cook:

1. Put in meat and cook for 5 minutes on each side.
2. Put in tomatoes and all the spices. Pour in the broth and securely lock the lid. Set the steam release handle and switch to "Manual' mode. Turn the timer to 25 minutes and cook on "High" pressure.
3. Have fun!
4. Open the pot and move the meat to a serving plate.
5. Turn on the Instant Pot and put in butter to the stainless steel insert. Switch your Instant Pot to "Sauté' mode and tenderly melt. Put in garlic and onions and cook for 3-4 minutes, or until onions translucent.
6. Thoroughly wash the meat under cold running water and pat dry with a kitchen paper. Move to a cutting board and chop into bite-sized pieces. Save for later.
7. When your instant pot sounds the end signal, depressurize using the natural release method.

Nutritional Info: (Calories 651 | Total Fats 49.2g | Net Carbs: 2.2g | Protein 46.2g |Fiber: 0.6g)

Italian Beef Dish

Aggregate Time to Prepare: **35 Minutes**

Yield: **4 Servings**

Ingredients:

- 1 Carrot, sliced thinly
- 1 pound Ground Beef

- 1 tbsp. Olive Oil
- 1 tsp Basil
- 1 tsp Oregano
- 14 ounces diced canned Tomatoes, undrained
- ½ cup shredded Mozzarella Cheese
- ½ cup Tomato Puree
- ½ Onion, diced

How to Cook:

1. Heat the oil in the Instant Pot using the "Sauté" mode.
2. Put in the onion and cook for 2 minutes.
3. Put in beef and cook until browned.
4. Stir in the canned tomatoes, tomato puree, basil, and oregano.
5. Shut and secure the lid and cook on HIGH for 15 minutes on MEAT/STEW.
6. Release the pressure using the quick release method and mix in the mozzarella.
7. Set to "Sauté" mode and cook for 5 additional minutes.
8. Your dish is ready! Have fun!

Nutritional Info: (Calories 330 | Total Fats 17g | Net Carbs 6g | Protein 28g |Fiber: 1.2g)

Italian Lamb Shanks

Aggregate Time to Prepare: **35 Minutes**

Yield: **4 Servings**

Ingredients:

- 1 large onion, thinly sliced

- 1 large tomato, roughly chopped
- 2 celery stalks, chopped
- 2 garlic cloves
- 3 cups beef broth
- 3 tbsp olive oil
- 4 lamb shanks
- 8 oz button mushrooms, sliced
- ¼ cup apple cider vinegar
- ¼ cup leeks, chopped

Spices:

- 1 tsp dried rosemary
- 2 tsp sea salt

How to Cook:

1. Mix the ingredients in the pot and stir thoroughly. Shut and secure the lid and set the steam release handle to the "Sealing" position.
2. Switch your Instant Pot to "Manual" mode and turn the timer to 25 minutes on high pressure.
3. When finished, depressurize using the natural release method and open the lid.
4. Serve instantly.
5. If you want, you can also drizzle with some Parmesan prior to serving.

Nutritional Info: (Calories 536 | Total Fats: 26.5g | Net Carbs: 7.3g | Protein: 62.6g | Fiber: 2.2g)

Italian Roast

Aggregate Time to Prepare: 45 Minutes

Yield: 4 Servings

Ingredients:

- 1 cup olive oil
- 1 lb boneless pork loin, chopped into 4 pieces
- 1 lemon, sliced
- 2 tbsp Dijon mustard
- 3 tbsp butter
- ¼ cup apple cider vinegar

Spices:

- 1 tbsp dried rosemary
- 1 tsp white pepper, freshly ground
- 2 tsp garlic powder
- 2 tsp salt
- 2 tsp smoked paprika
- ½ tsp dried thyme

How to Cook:

1. In a medium-sized container, mix together olive oil, apple cider, Dijon, lemon slices, dried rosemary, garlic powder, smoked paprika, thyme, salt, and pepper. Combine thoroughly and put in pork.
2. Coat each piece with the mixture and place in a large Ziploc bag, refrigerate overnight.
3. Turn on your Instant Pot and pour in one cup of water. Set the trivet at the bottom of the stainless steel insert.
4. Take the meat out of the fridge approximately 30 minutes before cooking. Put in an oven-safe container and drizzle with some of the marinade – approximately 3 tablespoons.
5. Loosely cover with aluminium foil and shut and secure the lid. Make sure the steam release handle is

on the "Sealing" position and push the "Meat" button. Cook for 20 minutes.
6. When finished, depressurize using the natural release method and open the lid.
7. Preheat the oven to 400 degrees. Line some parchment paper over a baking sheet and put in the meat.
8. Liberally brush with the marinade and roast for 15 minutes.
9. When finished, remove from the oven and brush with butter. Serve instantly.

Nutritional Info: (Calories 351| Total Fats: 25.4g | Net Carbs: 0.2g | Protein: 29.9g |Fiber: 0.1g)

Jamaican Jerk Pork

Aggregate Time to Prepare: **55 Minutes**

Yield: **4 Servings**

Ingredients:

- 1 cup Beef Broth
- 1 tbsp. Olive Oil
- 2 pounds Pork Shoulder
- 2 tbsp. Jamaican Spice Rub

How to Cook:

1. Switch the Instant Pot to "Sauté" mode and heat the oil.
2. Put in pork and cook on all sides, until browned.
3. Mix the spices and broth and pour over.
4. Shut and secure the lid and switch your instant pot to "Manual" mode and cook for 45 minutes.

5. Depressurize quickly.
6. Shred the meat with forks inside the pot.
7. Your dish is ready! Have fun!

Nutritional Info: (Calories 720| Total Fats 58g | Net Carbs 1.7g | Protein 55g |Fiber: 0.3g)

Jerk Pork

Aggregate Time to Prepare: 10 Minutes

Yield: 16 Servings

Ingredients:

- 1 tbsp. Olive Oil
- 4 lbs. Pork Shoulder
- ¼ cup Jamaican Jerk Spice Blend
- ½ cup Beef Stock

Direction:

1. Slightly coat the pork with olive oil and then rub thoroughly with the Jamaican jerk spice blend.
2. Set the Instant Pot on "Sauté" and brown the meat on all sides, 2 minutes each.
3. Put in the beef broth and place and lock the lid.
4. Manually set the cooking time to 45 minutes at high pressure.
5. When finished, remove from instant pot, shred using a fork and serve.

Nutritional Info: (Calories: 282 | Total Fats: 20g | Net Carbs: 0g | Proteins: 23g |Fibers: 0g)

Juicy Pot Roast

Aggregate Time to Prepare: 80 Minutes

Yield: 4 Servings

Ingredients:

- 1 Onion, sliced
- 2 cups Bone Broth
- 2 pounds Chuck Roast
- 2 tbsp. Coconut Oil
- Salt and Pepper, to taste

How to Cook:

1. Melt the coconut oil in your Instant Pot using the "Sauté" mode.
2. Sprinkle the meat with some salt and pepper.
3. Put it in the pot and sear on all sides until browned.
4. Pour the broth over and lock the lid.
5. Switch the Instant Pot to "Manual" mode and cook for 70 minutes.
6. Release the pressure using the quick release method.
7. Your dish is ready! Have fun!

Nutritional Info: (Calories 760| Total Fats 50g | Net Carbs 2.5g | Protein 67g |Fiber: 0.7g)

Kaccha Meatballs

Aggregate Time to Prepare: 30 Minutes

Yield: 6 Servings

Ingredients:

- 1 cup tomatoes, diced
- 1 tbsp butter
- 2 green chili peppers, thinly sliced
- 2 large eggs
- 2 lbs minced beef
- ½ cup beef broth
- ½ cup coriander, chopped

Spices:

- 1 tsp fresh ginger, grated
- 1 tsp garam masala powder
- 1 tsp red chili powder
- 1 tsp salt
- 2 tsp poppy seeds
- ½ tsp turmeric powder

How to Cook:

1. In a large mixing container, mixmeat, green peppers, coriander, eggs, and all the spices. Combine with your hands until all thoroughly blended. Mould 1 ½-inch balls and save for later.
2. Turn on the Instant Pot and push the "Sauté" button. Melt the butter in the stainless steel insert and place the meatballs on the bottom. Cook for 5-7 minutes, or until browned from all sides.
3. After that, put in diced tomatoes and pour in the broth. Shut and secure the lid .
4. Close the steam release handle and push the "Manual"button. Turn the timer to 10 minutes and cook on "High" pressure.
5. When you hear the cooker's end signal, release the pressure using the quick release method of the pressure.

6. Open the pot and move meatballs along with sauce to a serving dish.
7. Drizzle with some fresh parsley prior to serving.

Nutritional Info: (Calories 339 | Total Fats 13.7g | Net Carbs: 1.5g | Protein: 49g | Fiber: 0.8g)

Keto Sambar

Aggregate Time to Prepare: 55 Minutes

Yield: 6 Servings

Ingredients:

- 1 cup coconut milk
- 1 cup eggplant, chopped into chunks
- 1 large onion, thinly sliced
- 2 chili peppers, whole
- 2 cups cauliflower, chopped into florets
- 2 lbs pork chops, chop into bite-sized pieces
- 2 small tomatoes, chopped
- 3 garlic cloves, crushed
- 4 cups vegetable stock
- 4 tbsp ghee

Spices:

- 1 tbsp jiggery powder
- 1 tsp black pepper
- 2 tbsp chili powder
- 2 tsp salt
- 2 tsp sambar powder
- 3 tbsp brown mustard seeds
- 3 tsp turmeric powder

- ¼ cup fresh parsley, thinly sliced

How to Cook:

1. Put vegetables in a large colander and rinse thoroughly. Drain and save for later.
2. Cut the meat into bite-sized pieces. Put in a deep container and drizzle with salt and pepper. Save for later.
3. Turn on your Instant Pot and coat the inner pot with ghee. Switch your Instant Pot to "Sauté' mode and put in mustard seeds. Cook for 1 minute and then put in onions, garlic, and chili pepper. Stir thoroughly and cook for 3-4 minutes.
4. After that put in cauliflower and eggplant. Pour in some of the stock and bring it to a boil. Simmer for 5 minutes.
5. Lastly, put in the rest of the ingredients and stir thoroughly. Shut and secure the lid and set the steam release handle to the "Sealing" position and switch to "Manual' mode.
6. Turn the timer to 35 minutes on high pressure.
7. When finished, depressurize using the natural release method and optionally drizzle with some more fresh parsley.
8. Serve instantly.

Nutritional Info: (Calories 600| Total Fats 46.3g | Net Carbs: 4.8g | Protein: 36.1g |Fiber: 3.8g)

Knorr Demi-Glace Beef

Aggregate Time to Prepare: 80 Minutes

Yield: 4 Servings

Ingredients:

- 1 ¼ cup Beef Broth
- 1 Onion, chopped
- 1 tbsp. Worcestershire Sauce
- 2 Bay Leaves
- 2 Celery Stalks, chopped
- 2 tbsp. Olive Oil
- 2 pounds Beef Brisket
- 2 tbsp. Knorr-Demi Glace
- 2 tsp minced Garlic
- ½ tsp Pepper
- ½ tsp Salt

How to Cook:

1. Heat ½ of the olive oil in your Instant Pot using the "Sauté" mode.
2. Sprinkle the beef with salt and pepper and sear it for approximately 2 minutes on each side. Move to a plate.
3. Heat the rest of the olive oil and put in onions and celery.
4. Cook for 3 minutes.
5. Put in garlic and cook for 1 additional minute.
6. Mix together the sauces and broth, and pour inside the Instant Pot.
7. Put in the bay leaves and return the beef to the pot.
8. Shut and secure the lid and cook on MEAT/STEW for 1 hour.
9. Depressurize using the natural release method.
10. Your dish is ready! Have fun!

Nutritional Info: (Calories 508| Total Fats 19g | Net Carbs 6g | Protein 48g |Fiber: 1g)

Lamb Chops with Vegetables

Aggregate Time to Prepare: **40 Minutes**

Yield: 5 Servings

Ingredients:

- 1 bell pepper, thinly sliced
- 1 cup cauliflower, chop into florets
- 1 cup onions, thinly sliced
- 1 cup vegetable stock
- 2 tbsp oil
- 5 lamb chump chops

Spices:

- 1 tsp sat
- 2 bay leaves
- ½ tsp black pepper

How to Cook:

1. Oil-coat the bottom of the stainless steel inert with oil and put in lamb chops- drizzle with some salt and pepper and then put in the cauliflower. Spread on top onions and peppers and pour in the stock.
2. Shut and secure the lid and set the steam release handle to the "Sealing" position. Switch your Instant Pot to "Manual" mode and turn the timer to 15 minutes on high pressure.
3. When finished, depressurize using the quick release method and open the lid. Allow it to sit for some time.
4. Preheat the oven to 400 degrees F.

5. Move the meat to a baking dish and put in vegetables. Roast in the oven for 10-12 minutes on each side.
6. Remove from the oven and serve.

Nutritional Info: (Calories 331 | Total Fats: 15.8g | Net Carbs: 3.8g | Protein: 40.3g |Fiber: 1.4g)

Lamb Neck with Broccoli

Aggregate Time to Prepare: **25 Minutes**

Yield: **4 Servings**

Ingredients:

- 1 cup cauliflower, chopped into florets
- 1 large tomato, roughly chopped
- 1 lb broccoli, chopped
- 1 lb lamb neck, chopped
- 2 celery stalks, thinly sliced
- 2 small onions, thinly sliced
- 2 tbsp olive oil
- ½ small sweet potato, thinly sliced

Spices:

- 1 tbsp cayenne pepper
- 2 tsp salt
- ½ tsp black pepper, freshly ground

How to Cook:

1. Thoroughly wash the meat and chop into bite-sized pieces. Put at the bottom of your pot and put in vegetables.

2. Drizzle with olive oil, salt, cayenne pepper, and black pepper. Pour in the stock and shut and secure the lid.
3. Make sure the steam release handle is on the "Sealing" position. Switch your Instant Pot to "Manual" mode and turn the timer to 17 minutes on high pressure.
4. When finished, depressurize using the natural release method and open the lid. Stir thoroughly and serve instantly.

Nutritional Info: (Calories 346 | Total Fats: 15.9g | Net Carbs: 10.4g | Protein: 36.5g |Fiber: 5.3g)

Lamb Riblets with Herbs

Aggregate Time to Prepare: 50 Minutes

Yield: 4 Servings

Ingredients:

- 1 cup beef broth
- 1 tbsp lemon zest
- 2 tsp capers
- 3 garlic cloves, crushed
- 4 slabs of lamb riblets, approximately 2 lbs
- 4 tbsp butter
- 4 tbsp olive oil
- ¼ cup shallots, chopped

Spices:

- 1 tsp dried oregano
- 1 tsp dried parsley
- 1 tsp fresh mint, thinly sliced

- ½ tsp sea salt

How to Cook:

1. Thoroughly wash the meat under cold running water and place on a clean work surface. Rub uniformly with salt, oregano, and lemon zest. Move to the pot and pour in the broth.
2. Shut and secure the lid and set the steam release handle to the "Sealing" position. Switch your Instant Pot to "Manual" mode and cook for 20 minutes on high pressure.
3. When finished, depressurize using the natural release method for 10 minutes and then move the pressure valve to the "Venting" position to release any rest of the pressure.
4. Open the lid and remove the riblets from the pot. Move to a container and save for later.
5. Switch your Instant Pot to "Sauté' mode and melt the butter.
6. Put in shallots and garlic. Cook for 3-4 minutes and then put in the meat.
7. Brown on both sides for 4-5 minutes.
8. Take out of the pot and drizzle with some fresh mint. Serve with capers.

Nutritional Info: (Calories 665 | Total Fats: 42.5g | Net Carbs: 2.8g | Protein: 65.5g | Fiber: 0.2g)

Lamb Ribs with Garlic Gravy

Aggregate Time to Prepare: 40 Minutes

Yield: 6 Servings

Ingredients:

- 1 cup heavy cream
- 2 cups beef stock
- 2 lbs lamb ribs
- 2 tbsp milk, full-fat
- 2 tbsp sour cream
- 3 tbsp butter
- 4 garlic cloves, crushed
- ¼ cup Parmesan cheese, grated

Spices:

- 1 tsp salt
- 3 tbsp fresh parsley, thinly sliced
- ¼ tsp garlic powder
- ¼ tsp onion powder

How to Cook:

1. Wash thoroughly the ribs and place in the pot. Pour in the stock and season with salt. Shut and secure the lid and set the steam release handle to the "Sealing" position.
2. Switch your Instant Pot to "Manual" mode and turn the timer to 20 minutes.
3. When finished, release the pressure using the quick release method and open the lid. Remove the ribs from the pot and save for later.
4. Remove the liquid but make sure to reserve approximately three tablespoons.
5. After that, Switch your Instant Pot to "'Sauté" mode and coat the inner pot with butter. Put in garlic and briefly fry for one minute.
6. Put in Heavy cream, sour cream, milk, and the reserved stock. Drizzle with parsley, garlic powder, and onions powder.
7. Cook for 5-6 minutes, stirring continuously.

8. Put in Parmesan and push the "Cancel" button. Remove the gravy from the pot and drizzle over ribs.
9. Serve warm.

Nutritional Info: (Calories 453 | Total Fats: 26.8g | Net Carbs: 1.7g | Protein: 49g |Fiber: 0g)

Lamb Shoulder Hash

Aggregate Time to Prepare: 35 Minutes

Yield: 3 Servings

Ingredients:

- 1 large tomato, thinly sliced
- 2 celery stalks, thinly sliced
- 2 green bell peppers, thinly sliced
- 2 tbsp butter
- 2 tbsp olive oil
- 3 large eggs
- ¼ cup almonds, minced
- ¼ cup beef broth
- oz lamb shoulder, chopped into bite-sized pieces

Spices:

- 1 tsp salt
- ¼ tsp black pepper, ground
- ½ tsp garlic powder

How to Cook:

1. Turn on your Instant Pot and coat the inner pot with oil. Put in chopped meat and season with salt.

2. Cook for 5-6 minutes and then put in bell peppers and celery stalks. Carry on cooking for 10 minutes, stirring intermittently.
3. After that pour in the stock and put in tomatoes. Bring it to a boil and simmer for 15 minutes.
4. When most of the liquid has evaporated, mix in the butter and season with garlic powder and black pepper. If you want, you can also put in some more salt.
5. Tenderly crack the eggs and continue to cook until completely set.

Nutritional Info: (Calories 465 | Total Fats: 32.6g | Net Carbs: 7.9g | Protein: 33.7g |Fiber: 3g)

Lamb with Port Wine and Garlic Gravy

Aggregate Time to Prepare: 30 Minutes

Yield: 4 Servings

Ingredients:

- 1 tbsp. Butter
- 1 tbsp. Olive Oil
- 1 tbsp. Tomato Paste
- 1 tsp Balsamic Vinegar
- 10 Garlic Cloves, peeled
- 2 pounds Lamb Shanks
- ½ cup Chicken Broth
- ½ cup Port Wine
- ½ tsp Thyme

How to Cook:

1. Switch the Instant Pot to "Sauté" mode and heat the oil.
2. Put in the garlic and cook until they turn brown.
3. Put in tomato paste, broth, thyme, and port wine.
4. Stir to mix and put in the lamb shanks.
5. Shut and secure the lid and cook on HIGH for 20 minutes.
6. Depressurize using the natural release method.
7. Move the lambs to a plate.
8. Stir in the butter and vinegar.
9. Pour the sauce over the shanks.
10. Your dish is ready! Have fun!

Nutritional Info: (Calories 600| Total Fats 35g | Net Carbs 8.2g | Protein 58 |Fiber: 0.5g)

Lasagne

Aggregate Time to Prepare: 60 Minutes

Yield: 6 Servings

Ingredients:

- 1 cup Parmesan cheese (grated)
- 1 medium Eggplant
- 1 medium Red Onion (diced)
- 1 Red Bell Pepper (diced)
- 1 tbsp. Basil (chopped)
- 16 oz. Cottage Cheese
- 16 oz. Marinara Sauce
- 2 large Eggs
- 2 medium Zucchini
- 2 tbsp. Olive Oil
- 3 tsp Salt

- 8 oz. Mozzarella (shredded)

How to Cook:

1. Cut the zucchini and eggplant into ¼ inch slices lengthwise. Lay on a kitchen towel and drizzle with salt, and cover with another kitchen towel. Save for later for 15 minutes, and then pat dry.
2. Set the oven to broil at 500 degrees F. Put zucchini and eggplant on a baking sheet in single layer, and lightly brush them with olive oil. Broil for 8 minutes on the top rack, then flip them and broil for an additional 8 minutes.
3. In a container whisk two eggs and put into the cottage cheese. Combine thoroughly to mix.
4. Lightly brush the Instant Pot insert with olive oil and spread one-third of marinara sauce on the bottom.
5. Put a layer of eggplant slices in the Instant Pot. Spread half of the cottage cheese mixture over it, then half of bell peppers and onions. Then place a third of mozzarella.
6. Layer the zucchini slices, and spread over them one-third of the marinara sauce, followed by the rest of bell peppers and onions, and the third of mozzarella.
7. Layer the eggplant slices, and spread over them the last third of marinara sauce followed by mozzarella. Drizzle with half of the cup parmesan.
8. Shut and secure the lid and turn the timer and cook for 20 minutes at high pressure.
9. When finished depressurize using the quick release method. Serve drizzled with parmesan and chopped basil.

Nutritional Info: (Calories: 273 | Total Fats: 12g | Net Carbs: 12g | Proteins: 23g | Fibers: 6g)

Machaca

Aggregate Time to Prepare: 75-80 Minutes

Yield: 6 Servings

Ingredients:

- 1 cup Beef Broth
- 1 tsp Cumin
- 1 tsp Ground Black Pepper
- 1 tsp Salt
- 2 cups Salsa
- 2 tbsp. Tomato Paste
- 2 tbsp. Worcester Sauce
- 2 tsp Garlic Powder
- 3 tbsp. Rendered Pork Fat
- 3½ lbs. Beef Chuck Arm
- ½ tsp Ground Coriander Seeds

How to Cook:

1. Put in a container the garlic powder, cumin, coriander seeds, salt and pepper, and Combine thoroughly. Put in the chuck and rub thoroughly.
2. Switch your Instant Pot to "Sauté" mode and put in the pork fat.
3. When the fat has melted place in the chick and brown on four sides, 2 minutes on each.
4. While Chuck is browning mix together in a container the tomato paste, Worcester sauce, salsa and beef broth. Pour it over the chuck when it has browned.
5. Shut and secure the lid, and turn the timer and cook for 70 minutes at high pressure.

6. When finished allow the pressure to be released naturally.
7. Shred the chuck using a fork and mix thoroughly to reabsorb the juices.
8. Serve hot.

Nutritional Info: (Calories: 608 | Total Fats: 44g | Net Carbs: 6g | Proteins: 44g | Fibers: 1g)

Marinated Beef Shank

Aggregate Time to Prepare: **40 Minutes**

Yield: 8 Servings

Ingredients:

- 1 cup green onions
- 3 cups beef broth
- 3 lbs beef shank

For the marinade:

- 1 cup olive oil
- 1 tbsp fresh rosemary, chopped
- 1 tsp black pepper, ground
- 1 tsp salt
- 2 garlic cloves, crushed
- 2 tsp fresh thyme, chopped
- ½ tsp smoked paprika, ground

How to Cook:

1. In a large container, mix all marinade ingredients. Combine until thoroughly blended and save for later.
2. Thoroughly wash the meat under cold running water and pat dry with a kitchen paper. Put in a large Ziploc

bag and pour in the marinade. Shake thoroughly to coat the meat uniformly with the marinade. Refrigerate for 1 hour.
3. Turn on the Instant Pot and Switch your Instant Pot to "'Sauté" mode. Drain the meat and place in the stainless steel insert. Cook for 5 minutes on each side, or until golden brown.
4. Pour in the broth and securely lock the lid. Close the steam release handle and switch to "Manual' mode. Turn the timer to 20 minutes and cook on "High" pressure.
5. When your instant pot sounds the end signal, depressurize using the natural release method.
6. Open the pot and move the meat to a serving plate. Drizzle with some marinade and garnish with green onions.

Nutritional Info: (Calories 369 | Total Fats 14.7g | Net Carbs: 1.5g | Protein 53.8g | Fiber: 0.7g)

Marinated Pork

Aggregate Time to Prepare: 20 Minutes

Yield: 3 Servings

Ingredients:

- 1 celery stalk, thinly sliced
- 1 cup olive oil
- 1 lb pork pork butt, sliced
- 2 small onions, thinly sliced
- 2 tbsp fresh parsley, thinly sliced
- 2 tbsp lemon juice
- 4 garlic cloves, whole

- ¼ cup apple cider vinegar
- ½ cup sun-dried tomatoes

Spices:

- 1 tsp chili pepper
- 1 tsp white pepper, freshly ground
- 2 bay leaves
- 2 tsp fresh rosemary, thinly sliced
- 2 tsp salt

How to Cook:

1. In a medium-sized container, mix olive oil, cider, chopped onions, garlic, celery, tomatoes, lemon juice, and parsley. Sprinkle with rosemary, chili pepper, salt, white pepper, and bay leaves.
2. Combine thoroughly and submerge the meat into this mixture. Tightly cover with aluminium foil and marinate overnight.
3. Turn on your Instant Pot and position the trivet at the bottom of the inner pot. Put the meat directly on the trivet and drizzle with some of the marinade.
4. Shut and secure the lid and set the steam release handle to the "Sealing" position.
5. Switch your Instant Pot to "Manual" mode and cook for 15 minutes on high pressure.
6. When finished, depressurize using the quick release method and open the lid. Take the meat out of the pot and drizzle with some more marinade prior to serving.

Nutritional Info: (Calories 381 | Total Fats: 22.3g | Net Carbs: 3.1g | Protein: 40.3g | Fiber: 0.9g)

Meatballs in Enchilada Sauce

Aggregate Time to Prepare: **40 Minutes**

Yield: **4 Servings**

Ingredients:

- 1 Egg
- 1 pound Ground Beef
- 1 tbsp. Olive Oil
- 1 tsp Cumin
- ½ cup Almond Flour
- ½ tsp dried Parsley
- ½ tsp Garlic Powder

Enchilada Sauce:

- 1 ½ cups Salsa Verde
- 1 cup Chicken Broth
- 1 cup diced Onion
- 2 Garlic Cloves
- 2 tbsp. Adobo Sauce
- 2 tbsp. Olive Oil

How to Cook:

1. Heat 1 tbsp. oil in your Instant Pot using the "Sauté" mode.
2. Mix the ingredients for the meatballs in a container.
3. Mould mixtures.
4. Put them in the Instant Pot and cook until browned. Move to a plate.
5. Heat the rest of the 2 tbsp. oil.
6. Put in onion and cook for 3 minutes.
7. In the mean time, place the rest of the sauce ingredients in a blender and blend until smooth.

8. Pour the sous into the pot and cook for 2 additional minutes.
9. Put in the meatballs and shut and secure the lid.
10. Switch the Instant Pot to "High" and cook for 7 minutes.
11. Depressurize naturally and serve.

Nutritional Info: (Calories 440| Total Fats 38g | Net Carbs 2.2g | Protein 22g |Fiber: 1.6g)

Meatballs in Tomato Sauce

Aggregate Time to Prepare: 25 Minutes

Yield: 5 Servings

Ingredients:

- 1 tsp Olive Oil
- 1 tsp Onion Flakes
- 1 tsp Salt
- 1½ lbs. Ground Beef (85%)
- 2 Eggs
- 2 tbsp. Parsley Leaves (chopped)
- 3 Sugar-Free Marinara Sauce
- ¼ tsp Garlic Powder
- ¼ tsp Ground Black Pepper
- ¼ tsp Oregano
- ⅓ cup Warm Water
- ½ cup Almond Flour
- ¾ cup Parmesan (grated)

How to Cook:

1. Put all ingredients, except olive oil and marinara, in a container and mix thoroughly to mix. Make into fifteen roughly two inch balls.
2. Line the bottom of the Instant Pot insert with the olive oil.
3. Switch your Instant Pot to "Sauté" mode and brown the meatballs on all sides for 2 minutes, in three batches.
4. Return all meatballs in the pot and pour over the marinara sauce.
5. Shut and secure the lid, and turn the timer and cook for 10 minutes at low pressure.
6. When finished depressurize using the quick release method.
7. Serve warm with spaghetti squash.

Nutritional Info: (Calories: 455 | Total Fats: 33g | Net Carbs: 5g | Proteins: 34g | Fibers: 1g)

Mediterranean Beef Meatballs

Aggregate Time to Prepare: 30 Minutes

Yield: 6 Servings

Ingredients:

- 1 cup beef broth
- 1 cup fresh parsley, thinly sliced
- 1 cup tomatoes, diced
- 1 medium-sized yellow bell pepper, chopped
- 1 small red onion, chopped
- 1 tbsp olive oil
- 2 lbs ground beef
- 3 garlic cloves

- 3 large eggs
- ¼ cup feta cheese

Spices:

- 1 tsp sea salt
- ¼ tsp dried thyme, ground
- ½ tsp dried oregano, ground
- ½ tsp red pepper flakes

How to Cook:

1. In a large mixing container, mix beef, eggs, parsley, and cheese. Put in approximately 1-2 tablespoons of lukewarm water mix with your hands. Put in all the spices and mix until thoroughly blended.
2. Mould balls with the mixture, about 1-inch in diameter. Save for later,
3. Turn on the Instant Pot and coat the stainless steel insert with olive oil. Switch your Instant Pot to "Sauté' mode and put in onions and garlic. Stir-fry for 3-4 minutes, or until the onions translucent. Stir in the tomatoes and pour in the broth. Cautiously place the meatballs in the pot and shut and secure the lid.
4. Close the steam release handle and switch to "Manual' mode. Turn the timer to 10 minutes and cook on "High" pressure.
5. When your instant pot sounds the end signal, release the pressure using the quick release method and open the pot.
6. Move the meatballs to a serving container and drizzle with the rest of the sauce from the pot.
7. If you want, you can also brown the meatballs on each side before cooking in your instant pot.

Nutritional Info: (Calories 383 | Total Fats 16.1g | Net Carbs: 4.3g | Protein 51.7g |Fiber: 1.4g)

Mediterranean Pork

Aggregate Time to Prepare: **35 Minutes**

Yield: **4 Servings**

Ingredients:

- 1 lb pork neck, chopped into bite-sized pieces
- 1 onion, thinly sliced
- 2 medium-sized tomatoes, roughly chopped
- 2 tbsp apple cider vinegar
- 2 tbsp fresh parsley leaves, thinly sliced
- 2 tbsp salted capers
- 3 garlic cloves, crushed
- 4 kalamata olives
- 4 tbsp olive oil

Spices:

- 1 tsp dried rosemary
- ¼ tsp chili flakes
- ½ tsp pepper, ground
- ½ tsp salt

How to Cook:

1. Turn on your Instant Pot and Switch your Instant Pot to "'Sauté" mode. Heat up the olive oil and put in onions and garlic. Stir-fry for 3-4 minutes and then put in tomatoes. Carry on cooking until completely soft.
2. After that put in the meat and drizzle with apple cider vinegar. Drizzle with salt, pepper, rosemary, and chili.

3. Give it a food stir and cook for 4-5 minutes.
4. Lastly, pour in the stock and capers and olives. Shut and secure the lid and set the steam release handle. Switch your Instant Pot to "Manual" mode and turn the timer to 15 minutes on high pressure.
5. When finished, depressurize using the natural release method and open the lid. Drizzle with parsley and serve instantly.

Nutritional Info:(Calories 317 | Total Fats: 18.6g | Net Carbs: 5.1g | Protein: 30.8g |Fiber: 1.6g)

Mediterranean Tenderloin

Aggregate Time to Prepare: **55 Minutes**

Yield: 4 Servings

Ingredients:

- 1 cup cherry tomatoes, chopped
- 1 red pepper, thinly sliced
- 2 lbs lamb tenderloin, chopped
- 3 garlic cloves
- 4 tbsp olive oil
- ¼ cup fresh parsley, thinly sliced
- ¼ cup swerve
- ½ cup beef broth

Spices:

- 1 tsp dried oregano
- 1 tsp salt
- ¼ tsp onion powder

- ½ tsp dried thyme

How to Cook:

1. Put the meat in the pot and pour in enough water to cover. Drizzle with salt and shut and secure the lid.
2. Make sure the steam release handle is on the "Sealing" position and push the "Meat" button.
3. When finished, depressurize using the natural release method and cautiously open the lid. Remove the meat and the liquid from the pot and Switch your Instant Pot to "'Sauté" mode.
4. Heat the inner pot and put in olive oil. Put in garlic, bell peppers, and season with some salt, oregano, thyme, and onion powder. Stir thoroughly and simmer for 5 minutes.
5. After that put in tomatoes and pour in some of the broth. Cook until tomatoes have completely softened.
6. Stir in swerve and mix thoroughly. Push the "Cancel" button.
7. Move the mixture to a food processor or a blender and pulse until completely smooth.
8. Preheat the oven to 400 degrees. Line some parchment paper over a baking sheet and put in the meat. Drizzle with the tomato sauce and drizzle with parsley.
9. Bake for 15 minutes.

Nutritional Info: (Calories 569 | Total Fats: 31g | Net Carbs: 4g | Protein: 65.3g | Fiber: 1.1g)

Mexican Pork Carnitas

Aggregate Time to Prepare: 60 Minutes

Yield: 11 Serving

Ingredients:

- 1 tsp Ground Black Pepper
- 1½ tsp Cumin
- 2 Bay Leaves
- 2 Chipotle Peppers in Adobo Sauce
- 2 tsp Salt
- 2½ lbs. Pork Shoulder
- 6 cloves Garlic (chop in quarters lengthwise)
- ¼ tsp Dry Adobo Seasoning
- ¼ tsp Dry Oregano
- ½ tsp Garlic Powder
- ¾ cup Chicken Broth

How to Cook:

1. Sprinkle the pork shoulder with salt and pepper.
2. Put in the Instant Pot and set it to "Sauté". Brown the pork on both sides for around 5 minutes and then remove from pot and leave to cool enough to handle, some 10 minutes.
3. While meat is cooling mix together cumin, oregano, adobo and garlic powder in a container.
4. With a smaller knife make an inch deep incisions on all sides of the meat and stuff in them pieces of garlic.
5. Rub the pork with the mixture of dry spices, and save for later.
6. Put in the Instant Pot the broth, chipotle pepper and bay leave, and stir to mix.
7. Put in the pork to the Instant Pot and set it on "Meat/Stew" settings. Manually turn the timer and cook for 50 minutes at high pressure.
8. When finished allow to naturally releases pressure.

9. Remove the lid and bay leaves, and shred the meat using a fork. Then stir thoroughly so that meat would reabsorb the juices.
10. Serve warm.

Nutritional Info: (Calories: 160 | Total Fats: 7g | Net Carbs: 1g | Proteins: 20g | Fibers: 0g)

Milk Braised Pork Loin

Aggregate Time to Prepare: **55 Minutes**

Yield: **4 Servings**

Ingredients:

- 1 Bay Leaf
- 1 tsp Pepper
- 2 ½ cups Milk
- 2 pounds Pork Loin
- 2 tbsp. Butter
- 2 tbsp. Olive Oil
- 2 tsp Salt

How to Cook:

1. Heat the oil in the Instant Pot using the "Sauté" mode.
2. Sprinkle the meat with salt and pepper and sear on all sides.
3. Pour the milk over and put in butter and bay leaf.
4. Shut and secure the lid and cook on HIGH for 30 minutes.
5. Wait for about 2 minutes before doing a quick pressure release.
6. Your dish is ready! Have fun!

Nutritional Info: (Calories 380| Total Fats 19g | Net Carbs 2.5g | Protein 380g |Fiber: 1.5g)

Minty Lamb and Spinach Salad

Aggregate Time to Prepare: 50 Minutes

Yield: 4 Servings

Ingredients:

- 1 ½ pounds boneless Lamb
- 1 ½ tbsp. Lemon Juice
- 1 cup chopped Mint
- 1 tsp Cumin
- 2 cups Baby Spinach
- 2 cups Beef Stock
- 4 ounces Feta Cheese, crumbled
- ¼ cup plus 1 tbsp. Olive Oil
- ¼ cup toasted Pecans
- ¼ tsp Thyme
- Salt and Pepper, to taste

How to Cook:

1. Rub the lamb with salt, pepper, garlic, thyme, and 1 tbsp. oil.
2. Put in the Instant Pot and pour the broth over.
3. Switch the Instant Pot to "High" and cook for 40 minutes.
4. Allow it to cool and slice.
5. Put the spinach in a large serving container.
6. Spread on top lamb and drizzle with mint.
7. Scatter the pecans over and spread on top feta cheese.

8. Combine together the rest of the olive oil and lemon juice, and season with some salt and pepper.
9. Drizzle over the salad.
10. Your dish is ready! Have fun!

Nutritional Info: (Calories 240| Total Fats 21g | Net Carbs 8.1g | Protein 14g |Fiber: 2.9g)

Mustard Cheese Meatballs

Aggregate Time to Prepare: 20 Minutes

Yield: 6 Servings

Ingredients:

- 1 cup beef stock
- 1 small Jalapeno pepper, chopped
- 1 tbsp butter
- 1 tbsp Dijon mustard
- 1 tbsp fresh parsley, thinly sliced
- 2 garlic cloves, crushed
- 2 large eggs, beaten
- 2 lbs lean ground beef
- 3 oz cheddar cheese

Spices:

- 1 tsp salt
- ¼ tsp smoked paprika, ground
- ½ tsp black pepper, ground

How to Cook:

1. In a large mixing container, mix ground beef, cheese, eggs, garlic, Jalapeno pepper, parsley, mustard, paprika, salt, and pepper.

2. Combine until thoroughly blended.
3. Mould the meatballs, approximately 1 to 1 1/2 –inch in diameter and save for later.
4. Turn on your Instant Pot and put in butter to the stainless steel insert. Tenderly melt over the "Sauté" mode, stirring continuously.
5. Spread the meatballs on the bottom of the pot and gradually pour in the beef stock.
6. Shut and secure the lid and set the steam release the handle by moving the valve to the "Sealing" position.
7. Switch your Instant Pot to "Manual" mode and turn the timer to 10 minutes. Cook on "High" pressure.
8. When finished, release the pressure using the quick release method and open the pot.
9. Move the meatballs to a serving platter and drizzle with some of the liquid from the pot.
10. If you want, you can also garnish with some thinly sliced cilantro prior to serving.

Nutritional Info: (Calories 387 | Total Fats 17.9g | Net Carbs: 0.9g | Protein 52.2g |Fiber: 0.3g)

Parsi Veal with Eggs

Aggregate Time to Prepare: 30 Minutes

Yield: 4 Servings

Ingredients:

- 1 cup tomatoes, chopped
- 1 medium-sized red onion, diced
- 2 garlic cloves, thinly sliced

- 2 lbs minced veal
- 2 tbsp butter
- 2 tsp apple cider vinegar
- 3 large eggs, free-range

Spices:

- 1 tbsp fresh ginger, grated
- 1 tsp cayenne pepper, ground
- 1 tsp salt
- ½ tsp chili powder
- ½ tsp turmeric powder

How to Cook:

1. Turn on the Instant Pot and push the "Sauté" button. Melt the butter in the stainless steel insert and onions and garlic. Stir-fry for 6-8 minutes, or until caramelized.
2. Put in minced veal and break with a wooden spatula. Cook for 10 minutes, stirring intermittently.
3. After that, put in tomatoes, vinegar, and all the spices. Pour in ½ cup of water and stir thoroughly. Shut and secure the lid .
4. Close the steam release handle and push the "Manual" button. Turn the timer to 5 minutes and cook on "High" pressure.
5. When you hear the cooker's end signal, release the pressure using the quick release method and open the pot.
6. Push the "Sauté" button and continue to cook for 5 additional minutes, or until the mixture almost evaporated.
7. Poach the eggs on the top of the mixture and cook for 2-3 minutes without stirring.
8. Turn off your Instant pot and move to a serving dish.

9. Garnish with some cilantro, parsley, and lime prior to serving.
10. Have fun!

Nutritional Info: (Calories 524 | Total Fats 28.8g | Net Carbs: 5.1g | Protein: 61g | Fiber: 1.6g)

Pepper Curry

Aggregate Time to Prepare: 55 Minutes

Yield: 5 Servings

Ingredients:

- 1 cup sun-roasted tomatoes, diced
- 1 lb beef stew meat
- 2 red bell peppers, sliced
- 3 green chili peppers, chopped
- 4 tbsp butter
- 5 garlic cloves, crushed

Spices:

- 1 tbsp cayenne pepper
- 1 tsp cumin powder
- 2 tbsp fresh ginger, grated
- 2 tsp coriander powder
- 2 tsp garam masala

How to Cook:

1. Mix the ingredients in the pot and stir thoroughly
2. Shut and secure the lid and set the steam release handle to the "Sealing" position. Switch your Instant Pot to "Manual" mode and turn the timer to 30 minutes.

3. When finished, depressurize using the natural release method and cautiously open the lid. If you want, you can also drizzle with some fresh parsley prior to serving.

Nutritional Info:(Calories 278 | Total Fats: 15g | Net Carbs: 5.2g | Protein: 28.5g | Fiber: 1.2g)

Pepper Short Ribs

Aggregate Time to Prepare: **40 Minutes**

Yield: **8 Servings**

Ingredients:

- 1 cup heavy cream
- 1 medium-sized red onion, diced
- 2 cups beef stock
- 3 lbs beef short ribs
- 4 garlic cloves, crushed

Spices:

- 1 tsp fresh sage, chopped
- 1 tsp fresh thyme, chopped
- 1 tsp Italian seasoning
- 2 tsp black pepper, ground

How to Cook:

1. Turn on your Instant Pot and put in onions and garlic to the stainless steel insert. Cook for 3-4 minutes, or until onions translucent.
2. Put in the ribs and pour in the broth. Drizzle with Italian seasoning, thyme, and sage.

3. Shut and secure the lid and set the steam release handle by moving the valve to the "Sealing" position. Switch your Instant Pot to "Manual" mode and turn the timer to 20 minutes. Cook on "High" pressure.
4. When finished, depressurize using the quick release method and open the pot.
5. Stir in the heavy cream and Switch your Instant Pot to "'Sauté" mode. Simmer for 10 additional minutes.
6. Move the meat to a serving plate and drizzle over with the cream sauce.

Nutritional Info: (Calories 416 | Total Fats 21.2g | Net Carbs: 2.3g | Protein 20.4g |Fiber: 21.2g)

Pepperoncini Pot Roast

Aggregate Time to Prepare: 120 Minutes

Yield: 8 Servings

Ingredients:

- 1 envelope Gravy Combine
- 5 pounds Beef Roast
- 6 Pepperoncini
- ¼ cup Butter
- ½ cup Beef Broth
- ½ cup Pepperoncini Juice

How to Cook:

1. Put all of the ingredients in the Instant Pot and shut and secure the lid.
2. Switch your Instant Pot to "Manual" mode and cook on HIGH for 90 minutes.
3. Allow the pressure to drop naturally.

4. Slice the meat and drizzle with the gravy.
5. Your dish is ready! Have fun!

Nutritional Info: (Calories 600| Total Fats 58g | Net Carbs 6.5g | Protein 63g |Fiber: 1.5g)

Picadillo

Aggregate Time to Prepare: 20 Minutes

Yield: 6 Servings

Ingredients:

- 1 Bay Leaf
- 1 tbsp. Olive Oil
- 1 tsp Cumin
- 1 tsp Ground Black Pepper
- 1 tsp Salt
- 1½ lbs. Lean Ground Beef
- 2 cloves Garlic (minced)
- 2 tbsp. Coriander Leaves (chopped)
- 3½ oz. Onion (diced)
- 4 oz. Tomato Sauce
- 5 tbsp. Water
- 6 Capers
- 6 Olives (stuffed with pepper)
- 6 oz. Tomato (diced)
- ½ Red Bell Pepper (diced)

How to Cook:

1. Switch your Instant Pot to "Sauté" mode and pour in it one tablespoon of olive oil. Put in beef to it and

lightly brown it while breaking up bigger chunks with a spatula, some 3-4 minutes.
2. Put in the onion, garlic, chopped tomato, salt, pepper and coriander leaves. Stir and cook for a minute.
3. Put in the olives, capers, cumin, bell pepper, tomato sauce, bay leaf and water. Stir to mix.
4. Shut and secure the lid and manually turn the timer and cook for 15 minutes at high pressure.
5. When finished allow the pressure to be released naturally. Serve warm.

Nutritional Info: (Calories: 207 | Total Fats: 8.5g | Net Carbs: 4g | Proteins: 25g | Fibers: 1g)

Pork and Brussel Sprouts

Aggregate Time to Prepare: **40 Minutes**

Yield: **4 Servings**

Ingredients:

- 1 cup Beef Flour
- 1 cup sliced Onions
- 1 tbsp. Arrowroot
- 1 tbsp. Coconut Oil
- 2 cups Brussel Sprouts
- 2 tsp Garlic Cloves
- 4 Pork Chops, boneless
- ½ tsp Thyme

How to Cook:

1. Melt the coconut oil in the Instant Pot using the "Sauté" mode.

2. Put in the pork and cook until browned on all sides. Move to a plate.
3. Put in the onions, garlic, and thyme, and cook for one additional minute.
4. Put in the beef and return the chops to the pot.
5. Shut and secure the lid and cook for 15 minutes on MANUAL.
6. Release the pressure using the quick release method.
7. Put in the Brussel sprouts and shut and secure the lid again.
8. Switch the Instant Pot to "High" and cook for 3 minutes.
9. Move the pork and Brussel sprouts to a plate.
10. Stir in the arrowroot and cook the sauce using the "Sauté" mode until thickens.
11. Drizzle over the meat and Brussel sprouts.
12. Your dish is ready! Have fun!

Nutritional Info: (Calories 320 | Total Fats 18g | Net Carbs 8g | Protein 24g |Fiber: 1.6g)

Pork Butt Chops in Creamy Gravy

Aggregate Time to Prepare: 20 Minutes

Yield: 3 Servings

Ingredients:

- 1 cup cauliflower, chopped into florets
- 10 oz pork butt, chopped into bite-sized pieces
- 4 tbsp olive oil
- ¼ tsp dried rosemary

For the sauce:

- 1 cup spinach, torn
- 1 tsp sea salt
- ¼ cup almond flour
- ¼ cup button mushrooms
- ½ cup milk, full-fat
- ½ tsp black pepper, ground

How to Cook:

1. Mix the sauce ingredients using a food processor and process until smooth. Save for later.
2. Turn on the Instant Pot and coat the stainless steel insert with some olive oil. Put in the meat and cauliflower. Drizzle with rosemary and stir thoroughly. Cook for 3 minutes.
3. Pour in the sauce and ½ cup of milk.
4. Shut and secure the lid and close the steam release handle. Switch the Instant pot to "Manual" mode and turn the timer to 5 minutes. When finished, release the pressure using the quick release method and open the pot.
5. Serve instantly.

Nutritional Info:(Calories 389 | Total Fats 27g | Net Carbs: 3.5g | Protein 32.4g | Fiber: 1.4g)

Pork Butt in Garlic Gravy

Aggregate Time to Prepare: 50 Minutes

Yield: 5 Servings

Ingredients:

- 1 ½ cups beef stock
- 2 large celery stalks, thinly sliced

- 2 lbs pork butt, chop into 5 smaller pieces
- 2 tbsp soy sauce
- 3 garlic cloves, crushed
- 4 bacon slices, chopped
- 4 tbsp olive oil
- 6 pickles, sliced
- ¼ cup balsamic vinegar

Spices:

- 1 tsp garlic powder
- 1 tsp salt
- ½ tsp black pepper, freshly ground
- ½ tsp chili powder
- ½ tsp dried basil
- ½ tsp dried marjoram

How to Cook:

1. Wash thoroughly the meat and pat dry with some kitchen paper. Put on a large cutting board. Using a sharp knife, make 7-8 incisions in each part. Stuff each with celery, garlic, and pickles. Drizzle with salt, pepper, and chili powder. Save for later.
2. Turn on your Instant Pot and coat the inner pot with oil. Heat up and put in the rest of the celery. Cook for 2-3 minutes and then put in bacon.
3. Carry on cooking for an additional 5 minutes.
4. After that put in the pork and pour in the beef stock. Shut and secure the lid and set the steam release handle. Switch your Instant Pot to "Manual" mode and turn the timer to 15 minutes.
5. When finished, depressurize using the quick release method and open the lid. Switch your Instant Pot to "Sauté' mode again and pour in the soy sauce. Drizzle

with basil, marjoram, and garlic powder. Cook for 6-7 minutes.
6. When finished, push the "Cancel" button and serve instantly.

Nutritional Info: (Calories 461 | Total Fats: 24.3g | Net Carbs: 2.3g | Protein: 54.8g |Fiber: 1.1g)

Pork Carnitas

Aggregate Time to Prepare: 70 Minutes

Yield: 4 Servings

Ingredients:

- 1 Jalapeno, diced
- 1 Onion, chopped
- 1 tbsp. Olive Oil
- 1 tsp Cumin
- 1 tsp Oregano
- 2 cups Beef Broth
- ½ cup Water
- 2 pounds Pork Shoulder
- 2 tsp minced Garlic
- Juice of 2 Limes

How to Cook:

1. Switch the Instant Pot to "Sauté" mode and heat the oil.
2. Put in the pork and sear on all sides until browned.
3. Put the rest of the ingredients in the pot and stir to mix.
4. Shut and secure the lid and choose MANUAL.

5. Switch the Instant Pot to "High" and cook for 30 minutes.
6. Depressurize using the natural release method, for 20 minutes.
7. Open the lid and shred the pork with two forks.
8. Cook some more using the "Sauté" mode if you want a thicker sauce.
9. Your dish is ready! Have fun!

Nutritional Info: (Calories 650| Total Fats 35g | Net Carbs 7g | Protein 55g |Fiber: 1.8g)

Pork Chops

Aggregate Time to Prepare: 30 Minutes

Yield: 8 Servings

Ingredients:

- 3 tbsp. Butter (chop into pieces)
- 3⅓ lbs. Pork Chops
- 5 tbsp. Lime Juice
- ½ cup Salsa
- ½ tsp Ground Cumin
- ¾ tsp Garlic Powder
- ¾ tsp Ground Black Pepper
- ¾ tsp Salt

How to Cook:

1. Combine salsa and lemon juice and save for later.
2. Combine cumin, garlic powder, salt and pepper, and rub in the pork chops.
3. Switch your Instant Pot to "Sauté" mode and put in butter.

4. When butter has melted brown pork chops in 2-3 batches, 2-3 minutes on each side.
5. Layer the chops in the Instant Pot in two layers, covering each with salsa.
6. Shut and secure the lid and turn the timer and cook for 15 minutes at high pressure.
7. Release the pressure using the "quick release" method and serve.

Nutritional Info: (Calories: 364 | Total Fats: 17g | Net Carbs: 3g | Proteins: 51g |Fibers: 0g)

Pork Chops with Cheese and Prosciutto

Aggregate Time to Prepare: **55 Minutes**

Yield: **5 Servings**

Ingredients:

- 1 onion, thinly sliced
- 2 garlic cloves, crushed
- 2 tbsp balsamic vinegar
- 3 oz prosciutto
- 4 tbsp olive oil
- 5 pork chops, boneless
- ½ cup cottage cheese
- ½ cup diced canned tomatoes, sugar-free

Spices:

- 1 tsp dried basil
- 1 tsp salt
- ½ tsp black pepper, freshly ground

How to Cook:

1. Wash thoroughly the meat and pat dry with a kitchen towel. Put on a cutting board and remove the bones. Rub thoroughly with some olive oil, salt, pepper, and basil. Allow it to sit for 15 minutes.
2. Turn on your Instant Pot and position a trivet at the bottom of the inner pot. Pour in one cup of water and save for later.
3. Move the meat into a small baking pan. Drizzle with some more olive oil and put in cheese and prosciutto. Loosely cover with aluminium foil and place in the pot.
4. Switch your Instant Pot to "Manual" mode and set the steam release handle. Turn the timer to 20 minutes on high pressure.
5. When finished, depressurize using the quick release method and open the lid. Remove the pan and save for later.
6. After that Switch your Instant Pot to "'Sauté" mode and coat the inner pot with some oil. Put in onions and cook until translucent. Pour in tomatoes and cook for 10-12 minutes, stirring intermittently. If you want, you can also season with some more salt or dried basil.
7. Take out of the pot and drizzle over meat. Serve instantly.

Nutritional Info: (Calories 416 | Total Fats: 19g | Net Carbs: 3.6g | Protein: 54.6g | Fiber: 0.7g)

Pork Chops with Sautéed Peppers

Aggregate Time to Prepare: **35 Minutes**

Yield: 5 Servings

Ingredients:

- 1 cup beef broth
- 1 lb pork chops, chop into bite-sized pieces
- 2 bacon slices, chopped
- 2 chili peppers, chopped
- 2 red bell peppers, sliced
- 2 small onions, thinly sliced
- 2 tbsp butter, unsalted

Spices:

- 2 tsp Italian seasoning
- ¼ tsp salt

How to Cook:

1. Thoroughly wash the meat under cold running water and drizzle with one teaspoon of Italian seasoning. Put in the instant pot and pour in the broth.
2. Shut and secure the lid and set the steam release handle. Switch your Instant Pot to "Manual" mode and turn the timer to 10 minutes on high pressure.
3. When finished, release the pressure by moving the handle to the "Venting" position and cautiously open the lid.
4. Take the meat out of the pot along with the broh and Switch your Instant Pot to "'Sauté" mode.
5. Oil-coat the inner pot with butter and put in onion. Sauté for 2 minutes and then put in peppers. Drizzle with salt and the rest of the Italian seasoning and cook for 2-3 minutes.
6. After that put in bacon and stir thoroughly. If you want, you can also put in some more salt or Italian

seasoning and cook for 5 minutes. If needed, put in some beef broth – approximately 2 tablespoons at the time.
7. Lastly, put in the meat and stir thoroughly. Cook for 5 minutes.
8. Push the "Cancel" button and serve instantly.

Nutritional Info: (Calories 407| Total Fats: 30.8g | Net Carbs: 5.4g | Protein: 25g |Fiber: 1.3g)

Pork Cutlets with Avocado Sauce

Aggregate Time to Prepare: 25 Minutes

Yield: 4 Servings

Ingredients:

- 1 cup beef broth
- 1 tsp salt
- 3 tbsp butter
- 4 pork cutlets, boneless

For the sauce:

- 1 avocado, chopped into chunks
- 1 cup onions, thinly sliced
- 1 tbsp lemon juice
- 1 tsp fresh basil, thinly sliced
- 2 garlic cloves, crushed
- 2 tbsp olive oil
- ¼ cup heavy cream
- ½ tsp cayenne pepper

How to Cook:

1. Turn on your Instant Pot and coat the inner pot with butter. Heat up and put in cutlets. Brown for 2-3 minutes on both sides and then start put ining broth, two tablespoons at the time. Simmer for 10-12 minutes or until you have used all the broth.
2. Remove the cutlets from the pot and save for later.
3. After that put in onions to the same pot and stir fry for about 2 minutes. Then put in avocado and approximately ¼ cup of water. Simmer until completely tender and then put in garlic, olive oil, cayenne pepper, basil, and lemon juice. Stir thoroughly and take out of the pot.
4. Move the sauce to a food processor and put in heavy cream. Process until smooth.
5. Drizzle over cutlets and serve.

Nutritional Info: (Calories 540 | Total Fats: 34.8g | Net Carbs: 4.1g | Protein: 48.7g | Fiber: 4.1g)

Pork Cutlets with Mushrooms

Aggregate Time to Prepare: 25 Minutes

Yield: 4 Servings

Ingredients:

- 1 cup shiitake mushrooms, sliced
- 1 onion, thinly sliced
- 2 cups button mushrooms, sliced
- 2 garlic cloves, crushed
- 2 pork cutlets, boneless
- 2 tbsp fresh parsley, thinly sliced
- 4 tbsp oil
- ½ cup heavy cream

Spices:

- 1 tsp dried thyme
- 1 tsp salt
- ½ tsp black pepper, freshly ground

How to Cook:

1. Thoroughly wash the meat and pat dry with a kitchen paper. Using a sharp knife, cautiously chop the meat into bite-sized pieces. Sprinkle with salt and pepper. Save for later.
2. Turn on your Instant Pot and Switch your Instant Pot to "'Sauté" mode. Oil-coat the inner pot with oil and put in onions and garlic. Sauté for 3-4 minutes and then put in mushrooms. Pour in the heavy cream and cook for 2-3 minutes.
3. After that put in the meat and season with thyme. Stir thoroughly and pour in ¼ cup of water.
4. Cook for 12-15 minutes, stirring intermittently. Stir in the parsley and push the "Cancel" button.
5. Optionally drizzle with some grated Parmesan cheese prior to serving.

Nutritional Info: (Calories 356 | Total Fats: 22.9g | Net Carbs: 8g | Protein: 28.6g |Fiber: 1.8g)

Pork in Tomato Sauce

Aggregate Time to Prepare: **20 Minutes**

Yield: **4 Servings**

Ingredients:

- 1 cup broccoli, thinly sliced

- 1 large onion, thinly sliced
- 1 lb pork loin, chopped
- 2 cups cherry tomatoes, thinly sliced
- ¼ cup olive oil

Spices:

- 1 rosemary sprig, fresh
- 1 tsp salt
- ¼ tsp chili powder
- ½ tsp black pepper, freshly ground

How to Cook:

1. Wash thoroughly the meat and drizzle with salt and pepper. Put in the pot and drizzle with oil. Pour in the broth and put in onions, broccoli, and tomatoes. Sprinkle with come chili powder and put in rosemary.
2. Stir thoroughly and shut and secure the lid. Make sure the steam release handle is on the "Sealing" position and push the "Stew" button.
3. When finished, depressurize using the natural release method and open the lid.
4. Remove the rosemary sprig and optionally drizzle with some more chili pepper.

Nutritional Info: (Calories 421 | Total Fats: 28.1g | Net Carbs: 6g | Protein: 32.8g | Fiber: 2.5g)

Pork Keto Risotto with Eggs

Aggregate Time to Prepare: **45 Minutes**

Yield: **4 Servings**

Ingredients:

- 1 cup cauliflower, thinly sliced
- 1 green chili pepper, thinly sliced
- 1 large onion, thinly sliced
- 1 small zucchini, sliced
- 10 oz pork neck, chopped into bite-sized pieces
- 2 eggs
- 4 tbsp olive oil
- 4 tbsp soy sauce

Spices:

- 1 tsp dried marjoram
- 1 tsp salt
- ½ tsp black pepper, freshly ground

How to Cook:

1. Put the meat in a deep container and season with salt, pepper, and marjoram. Drizzle with some olive oil and place in the pot.
2. Switch your Instant Pot to "Sauté' mode and cook for 5-6 minutes, stirring continuously. After that put in onions, zucchini, and pepper. Carry on cooking for an additional 5-6 minutes.
3. Push the "Cancel" button and pour in 1 cup of water. Shut and secure the lid and set the steam release handle. Cook for 7 minutes on the "Manual" mode.
4. When finished, depressurize using the quick release method and open the lid. Put in cauliflower and shut and secure the lid again.
5. Turn the timer to 3 minutes on high pressure. When you hear the end signal, depressurize using the quick release method and open the lid.
6. Stir in the soy sauce and crack eggs. Stir thoroughly and cover with the lid. Allow it to sit for some time prior to serving.

Nutritional Info:(Calories 288 | Total Fats: 18.8g | Net Carbs: 5.4g | Protein: 23.6g |Fiber: 1.9g)

Pork Leg Roast

Aggregate Time to Prepare: 55 Minutes

Yield: 6 Servings

Ingredients:

- 2 spring onions, thinly sliced
- 2 tbsp mustard
- 3 lbs pork leg
- 3 tbsp soy sauce
- 4 tbsp olive oil

Spices:

- 1 tsp coriander seeds
- 1 tsp white peppercorn
- 2 bay leaves
- ½ tsp dried rosemary
- ½ tsp dried sage

How to Cook:

1. Oil-coat the inner pot with two tablespoons of olive oil and Switch your Instant Pot to "'Sauté" mode. Heat up and put in spring onions and coriander seeds. Cook for 2-3 minutes and then put in the meat.
2. Pour in 5-6 cups of water and put in bay leaves. Shut and secure the lid. Make sure the steam release handle is on the "Sealing" position and push the "Meat" button.
3. Cook for 25 minutes on high pressure.

4. When finished, depressurize using the natural release method and open the lid. Take the meat out of the pot and chill for some time.
5. Preheat the oven to 450 degrees F. Oil-coat a baking sheet with the rest of the oil and save for later.
6. Rub the meat with sage and rosemary and place on a baking sheet. Pour in approximately one cup of water.
7. Put in the oven and reduce the heat to 400. Roast for 20 minutes.

Nutritional Info:(Calories 428 | Total Fats: 18.4g | Net Carbs: 1.6g | Protein: 60.9g |Fiber: 0.7g)

Pork Loin with Leeks

Aggregate Time to Prepare: **45 Minutes**

Yield: **4 Servings**

Ingredients:

- 1 celery stalk, chopped
- 1 lb pork loin, boneless
- 1 onion, thinly sliced
- 2 cups beef broth
- 2 large leeks, chopped
- 4 tbsp olive oil
- ¼ cup apple cider vinegar

Spices:

- 1 ½ tsp sea salt
- 2 tbsp stevia crystal (or powder)
- 2 tsp dried celery
- ¼ tsp chili powder

- ¼ tsp dried thyme

How to Cook:

1. Rub the meat with salt and place in the pot. Pour in enough water to cover and shut and secure the lid.
2. Set the steam release handle and push the "Maual" button. Turn the timer to 25 minutes on high pressure.
3. When finished, depressurize using the quick release method and open the lid. Move the meat to a container and remove the water. Save for later.
4. Switch your Instant Pot to "Sauté' mode and heat up the oil. Put in onions, leeks, and celery. Stir thoroughly and cook for 3-4 minutes.
5. In the mean time, place the meat on a cutting board and chop into bite-sized pieces. Put in to the pot and stir thoroughly. Drizzle with apple cider vinegar and season with spices.
6. Brown for 4-5 minutes, stirring intermittently.
7. Push the "Cancel" button and serve instantly.

Nutritional Info: (Calories 456| Total Fats: 30.6g | Net Carbs: 8.1g | Protein: 34.4g |Fiber: 1.5g)

Pork Neck with Jalapeno Peppers

Aggregate Time to Prepare: **40 Minutes**

Yield: **4 Servings**

Ingredients:

- 1 onion, thinly sliced
- 2 cups cherry tomatoes, sliced

- 2 jalapeno peppers, chopped
- 2 lbs pork neck, chopped
- 3 tbsp butter, melted
- 3 tbsp olive oil
- 4 cups beef broth

Spices:

- 1 tbsp cayenne pepper
- 1 tsp chili powder
- 1 tsp salt
- 2 bay leaves

How to Cook:

1. Thoroughly wash the meat under cold running water and pat dry with a kitchen paper. Put on a cutting board and chop into bite-sized pieces.
2. Turn on the Instant Pot and grease the bottom of the inner pot with olive oil. Put in the meat and drizzle with salt. After that put in vegetables and season with the rest of the spices.
3. Pour in the broth and put in butter. Make sure the steam release handle is on the "Sealing" position and push the "Meat" button. Cook for 2 minutes.
4. Turn off the Instant Pot by pressing the "Cancel" button. Perform a quick pressure release and open the lid.
5. Serve warm.

Nutritional Info:(Calories 559| Total Fats 28.8g | Net Carbs: 5.5g | Protein: 65.5g |Fiber: 2g)

Pork Neck with Sesame Seeds and Soy Sauce

Aggregate Time to Prepare: **45 Minutes**

Yield: **4 Servings**

Ingredients:

- 1 large onion, thinly sliced
- 1 lb pork neck, chopped into bite-sized pieces
- 3 tbsp oil
- 3 tbsp sesame seeds
- 4 garlic cloves, whole
- ½ cup canned tomatoes, sugar-free
- ½ cup dark soy sauce

Spices:

- 1 tsp salt
- 2 tsp stevia powder
- ½ tsp ginger powder

How to Cook:

1. Turn on your Instant Pot and Switch your Instant Pot to "'Sauté" mode. Oil-coat the inner pot with oil and heat up. Put in onions and cook until translucent.
2. After that put in garlic and chopped meat. Pour in approximately ¼ cup of water and cook for 20 minutes, stirring intermittently.
3. Lastly, put in tomatoes, soy sauce, and sesame seeds. Sprinkle with salt, ginger powder, and stevia powder. Stir thoroughly and continue to cook for 10 minutes.
4. Push the "Cancel" button and serve instantly. If you want, you can also drizzle with some freshly chopped parsley or spring onions.

Nutritional Info: (Calories 328| Total Fats: 17.6g | Net Carbs: 8.3g | Protein: 31.8g |Fiber: 1.9g)

Pork Shoulder with Sweet Potatoes

Aggregate Time to Prepare: 30 Minutes

Yield: 5 Servings

Ingredients:

- 1 celery stalk, chopped
- 1 cup cauliflower, chopped into florets
- 1 cup purple cabbage, shredded
- 1 large sweet potato, chopped into bite-sized chunks
- 2 chili peppers, sliced
- 2 lbs pork shoulder, chop into bite-sized pieces
- 4 garlic cloves, whole
- 4 tbsp butter

Spices:

- 1 tsp dried thyme
- 1 tsp white pepper, freshly ground
- 2 bay leaves, whole
- 2 tsp salt

How to Cook:

1. Put the meat in the pot and pour in enough water to cover. Shut and secure the lid and set the steam release handle. Push the "Meat" button.
2. When finished, depressurize using the quick release method and open the lid.
3. After that put in the rest of the ingredients and optionally pour in one more cup of water. Stir

thoroughly and season with salt, pepper, thyme, and bay leaves.
4. Shut and secure the lid again and set the steam release handle to the "Sealing" position. Switch your Instant Pot to "Manual" mode and turn the timer to 7 minutes on high pressure.
5. When you hear the cooker's end signal, depressurize using the natural release method for 10-15 minutes and then cautiously open the lid.
6. Serve instantly.

Nutritional Info: (Calories 657| Total Fats: 48.1g | Net Carbs: 8.2g | Protein: 43.8g |Fiber: 2.2g)

Pork Steak in Mushroom Sauce

Aggregate Time to Prepare: 30 Minutes

Yield: 4 Servings

Ingredients:

- 1 celery stalk, chopped
- 1 cup button mushrooms, sliced
- 1 small onion, roughly chopped
- 2 cups heavy cream
- 3 tbsp butter
- 3 tbsp Parmesan, grated
- 4 cups beef broth
- 4 pork steaks (approximately 8oz each)
- ¼ cup apple cider vinegar
- ¼ cup cottage cheese
- ¼ cup crumbled feta cheese
- ½ cup celery leaves, whole

Spices:

- 1 tbsp peppercorn
- 1 thyme sprig, fresh
- 2 bay leaves
- 2 tsp salt

How to Cook:

1. Thoroughly wash the meat under cold running water and place at the bottom of the instant pot. Pour in the broth and apple cider. Put in salt, peppercorn, by leaves, thyme sprig, onion, celery stalk, and celery leaves. Shut and secure the lid and set the steam release handle.
2. Push the "Meat" button and cook for 15 minutes.
3. When finished, depressurize using the quick release method and open the lid. Remove the meat along with the broth from the pot and set aside.
4. After that Switch your Instant Pot to "'Sauté" mode and coat the inner pot with butter. Put in pre-cooked onions from the broth and stir thoroughly. Sprinkle with salt and put in mushrooms.
5. Cook for 5-6 minutes and then put in the cheese and heavy cream. Stir thoroughly and take out of the pot.
6. Drizzle over the meat and serve.

Nutritional Info: (Calories 721 | Total Fats: 44g | Net Carbs: 5.6g | Protein: 71.8g | Fiber: 0.6g)

Portobello Pork Butt

Aggregate Time to Prepare: **45 Minutes**

Yield: 2 Servings

Ingredients:

- 1 cup Portobello mushrooms, sliced
- 1 lb pork butt
- 2 garlic cloves, crushed
- 2 tbsp apple cider vinegar
- 3 tbsp oil
- 4 tbsp soy sauce
- ½ cup dried shiitake

Spices:

- 1 tsp salt
- 1 tsp turmeric powder
- 2 tsp stevia powder

How to Cook:

1. Put the meat on a cutting board and chop 2-inch long strips. Save for later.
2. Put shiitake in a container and pour in enough water to cover. Soak for 10-15 minutes. Drain and save for later.
3. Turn on your Instant Pot and heat the oil. Put in the meat and season with salt, turmeric, and stevia. Stir thoroughly and cook for 10 minutes.
4. Stir in Portobello mushrooms, soaked shiitake, and garlic. Carry on cooking for 7-8 minutes, stirring continuously.
5. Lastly, pour in the soy sauce and stir thoroughly. Carry on cooking for an additional 5 minutes. If needed, put in approximately 2-3 tablespoons of water.
6. Push the "Cancel" button and serve instantly.

Nutritional Info: (Calories 545| Total Fats: 28.4g | Net Carbs: 6.1g | Protein: 62.4g |Fiber: 0.8g)

Pressure Cooked Pastrami

Aggregate Time to Prepare: **60 Minutes**

Yield: **4 Servings**

Ingredients:

- 1 ½ tbsp. Pepper
- 1 tsp Paprika
- 2 cups Water
- 2 pounds Corned Beef
- 2 tbsp. Oil
- ½ tbsp. Garlic Powder
- ½ tbsp. Onion Powder
- ½ tbsp. Salt
- ½ tbsp. Sweetener
- ½ tsp ground Cloves

How to Cook:

1. Pour the water into the Instant Pot.
2. Put in the beef and shut and secure the lid.
3. Switch the Instant Pot to "High" and cook for 45 minutes.
4. Allow it to cool somewhat until safe to handle.
5. Mix the oil and spices and Massage the mixture onto the beef.
6. Switch your Instant Pot to "Sauté" mode and put in the meat.
7. Cook until browned on all sides.
8. Your dish is ready! Have fun!

Nutritional Info: (Calories 450| Total Fats 20g | Net Carbs 1.5g | Protein 40g |Fiber: 0g)

Puerto Rican Pork

Aggregate Time to Prepare: **110 Minutes**

Yield: **4 Servings**

Ingredients:

- 1 ½ cup Beef Broth
- 1 Chili, deseeded
- 1 tsp Pepper
- 2 Garlic Cloves, peeled
- 2 pounds Pork Shoulder
- 2 tbsp. Olive Oil
- ½ Onion, chopped
- Juice of 1 Lime

How to Cook:

1. Put the garlic, chili, lime juice, pepper, and half of the oil, in your food processor.
2. Process until smooth.
3. Rub the chili mixture into the pork shoulder.
4. Heat the rest of the oil in the Instant Pot using the "Sauté" mode.
5. Put in pork and cook until browned on all sides.
6. Pour the broth around (NOT over) the pork.
7. Shut and secure the lid and switch your instant pot to "Manual" mode and cook for 60 minutes.
8. Depressurize naturally.
9. Serve sliced and drizzled with the juices.
10. Your dish is ready! Have fun!

Nutritional Info: (Calories 830| Total Fats 61g | Net Carbs 6.1g | Protein 57g |Fiber: 2g)

Pulled BBQ Pork

Aggregate Time to Prepare: 105 Minutes

Yield: 8 Servings

Ingredients:

- 2 ½ pounds Pork Roast
- 2 cups Chicken Stock
- 8 ounces sugar-free Barbecue Sauce
- ¼ cup Olive Oil
- Salt and

How to Cook:

1. Heat the oil in the Instant Pot using the "Sauté" mode.
2. Sprinkle the pork with some salt and pepper and place it the Instant Pot.
3. Cook for approximately 3 minutes on each side.
4. Pour the broth over and shut and secure the lid.
5. Switch your Instant Pot to "Meat/Stew" mode and cook for 90 minutes.
6. Release the pressure using the quick release method.
7. Shred the meat with two forks inside the pot.
8. Put in the barbecue sauce and stir to coat thoroughly.
9. Shut and secure the lid and cook on HIGH for 5 minutes.
10. Your dish is ready! Have fun!

Nutritional Info: (Calories 400| Total Fats 16g | Net Carbs 2.5g | Protein 50 g |Fiber: 0.6g)

Quick Cheddar Beef Hash

Aggregate Time to Prepare: **20 Minutes**

Yield: **4 Servings**

Ingredients:

- 1 cup cauliflower, chopped
- 1 cup cheddar cheese
- 1 lb ground beef
- 1 medium-sized green bell pepper, chopped
- 1 small celery stalk, chopped
- 1 tbsp fresh parsley, thinly sliced
- 1 tbsp olive oil

Spices:

- 1 tsp sea salt
- ½ tsp black pepper, freshly ground
- ½ tsp smoked paprika, ground

How to Cook:

1. Plug the instant pot and Switch your Instant Pot to "'Sauté" mode. Oil-coat the stainless steel insert with olive oil. Put in ground beef and cook for 5 minutes, or until lightly browned.
2. After that, put in bell pepper, cauliflower, and parsley. Put in approximately ¼ cup of water and continue to cook for an additional 5 minutes, or until vegetables are tender. Drizzle all with smoked paprika, salt, and pepper.
3. Put in the cheese on top and allow it to melt.
4. Turn off your Instant pot and move all to a serving dish, using a large slotted spoon.

5. If you want, you can also spread on top sour cream and have fun instantly.

Nutritional Info: (Calories 373 | Total Fats 2.1g | Net Carbs: 3.1g | Protein 42.4g | Fiber: 1.3g)

Ribs and Kielbasa with Sauerkraut

Aggregate Time to Prepare: **35 Minutes**

Yield: **4 Servings**

Ingredients:

- 1 pound Pork Ribs
- 1 tbsp. Olive Oil
- 1 tbsp. Sweetener
- 14 ounces Kielbasa, sliced
- 2/3 cup Water
- 24 ounces Sauerkraut

How to Cook:

1. Switch the Instant Pot to "Sauté" mode and heat the oil.
2. Put in the ribs and cook until browned on all sides.
3. Put in the kielbasa on top and pour the water over.
4. Drizzle with the sweetener.
5. Position the kielbasa slices on top and shut and secure the lid.
6. Switch the Instant Pot to "Manual" mode and cook for 15 minutes.
7. Release the pressure using the quick release method.
8. Your dish is ready! Have fun!

Nutritional Info: (Calories 730| Total Fats 57g | Net Carbs 8g | Protein 40g |Fiber: 3.3g)

Rosemary Beef Roast

Aggregate Time to Prepare: 40 Minutes

Yield: 6 Servings

Ingredients:

- 1 cup bone broth
- 1 medium-sized red bell pepper, stripped
- 1 small onion, thinly sliced
- 1 tsp balsamic vinegar
- 1 tsp olive oil
- 2 lbs beef chuck roast, chop into large pieces
- 3 garlic cloves, crushed
- ½ cup heavy cream

Spices:

- 1 tsp black pepper, freshly ground
- 1 tsp dried marjoram, ground
- 1 tsp fresh rosemary, thinly sliced
- 1 tsp salt
- ½ tsp dried parsley, ground

How to Cook:

1. Turn on the Instant Pot and coat the stainless steel insert with olive oil. Switch your Instant Pot to "Sauté' mode and put in onions and garlic. Stir-fry for 3-4 minutes, or until translucent.
2. Put in meat and liberally drizzle with salt. Cook for 3-4 minutes on each side, or until lightly browned. After

that, put in all the rest of the ingredients and spices. Shut and secure the lid and close the steam release handle. Switch your Instant Pot to "Manual" mode and turn the timer to 25 minutes. Cook on "High" pressure.
3. When your instant pot sounds the end signal, release the pressure using the quick release method and open the pot. Move all to a serving container and garnish with fresh rosemary prior to serving.

Nutritional Info: (Calories 619 | Total Fats 46.7g | Net Carbs: 3g | Protein 43.6g | Fiber: 0.8g)

Rosemary Pork Shoulder

Aggregate Time to Prepare: **40 Minutes**

Yield: **4 Servings**

Ingredients:

- 2 shallots, sliced
- 2lbs pork shoulder roast
- 3 tbsp Dijon mustard
- 3 tbsp olive oil
- 4 garlic cloves, crushed

Spices:

- 1 tbsp fresh rosemary, thinly sliced
- 1 tsp salt
- ½ tsp white pepper, freshly ground

How to Cook:

1. Wash thoroughly the meat and drizzle with salt and pepper. Save for later.

2. Take a round oven-safe container and coat with olive oil. Make a layer with shallots and drizzle with garlic and fresh rosemary.
3. Put the meat on top and liberally brush with Dijon mustard. Loosely cover with aluminium foil and save for later.
4. Turn on your Instant Pot and set the trivet in the inner pot. Pour in one cup of water and place the container on the trivet.
5. Shut and secure the lid and set the steam release handle to the "Sealing" position and switch to "Manual' mode.
6. Turn the timer to 25 minutes on high pressure.
7. When finished, depressurize using the natural release method and open the lid. Remove the container from the pot and chill for some time.
8. Serve instantly.

Nutritional Info: (Calories 430 | Total Fats: 19g | Net Carbs: 2g | Protein: 60.2g |Fiber: 0.5g)

Saffron Cauliflower Rice with Pork

Aggregate Time to Prepare: 60 Minutes

Yield: **4 Servings**

Ingredients:

- 1 lb pork leg roast, boneless and chop into bite-sized pieces
- 2 cups cauliflower florets
- 2 cups vegetable stock
- 2 small onions, thinly sliced
- 2 tbsp sesame seeds

- 3 garlic cloves
- 3 tbsp oil
- 4 tbsp ghee
- ¼ cup apple cider vinegar

Spices:

- 1 ½ tsp salt
- 1 cinnamon stick
- 1 tsp black pepper, freshly ground
- 1 tsp cinnamon powder
- 1 tsp cumin powder
- 1 tsp turmeric powder
- 2 bay leaves
- 2 cardamom pods, bruised
- 2 tsp saffron threads
- 2 tsp turmeric power
- ½ tsp ginger powder

How to Cook:

1. Mix together oil, turmeric powder, ginger powder, and cinnamon powder until a smooth paste. Save for later.
2. Thoroughly wash the meat and pat dry with a kitchen towel. Put on a large cutting board and chop into bite-sized pieces. Lightly brush each piece with the oil mixture and save for later.
3. Plug the instant pot and Switch your Instant Pot to "'Sauté" mode. Oil-coat the inner pot with ghee and heat up. Put in onions and cook until translucent, stirring continuously with a wooden spatula. Take out of the pot and save for later.
4. After that put in the meat and brown for 7-8 minutes, stirring intermittently.

5. Pour in the stock and put in onions along with the rest of the ingredients. Shut and secure the lid and cook for 20 minutes on the "Manual" mode.
6. When finished, depressurize using the quick release method and open the lid.
7. Preheat the oven to 450 degrees. Move the mixture to an oil-coated baking dish and bake for 15 minutes.
8. Remove from the oven and chill for some time. Drizzle with saffron and serve.

Nutritional Info:(Calories 426 | Total Fats: 29.3g | Net Carbs: 5.5g | Protein: 32.2g |Fiber: 2.8g)

Sage and Marjoram Lamb

Aggregate Time to Prepare: 80 Minutes

Yield: 4 Servings

Ingredients:

- 1 ½ cups Chicken Broth
- 1 ½ tsp Marjoram
- ¼ tsp Thyme
- 1 ½ tsp Sage
- 1 Bay Leaf
- 2 tbsp. Arrowroot
- 2 tsp minced Garlic
- 6 pounds Leg of Lamb
- Salt and Pepper, to taste

How to Cook:

1. Switch the Instant Pot to "Sauté" mode and heat the oil.

2. Mix the herbs with garlic and salt and pepper, and rub into the meat.
3. Put the lamb in the Instant Pot and sear on all sides, until browned.
4. Pour the broth over and put in the bay leaf.
5. Shut and secure the lid and cook for 60 minutes on MEAT/STEW.
6. Depressurize quickly and move the lamb to a plate.
7. Switch your Instant Pot to SATE and whisk in the arrowroot.
8. Cook until the sauce is thickened.
9. Drizzle over the lamb.
10. Your dish is ready! Have fun!

Nutritional Info: (Calories 620| Total Fats 26g | Net Carbs 3g | Protein 58g |Fiber: 0.1g)

Savory Cauliflower Beef Roast

Aggregate Time to Prepare: **50 Minutes**

Yield: **6 Servings**

Ingredients:

- 1 cup beef broth
- 1 cup cauliflower, chopped
- 1 medium-sized onion, chopped
- 1 tbsp olive oil
- 2 lbs beef chuck roast, chop into small chunks
- 2 tbsp butter
- ½ cup heavy cream

Spices:

- 1 tsp sea salt

- ¼ tsp dried rosemary, ground
- ½ tsp black pepper, ground
- ½ tsp dried thyme, ground
- ½ tsp smoked paprika, ground

How to Cook:

1. Turn on the Instant Pot and coat the stainless steel insert with olive oil. Switch your Instant Pot to "Sauté' mode and put in the meat chunks and onions. Drizzle with smoked paprika, salt, and pepper. Cook for 5 minutes, or until golden brown.
2. Pour in the beef broth and shut and secure the lid. Set the steam release handle by moving the valve to the "Sealing" position. Switch your Instant Pot to "Manual" mode and turn the timer to 25 minutes. Cook on "High" pressure.
3. When finished, release the pressure using the quick release method by turning the valve to the "Venting" position.
4. Open the pot and Switch your Instant Pot to "'Sauté" mode. Put in cauliflower and heavy cream. Drizzle with dried thyme and rosemary. Stir thoroughly and bring it to a simmer. Cook for 10 minutes more, stirring intermittently.

Nutritional Info: (Calories 657 | Total Fats 52.3g | Net Carbs: 2.3g | Protein 52.3g |Fiber: 1g)

Seasoned Apple Cider Vinegar Beef

Aggregate Time to Prepare: **110 Minutes**

Yield: 6 Servings

Ingredients:

- 1 cup Beef Broth
- 1 tsp Basil
- 1 tsp Marjoram
- 1 tsp Onion Powder
- 1 tsp Oregano
- 1 tsp Salt
- 3 pounds Chuck Roast
- 6 Garlic Cloves
- ¼ cup Apple Cider Vinegar
- ½ tsp ground Ginger

How to Cook:

1. With a knife, chop a few sliced in the meat and push the garlic inside.
2. Mix the herbs and spices in a small container and rub this mixture into the meat.
3. Put the meat in the Instant Pot.
4. Pour the vinegar and broth over and shut and secure the lid.
5. Switch the Instant Pot to "High" and cook for 90 minutes.
6. Depressurize naturally.
7. Your dish is ready! Have fun!

Nutritional Info: (Calories 408| Total Fats 26g | Net Carbs 2g | Protein 40g |Fiber: 0g)

Shredded Beef with Pepper Rings

Aggregate Time to Prepare: 85 Minutes

Yield: 6 Servings

Ingredients:

- 1 tbsp. Garlic Powder
- 16 ounces jarred Pepper Rings
- 3 pounds Beef
- ½ cup Beef Broth
- Salt and Pepper, to taste

How to Cook:

1. Sprinkle the beef with salt, pepper, and garlic powder.
2. Put in the Instant Pot.
3. Put in the pepper rings and pour the broth over.
4. Shut and secure the lid and select MANUAL.
5. Switch the Instant Pot to "High" and cook for 70 minutes.
6. Depressurize using the natural release method.
7. Shred the beef with two forks inside the pot.
8. Stir thoroughly to mix.
9. Your dish is ready! Have fun!

Nutritional Info: (Calories 442| Total Fats 18 | Net Carbs 3g | Protein 65g |Fiber: 0.1g)

Simple Beef and Broccoli Dish

Aggregate Time to Prepare: 50 Minutes

Yield: 4 Servings

Ingredients:

- 1 Onion, quartered
- 1 pound Beef, chopped

- 1 tsp ground Ginger
- 1 tsp minced Garlic
- 12 ounces Broccoli Florets
- 2 tbsp. Fish Sauce
- ¼ cup Coconut Aminos
- ¼ tsp Pepper
- ½ tsp Salt

How to Cook:

1. Put all of the ingredients, except the broccoli, in your Instant Pot.
2. Shut and secure the lid and choose MEAT/STEW.
3. Cook on default.
4. Depressurize quickly.
5. Stir in broccoli and cook using the "Sauté" mode for 5 minutes.
6. Your dish is ready! Have fun!

Nutritional Info: (Calories 270| Total Fats 8g| Net Carbs 7g | Protein 38.5g |Fiber: 2g)

Simple Butter Lamb

Aggregate Time to Prepare: 50 Minutes

Yield: 6 Servings

Ingredients:

- 2 lbs lamb shoulder, chop into 3 pieces
- 3 tbsp butter, softened
- 4 cups beef broth
- ¼ cup balsamic vinegar

Spices:

- 1 tsp black pepper, freshly ground
- 2 rosemary sprigs
- 2 tsp salt

How to Cook:

1. Wash thoroughly the meat and rub each piece with salt and pepper. Put at the bottom of the pot and put in rosemary sprigs.
2. Pour in the broth and vinegar. Shut and secure the lid. Make sure the steam release handle is on the "Sealing" position and switch to "Manual' mode.
3. Cook for 25 minutes on high pressure.
4. When your instant pot sounds the end signal, depressurize using the quick release method and open the lid.
5. In the mean time, preheat the oven to 450 degrees.
6. Take the meat out of the pot and brush with butter. If you want, you can also drizzle with some more salt and pepper and place ona baking sheet lined with some parchment paper.
7. Roast for 15-20 minutes, turning once.

Nutritional Info: (Calories 360 | Total Fats: 17.8g | Net Carbs: 0.7g | Protein: 45.8g | Fiber: 0g)

Simple Holiday Roast

Aggregate Time to Prepare: 50 Minutes

Yield: 6 Servings

Ingredients:

- 1 cup Beef Broth
- 1 cup Red Wine

- 2 ½ pounds Beef Roast
- 1 Onion, sliced
- 2 Garlic Cloves, sliced
- 2 Celery Stalks, chopped
- 1 Bell Pepper, chopped
- 2 tbsp. Italian Seasoning
- 2 tbsp. Olive Oil
- 2 tbsp. sugar-free Steak Sauce

How to Cook:

1. Heat ½ of the olive oil in your Instant Pot using the "Sauté" mode.
2. Put in the beef and sear on all sides for approximately 5 minutes in total. Move to a plate.
3. Heat the rest of the olive oil and put in the onions, celery, and peppers.
4. Cook for 3 minutes.
5. Stir in garlic and seasonings and cook for an additional minute.
6. Return the beef to the pot.
7. Mix together the broth, sauce, and red wine, and pour this mixture over the beef.
8. Shut and secure the lid and cook on HIGH for 40 minutes.
9. Depressurize using the natural release method.
10. Your dish is ready! Have fun!

Nutritional Info: (Calories 415| Total Fats 18g | Net Carbs 6g | Protein 42g |Fiber: 1g)

Simple Tomato Pork Chops

Aggregate Time to Prepare: **40 Minutes**

Yield: 2 Servings

Ingredients:

- 1 cup beef broth
- 1 cup cherry tomatoes
- 1 green bell pepper, sliced
- 1 small onion, thinly sliced
- 2 pork chops, with bones
- 4 tbsp olive oil

Spices:

- ¼ tsp garlic powder
- ½ tsp salt
- ½ tsp white pepper, freshly ground

How to Cook:

1. Put the meat in the pot and season with salt. Pour in the broth and shut and secure the lid. Make sure the steam release handle is on the "Sealing" position and switch to "Manual' mode.
2. Turn the timer to 15 minutes on high pressure. When finished, depressurize using the natural release method and open the lid.
3. Take the meat out of the pot and move to a deep container. Save for later.
4. After that, Switch your Instant Pot to "'Sauté" mode and coat the inner pot with olive oil. Heat up and put in onions and peppers. Drizzle with some more salt. Cook for 5-6 minutes and then put in cherry tomatoes. Pour in approximately ¼ cup of the broth and simmer for 10-12 minutes, stirring intermittently.
5. Sprinkle with pepper and garlic powder. If you want, you can also put in some red pepper flakes. Move the

mixture to a food processor and process until smooth. Drizzle over pork chope and serve instantly.

Nutritional Info: (Calories 633| Total Fats: 37g | Net Carbs: 9.1g | Protein: 63.6g |Fiber: 2.6g)

Slowly Cooked Lamb Shoulder Kebab

Aggregate Time to Prepare: 8 HOURS 20 Minutes

Yield: 5 Servings

Ingredients:

- 1 cup Greek yogurt
- 1 cup tomatoes, chopped
- 1 garlic head, whole
- 1 onion, whole
- 2 celery stalks, chopped
- 2 lbs lamb shoulder, chopped into smaller pieces
- 3 tbsp butter
- 3 tbsp olive oil
- ¼ cup fresh parsley, thinly sliced

Spices:

- 1 tsp black pepper
- 1 tsp salt
- ½ tsp red chili flakes

How to Cook:

1. Oil-coat the bottom of the pot with olive oil. Put in the meat along with tomatoes, celery stalks, onion, and garlic. Drizzle with salt, pepper, and chili flakes.
2. Pour in enough water to cover and shut and secure the lid. Make sure the steam release handle is on

the "Sealing" position and push the "Slow Cook" button.
3. Turn the timer to 8 hours on low pressure.
4. When finished, depressurize using the natural release method and open the lid. Take the meat out of the pot and place on a large cutting board. Using a sharp cutting knife, chop into bite-sized pieces and save for later.
5. Remove the liquid and vegetables from the pot and Switch your Instant Pot to "'Sauté" mode. Oil-coat the inner pot with butter and put in the meat. Cook for 5-6 minutes, stirring intermittently.
6. Take out of the pot and chill for some time. Spread on top Greek yogurt and drizzle with freshly chopped parsley.
7. Serve instantly.

Nutritional Info: (Calories 527 | Total Fats: 29.6g | Net Carbs: 6.2g | Protein: 56.1g |Fiber: 1.2g)

Slowly Cooked Pork with Leeks

Aggregate Time to Prepare: 8 HOURS

Yield: 6 Servings

Ingredients:

- 1 cup cherry tomatoes, sliced
- 1 green bell pepper, sliced
- 2 large leeks, chopped into 2-inch long pieces
- 2 lbs pork butt, chopped into smaller pieces
- 4 tbsp olive oil
- 5 cups beef broth

Spices:

- 1 tsp salt
- 2 tsp cayenne pepper
- 3 bay leaves
- ½ tsp black pepper, freshly ground

How to Cook:

1. Mix the ingredients in the pot and shut and secure the lid.
2. Make sure the steam release handle is on the "Sealing" position and push the "Slow Cook" button.
3. Turn the timer to 8 hours on low pressure.
4. When finished, depressurize using the natural release method for 10-15 minutes and then move the pressure valve to release the rest of the pressure.
5. Cautiously open the lid and serve instantly.
6. If you want, you can also drizzle with some Parmesan prior to serving.

Nutritional Info: (Calories 434 | Total Fats: 20.8g | Net Carbs: 6.4g | Protein: 52g | Fiber: 1.2g)

Spicy and Smokey Pork

Aggregate Time to Prepare: 75 Minutes

Yield: 4 Servings

Ingredients:

- 1 ½ cups Beef Broth
- 1 tbsp. Coconut Oil
- 1 tsp Cumin
- 1 tsp Garlic Powder

- 1 tsp ground Ginger
- 1 tsp Oregano
- 1 tsp Smoked Paprika
- 1 tsp Sweetener
- 1 tsp Thyme
- 2 pounds Pork Roast
- ½ tsp Chili Powder
- ½ tsp Onion Powder
- ½ tsp Pepper

How to Cook:

1. Melt the coconut oil in your Instant Pot using the "Sauté" mode.
2. Mix all of the herbs and spices and Massage the mixture onto the pork.
3. Put the pork in the Instant Pot and sear on all sides, until browned.
4. Mix the liquid smoke with the broth and pour over.
5. Shut and secure the lid and cook for 45 minutes on HIGH.
6. Depressurize naturally.
7. Your dish is ready! Have fun!

Nutritional Info: (Calories 760| Total Fats 40g | Net Carbs 2.2g | Protein 75g |Fiber: 0.2g)

Spicy Burgers

Aggregate Time to Prepare: **15 Minutes**

Yield: 6 Servings

Ingredients:

- 1 lb ground pork

- 1 red chili pepper
- 2 onions
- 3 tbsp almond flour
- ½ cup fresh parsley, thinly sliced

Spices:

- ¼ tsp black pepper, freshly ground
- ¼ tsp garlic powder
- ½ tsp salt

How to Cook:

1. Put the onions and chili pepper using a food processor and process for 30 seconds. Move to a container and put in the meat. Drizzle with parsley, almond flour, and spices.
2. Combine thoroughly and shape burgers, approximately 2-inch in diameter.
3. Put burgers in the steam basket and pour in one cup of water in the inner pot.
4. Shut and secure the lid and set the steam release handle to the "Sealing" position. Switch your Instant Pot to "Manual" mode and turn the timer to 7 minutes on high pressure.
5. When finished, depressurize using the quick release method and open the lid.
6. Remove burgers from the pot and serve instantly.

Nutritional Info: (Calories 198 | Total Fats: 4.9g | Net Carbs: 4.4g | Protein: 30.9g | Fiber: 1.7g)

Spicy Garam Masala Beef Roast

Aggregate Time to Prepare: **40 Minutes**

Yield: 4 Servings

Ingredients:

- 1 cup of cherry tomatoes, diced
- 1 egg, beaten
- 1 small onion, diced
- 1 small red chili pepper, chopped
- 2 cups chicken broth
- 2 lbs beef shoulder roast
- 2 tbsp olive oil
- 4 garlic cloves, crushed

Spices:

- 1 tsp salt
- ¼ tsp cardamom, ground
- ¼ tsp cinnamon, ground
- ¼ tsp nutmeg, ground
- ½ tsp black pepper, ground

How to Cook:

1. Thoroughly wash the meat under cold running water and pat dry with a kitchen paper. Cut into bite-sized pieces and save for later.
2. In a large mixing container, mix all spices and mix until blend. Put in meat and stir thoroughly until all thoroughly coated.
3. Turn on the Instant Pot and coat the stainless steel insert with olive oil. Switch your Instant Pot to "Sauté' mode and put in chili pepper, onions, and garlic. Cook for 2-3 minutes, or until onions translucent.
4. After that, put in meat and continue to cook for an additional 10 minutes, stirring intermittently.

5. Pour in the broth and shut and secure the lid. Set the steam release handle by moving the valve to the "Sealing" position. Push the "Manual button and turn the timer to 15 minutes. Cook on "High" pressure.
6. When finished, depressurize using the natural release method and open the pot. Stir in the tomatoes and simmer for 5 minutes. The liquid should be reduced by half. Poach the egg on top and cook for additional 2 minutes.
7. Move to a serving dish and serve instantly.

Nutritional Info: (Calories 458 | Total Fats 25g | Net Carbs: 4.2g | Protein 50.8g |Fiber: 1.2g)

Spicy Goulash

Aggregate Time to Prepare: 40 Minutes

Yield: 4 Servings

Ingredients:

- 1 small chili pepper, sliced
- 12 oz. button mushrooms
- 14 oz. venison neck, chopped into bite-sized pieces
- 4 cups beef broth
- 5 tbsp. olive oil

Spices:

- 1 tbsp. cayenne pepper
- 1 tsp chili pepper powder
- 1 tsp salt
- ½ tsp freshly ground pepper

How to Cook:

1. Oil-coat the bottom of your instant pot and push the "Sautée" button. Put in onions and cook for two minutes. After that, put in chili pepper, chili powder, and cayenne pepper. Carry on cooking for two additional minutes, stirring continuously.
2. Push "Cancel" button and put in meat, mushrooms, beef broth, and water. Shut and secure the lid and set the steam release handle. Push "Manual" button and turn the timer to 30 minutes.
3. When your instant pot sounds the end signal, release the pressure using the quick release method and open the lid.
4. Serve warm.

Nutritional Info: (Calories 353 | Total Fats 22.8g | Net Carbs: 3.3g | Protein 33.7g |Fiber: 1.3g)

Spicy Lamb

Aggregate Time to Prepare: **45 Minutes**

Yield: **6 Servings**

Ingredients:

- 2 cups cherry tomatoes, chopped
- 2 lbs boneless leg of lamb, chop into bite-sized pieces
- 2 tbsp ghee
- 3 cups vegetable stock
- ¼ cup heavy cream

Spices:

- 1 ½ tsp cumin seeds

- 1 cinnamon stick
- 1 tbsp coriander powder
- 1 tsp cumin powder
- 1 tsp garam masala
- 1 tsp ginger powder
- 1 tsp salt
- 2 tbsp chili powder
- 2 tsp fennel seeds
- 3 bay leaves
- 3 cloves, whole
- ½ tsp garlic powder

How to Cook:

1. Thoroughly wash the meat under cold running water and pat dry with a kitchen paper. Put on a clean work surface and chop into bite-sized pieces. Put in a deep container and put in heavy cream and garam masala. Stir thoroughly and tightly cover with aluminium foil. Refrigerate overnight.
2. Turn on your Instant Pot and Switch your Instant Pot to "'Sauté" mode. Oil-coat the inner pot with ghee and put in bay leaves, cardamom, cinnamon, cloves, cumin seeds, and fennel seeds. Briefly cook for 1-2 minutes, stirring continuously with a wooden spatula.
3. After that put in the rest of the spices and stir thoroughly again. Carry on cooking for an additional minute.
4. Lastly, put in the meat along with the heavy cream. Pour in the stock and put in cherry tomatoes. Stir thoroughly and shut and secure the lid. Set the steam release handle and switch to "Manual' mode.
5. Turn the timer to 25 minutes on high pressure.

6. When finished, depressurize using the natural release method and open the lid. Stir thoroughly again and serve instantly.

Nutritional Info: (Calories 350| Total Fats 17.4g | Net Carbs: 1.9g | Protein: 43.3g |Fiber: 1g)

Spicy Lamb Coriander Curry

Aggregate Time to Prepare: **60 Minutes**

Yield: **4 Servings**

Ingredients:

- 1 cup tomatoes, diced
- 1 medium-sized onion
- 1 medium-sized red bell pepper
- 1 tbsp olive oil
- 2 cups beef stock
- 2 lbs leg of lamb
- 4 garlic cloves, thinly sliced
- ½ cup fresh coriander, chopped

Spices:

- 1 tsp cumin seeds
- 1 tsp fennel seeds
- 1 tsp garam masala powder
- 1 tsp red chili powder
- 1 tsp salt
- 2 tsp fresh ginger, grated
- ½ tsp black pepper, ground

How to Cook:

1. Turn on the Instant Pot and coat the stainless steel insert with olive oil. Push the "Sauté" button and put in onions, cumin seeds, and fennel seeds. Cook for 3-4 minutes, or until the onions translucent.
2. Put in bell pepper and tomatoes. Stir thoroughly and bring it to a ligh simmer. Drizzle with garam masala, ginger, and red chili powder.
3. Lastly, put in meat and pour in the beef stock. Stir in the coriander and shut and secure the lid.
4. Set the steam release handle and push the "Manual" button. Turn the timer to 40 minutes and cook on "High" pressure.
5. When your Instant Pot sounds the end signal, release the pressure using the quick release method of the pressure. Open the pot and push the "Sauté" button. Cook for 10 additional minutes, or until the liquid reduces to a favoured consistency.
6. If you want, you can also drizzle with some thinly sliced cilantro prior to serving.

Nutritional Info:(Calories 503 | Total Fats 21g | Net Carbs: 7g | Protein: 66.7g |Fiber: 2.3g)

Spicy Lamb Patties

Aggregate Time to Prepare: 25 Minutes

Yield: 6 Servings

Ingredients:

- 1 medium-sized onion, thinly sliced
- 1 small green chili pepper, thinly sliced
- 1 tbsp olive oil
- 2 garlic cloves, minced

- 2 lbs minced lamb
- 4 large eggs, beaten
- ½ cup almonds, minced

Spices:

- 1/2 tsp garam masala powder
- 1 tsp dried mint, ground
- 1 tsp salt
- ½ tsp chili powder

How to Cook:

1. In a large mixing container, mix meat, garlic, green chili pepper, 3 eggs, and all spices. Combine with your hands until all thoroughly blended.
2. Mould the patties of favoured size and roll them in the rest of the egg, and then in minced almonds. Save for later.
3. Turn on the Instant Pot and put in butter to the stainless steel insert. Push the "Sauté" button and tenderly spread the patties on the bottom of the pot. Cook in batches if needed.
4. Cook for 5-7 minutes on each side, or until nicely brown.
5. Take out of the pot and move to a serving plate.
6. If you want, you can also serve with plain yogurt and have fun!

Nutritional Info:(Calories 405 | Total Fats 20.8g | Net Carbs: 2.7g | Protein: 48.6g |Fiber: 1.5g)

Spicy Pork Butt

Aggregate Time to Prepare: **75 Minutes**

Yield: **6 Servings**

Ingredients:

- 1 ½ cups Water
- 1 tbsp. Olive Oil
- 1 tsp Cayenne Pepper
- 1 tsp Oregano
- 1 tsp Thyme
- 2 tsp Chili Powder
- 2 tsp Cumin
- 2 tsp granulated Sweetener
- 2 tsp Paprika
- 2 tsp Pepper
- 4 pounds Pork Butt

How to Cook:

1. Slightly coat the pork butt with the olive oil.
2. Mix the spices in a small container and rub this mixture into the meat.
3. Pour the water into the Instant Pot and place the meat inside.
4. Shut and secure the lid and choose MANUAL.
5. Switch the Instant Pot to "High" and cook for 65 minutes.
6. Release the pressure using the quick release method.
7. Your dish is ready! Have fun!

Nutritional Info: (Calories 780| Total Fats 55g | Net Carbs 1g | Protein 60g |Fiber: 0g)

Spicy Pork with Celery

Aggregate Time to Prepare: **40 Minutes**

Yield: 4 Servings

Ingredients:

- 1 cup cauliflower florets
- 1 cup celery stalks, thinly sliced
- 1 large leek, thinly sliced
- 1 large onion, sliced
- 2 lbs pork ribs, chop into smaller pieces
- 3 tbsp olive oil
- 4 cups beef broth
- ¼ cup fresh parsley, thinly sliced

Spices:

- 1 bay leaf
- 1 tsp chili powder
- 1 tsp salt
- ½ tsp red pepper flakes

How to Cook:

1. Turn on your Instant Pot and Switch your Instant Pot to "'Sauté" mode. Heat up the oil and then put in ribs in several batches. Brown for 2-3 minutes on each side and take out of the pot. Repeat with the rest of the meat.
2. After that put in onions and celery stalk. Drizzle with some salt and sauté for 4-5 minutes, stirring continuously.
3. Lastly, put in the pork and the rest of the ingredients. Pour in the broth and shut and secure the lid. Make sure the steam release handle is on the "Sealing" position and switch to "Manual' mode.
4. Cook for 20 minutes on high pressure.
5. When finished, depressurize using the natural release method and serve instantly.

Nutritional Info: (Calories 493 | Total Fats: 20g | Net Carbs: 7.5g | Protein: 65.7g | Fiber: 2.4g)

Spinach Beef with Bell Peppers

Aggregate Time to Prepare: 35

Yield: 4 Servings

Ingredients:

- 1 cup fresh spinach, chopped
- 1 cup tomatoes, diced
- 1 medium-sized red bell pepper, chopped
- 1 medium-sized yellow bell pepper, chopped
- 1 tbsp balsamic vinegar
- 2 cups beef stock
- 2 lbs lean ground beef
- 2 tsp olive oil
- 4 tbsp fresh parsley, thinly sliced
- ½ cup mozzarella cheese

Spices:

- 1 tsp dried oregano, ground
- 1 tsp onion powder
- 1 tsp salt
- ¼ tsp black pepper, ground
- ½ tsp cayenne pepper, ground
- ½ tsp dried thyme, ground
- ½ tsp garlic powder

How to Cook:

1. Prepare the vegetables and mix all in a large container. Drizzle with salt, pepper, vinegar, and stir thoroughly. Save for later.
2. Turn on your Instant Pot and coat the stainless steel insert with olive oil. Switch your Instant Pot to "Sauté' mode and put in ground beef. Using a large spatula, break until no lumps. Drizzle with onion powder, garlic powder, cayenne pepper, oregano, and thyme. Cook for 3-4 minutes and pour in the broth. Shut and secure the lid and set the steam release handle. Switch your Instant Pot to "Manual" mode and turn the timer to 8 minutes. Cook on "High" pressure.
3. When your instant pot sounds the end signal, depressurize using the quick release method and open the pot. Stir in the vegetables and Switch your Instant Pot to "'Sauté" mode. Carry on cooking for 10 additional minutes, or until vegetables are tender.
4. Spread on top mozzarella and cook for a minute, or until melts. Turn off your Instant pot and move all to a serving dish.
5. Have fun!

Nutritional Info: (Calories 497 | Total Fats 17.8g | Net Carbs: 6.2g | Protein 72.7g | Fiber: 2g)

Spring Lamb Neck with Greens

Aggregate Time to Prepare: 40 Minutes

Yield: 6 Servings

Ingredients:

- 1 cup cauliflower, chopped into small florets

- 1 cup Feta cheese, crumbled
- 1 large leek, thinly sliced
- 1 lb lamb neck, chopped into smaller pieces
- 2 cups spinach, torn
- 2 cups Swiss chard, chopped
- 2 garlic cloves, crushed
- 2 lbs collard greens, chopped
- ¼ cup fresh mint, chopped
- ¼ cup olive oil

Spices:

- 2 tsp salt

How to Cook:

1. Thoroughly wash the meat and pat dry with a kitchen towel. Put on a large cutting board and chop into smaller pieces. Liberally drizzle with salt and place in the pot.
2. Pour in enough water to cover and shut and secure the lid. If you want, you can also put in 1 bay leaf.
3. Make sure the steam release handle is on the "Sealing" position and switch to "Manual' mode.
4. Turn the timer to 25 minutes on high pressure.
5. When finished, depressurize using the quick release method and open the lid. Remove the meat along with the rest of the liquid. Save for later.
6. In the mean time, rinse thoroughly the greens and drain in a large colander.
7. Switch your Instant Pot to "Sauté' mode and put in oil. Put in the greens, garlic, and cauliflower. Pour in 1 cup of the reserved liquid and spread on top the meat.
8. Shut and secure the lid again and turn the timer to 2 minutes on the "Manual" mode.

9. When finished, depressurize using the quick release method and open the lid.
10. Drizzle with feta cheese and serve.

Nutritional Info: (Calories 341 | Total Fats: 20.5g | Net Carbs: 7.4g | Protein: 29.4g | Fiber: 6.4g)

Spring Onion Pork

Aggregate Time to Prepare: 30 Minutes

Yield: 2 Servings

Ingredients:

- 1 cup beef stock
- 14oz pork neck, chopped into bite-sized pieces
- 2 tbsp butter
- 3 spring onions, thinly sliced
- 3 tbsp olive oil

Spices:

- 1 ½ tsp salt
- 1 tsp peppercorn
- 2 tsp cayenne pepper
- ½ tsp black pepper, freshly ground

How to Cook:

1. Turn on your Instant Pot and Switch your Instant Pot to "'Sauté" mode. Oil-coat the inner pot with oil and heat up. Put in onions and drizzle with some salt.
2. Cook for 2-3 minutes and then put in the meat. Sprinkle with pepper, cayenne pepper, and drizzle with peppercorn.

3. Cook for 5-6 minutes, stirring continuously. Put in butter and pour in the stock.
4. Shut and secure the lid and set the steam release handle. Switch your Instant Pot to "Manual" mode and turn the timer to 12 minutes.
5. When finished, depressurize using the natural release method and open the lid.
6. Serve instantly.

Nutritional Info: (Calories 581 | Total Fats: 39.8g | Net Carbs: 1.1g | Protein: 53.8g |Fiber: 0.6g)

Spring Vegetable Pork

Aggregate Time to Prepare: 30 Minutes

Yield: 2 Servings

Ingredients:

- 1 cup broccoli, thinly sliced
- 1 lb pork neck, chopped into bite-sized pieces
- 1 small chili pepper, thinly sliced
- 1 tbsp Dijon mustard
- 1 tbsp tomato paste
- 2 spring onions, thinly sliced
- 2 tbsp apple cider vinegar
- 2 tbsp butter
- 4 cups beef stock
- ¼ cup celery stalk, thinly sliced

Spices:

- 1 tsp dried celery
- 1 tsp pink Himalayan salt
- ½ tsp garlic powder

- ½ tsp pepper

How to Cook:

1. Oil-coat the bottom of the inner pot with butter and put in the meat. Sprinkle with salt and pepper and put in vegetables. Stir in tomato paste and drizzle with dried celery and garlic powder. Stir thoroughly and pour in the stock.
2. Shut and secure the lid and set the steam release handle to the "Sealing" position. Switch your Instant Pot to "Manual" mode and turn the timer to 20 minutes on high pressure.
3. When finished, depressurize using the natural release method and open the lid. Stir in Dijon and optionally drizzle with some more salt or pepper.
4. Serve instantly.

Nutritional Info: (Calories 498 | Total Fats: 21.1g | Net Carbs: 4.5g | Protein: 67.3g | Fiber: 2.4g)

Steamed Pork Neck

Aggregate Time to Prepare: **40 Minutes**

Yield: 3 Servings

Ingredients:

- 1 lb pork neck, chop into 3 pieces
- 2 cups cauliflower florets
- 3 garlic cloves, crushed
- 3 tbsp apple cider vinegar
- 4 tbsp olive oil

Spices:

- 1 tbsp cayenne pepper
- 1 tbsp dried celery
- 1 tsp white pepper, freshly ground
- 2 tsp sea salt

How to Cook:

1. Thoroughly wash the meat under cold running water and place on a cutting board. Using a sharp cutting knife, chop into 3 equivalent pieces. Rub each piece with salt, white pepper, cayenne pepper, and celery. Save for later.
2. Oil-coat a small round baking pan with oil and put in cauliflower. Spread on top pork and drizzle with apple cider vinegar.
3. Turn on your Instant Pot and position a trivet at the bottom of the inner pot. Put the baking pan on the trivet and pour in 2 cups of water in the inner pot.
4. Shut and secure the lid and set the steam release handle to the "Sealing" position. Switch your Instant Pot to "Manual" mode and turn the timer to 25 minutes on high pressure.
5. When finished, depressurize using the quick release method and open the lid.
6. Remove the baking pan from the pot and chill for some time. Serve with some Greek yogurt or cottage cheese.

Nutritional Info: (Calories 401| Total Fats: 24.1g | Net Carbs: 3g | Protein: 41.1g |Fiber: 1.7g)

Sweet and Balsamic Glazed Pork Loin

Aggregate Time to Prepare: 80 Minutes

Yield: 4 Servings

Ingredients:

- 1 tsp minced Garlic
- 1 tsp Sage
- 2 pounds Pork Loin
- ½ cup Beef Broth
- ½ tsp Pepper

Glaze:

- 1 tbsp. Arrowroot
- 2 tbsp. Coconut Aminos
- ¼ cup Balsamic Vinegar
- ½ cup Sweetener
- ½ cup Water

How to Cook:

1. Mix the garlic, pepper, and sage, and rub into the meat.
2. Pour the broth into the Instant Pot and place the meat inside.
3. Shut and secure the lid and cook on HIGH for 60 minutes.
4. Allow the pressure to release for 10 minutes.
5. Move the meat to a plate and Shred using two forks.
6. In the Instant Pot, whisk together the glaze ingredients.
7. Cook using the "Sauté" mode for 3 minutes.
8. Drizzle the glaze over the meat.
9. Your dish is ready! Have fun!

Nutritional Info: (Calories 510| Total Fats 23g | Net Carbs 9g | Protein 60g |Fiber: 0.3g)

Sweet and Sour Pork Ribs

Aggregate Time to Prepare: 25 Minutes

Yield: 10 Servings

Ingredients:

- 1 large Onion (sliced)
- 1 tbsp. Sesame Seeds
- 1 tbsp. White Vinegar
- 1 tsp Ground Ginger
- 1 tsp Salt
- 3 cloves Garlic (minced)
- 5 lb. Bone-in Country Style Pork Ribs
- ¼ cup Sugar-Free Maple Syrup
- ½ cup Soy Sauce
- ½ cup Sugar-Free Ketchup
- ½ tsp Paprika Flakes
- ¾ cup Brown Sugar Substitute

How to Cook:

1. In a large container place the brown sugar substitute, soy sauce, maple syrup, ketchup, vinegar, garlic, ginger, salt, paprika. Combine thoroughly to mix.
2. Put the ribs in and toss to coat. Cover and refrigerate for at least 4 hours, but not longer than 24 hours.
3. Put the onion slices on bottom of the Instant Pot and place ribs on top of them.
4. Shut and secure the lid and manually turn the timer and cook for 60 minutes at high pressure.
5. Let naturally release the pressure.
6. Move the ribs on a serving platter and drizzle with sesame seeds.

Nutritional Info: (Calories: 603 | Total Fats: 34g | Net Carbs: 9g | Proteins: 63g | Fibers: 0g)

Sweet Coconut Lamb Shoulder

Aggregate Time to Prepare: **45 Minutes**

Yield: **5 Servings**

Ingredients:

- 1 onion, chop into 6 wedges
- 2 lbs lamb shoulder
- 2 tbsp avocado oil
- 2-inch piece of ginger, chopped
- 3 cups vegetable stock
- 4 garlic cloves, thinly sliced
- ½ cup coconut milk

Spices:

- 1 tsp coriander powder
- 1 tsp cumin powder
- 1 tsp salt
- ½ tsp white pepper, freshly ground

How to Cook:

1. Thoroughly wash the meat and place in the pot. Pour in the stock and shut and secure the lid. Make sure the steam release handle is on the "Sealing" position and switch to "Manual' mode.
2. Turn the timer to 30 minutes on high pressure.
3. When finished, depressurize using the quick release method and open the lid. Take the meat out of the pot and save for later.

4. Remove the stock and Switch your Instant Pot to "'Sauté" mode. Oil-coat the inner pot with oil and put in garlic, onions, and ginger. Cook for 5-6 minutes, stirring intermittently.
5. In the mean time, rub the meat with salt, coriander, cumin, and pepper. Put in the pot and pour in the coconut milk.
6. Tenderly simmer for 4-5 minutes and then push the "Cancel" button.
7. Put the meat on a large platter and drizzle with the coconut sauce.
8. Serve instantly.

Nutritional Info:(Calories 416 | Total Fats: 19.8g | Net Carbs: 3.4g | Protein: 52.2g |Fiber: 1.6g)

Sweet Coconut Pork

Aggregate Time to Prepare: **1 HOUR**

Yield: **6 Servings**

Ingredients:

- 1 chili pepper, thinly sliced
- 1 cup cauliflower, chopped into florets
- 1 cup heavy cream
- 1 large onion, thinly sliced
- 2 tbsp butter
- 2 tbsp coconut cream
- 3 tbsp almond flour
- 4 pork chops, with bones
- ¼ cup coconut milk

Spices:

- 1 tsp rum extract
- 1 tsp salt
- 2 tsp stevia powder
- ½ tsp white pepper, freshly ground

How to Cook:

1. In a medium-sized container, mix heavy cream, coconut milk, coconut cream, salt, pepper, stevia, and rum. Put in the meat and coat thoroughly with the mixture. Move to a large Ziploc bag. Seal the bag and refrigerate overnight.
2. Turn on your Instant Pot and set the trivet at the bottom of the inner pot. Remove the pork from the fridge and place in a deep oven-safe container along with the marinade.
3. Put the container in the pot and pour in approximately one cup of water in the inner pot. Shut and secure the lid and set the steam release handle to the "Sealing" posisiton.
4. Switch your Instant Pot to "Manual" mode and turn the timer to 20 minutes on high pressure.
5. When finished, depressurize using the quick release method and open the lid. Remove the container with the pork and Switch your Instant Pot to "'Sauté" mode.
6. Oil-coat the inner pot with butter and heat up. Put in onions, peppers, and cauliflower. Stir thoroughly and cook for 6-7 minutes.
7. After that put in the pork along with its sauce and mix in almond flour. Carry on cooking for an additional 3-4 minutes, coating the meat thoroughly with the sauce.
8. Push the "Cancel" button and serve instantly.

Nutritional Info: (Calories 462| Total Fats: 24.6g | Net Carbs: 7.9g | Protein: 49.4g |Fiber: 1.6g)

Sweet Dijon Pork Chops

Aggregate Time to Prepare: 25 Minutes

Yield: 4 Servings

Ingredients:

- 1 cup Chicken Broth
- 1 tbsp. Olive Oil
- 2 pounds Pork Chops
- 2 tbsp. Dijon Mustard
- 2 tbsp. Sweetener
- ¼ tsp Pepper
- ½ tsp Cinnamon
- ½ tsp grated Ginger
- ½ tsp Salt

How to Cook:

1. Sprinkle the meat with salt and pepper.
2. Heat the oil in the Instant Pot using the "Sauté" mode.
3. Put in the pork chops and cook until browned.
4. In the mean time, whisk the rest of the ingredients in a container.
5. Pour the mixture over the pork.
6. Shut and secure the lid and choose MANUAL.
7. Switch the Instant Pot to "High" and cook for 15 minutes.
8. Your dish is ready! Have fun!

Nutritional Info: (Calories 650| Total Fats 40g | Net Carbs 3g | Protein 57g |Fiber: 1g)

Sweet Garlic Pork

Aggregate Time to Prepare: 45 Minutes

Yield: 6 Servings

Ingredients:

- 1 cup cherry tomatoes
- 2 large onions, thinly sliced
- 2 lbs pork chops
- 3 tbsp apple cider vinegar
- 3 tbsp butter
- 4 garlic cloves
- ¼ cup soy sauce
- ½ cup celery stalks, chopped

Spices:

- 1 tsp salt
- 2 tbsp stevia crystal
- ½ tsp chili flakes
- ½ tsp ginger powder

How to Cook:

1. Wash thoroughly the meat and pat dry each piece with some kitchen paper. Put on a large cutting board and remove the bones. Chop into bite-sized pieces and place in a deep container. Drizzle with salt, ginger, and chili flakes. Drizzle with soy sauce and save for later.

2. Turn on your Instant Pot and Switch your Instant Pot to "'Sauté" mode. Oil-coat the inner pot with butter and heat up. Put in onions, garlic, and celery stalks. Cook for 3-4 minutes, stirring continuously. After that put in cherry tomatoes and drizzle with stevia. Carry on cooking for 5 minutes or until soft.
3. Lastly, put in the meat and drizzle with apple cider vinegar. Stir fry for an additional 4-5 minutes and then pour in one cup of water.
4. Push the "Cancel" button and shut and secure the lid. Make sure the steam release handle is on the "Sealing" position and switch to "Manual' mode.
5. Turn the timer to 10 minutes on high pressure.when done, depressurize using the natural release method and open the lid.
6. If you want, you can also drizzle with freshly chopped parsley and serve instantly.

Nutritional Info: (Calories 569| Total Fats: 43.5g | Net Carbs: 5.3g | Protein: 35.6g |Fiber: 1.7g)

Sweet Pork with Cauliflower

Aggregate Time to Prepare: **40 Minutes**

Yield: **6 Servings**

Ingredients:

- 1 small onion, thinly sliced
- 2 celery stalks, chopped
- 2 cups cauliflower, chop into florets
- 2 lbs pork shoulder, chop into bite-sized pieces
- 4 cups beef broth
- 4 tbsp olive oil

- 5 bacon slices, chopped

Spices:

- 1 ½ tsp salt
- 1 tsp onion powder
- 2 tsp peppercorn
- ¼ cup stevia crystal
- ½ tsp garlic powder

How to Cook:

1. Oil-coat the bottom of the instant pot with oil and make the first layer with meat. Sprinkle with some salt and then put in onions and celery stalks. If you want, you can also drizzle with some more salt and put in cauliflower. Spread on top bacon and tenderly pour in the broth.
2. Shut and secure the lid and set the steam release handle to the "Sealing" position. Switch your Instant Pot to "Manual" mode and turn the timer to 15 minutes on high pressure.
3. When finished, depressurize using the natural release method and open the lid. Remove the meat and vegetables from the pot but keep the broth.
4. After that Switch your Instant Pot to "'Sauté" mode and put in stevia crystal, some more salt, peppercorn, onion powder, and garlic powder.
5. Tenderly simmer until the liquid has reduced in half.
6. Remove the peppercorn from the pot and put in the meat. Coat thoroughly with the sauce and serve with cauliflower.
7. Drizzle with some more sweet sauce prior to serving.

Nutritional Info: (Calories 647 | Total Fats: 49.2g | Net Carbs: 2.7g | Protein: 45.1g | Fiber: 1.2g)

Sweet Ribs

Aggregate Time to Prepare: 45 Minutes

Yield: 5 Servings

Ingredients:

- 1 celery stalk, chopped
- 1 green bell pepper, sliced
- 1 tbsp almond flour
- 1 tbsp apple cider
- 2 lbs pork ribs, chopped
- 2 red bell peppers, sliced
- 3 tbsp oil
- ¼ cup soy sauce

Spices:

- 1 bay leaf
- 1 rosemary sprig, fresh
- 1 tsp salt
- ½ tsp dried basil

How to Cook:

1. Put the ribs in the pot and pour in enough water to cover. Drizzle with salt, put in basil, bay leaf, and rosemary. Shut and secure the lid.
2. Make sure the steam release handle is on the "Sealing" position and switch to "Manual' mode. Cook for 25 minutes on high pressure.
3. When finished, depressurize using the natural release method and open the lid. Remove the ribs from the pot and chill for some time.

4. Oil-coat the inner pot with oil and Switch your Instant Pot to "'Sauté" mode. Put in bell peppers and celery stalks. Sauté for 5-6 minutes, stirring continuously.
5. Rub the ribs with soy sauce and put into the pot. Pour in the rest of the soy sauce and approximately ¼ cup of water.
6. Stir in the almond flour and simmer for 4-5 minutes.
7. Push the "Cancel" button and serve instantly.

Nutritional Info: (Calories 367 | Total Fats: 15g | Net Carbs: 5.8g | Protein: 49.1g | Fiber: 1.2g)

Tender Venison

Aggregate Time to Prepare: 80 Minutes

Yield: 8 Servings

Ingredients:

- 1 garlic head, separated into cloves
- 1 tbsp. butter, unsalted
- 3 lbs. venison shoulder, boneless

Spices:

- 1 tsp ginger powder
- 1 tsp salt
- 3 tbsp. apple cider vinegar
- ½ tsp black pepper, freshly ground
- ½ tsp garlic powder
- ½ tsp red pepper flakes

How to Cook:

1. In a small container, mixed apple cider, garlic powder, and ginger powder. Slightly coat the meat with this mixture and save for later.
2. Turn on the Instant Pot and switch to 'Sauté' mode. Put in pork in batches and brown uniformly on all sides. After that, put in one cup of water and garlic. Shut and secure the lid and close the steam release handle. Switch the Instant pot to "Manual" mode and turn the timer to 35 minutes.
3. When finished, push "Cancel" button and release the pressure using the quick release method. Open the lid and switch to 'Sauté' mode again. Drizzle the meat with salt, pepper, and red pepper flakes. Put in butter and cook until all the liquid evaporates – approximately 10 minutes.
4. Chill for 15 minutes prior to serving.

Nutritional Info: (Calories 524 | Total Fats 37.9g | Net Carbs: 2.8g | Protein 40g | Fiber: 0.3g)

Thai Pork with White Pepper Gravy

Aggregate Time to Prepare: 15 Minutes

Yield: 2 Servings

Ingredients:

- 1 cup dried black mushrooms, chopped
- 1 small onion, sliced
- 10 oz pork fillet, chop into strips
- 2 spring onion, chopped
- 2 tbsp fish sauce
- 2 tbsp oyster sauce
- 3 garlic cloves

- 3 tbsp peanut oil

Spices:

- 1 tsp white pepper, freshly ground
- ½ tsp sea salt

How to Cook:

1. Soak the mushrooms approximately 10-15 minutes before cooking.
2. Turn on your Instant Pot and heat the oil. Put in sliced pork, onions, and garlic. Cook 1-2 minutes and then put in spring onions. Carry on cooking for an additional 2-3 minutes, stirring continuously
3. After that put in mushrooms and stir thoroughly. Drizzle with fish sauce and oyster sauce. Carry on cooking for 2-3 minutes, stirring continuously.
4. Drizzle with white pepper and pour in approximately ¼ cup of water. Tenderly simmer for 10 minutes,
5. Push the "Cancel" button and serve instantly.

Nutritional Info: (Calories 423 | Total Fats: 25.4g | Net Carbs: 6.5g | Protein: 40.1g |Fiber: 1.6g)

Tomato Lamb Shanks with Thyme

Aggregate Time to Prepare: 30 Minutes

Yield: 4 Servings

Ingredients:

- 1 cup cherry tomatoes
- 1 large onion, thinly sliced
- 1 tbsp fish sauce
- 2 celery stalks, chopped

- 2 cups beef broth
- 2 tbsp balsamic vinegar
- 2 tbsp butter
- 4 garlic cloves, crushed
- 4 lamb shanks

Spices:

- 1 tsp dried thyme
- 1 tsp sea salt
- 2 bay leaves

How to Cook:

1. Turn on your Instant Pot and Switch your Instant Pot to "'Sauté" mode. Oil-coat the inner pot with butter and heat up.
2. Put in the meat and brown on all sides for 2-3 minutes. You will probably have to do this in several batches.
3. When finished, take out of the pot and move to a large platter. Loosely cover with some aluminium foil and save for later.
4. Put in some more olive oil in the pot and put in garlic, onions, and celery stalk. Stir thoroughly and cook for 4-5 minutes.
5. After that, pour in the balsamic vinegar and continue to cook until the vinegar has completely evaporated.
6. Lastly, put in the meat along with the rest of the ingredients. Stir thoroughly and shut and secure the lid. Make sure the steam release handle is on the "Sealing" position and push the "Stew" button.
7. When finished, depressurize using the quick release method and open the lid.
8. Serve instantly.

Nutritional Info: (Calories 474 | Total Fats: 21.3g | Net Carbs: 5.7g | Protein: 59.9g | Fiber: 1.5g)

Tomato Lamb with Brussels Sprouts

Aggregate Time to Prepare: 30 Minutes

Yield: 4 Servings

Ingredients:

- 1 cup Brussels sprouts
- 1 cup cherry tomatoes, whole
- 1 cup sour cream
- 2 celery stalks
- 2 racks of lamb
- 2 tbsp olive oil
- 3 cups vegetable stock
- ½ cup button mushrooms

Spices:

- 1 tsp dried rosemary
- 1 tsp salt
- ½ tsp black pepper, freshly ground
- ½ tsp chili powder
- ½ tsp dried sage

How to Cook:

1. Thoroughly wash the lamb under cold running water and drizzle with salt, rosemary, and sage. Put at the bottom of the instant pot and pour in the stock.
2. Shut and secure the lid and set the steam release handle to the "Sealing" position. Switch your Instant

Pot to "Manual" mode and turn the timer to 15 minutes on high pressure.
3. When finished, depressurize using the quick release method and open the lid.
4. After that put in sprouts, tomatoes, mushrooms, celery stalks, and oil. Sprinkle with some more salt, and chili powder.
5. Shut and secure the lid again and continue to cook for an additional 5 minutes on the "Manual" mode.
6. Cautiously open the lid when done and serve with sour cream.

Nutritional Info: (Calories 487 | Total Fats: 30.3g | Net Carbs: 5.4g | Protein: 45.7g | Fiber: 2g)

Tomato Pork Roast

Aggregate Time to Prepare: 50 Minutes

Yield: 5 Servings

Ingredients:

- 2 cups cauliflower, chopped into florets
- 2 large onions, sliced
- 2 large tomatoes, sliced
- 2 lbs pork butt, sliced
- 3 tbsp butter
- 4 cups beef broth
- 4 tbsp olive oil

Spices:

- 1 ½ tsp salt
- 1 tsp freshly ground black pepper
- ½ tsp nutmeg

How to Cook:

1. Rub the meat with olive oil and season with salt, pepper, and nutmeg. Put in the instant pot and pour in the broth.
2. Shut and secure the lid and set the steam release handle to the "Sealing" position. Switch your Instant Pot to "Manual" mode and cook for 20 minutes on high pressure.
3. In the mean time, preheat the oven to 400 degrees. Slightly coat a baking pan with butter and save for later.
4. When your instant pot sounds the end signal, depressurize using the quick release method and open the lid. Move to the readied baking pan and put in cauliflower, onions, and tomatoes.
5. Pour in approximately one cup of the broth and roast for approximately 15-20 minutes or until the meat is lightly charred and the vegetables fork-tender.

Nutritional Info: (Calories 494 | Total Fats: 25.8g | Net Carbs: 8.1g | Protein: 53.5g | Fiber: 3.2g)

Tomato Rasam

Aggregate Time to Prepare: 60 Minutes

Yield: 5 Servings

Ingredients:

- 1 lb beef stew meat
- 1 small onion, thinly sliced
- 2 garlic cloves, crushed
- 2 large tomatoes, chopped

- 2 red chilies, thinly sliced
- 4 tbsp ghee
- 5 cups vegetable stock

Spices:

- 2 tbsp chili powder
- 2 tsp coriander powder
- 2 tsp hing
- 2 tsp mustard seeds
- 2 tsp salt
- 2 tsp stevia powder
- 2 tsp turmeric powder

How to Cook:

1. Turn on your Instant Pot and pour in the stock. Put in tomatoes, onions, and chili peppers. Stir thoroughly and Switch your Instant Pot to "'Sauté" mode. Bring it to a boil and tenderly simmer for 15 minutes.
2. After that mix in the meat and season with all spices. Put in the rest of the ingredients and stir thoroughly.
3. Shut and secure the lid and set the steam release handle to the "Sealing" position. Switch your Instant Pot to "Manual" mode and turn the timer to 40 minutes on high pressure.
4. When finished, depressurize using the natural release method and open the lid. Stir thoroughly again and serve instantly.

Nutritional Info:(Calories 285| Total Fats 16.1g | Net Carbs: 5.6g | Protein: 28.8g |Fiber: 1.8g)

Tomato Ribs

Aggregate Time to Prepare: **45 Minutes**

Yield: 6 Servings

Ingredients:

- 1 cup sun-dried tomatoes
- 1 large onion, thinly sliced
- 2 cups cherry tomatoes, whole
- 2 lbs pork ribs, chopped
- 4 cups beef broth
- 4 tbsp butter

Spices:

- 1 tsp dried thyme
- 1 tsp sea salt
- 3 tbsp stevia or swerve
- ½ tsp dried oregano
- ½ tsp garlic powder

How to Cook:

1. Turn on your Instant Pot and put in ribs. Pour in the broth and shut and secure the lid. Set the steam release handle and switch to "Manual' mode.
2. Turn the timer to 20 minutes on high pressure.
3. When finished, depressurize using the natural release method and open the lid. Remove the meat along with the broth from the pot and Switch your Instant Pot to "'Sauté" mode.
4. Oil-coat the inner pot with butter and put in onions. Drizzle with some salt and cook until translucent.

5. After that put in tomatoes and pour in 2 cups of broth. Drizzle with the rest of the spices and cook until tomatoes have softened. Stir intermittently.
6. When finished, push the "Cancel" button and put in the meat. Coat thoroughly with the sauce and cover.
7. Allow it to sit for approximately 10 minute prior to serving.

Nutritional Info: (Calories 532 | Total Fats: 35.6g | Net Carbs: 4.9g | Protein: 44.4g | Fiber: 1.6g)

Veal Masala Curry

Aggregate Time to Prepare: 30 Minutes

Yield: 4 Servings

Ingredients:

- 1 cup tomatoes, diced
- 1 medium-sized onion, chopped
- 1 tbsp olive oil
- 2 cups beef stock
- 2 garlic cloves, crushed
- 2 lbs veal tenderloin, chop into bite-sized pieces
- ½ cup fresh parsley, thinly sliced

Spices:

- 1 tsp garam masala powder
- 1 tsp lime zest, freshly grated
- 1 tsp salt
- 1 tsp smoked paprika, ground
- ½ tsp coriander powder
- ½ tsp cumin powder

- ½ tsp curry powder

How to Cook:

1. Turn on the Instant Pot and coat the stainless steel insert with olive oil. Push the "Sauté" button and put in onions, garlic, and all the spices. Stir-fry for 3-4 minutes, or until the onions translucent.
2. Put in meat, tomatoes, and parsley. Pour in the beef stock and stir thoroughly.
3. Shut and secure the lid and close the steam release handle. Push the "Manual" button and turn the timer to 25 minutes. Cook on "High" pressure.
4. When you hear the cooker's end signal release the pressure using the quick release method by moving the valve to the "Venting" position.
5. Open the pot and move all to a serving dish.
6. Drizzle with some fresh parsley and garnish with some lemon slices prior to serving.
7. Have fun!

Nutritional Info: (Calories 462 | Total Fats 19.8g | Net Carbs: 4.1g | Protein: 62.2g | Fiber: 1.7g)

Veal with Garlic

Aggregate Time to Prepare: 50 Minutes

Yield: 4 Servings

Ingredients:

- 1 cup tomatoes, diced
- 1 medium-sized onion, chopped
- 1 medium-sized red bell pepper, chop into strips
- 1 tbsp butter
- 1 tbsp olive oil
- 2 lbs veal tenderloin, chop into bite-sized pieces
- 3 cups bone broth
- 5 garlic cloves, thinly sliced

Spices:

- 1 tsp smoked paprika, ground
- 1 tsp sea salt
- ½ tsp black pepper, ground
- ½ tsp dried thyme, ground
- ¼ tsp dried rosemary, ground

How to Cook:

1. Thoroughly wash the meat under running water and pat dry with a kitchen paper. Move to a cutting board and chop into bite-sized pieces using a sharp knife. Rub with salt and pepper and save for later.
2. Turn on the Instant Pot and coat the stainless steel insert with olive oil. Switch your Instant Pot to "Sauté' mode and put in meat. Cook for 5 minutes, or until golden brown. Remove the meat to a plate and save for later.

3. Put in butter and stir until melts. Put in onions, garlic, and bell peppers. Stir-fry for 3-4 minutes or until onions translucent.
4. After that, return the meat and drizzle all with smoked paprika, thyme, and rosemary. Pour in the broth and mix in the tomatoes. Shut and secure the lid and close the steam release handle. Switch your Instant Pot to "Manual" mode and turn the timer to 35 minutes. Cook on "High" pressure.
5. When your instant pot sounds the end signal, release the pressure using the quick release method and turn off the pot.
6. Open the lid and move to a serving pot, or directly to a serving containers.
7. Have fun!

Nutritional Info: (Calories 553 | Total Fats 22.4g | Net Carbs: 6.4g | Protein: 76.1g |Fiber: 2g)

Venison with Béarnaise Sauce

Aggregate Time to Prepare: 30 Minutes

Yield: 6 Servings

Ingredients:

- 1 cup beef stock
- 1 large onion, thinly sliced
- 2 lbs. shoulder of venison, chopped into smaller pieces
- 3 tbsp. oil
- 4 egg yolks
- 6 tbsp. butter

Spices:

- 1 tsp fresh basil, thinly sliced
- 1 tsp lemon extract
- 1 tsp salt
- 5 peppercorns

How to Cook:

1. Put butter at the bottom of your pot and switch your Instant Pot to 'Sauté' mode. Melt the butter and put in onions. Stir-fry until translucent. Put in stock, basil, peppercorn, and lemon extract. Stir thoroughly and shut and secure the lid. Set the steam release handle and push the 'Manual' button. Set the time for 5 minutes.
2. After you hear the cooker's end signal, release the pressure using the quick release method and open the lid. Stir in egg yolks and put in the meat. Pour in 2 cups of water and shut and secure the lid.
3. Set the steam release handle again and push the 'Manual' button. Cook for 25 minutes on high pressure.
4. Serve warm with the sauce.

Nutritional Info: (Calories 374 | Total Fats 23g | Net Carbs: 2.3g | Protein 35.9g | Fiber: 0.5g)

Vinegary Lamb Shanks

Aggregate Time to Prepare: 50 Minutes

Yield: 4 Servings

Ingredients:

- 1 ½ cups Beef Broth
- 1 ½ tsp ground Ginger
- 1 Onion, sliced
- 2 Garlic Cloves, minced
- 2 tbsp. Apple Cider Vinegar
- 2 tbsp. Coconut Aminos
- 2 tbsp. Coconut Oil
- 4 Lamb Shanks
- ½ tsp Pepper

How to Cook:

1. Melt half of the olive oil in your Instant Pot using the "Sauté" mode.
2. Put in the lamb shanks and cook until browned on all sides (you may need to work in batches).
3. Put in onion and cook for 2 additional minutes,
4. Stir in the garlic and ginger and cook for 1 minute.
5. Stir in the rest of the ingredients and shut and secure the lid.
6. Switch the Instant Pot to "High" and cook for 7 minutes.
7. Turn off the Instant Pot and let sit covered for 20 minutes.
8. Depressurize and serve.
9. Have fun!

Nutritional Info: (Calories 280| Total Fats 14g | Net Carbs 5g | Protein 25g |Fiber: 1g)

White Wine Pork Belly

Aggregate Time to Prepare: 60 Minutes

Yield: 4 Servings

Ingredients:

- 1 Garlic Clove
- 1 pound Pork Belly
- 1 Rosemary Sprig
- 3 tbsp. Olive Oil
- ½ cup White Wine
- Salt and Pepper, to taste

How to Cook:

1. Heat the olive oil in the Instant Pot using the "Sauté" mode.
2. Put in the pork belly and cook for approximately 3 minutes on each side.
3. Pour the wine over.
4. Put the rosemary sprig and garlic inside.
5. Drizzle with salt and pepper.
6. Shut and secure the lid and switch your instant pot to "Manual" mode and cook for 40 minutes.
7. Release the pressure using the quick release method.
8. Your dish is ready! Have fun!

Nutritional Info: (Calories 610| Total Fats 60g | Net Carbs 1g | Protein 40g |Fiber: 0g)

Wontons

Aggregate Time to Prepare: 85-90 Minutes

Yield: 4 Servings

Ingredients:

- 1 lbs. Ground Pork
- 1 tbsp. Garlic (minced)

- 1 tbsp. Ginger (minced)
- 1 tsp Ground Black Pepper
- 1 tsp Oyster Sauce
- 2 cups Water
- 2 Eggs
- 2 tsp Soy Sauce
- ¼ cup Coriander (chopped)
- ¼ cup Spring Onions (chopped)
- ½ tsp Salt

How to Cook:

1. Put all ingredients, except water, in a container and mix thoroughly.
2. Take an oven safe silicone baby food container with twelve 2.5 ounces cavities, and fill them ¾ full.
3. Pour two cups of water in the Instant Pot and place the steamer rack in it, and then set the food container on it.
4. Shut and secure the lid and set Instant Pot to "Steam" and cooking time to 10 minutes.
5. When finished allow the pressure to be released naturally for 5 minutes and then quick release it.
6. Remove the wontons from food containers and serve with soy or other dipping sauce.

Nutritional Info: (Calories: 340 | Total Fats: 23g | Net Carbs: 2g | Proteins: 22g | Fibers: 0g)

Zucchini Noodles with Sesame Seeds

Aggregate Time to Prepare: **50 Minutes**

Yield: **4 Servings**

Ingredients:

- 1 large tomato, chopped
- 1 large zucchini, spiralized
- 1 lb lamb tenderloin
- 1 onion, thinly sliced
- 2 celery stalks, chopped
- 3 garlic cloves, crushed
- 3 tbsp butter
- 4 tbsp sesame seeds

Spices:

- 1 bay leaf
- 1 tsp black pepper, ground
- 2 tsp salt
- ½ tsp dried thyme

How to Cook:

1. Put the meat in the instant pot and pour in enough water to cover. Put in celery stalks, one teaspoon of salt, and bay leaf.
2. Shut and secure the lid and set the steam release handle to the "Sealing" position. Switch your Instant Pot to "Manual" mode and cook for 25 minutes on high pressure.
3. When finished, depressurize using the quick release method and open the lid. Take the meat out of the pot along with the liquid. Make sure to reserve some of the liquid.
4. After that Switch your Instant Pot to "'Sauté" mode. Oil-coat the inner pot with butter and put in onions and garlic. Cook for 3-4 minutes, stirring continuously. After that put in sesame seeds and tomato. Sprinkle with some more salt and thyme.

Carry on cooking for 6-7 minutes, stirring intermittently.
5. In the mean time, run the zucchini through spiralizer to create noodles. Put in noodles to the pot and pour in approximately ¼ cup of the reserved liquid. Carry on cooking for an additional 4-5 minutes.
6. Put the meat on a cutting board and chop into bite-sized pieces. Put in to the pot and coat thoroughly with the sauce and noodles.
7. Push the "Cancel" button and take out of the pot. Serve instantly.

Nutritional Info: (Calories 376 | Total Fats: 21.7g | Net Carbs: 6.9g | Protein: 35.4g | Fiber: 3.3g)

Zucchini Pork

Aggregate Time to Prepare: **1 HOUR|**

Yield: **4 Servings**

Ingredients:

- 1 cup button mushrooms, sliced
- 1 cup cauliflower florets
- 1 egg white
- 1 large tomato, roughly chopped
- 1 lb pork neck, chopped into bite-sized pieces
- 1 small onion, thinly sliced
- 1 zucchini, spiralized into noodles
- 2 garlic cloves, crushed
- 2 red bell peppers, chopped
- 2 tbsp apple cider vinegar
- 2 tbsp butter
- 2 tbsp soy sauce

Spices:

- 1 tbsp cayenne pepper
- 1 tsp salt
- 2 bay leaves
- 2 tbsp stevia powder
- ½ tsp ginger powder

How to Cook:

1. In a small container, mix egg whites, soy sauce, apple cider, salt, stevia, half of the cayenne pepper, and ginger powder.
2. Liberally brush the meat with this mixture and let it sit for 15-20 minutes.
3. Turn on your Instant Pot and put in butter. Heat up and put in the meat. Cook for 4-5 minutes, stirring continuously.
4. Take the meat out of the pot and put in onions, garlic, mushrooms, peppers, tomato, and cauliflower.
5. Carry on cooking for 10-12 minutes.
6. Lastly, put in the meat, bay leaf, and pour in 1 cup of water. Shut and secure the lid and set the steam release handle to the "Sealing" posisiton.
7. Switch your Instant Pot to "Manual" mode and turn the timer to 13 minutes on high pressure.
8. When finished, depressurize using the quick release method and open the lid. Stir in zuccnhini noodles and Switch your Instant Pot to "'Sauté" mode.
9. Cook for 7-8 minutes, stirring intermittently.
10. Serve with grated Parmesan cheese or freshly chopped parsley.

Nutritional Info: (Calories 277| Total Fats: 10.2g | Net Carbs: 9.5g | Protein: 34.1g |Fiber: 3.2g)

Zucchini Stew

Aggregate Time to Prepare: **30 Minutes**

Yield: **3 Servings**

Ingredients:

- 1 cup purple cabbage, shredded
- 1 large zucchini, sliced into 1-inch thick slices
- 1 lb lamb loin, chopped into bite-sized pieces
- 1 small chili pepper, thinly sliced
- 2 cups beef stock
- 3 tbsp olive oil
- 4 garlic cloves, crushed

Spices:

- 1 tsp oregano
- 1 tsp salt
- ¼ tsp dried thyme
- ½ tsp chili powder

How to Cook:

1. Turn on your Instant Pot and Switch your Instant Pot to "'Sauté" mode. Heat up the oil and put in garlic. Cook for one minute and then put in the meat. Sprinkle with salt, chili powder, oregano, and thyme. Stir thoroughly and continue to cook for 5-6 minutes, stirring intermittently.
2. After that put in zucchini and stir thoroughly. Stir-fry for 3 minutes.
3. Pour in the stock and put in chili pepper and cabbage. Shut and secure the lid and set the steam release handle to the "Sealing" position.

4. Switch your Instant Pot to "Manual" mode and turn the timer to 12 minutes on high pressure.
5. When finished, depressurize using the natural release method and open the lid.
6. If you want, you can also spread on top Greek yogurt prior to serving.

Nutritional Info: (Calories 442 | Total Fats: 25.7g | Net Carbs: 4.6g | Protein: 46.2g | Fiber: 1.9g)

Seafood Recipes

5-Minute Mussels Soup

Aggregate Time to Prepare: **5 Minutes**

Yield: **3 Servings**

Ingredients:

- 1 cup cherry tomatoes, chopped
- 2 tbsp butter
- 4 cups fish stock
- 7 oz mussels, defrosted and cleaned
- ¼ cup fish sauce

Spices:

- 2 tsp Italian seasoning
- ¼ tsp stevia powder

How to Cook:

1. Wash thoroughly and wash the mussels. Drain in a large sieve and place in the pot.
2. Drizzle with Italian seasoning and stevia extract. Pour in the fish stock and soy sauce and put in cherry tomatoes. Stir thoroughly and shut and secure the lid.
3. Make sure the steam release handle is on the "Sealing" position and switch to "Manual' mode.
4. When finished, depressurize using the quick release method and open the lid. Stir in the fish sauce and serve instantly.
5. If you want, you can also drizzle with freshly chopped parsley prior to serving.

Nutritional Info:(Calories 404| Total Fats 21.3g | Net Carbs: 5g | Protein: 44.6g |Fiber: 1.3g)

5-Minute Shrimp Soup

Aggregate Time to Prepare: 40 Minutes

Yield: 5 Servings

Ingredients:

- 1 cup broccoli, chop into florets
- 1 large tomato, roughly chopped
- 2 lbs shrimps, tail-on
- 3 tbsp butter
- 3 tbsp olive oil
- 4 cups fish stock
- 4 garlic cloves, minced
- ½ cup fresh parsley, thinly sliced

Spices:

- 1 tsp dried rosemary
- 2 tsp sea salt

How to Cook:

1. Plug in the instant pot. Heat up the olive oil on the "Sauté" mode and put in broccoli. Stir thoroughly and cook until golden brown. Drizzle with garlic and cook for one additional minute.
2. After that put in tomatoes and pour in some fish stock – approximately three tablespoons will be enough. Cook for 7-8 minutes, or until most of the liquid evaporates.

3. After that put in shrimps and briefly brown. Stir thoroughly and season with salt and rosemary.
4. Put in the rest of the ingredients and stir thoroughly. Shut and secure the lid and set the steam release handle and switch to "Manual' mode.
5. Turn the timer to 15 minutes.
6. When finished, depressurize using the quick release method and open the lid. If you want, you can also drizzle with some more herbs or spices and serve instantly.

Nutritional Info:(Calories 399 | Total Fats 20.1g | Net Carbs: 5.4g | Protein: 46.8g |Fiber: 1.2g)

Adobo Shrimps

Aggregate Time to Prepare: **50Minutes**

Yield: **4 Servings**

Ingredients:

- 1 lb shrimps, peeled and deveined
- 1 red chili pepper, thinly sliced
- 1 small onion, thinly sliced
- 2 cups fish stock
- 2 tbsp fish sauce
- 2 tbsp green onions, thinly sliced
- 5 garlic cloves, crushed
- ¼ cup olive oil
- ¼ cup rice vinegar
- ¼ cup soy sauce

Spices:

- 1 tbsp peppercorn

- 1 tsp stevia powder
- 2 tsp salt

How to Cook:

1. In a large container, whisk together olive oil, rice vinegar, soy sauce, green onions, garlic, fish sauce, chopped onion, chili pepper, salt, peppercorn, and stevia.
2. Put in shrimps and stir thoroughly ensuring to coat shrimps thoroughly in the marinade. Move to a large Ziploc bag and refrigerate for at least 30 minutes (up to 2 hours).
3. Turn on your Instant Pot and pour in the stock. Remove the shrimps from the Ziploc and place in the pot along with ¼ cup of the marinade.
4. Stir thoroughly and shut and secure the lid. Make sure the steam release handle is on the "Sealing" position and switch to "Manual' mode.
5. Turn the timer to 10 minutes.
6. When finished, release the pressure using the quick release method and serve instantly.

Nutritional Info:(Calories 298 | Total Fats 15.5g | Net Carbs: 5.7g | Protein: 30.4g |Fiber: 0.7g)

Almond and Dijon Tilapia

Aggregate Time to Prepare: 10 Minutes

Yield: 4 Servings

Ingredients:

- 1 cup Water
- 1 tsp Olive Oil

- 2 tbsp. Dijon Mustard
- 2/3 cup sliced Almonds
- 4 Tilapia Fillets
- ¼ tsp Pepper

How to Cook:

1. Pour the water into the Instant Pot.
2. Mix together the mustard, oil, and pepper.
3. Slightly coat over the tilapia fillets.
4. Line the tilapia with almond slices and place on the rack.
5. Shut and secure the lid and set the Instant Pot to MANUAL.
6. Cook on High for 5 minutes.
7. Release the pressure using the quick release method.
8. Your dish is ready! Have fun!

Nutritional Info: (Calories 327| Total Fats 15g | Net Carbs 1.3g | Protein 46g |Fiber: 2.8g)

Bacon Shrimps

Aggregate Time to Prepare: 20 Minutes

Yield: 5 Servings

Ingredients:

- 1 lb shrimps, peeled and deveined
- 10 slices bacon, chopped
- 2 small onions, chopped
- 2 tbsp soy sauce
- 4 garlic cloves, crushed
- 5 cups fish stock
- 6 tbsp butter, unsalted

Spices:

- 1 tsp Old Bay seasoning
- 1/8 tsp lemon pepper
- ¼ tsp chili powder

How to Cook:

1. Melt the butter and heat up on the "Sauté" mode. Put in onions and cook for 3-4 minutes, stirring continuously.
2. After that put in garlic and cook for one additional minute. Push the "Cancel" button and put in the rest of the ingredients.
3. Stir thoroughly and shut and secure the lid. Set the steam release handle and switch to "Manual' mode.
4. Turn the timer to 7 minutes on high pressure.
5. When finished, depressurize using the natural release method and open the lid.
6. Serve instantly.

Nutritional Info: (Calories 493 | Total Fats 33.2g | Net Carbs: 5.1g | Protein: 41g | Fiber: 0.7g)

Black Cauliflower Pasta

Aggregate Time to Prepare: 20 Minutes

Yield: 3 Servings

Ingredients:

- 1 lb frozen seafood mix, defrosted
- 1 tsbp squid ink
- 2 cups cauliflower, chopped into florets
- 2 tbsp apple cider vinegar

- 4 garlic cloves, crushed
- ¼ cup Parmesan cheese
- ½ cup olive oil

Spices:

- 1 tbsp fresh parsley, thinly sliced
- 1 tsp fresh rosemary, thinly sliced
- 1 tsp sea salt

How to Cook:

1. Turn on your Instant Pot and coat the inner pot with three tablespoons of olive oil.
2. Switch your Instant Pot to "Sauté" mode and heat up. Put in crushed garlic and stir-fry for one minute.
3. After that, put in seafood mix, parsley, chopped rosemary, and drizzle with salt. Stir thoroughly and pour in the rest of the olive oil along with ¼ cup of water.
4. Put in chopped cauliflower and mix in the squid ink. Shut and secure the lid . Set the steam release handle and switch to "Manual' mode.
5. Turn the timer to 5 minutes on high pressure.
6. When finished, depressurize using the natural release method for approximately 10 minutes and then move the pressure valve to the "Venting" position to release the rest of the pressure.
7. Cautiously open the lid and drizzle with Parmesan cheese.
8. Serve warm.

Nutritional Info:(Calories 476| Total Fats 37g | Net Carbs: 6.8g | Protein: 25.9g |Fiber: 1.8g)

Caramelized Tilapia

Aggregate Time to Prepare: 55 Minutes

Yield: 4 Servings

Ingredients:

- 1 pound tilapia Fillets
- 1 Red Chili, minced
- 1 Spring Onion, minced
- 1/3 cup Water
- 3 tbsp. Fish Sauce
- 3 tsp minced Garlic
- ¼ cup Granulated Sweetener
- ¾ cup Coconut Water
- Salt and Pepper, to taste

How to Cook:

1. In a container, mix the fish sauce, garlic, salt, and pepper.
2. Put the tilapia inside and mix to coat.
3. Cover and let sit in the fridge for 30 minutes.
4. In the mean time, mix the water and sweetener in the Instant Pot.
5. Cook using the "Sauté" mode until caramelized.
6. Put in fish and pour the coconut water over.
7. Shut and secure the lid and cook on HIGH for 10 minutes.
8. Release the pressure using the quick release method.
9. Top the fish with spring onion and chili.
10. Your dish is ready! Have fun!

Nutritional Info: (Calories 150| Total Fats 4g | Net Carbs 3g | Protein 21g |Fiber: 0.6g)

Catfish with Soy Sauce and Dill

Aggregate Time to Prepare: **15 Minutes**

Yield: **4 Servings**

Ingredients:

- 1 tbsp. chopped Dill
- 1 tbsp. Olive Oil
- 2 tbsp. Soy Sauce
- 2 tsp minced Garlic
- 4 Catfish Fillets
- ¼ cup Water

How to Cook:

1. Heat the oil in the Instant Pot using the "Sauté" mode.
2. Put in garlic and cook for approximately 30-60 seconds.
3. Put in the dill and soy sauce and stir to mix.
4. Put the catfish fillets inside and cook for 4 minutes on each side.
5. Pour the water over and shut and secure the lid.
6. Switch the Instant Pot to "High" and cook for 1 minute.
7. Your dish is ready! Have fun!

Nutritional Info: (Calories 103| Total Fats 5g | Net Carbs 2.5g | Protein 11g |Fiber: 0g)

Cheesy Tuna and Noodles

Aggregate Time to Prepare: 10 Minutes

Yield: 4 Servings

Ingredients:

- 1 cup Water
- 2 Tuna cans, drained
- 4 tbsp. Cheddar Cheese
- 4 Zucchini Noodles
- ½ cup Heavy Cream
- ½ cup shredded Cheddar Cheese

How to Cook:

1. Pour the water into the Instant Pot.
2. Put the zoodles, heavy cream, tuna, and cheddar, in a baking dish.
3. Stir to mix.
4. Put the dish inside the Instant Pot.
5. Shut and secure the lid and cook on HIGH for 3 minutes.
6. Separate between 4 containers.
7. Spread on top parmesan cheese.
8. Your dish is ready! Have fun!

Nutritional Info: (Calories 210| Total Fats 9.3g | Net Carbs 2g | Protein 15g |Fiber: 0g)

Chili Anchovy

Aggregate Time to Prepare: 25 Minutes

Yield: 2 Servings

Ingredients:

- 1 Red Chili, sliced
- 1 tbsp. Basil
- 1 tsp Chili Flakes
- 1 tsp Dill
- 1/3 cup Ground Almond
- 10 ounces Anchovy
- 4 tbsp. Butter
- ½ tsp Paprika
- Salt and Pepper, to taste

How to Cook:

1. Melt the butter in the Instant Pot using the "Sauté" mode.
2. Mix the chili and all of the spices in a container.
3. Put in anchovy and coat thoroughly.
4. Put in anchovy to the Instant Pot and cook for 4-5 minutes on each side.
5. Drain on paper towels.
6. Your dish is ready! Have fun!

Nutritional Info: (Calories 350| Total Fats 25g | Net Carbs 3.1g | Protein 28g |Fiber: 0.3g)

Chili Hake Fillets

Aggregate Time to Prepare: **45 Minutes**

Yield: **6 Servings**

Ingredients:

- 1 red onion, thinly sliced
- 2 lbs hake fillets, skinless

- 3 cups fish stock
- 3 garlic cloves, minced
- ¼ cup apple cider vinegar
- ¼ cup soy sauce
- ½ cup olive oil

Spices:

- 1 tsp sea salt
- 2 tbsp fresh dill, thinly sliced
- 2 tsp chili powder
- 2 tsp fresh rosemary

How to Cook:

1. Thoroughly wash fillets under cold running water and place them in a deep container. Drizzle with olive oil and apple cider vinegar. Drizzle with rosemary, salt, dill, and chili powder. Cover with the lid and save for later.
2. Turn on your Instant Pot and coat the inner pot with some oil. Switch your Instant Pot to "Sauté' mode and put in onions and garlic. Stir-fry for 3-4 minutes and season with some salt and optionally some pepper.
3. Remove the fillets from the container and place in the pot. Drizzle with approximately two tablespoons of the marinade and pour in the stock. Shut and secure the lid and set the steam release handle.
4. Switch your Instant Pot to "Manual" mode and turn the timer to 12 minutes on HIGH pressure.
5. When finished, release the pressure using the quick release method and cautiously open the lid. Switch your Instant Pot to "Sauté' mode and pour in the soy sauce.
6. Tenderly stir again and cook for 3-4 minutes.

7. Turn off your Instant pot and serve instantly.

Nutritional Info:(Calories 468| Total Fats 30.6g | Net Carbs: 2.6g | Protein: 43.9g |Fiber: 0.5g)

Chili Lime Salmon

Aggregate Time to Prepare: 15 Minutes

Yield: 1 Serving

Ingredients:

- 1 cup fish stock
- 1 jalapeno pepper, chopped
- 1 tbsp freshly squeezed lime juice
- 1 tbsp olive oil
- 1 tbsp swerve
- 2 garlic cloves, crushed
- 7 oz salmon fillets

Spices:

- 1 tbsp fresh parsley, thinly sliced
- 1 tsp sea salt
- ¼ tsp cumin powder
- ½ tsp black pepper
- ½ tsp smoked paprika

How to Cook:

1. Thoroughly wash the fillets under cold running water and rub with salt and pepper. Put in the steam basket and pour in one cup of water.
2. Shut and secure the lid and set the steam release handle to the "Sealing" position. Push the "Steam"

button and turn the timer to 4 minutes on high pressure.
3. When finished, release the pressure using the quick release method and open the lid.
4. In the mean time, in a small container, mix olive oil, swerve, garlic, lime juice, cumin powder, paprika, and parsley.
5. Switch your Instant Pot to "Sauté' mode and pour the mixture in the pot. Heat up and put in chopped pepper. Stir in the salmon and cook for 2 minutes.
6. Turn off the Instant Pot by pressing the "Cancel" button. Serve instantly.

Nutritional Info:(Calories 399 | Total Fats 26.5g | Net Carbs: 2.5g | Protein: 39.2g |Fiber: 0.6g)

Chili Mahi-Mahi

Aggregate Time to Prepare: 20 Minutes

Yield: 4 Servings

Ingredients:

- 1 ½ cups Water
- 1/3 cup chopped Green Chilies
- 2 tbsp. Butter, melted
- 4 Mahi Mahi Fillets
- ¼ tsp Pepper
- ¼ tsp Salt

How to Cook:

1. Melt the butter in the Instant Pot using the "Sauté" mode.

2. Drizzle the fish with salt and pepper and cook for a minute on each side.
3. Move to a steaming basket.
4. Pour the water into the Instant Pot.
5. Top the fish with chopped chilies and lower the basket.
6. Shut and secure the lid and cook for 5 minutes on HIGH.
7. Release the pressure using the quick release method.
8. Your dish is ready! Have fun!

Nutritional Info: (Calories 325| Total Fats 22g | Net Carbs 3g | Protein 20g |Fiber: 0.4g)

Clams in a White Wine Sauce

Aggregate Time to Prepare: 15 Minutes

Yield: 4 Servings

Ingredients:

- 2 ½ pounds Clams
- 2 cups Veggie Broth
- 2 tbsp. Lemon Juice
- 2 tsp minced Garlic
- ¼ cup chopped Basil
- ¼ cup Olive Oil
- ¼ cup White Wine

How to Cook:

1. Heat the oil in the Instant Pot using the "Sauté" mode.
2. Put in garlic and cook for 1 minute.
3. Stir in the lemon juice, white wine, broth, and basil.

4. Bring to a boil.
5. Put the clams in the steamer basket and lower it into the pot.
6. Shut and secure the lid and cook for 4 minutes on HIGH.
7. Serve drizzled with the cooking liquid.
8. Have fun!

Nutritional Info: (Calories 224| Total Fats 15g | Net Carbs 5.7g | Protein 16g |Fiber: 0.1g)

Classic Fish Stew

Aggregate Time to Prepare: 30 Minutes

Yield: 6 Servings

Ingredients:

- 1 cup fresh parsley, thinly sliced
- 1 lb king prawns, raw shelled
- 2 celery stalks, thinly sliced
- 2 lbs pollock fillets, skinless
- 2 small onions, thinly sliced
- 3 cups fish stock
- 3 garlic cloves, crushed
- ½ cup extra virgin olive oil

Spices:

- 1 tbsp fresh rosemary, thinly sliced
- 1 tsp sea salt

How to Cook:

1. Turn on your Instant Pot and coat the inner pot with three tablespoons of olive oil.

2. Put in onions and crushed garlic. Switch your Instant Pot to "Sauté' mode and cook for 4-5 minutes, stirring continuously.
3. After that, put in the rest of the ingredients and stir all thoroughly. Push the "Cancel" button to turn off the "Sauté" mode.
4. Shut and secure the lid and set the steam release handle. Switch your Instant Pot to "Manual" mode and turn the timer to 10 minutes.
5. When finished, push the "Cancel" button again and depressurize using the quick release method.
6. Cautiously open the lid and drizzle the stew with some freshly squeezed lemon juice prior to serving.

Nutritional Info:(Calories 557| Total Fats 32g | Net Carbs: 3.6g | Protein: 60.8g |Fiber: 1g)

Classic Lobster Tomato Stew

Aggregate Time to Prepare: **15 Minutes**

Yield: **4 Servings**

Ingredients:

- 1 cup celery, thinly sliced
- 2 cups cherry tomatoes, chopped
- 2 cups fish stock
- 2 cups heavy cream
- 2 shallots, diced
- 2 tbsp butter
- 3 tbsp olive oil
- 4 lobster tails, defrosted

Spices:

- 1 tbsp Old Bay seasoning
- 1 tsp black pepper, freshly ground
- 1 tsp dill
- ½ tsp smoked paprika

How to Cook:

1. In a large container, mix tomatoes, celery, shallots, olive oil, and dill. Combine until thoroughly blended and save for later.
2. Turn on your Instant Pot and Switch your Instant Pot to "'Sauté" mode. Oil-coat the inner pot with butter and put in lobster tails. Sprinkle with salt, pepper, and Old Bay seasoning. Cook for 3-4 minutes on each side.
3. Pour in the tomato mixture, fish stock, and drizzle with smoked paprika.
4. Stir thoroughly and shut and secure the lid. Set the steam release handle and switch to "Manual' mode. Turn the timer to 5 minutes on high pressure.
5. When finished, push the "Cancel" button and depressurize using the natural release method. Cautiously open the lid and mix in the heavy cream.
6. Chill for some time and serve.

Nutritional Info:(Calories 468| Total Fats 40.3g | Net Carbs: 5.3g | Protein: 21.2g |Fiber: 1.5g)

Coconut Milk Cod

Aggregate Time to Prepare: 20 Minutes

Yield: 4 Servings

Ingredients:

- 1 pound Cod Fillets
- 1 tbsp. Butter
- 1 tbsp. Lime Zest
- 1 tsp minced Garlic
- 1/2 cup Coconut Milk
- 2 tbsp. Soy Sauce
- 3 tbsp. Almond Flour
- ¼ cup Fish Sauce

How to Cook:

1. Chop the cod and insert in the Instant Pot.
2. Put in the rest of the ingredient and stir to mix.
3. Set the Instant Pot to "Sauté" mode and shut and secure the lid.
4. Let cook using the "Sauté" mode with the lid on, for approximately 10 minutes.
5. Open the lid and cook for 3 additional minutes.
6. Your dish is ready! Have fun!

Nutritional Info: (Calories 260| Total Fats 14g | Net Carbs 6.1g | Protein 24g |Fiber: 1g)

Cod Chowder with Bacon

Aggregate Time to Prepare: 25 Minutes

Yield: 5 Servings

Ingredients:

- 1 cup button mushrooms, sliced
- 1 cup full-fat milk
- 1 lb cod fillets
- 2 cups cauliflower, chop into florets
- 3 cups fish stock

- 3 tbsp butter
- 5 bacon slices, chopped
- ¼ cup fish sauce
- ¼ cup heavy cream
- ½ cup onions, thinly sliced

Spices:

- 1 tsp dried basil
- 1 tsp salt
- ½ tsp black pepper, freshly ground

How to Cook:

1. Turn on your Instant Pot and Switch your Instant Pot to "'Sauté" mode. Oil-coat the inner pot with butter and heat up. Put in onions and mushrooms and stir thoroughly. Cook for 5 minutes, stirring intermittently.
2. After that put in the fish stock and cauliflower. Put in cod fillets and season with salt, pepper, and basil.
3. Put in bacon and stir thoroughly again.
4. Shut and secure the lid and set the steam release handle to the "Sealing" position. Switch your Instant Pot to "Manual" mode and turn the timer to 8 minutes on high pressure.
5. When finished, depressurize using the quick release method and cautiously open the lid.
6. Stir in the milk and heavy cream. Drizzle with the fish sauce and chill for some time.
7. Serve with some freshly chopped parsley.

Nutritional Info:(Calories 333| Total Fats 20.7g | Net Carbs: 5.6g | Protein: 30.1g |Fiber: 1.4g)

Cod with Coriander

Aggregate Time to Prepare: 15 Minutes

Yield: 4 Servings

Ingredients:

- 1 cup coriander leaves, chopped
- 1 medium-sized yellow bell pepper, chopped
- 1 small green chili pepper, chopped
- 1 tbsp butter, melted
- 1 whole lemon, freshly juiced
- 2 lbs cod fillets
- 4 cherry tomatoes, chopped
- 4 garlic cloves, minced

Spices:

- 1 tsp garam masala powder
- 1 tsp mustard seeds
- 1 tsp sea salt
- ¼ tsp turmeric powder
- ½ tsp fenugreek seeds

How to Cook:

1. Turn on the Instant Pot and coat the stainless steel insert with melted butter. Push the "Sauté" button and put in garlic, green chili pepper, and all the spices. Stir-fry for 5 minutes, or until the onions translucent.
2. After that, put in tomatoes, bell pepper, and coriander. Spread on top fillets and pour in 2 cups of water. Shut and secure the lid and close the steam release handle by moving the valve to the "Sealing" position.

3. Push the "Manual" button and turn the timer to 8 minutes. Cook on "High" pressure.
4. When you hear the cooker's end signal, release the pressure using the quick release method and open the pot.
5. Move all to a serving dish and drizzle with fresh lemon juice.
6. Have fun!

Nutritional Info:(Calories 255 | Total Fats 5.6g | Net Carbs: 7.5g | Protein: 42.7g |Fiber: 2.8g)

Creamy Crabmeat

Aggregate Time to Prepare: 12 Minutes

Yield: 4 Servings

Ingredients:

- 1 pound Lump Crabmeat
- 1/2 Red Onion, chopped
- ¼ cup Butter
- ¼ cup Chicken Broth
- ½ Celery Stalk, chopped
- ½ cup Heavy Cream

How to Cook:

1. Melt the butter in the Instant Pot using the "Sauté" mode.
2. Put in onion and celery and cook for 4 minutes.
3. Put in crabmeat and broth.
4. Stir to mix and shut and secure the lid.
5. Switch the Instant Pot to "High" and cook for 3 minutes.

6. Release the pressure using the quick release method.
7. Stir in the cream.
8. Your dish is ready! Have fun!

Nutritional Info: (Calories 400| Total Fats 10g | Net Carbs 6g | Protein 40g |Fiber: 0.3g)

Creamy Mussel Soup

Aggregate Time to Prepare: 15 Minutes

Yield: 4 Servings

Ingredients:

- 1 cup broccoli, chopped
- 1 cup heavy cream
- 1 lb cauliflower, chopped into florets
- 1 tbsp soy sauce
- 2 cups fish stock
- 2 cups mussels, defrosted
- 2 tbsp butter, unsalted
- ¼ cup Parmesan cheese

Spices:

- 2 bay leaves
- ½ tsp fresh pepper, ground

How to Cook:

1. Put mussels in a large sieve and rinse thoroughly under cold running water. Drain and place in a deep container. Sprinkle with pepper and save for later.
2. Turn on your Instant Pot and Switch your Instant Pot to "'Sauté" mode. Put in cauliflower and broccoli. Stir thoroughly and cook for 5 minutes.

3. After that put in mussels and pour in the fish stock. Drizzle with soy sauce and put in bay leaves.
4. Shut and secure the lid and set the steam release handle to the "Sealing" position. Switch your Instant Pot to "Manual" mode and turn the timer to 5 minutes on high pressure.
5. When finished, release the pressure using the quick release method and open the lid. Remove the bay leaves and mix in the heavy cream and Parmesan.
6. Chill for some time prior to serving.

Nutritional Info:(Calories 283| Total Fats 20g | Net Carbs: 8g | Protein: 15.9g |Fiber: 3.5g)

Creamy Shrimp Stew

Aggregate Time to Prepare: **35 Minutes**

Yield: **4 Servings**

Ingredients:

- 1 cup cherry tomatoes, sliced in half
- 1 cup onion, thinly sliced
- 1 lb shrimps, peeled and deveined
- 2 cups fish stock
- 3 bacon slices, chopped
- 4 tbsp olive oil
- ¼ cup bell peppers, diced
- ¼ cup scallions, chopped
- ½ cup heavy cream

Spices:

- 1 tsp Old Bay seasoning
- 2 tsp apple cider vinegar

- ¼ tsp white pepper, freshly ground
- ½ tsp garlic powder
- ½ tsp salt

How to Cook:

1. Turn on your Instant Pot and Switch your Instant Pot to "'Sauté" mode. Oil-coat the inner pot with olive oil and put in bacon. Cook for 3-4 minutes or until lightly golden brown and crisp. Remove the bacon from the pot and save for later.
2. After that put in onions and bell peppers. Cook until translucent and put in cherry tomatoes and scallions. Carry on cooking for 10 minutes, stirring intermittently. If needed, pour in some of the stock.
3. After that put in shrimps and stir thoroughly. Pour in the rest of the stock and season with Old Bay seasoning, garlic powder, salt, and pepper. Drizzle with some apple cider and shut and secure the lid.
4. Make sure the steam release handle is on the "Sealing" position and switch to "Manual' mode. Cook for 8 minutes on high pressure.
5. When finished, depressurize using the natural release method and open the lid. Serve instantly.

Nutritional Info:(Calories 427| Total Fats 28.5g | Net Carbs: 6.4g | Protein: 35g |Fiber: 1.4g)

Crunchy Almond Tuna

Aggregate Time to Prepare: 10 Minutes

Yield: 4 Servings

Ingredients:

- 1 cup grated Cheddar Cheese
- 1 cup shaved Almonds
- 1 tsp Garlic Powder
- 2 cans of Tuna, drained
- 2 tbsp. Butter

How to Cook:

1. Melt the butter in the Instant Pot using the "Sauté" mode.
2. Put in tuna, almonds, and cheddar.
3. Cook using the "Sauté" mode for 3 minutes.
4. Serve instantly over cauliflower rice or on its own.
5. Have fun!

Nutritional Info: (Calories 150| Total Fats 5g | Net Carbs 4g | Protein 10g |Fiber: 2g)

Easy Catfish Stew

Aggregate Time to Prepare: 10 Minutes

Yield: 2 Servings

Ingredients:

- 10 oz catfish fillets, chop into bite-sized pieces
- 2 cups cherry tomatoes, chopped
- 2 cups collard greens, thinly sliced (can be replaced with spinach or kale)
- 2 cups fish stock
- 3 tbsp olive oil

Spices:

- 1 tsp dried dill
- 1 tsp garlic powder

- 1 tsp Italian seasoning
- ¼ tsp chili flakes
- ½ tsp sea salt

How to Cook:

1. Mix the ingredients in the instant pot and stir thoroughly. Shut and secure the lid and set the steam release handle to the "Sealing" position.
2. Switch your Instant Pot to "Manual" mode and turn the timer to 7 minutes on high pressure.
3. When finished, release the pressure for approximately 10 minutes and then move the pressure valve to the "Venting" position.
4. Cautiously open the lid and optionally drizzle with some fresh parsley or grated Parmesan prior to serving.

Nutritional Info:(Calories 456 | Total Fats 34.3g | Net Carbs: 5.8g | Protein: 29.9g | Fiber: 3.7g)

Easy Shrimp Cauliflower Risotto

Aggregate Time to Prepare: 15

Yield: 4 Servings

Ingredients:

- 1 cup cherry tomatoes, chopped
- 1 lb fresh shrimps, peeled and deveined
- 2 cups cauliflower florets
- 2 tbsp olive oil
- 3 garlic cloves, crushed
- 4 tbsp butter
- ¼ cup tomato puree, sugar-free

- ¾ cup fish stock

Spices:

- 1 tsp salt
- 2 tbsp fresh parsley, thinly sliced
- 2 tsp smoked paprika
- ½ tsp black pepper

How to Cook:

1. Clean and rinse shrimps. Put in the instant pot and drizzle with olive oil. Switch your Instant Pot to "Sauté' mode and briefly fry for 1-2 minutes.
2. Put in cauliflower, garlic, and tomatoes. Stir thoroughly and season with smoked paprika, salt, and pepper. Carry on cooking for about 2 minutes more.
3. After that pour in the fish stock and put in the tomato puree. Shut and secure the lid and set the steam release handle to the "Sealing" position.
4. Switch your Instant Pot to "Manual" mode and turn the timer to 6 minutes on high pressure.
5. When finished, release the pressure using the quick release method by moving the pressure valve to the "Venting" position.
6. Cautiously open the lid and mix in the butter. Drizzle with fresh parsley and serve instantly.

Nutritional Info:(Calories 334| Total Fats 21g | Net Carbs: 6.2g | Protein: 28.7g |Fiber: 21g)

Fish Korma

Aggregate Time to Prepare: 20 Minutes

Yield: 6 Servings

Ingredients:

- 1 cup tomatoes, diced
- 1 lemon, freshly juiced
- 1 medium-sized onions, sliced
- 4 lbs trout fillets
- 5 garlic cloves, peeled
- ½ cup plain yogurt, full-fat

Spices:

- 1 tbsp fresh ginger, grated
- 1 tsp black pepper, ground
- 1 tsp salt
- 2 cardamom pods
- 2 tbsp coriander, thinly sliced

How to Cook:

1. In a food processor, mix yogurt, garlic, ginger, coriander, cardamom, salt, and pepper. Process until smooth and creamy. Save for later.
2. Thoroughly wash the fish under cold running water and pat dry with kitchen paper. Slightly coat the fish with previously readied paste and refrigerate for 20 minutes.
3. Turn on the Instant Pot and coat the stainless steel insert with olive oil. Put in fish and cook for 2 minutes on each side.
4. After that, put in onions and tomatoes. Pour in 1 cup of water and securely lock the lid.
5. Close the steam release handle and push the "Manual" button. Turn the timer to 10 minutes and cook on "High" pressure.

6. When you hear the cooker's end signal, release the pressure using the quick release method and open the pot.
7. Move all to serving dish and garnish with some lemon slices prior to serving.
8. Have fun!

Nutritional Info:(Calories 615 | Total Fats 26.1g | Net Carbs: 5.9g | Protein: 82.6g |Fiber: 1.5g)

Fish Pho

Aggregate Time to Prepare: **40 Minutes**

Yield: **6 Servings**

Ingredients:

- 1 cup Zucchini Noodles
- 1 Jalapeno Pepper, sliced
- 1 tbsp. Salt
- 1 tsp Chili Flakes
- 1 tsp minced Garlic, sliced
- 4 ounces Salmon, chopped
- 5 cups Water
- 5 ounces Bok Choy
- 7 ounces Squid, chopped
- ¼ cup Soy Sauce
- ½ cup Dill
- ½ tbsp. Coriander

How to Cook:

1. In your IP, mix the water, dill, soy sauce, salt, chili flakes, and coriander.

2. Switch your Instant Pot to "Sauté" mode and shut and secure the lid.
3. After 10 minutes, strain the mixture and return the liquid back to the pot.
4. Stir in the fish, garlic, bok choy, jalapeño, and noodles.
5. Shut and secure the lid and cook on HIGH for 6 minutes.
6. Do a natural pressure release
7. Your dish is ready! Have fun!

Nutritional Info: (Calories 140| Total Fats 5g | Net Carbs 3g | Protein 12g |Fiber: 1g)

Fish Sauce Squid

Aggregate Time to Prepare: 20 Minutes

Yield: 4 Servings

Ingredients:

- 1 ½ cups Water
- 1 pound Squid
- 1 tbsp. Chives
- 1 tbsp. Lemon Juice
- 1 tbsp. minced Garlic
- 1 tsp Onion Powder
- 1 tsp Salt
- 1 tsp White Pepper
- 2 tbsp. Butter, melted
- 3 tbsp. Fish Sauce
- ¼ tsp Chili Powder

How to Cook:

1. Pour the water into the Instant Pot and put the trivet into the Instant Pot.
2. In a baking dish, mix all of the rest of the ingredients.
3. Stir to coat thoroughly.
4. Put the dish in the Instant Pot and shut and secure the lid.
5. Switch your Instant Pot to "Meat/Stew" mode and cook for 13 minutes.
6. Release the pressure using the quick release method.
7. Your dish is ready! Have fun!

Nutritional Info: (Calories 180| Total Fats 7g | Net Carbs 3g | Protein 15g |Fiber: 0g)

Fish Soup

Aggregate Time to Prepare: **30 Minutes**

Yield: **4 Servings**

Ingredients:

- 1 Carrot, sliced
- 1 cup Water
- 1 Onion, chopped
- 1 pound skinless and boneless Halibut, chopped
- 1 tbsp. Coconut Oil
- 2 Celery Stalks, chopped
- 2 cups Chicken Stock
- 2 tbsp. minced Ginger
- Salt and Pepper, to taste

How to Cook:

1. Melt the coconut oil in the Instant Pot using the "Sauté" mode.

2. Put in onion and cook for 4 minutes.
3. Stir in the stock, ginger, carrot, celery, and water.
4. Switch the Instant Pot to "High" and cook for 5 minutes.
5. Put in halibut and cook for 4 additional minutes.
6. Do a natural pressure release.
7. Your dish is ready! Have fun!

Nutritional Info: (Calories 170| Total Fats 6g | Net Carbs 4g | Protein 12g |Fiber: 1.8g)

Fish Stock

Aggregate Time to Prepare: 65 Minutes

Yield: 6 Servings

Ingredients:

- 1 cup chopped Carrots
- 1 cup chopped Celery
- 1 tbsp. Olive Oil
- 2 Lemongrass Stalks, chopped
- 2 Salmon Heads, quartered
- 2 tsp minced Garlic
- A handful of Thyme

How to Cook:

1. Switch the Instant Pot to "Sauté" mode and heat the oil.
2. Put in salmon heads and cook for 2 minutes.
3. Put in the rest of the ingredients.
4. Pour water until the Instant Pot reaches 3 quarts.
5. Shut and secure the lid and choose SOUP.
6. Cook for 45 minutes.

7. Depressurize for 15 minutes.
8. Strain and store.
9. Have fun!

Nutritional Info: (Calories 42| Total Fats 2g | Net Carbs 0g | Protein 5.6g |Fiber: 0g)

Garlic Butter Crab Legs

Aggregate Time to Prepare: **10 Minutes**

Yield: **4 Servings**

Ingredients:

- 1 ½ cups Water
- 1 tsp Olive Oil
- 1/3 cup Butter
- 2 tsp minced Garlic
- 3 pounds Crab Legs

How to Cook:

1. Pour the water into the Instant Pot and lower the steamer basket.
2. Put the crab legs into the basket and shut and secure the lid.
3. Switch your Instant Pot to "Steam" mode and cook for 4 minutes.
4. Release the pressure using the quick release method and move the crab legs to a platter.
5. Discard the cooking water and put in oil and butter.
6. When the butter is melted, put in garlic and cook for 1 minute.
7. Drizzle the garlicky butter over the crab legs.

Nutritional Info: (Calories 300| Total Fats 9g | Net Carbs 2g | Protein 35g |Fiber: 0g)

Ginger Salmon with Vegetables

Aggregate Time to Prepare: 45 Minutes

Yield: 4 Servings

Ingredients:

- 1 cup chicken stock
- 1 garlic clove, crushed
- 2 tbsp rice vinegar
- 2 tbsp sesame oil
- 2 tbsp soy sauce
- 4 medium-sized salmon steaks
- 7 oz broccoli, chopped
- 7 oz kale, chopped

Spices:

- 1 tsp sea salt
- 2 tsp ginger, freshly grated
- ¼ tsp chili powder
- ½ tsp black pepper, freshly ground

How to Cook:

1. Rub steaks with garlic, ginger, and chili powder. Drizzle with some salt and pepper place in a small baking dish. Loosely cover with the aluminium foil and save for later.
2. Turn on your Instant Pot and put in vegetables. Pour in the chicken stock and season with salt and some

pepper. Shut and secure the lid and set the steam release handle.
3. Switch your Instant Pot to "Manual" mode and turn the timer to 10 minutes.
4. When finished, release the pressure using the quick release method and open the lid. Remove the vegetables and drain. Put in a deep container and drizzle with some sesame oil, soy sauce, and rice vinegar. Save for later.
5. Position a trivet in the inner pot and place the baking dish on top. Pour in 2 cups of water and shut and secure the lid.
6. Set the steam release handle again and switch to "Manual' mode. Turn the timer to 8 minutes on high pressure.
7. When finished, release the pressure using the quick release method and open the lid. Remove the steaks from the pot and save for later.
8. After that Switch your Instant Pot to "'Sauté" mode and put in the vegetable mixture. Briefly cook – for 3-4 minutes, stirring continuously. Push the "Cancel" button.
9. Remove the vegetables from the pot and place on a large serving platter. Spread on top salmon steaks and optionally season with some more salt or pepper to taste.
10. Serve instantly.

Nutritional Info:(Calories 313 | Total Fats 16.4g | Net Carbs: 7.4g | Protein: 32.7g |Fiber: 2.1g)

Ginger Tilapia Fillets

Aggregate Time to Prepare: 40 Minutes

Yield: 2 Servings

Ingredients:

- 1 cup fish stock
- 1 lb tilapia fillets, chopped
- 1 spring onion, thinly sliced
- 1 tbsp rice vinegar
- 2 tbsp peanut oil
- 3 tbsp soy sauce
- ¼ cup celery leaves, thinly sliced

Spices:

- 1 tbsp fresh ginger, grated
- 1 tsp garlic powder
- 1 tsp sea salt

How to Cook:

1. In a small container, whisk together peanut oil, soy sauce, rice vinegar, ginger, garlic powder, and sea salt. Rub the fish with this mixture and place in a large Ziploc bag. Seal the bag and refrigerate for at least 30 minutes.
2. Turn on your Instant Pot and pour in the stock. Remove the fish from the fridge and place in the pot along with the marinade. Drizzle with celery and shut and secure the lid.
3. Make sure the steam release handle is on the "Sealing" position and switch to "Manual' mode. Turn the timer to 6 minutes on high pressure.

Nutritional Info:(Calories 348 | Total Fats 16.5g | Net Carbs: 2.2g | Protein: 46.6g |Fiber: 0.6g)

Green Pesto Tuna Steak

Aggregate Time to Prepare: **40 Minutes**

Yield: 4 Servings

Ingredients:

- 1 cup basil leaves, thinly sliced
- 1 cup cauliflower, thinly sliced
- 2 garlic cloves
- 2 tuna steaks, approximately 1-inch thick
- 3 tbsp butter
- 3 tbsp mozzarella, shredded
- ¼ cup olive oil

Spices:

- 1 tsp sea salt

How to Cook:

1. Turn on your Instant Pot and set the steam basket. Pour in one cup of water and put in tuna steaks in the basket.
2. Sprinkle with salt and shut and secure the lid. Make sure the steam release handle is on the "Sealing" position and switch to "Manual' mode. Cook for 7 minutes on high pressure.
3. When finished, release the pressure using the quick release method and open the lid. Using oven mitts, tenderly remove the steam basket and save for later.
4. Remove the water from the pot and put in butter. Switch your Instant Pot to "Sauté' mode and heat up.
5. Briefly cook each tuna steak for 3-4 minutes on each side.
6. Take out of the pot and save for later.

7. After that, prepare the pesto. Mix the rest of the ingredients using a food processor and process until completely smooth. Coat each tuna steak with pesto and place on a small baking sheet lined with some parchment paper.
8. Bake for 15 minutes at 400 degrees or until lightly brown and crunchy.
9. Serve instantly.

Nutritional Info:(Calories 484 | Total Fats 32.9g | Net Carbs: 2g | Protein: 44.3g | Fiber: 0.8g)

Gruyere Lobster Keto Pasta

Aggregate Time to Prepare: 25 Minutes

Yield: 4 Servings

Ingredients:

- 1 cup Half and Half
- 1 tbsp. Arrowroot
- 1 tbsp. chopped Tarragon
- 1 tbsp. Worcestershire Sauce
- 2 cups Water
- 3 Lobster Tails
- 4 cups Zoodles
- ½ cup White Wine
- ¾ cup shredded Gruyere Cheese

How to Cook:

1. Put the lobster in the Instant Pot.
2. Pour the water over and shut and secure the lid.
3. Switch the Instant Pot to "High" and cook for 5 minutes.

4. Allow it to cool slightly. Spoon out the meat from the tails and place in a container.
5. Mix together the half and half, Worcestershire, wine, and arrowroot in the Instant Pot.
6. Cook using the "Sauté" mode for 2 minutes.
7. Stir in zoodles, lobster, and cheese.
8. Cook for 3 minutes.
9. Your dish is ready! Have fun!

Nutritional Info: (Calories 280| Total Fats 7g | Net Carbs 3g | Protein 17g |Fiber: 1.4g)

Haddock and Cheddar

Aggregate Time to Prepare: 30 Minutes

Yield: 4 Servings

Ingredients:

- 1 tbsp. Butter
- 12 ounces Haddock Fillets
- 3 tbsp. diced Onions
- 5 ounces Cheddar Cheese, grated
- ¼ tsp Garlic Salt
- ¼ tsp Pepper
- ½ cup Heavy Cream

How to Cook:

1. Melt the butter in the Instant Pot using the "Sauté" mode.
2. Sauté the onions for 2 minutes.
3. Sprinkle the fish with salt and pepper.
4. Put in the Instant Pot and cook for 2 minutes on each side.

5. Pour the cream over and spread on top the cheese.
6. Switch the Instant Pot to "Manual" mode and cook for 5 minutes.
7. Do a natural pressure release.
8. Your dish is ready! Have fun!

Nutritional Info: (Calories 195| Total Fats 18g | Net Carbs 5.5g | Protein 18g |Fiber: 1g)

Herbed Catfish

Aggregate Time to Prepare: **20 Minutes**

Yield: **4 Servings**

Ingredients:

- 1 tbsp. Olive Oil
- 1 tsp chopped Parsley
- 1 tsp Dill
- 1 tsp Salt
- 14 ounces Catfish Fillets
- 2 tbsp. Soy Sauce
- 2 tsp minced Garlic
- ¼ cup Fresh Thyme
- ¼ cup Water
- ½ cup Fish Stock

How to Cook:

1. Chop the fish and place in the Instant Pot.
2. Put in the rest of the ingredients and stir to mix.
3. Set the Instant Pot to MANUAL and shut and secure the lid.
4. Switch the Instant Pot to "High" and cook for 5 minutes.

5. Push CANCEL and release the pressure using the quick release method.
6. Switch your Instant Pot to "Sauté" mode and cook for 1 additional minute with the lid off.
7. Your dish is ready! Have fun!

Nutritional Info: (Calories 160| Total Fats 10g | Net Carbs 2.4g | Protein 18g |Fiber: 0g)

Hot and Lemony Salmon

Aggregate Time to Prepare: 10 Minutes

Yield: 4 Servings

Ingredients:

- 1 ½ cups Water
- 1 Lemon, sliced
- 2 tbsp. chopped Chili
- 4 Salmon Fillets
- ¼ tsp Pepper
- ¼ tsp Salt
- Juice of 1 Lemon

How to Cook:

1. Pour the water in your Instant Pot.
2. Position the salmon on the rack.
3. Drizzle with salt and pepper and drizzle with lemon juice.
4. Spread on top chili peppers and then with lemon slices.
5. Shut and secure the lid and select MANUAL.
6. Switch the Instant Pot to "High" and cook for 4 minutes.

7. Release the pressure using the quick release method.
8. Your dish is ready! Have fun!

Nutritional Info: (Calories 180| Total Fats 8g | Net Carbs 3g | Protein 25g |Fiber: 0g)

Indian Broccoli Shrimp

Aggregate Time to Prepare: 20 Minutes

Yield: 3 Servings

Ingredients:

- 1 cup broccoli, chopped
- 1 lb jumbo shrimps, frozen
- 1 medium-sized tomato, diced
- 1 tbsp almonds, chopped
- 2 cups fish stock
- 2 medium-sized red onions, chopped
- 2 tbsp coconut oil

Spices:

- 1 tsp salt
- 1 tsp smoked paprika, ground
- 1 whole clove
- 2 cardamom pods
- 4-5 curry leaves
- ¼ tsp garlic powder
- ¼ tsp ginger powder
- ½ tsp cumin seeds
- ½ tsp garam masala powder

How to Cook:

1. Turn on the Instant Pot and coat the stainless steel insert with coconut oil. Push the "Sauté" button and put in almonds. Cook for 2-3 minutes, stirring continuously. Take out of the pot and save for later.
2. After that, put in onions, cumin seeds, clove, and cardamom pods. Stir-fry for 3-4 minutes, or until onions translucent.
3. Put in smoked paprika, garam masala, salt, garlic powder, ginger powder, and curry leaves. Cook for a minute and then put in shrimps., broccoli, and tomato.
4. Pour in the fish stock and stir thoroughly. Shut and secure the lid and push the "Manual" button. Turn the timer to 8 minutes and cook on "High" pressure.
5. When your instant pot sounds the end signal, depressurize using the natural release method.
6. Open the pot and mix in the almonds.
7. Serve instantly.

Nutritional Info: (Calories 284 | Total Fats 12.1g | Net Carbs: 9.1g | Protein: 33.4g | Fiber: 4.3g)

Instant Lobster Tails

Aggregate Time to Prepare: 25 Minutes

Yield: 4 Servings

Ingredients:

- 1 cup Water
- 4 Lobster Tails
- ¼ cup Butter, melted
- ½ cup White Wine

How to Cook:

1. Wash the lobster tails and chop them in half.
2. Put in the steaming basket.
3. Pour the water and white wine into the Instant Pot and lower the basket.
4. Shut and secure the lid and set to MANUAL.
5. Cook on LOW for 4 minutes.
6. Let the pressure come down naturally.
7. Position on a platter and drizzle with melted butter.
8. Your dish is ready! Have fun!

Nutritional Info: (Calories 190| Total Fats 12g | Net Carbs 0g | Protein 19g |Fiber: 0g)

Instant Steamed Salmon

Aggregate Time to Prepare: **15Minutes**

Yield: **4 Servings**

Ingredients:

- 1 lb salmon fillets, sliced into 4 pieces
- 2 cups fish stock
- 2 lemons, juiced
- 4 tbsp butter
- ¼ cup Parmesan cheese, freshly grated

Spices:

- 1 tsp smoked salt
- 1 tsp white pepper, freshly ground

How to Cook:

1. Turn on your Instant Pot and pour in the stock. Drizzle with lemon juice and set the steam basket.
2. Thoroughly wash the salmon fillets and drizzle with salt and pepper. Put in the basket and shut and secure the lid.
3. Make sure the steam release handle is on the "Sealing" position and switch to "Manual' mode.
4. Turn the timer to 5 minutes.
5. When finished, release the pressure using the quick release method and open the lid. Remove the salmon fillets and save for later. Remove the stock from the pot.
6. Switch your Instant Pot to "Saute' mode and melt the butter. Put in salmon steaks and cook for 2-3 minutes on each side.
7. Drizzle with grated parmesan and serve instantly.

Nutritional Info:(Calories 257 | Total Fats 18.9g | Net Carbs: 0.1g | Protein: 22.7g | Fiber: 0g)

King Prawn Stew with Avocado

Aggregate Time to Prepare: 45 Minutes

Yield: 6 Servings

Ingredients:

- 1 avocado, chopped into bite-sized pieces
- 1 cup olive oil
- 1 small onion, thinly sliced
- 2 large celery stalks, chopped
- 2 lbs king prawns, whole
- 2 small tomatoes, roughly chopped
- 4 tbsp balsamic vinegar

- 5 cups fish stock
- 7 oz cauliflower, chopped into florets

Spices:

- 1 tsp chili flakes
- 1 tsp dried marjoram
- 1 tsp sea salt
- ½ tsp dried thyme

How to Cook:

1. Put prawns in a large colander and rinse thoroughly. Save for later.
2. In a medium-sized container, mix together oil, balsamic vinegar, salt, marjoram, thyme, and chili flakes. Stir thoroughly and put in prawns. If needed, put in some fish stock to the container and submerge prawns in this mixture. Refrigerate for 20 minutes.
3. In the mean time, prepare the vegetables and plug in the Instant pot. Switch your Instant Pot to "Sauté' mode and put in onions and celery stalks. Drizzle with some oil and cook for 4-5 minutes. After that put in avocado, cauliflower, and tomatoes. Stir thoroughly and continue to cook for an additional 5 minutes.
4. Remove the prawns from the fridge and move to the pot. Push the "Cancel" button and pour in the rest of the stock. Stir thoroughly and shut and secure the lid.
5. Set the steam release handle and switch to "Manual' mode. Turn the timer to 15 minutes.
6. When you hear the end signal, depressurize using the quick release method and cautiously open the lid.
7. Move the stew to serving containers and optionally drizzle with some pepper.
8. Serve instantly.

Nutritional Info:(Calories 593| Total Fats 44.4g | Net Carbs: 5.9g | Protein: 40.7g |Fiber: 4g)

Lemon Mussels with Asparagus

Aggregate Time to Prepare: 15 Minutes

Yield: 4 Servings

Ingredients:

- 1 cup sun-dried tomatoes
- 1 large green bell pepper, thinly sliced
- 1 lb mussels, cleaned
- 2 tsp lemon juice, freshly squeezed
- 3 tbsp avocado oil
- 4 cups fish stock
- 7 oz asparagus, chopped into bite-sized pieces

Spices:

- 1 ½ tsp smoked paprika
- 1 tsp sea salt
- ½ tsp garlic powder
- ½ tsp pepper

How to Cook:

1. Turn on your Instant Pot and Switch your Instant Pot to "'Sauté" mode. Oil-coat the stainless steel insert with avocado oil and heat up. If you want, you can also use olive oil.
2. Put in asparagus and stir-fry for 2-3 minutes. After that put in sun dried tomatoes and mussels. Drizzle with salt, pepper, garlic powder, and smoked paprika.
3. Carry on cooking for 4-5 minutes.

4. Lastly put in bell peppers and pour in the stock. Stir thoroughly and shut and secure the lid. Make sure the steam release handle is on the "Sealing" position and switch to "Manual' mode.
5. Turn the timer to 5 minutes on high pressure.
6. When finished, release the pressure using the quick release method and open the lid.
7. Serve instantly.

Nutritional Info:(Calories 179 | Total Fats 6g | Net Carbs: 8.2g | Protein: 20.7g | Fiber: 2.5g)

Lemon Pepper Wild Alaskan Cod

Aggregate Time to Prepare: 15 Minutes

Yield: 4 Servings

Ingredients:

- 1 ½ cups Water
- 1 tbsp. Olive Oil
- 1 tsp Lemon Pepper
- 2 tbsp. Butter, melted
- 4 Lemon Sliced
- 8 ounces Wild Alaskan Cod
- ¼ tsp Garlic Powder

How to Cook:

1. Pour the water into the Instant Pot.
2. Cut the cod in half and place each half on top of an aluminium foil piece.
3. Sprinkle with garlic powder and lemon pepper.
4. Spread on top the lemon slices, drizzle with oil, and cover in foil.

5. Put into the steamer basket.
6. Shut and secure the lid and cook on HIGH for 6 minutes.
7. Uncover and drizzle with melted butter.
8. Your dish is ready! Have fun!

Nutritional Info: (Calories 200| Total Fats 5g | Net Carbs 1g | Protein 21g |Fiber: 0g)

Lemony and Garlicky Prawns

Aggregate Time to Prepare: **10 Minutes**

Yield: **4 Servings**

Ingredients:

- 1 pound Prawns
- 1 tbsp. Ghee
- 2 tbsp. Lemon Juice
- 2 tbsp. Lemon Zest
- 2 tbsp. minced Garlic
- 2 tbsp. Olive Oil
- 2/3 cup Fish Stock
- Salt and Pepper, to taste

How to Cook:

1. Melt the ghee along with the oil in the Instant Pot using the "Sauté" mode.
2. Put in the rest of the ingredients and stir to mix.
3. Shut and secure the lid and cook on HIGH for 3 minutes.
4. Drain the prawns.
5. Your dish is ready! Have fun!

Nutritional Info: (Calories 160| Total Fats 2g | Net Carbs 2g | Protein 18g |Fiber: 0g)

Lime and Garlic Flavored Octopus

Aggregate Time to Prepare: 20 Minutes

Yield: 4 Servings

Ingredients:

- 1 tsp chopped Cilantro
- 10 ounces Octopus
- 2 tbsp. Olive Oil
- 2 tsp Garlic Powder
- 3 tbsp. Lime Juice
- Salt and Pepper, to taste

How to Cook:

1. Put the octopus in the steaming basket.
2. Sprinkle with garlic powder, salt, and pepper.
3. Drizzle with olive and lime juice.
4. Pour the water into the Instant Pot and lower the steaming basket.
5. Shut and secure the lid and cook for 8 minutes on HIGH.
6. Release the pressure using the quick release method.
7. Your dish is ready! Have fun!

Nutritional Info: (Calories 120| Total Fats 3g | Net Carbs 1.5g | Protein g |Fiber: 0g)

Lobster Tails in Butter Sauce

Aggregate Time to Prepare: **15 Minutes**

Yield: **4 Servings**

Ingredients:

- 1 cup water
- 1 lb fresh lobster tails, cleaned
- 1 tbsp apple cider vinegar
- 5 tbsp butter, unsalted
- ¼ cup fish stock
- ½ cup mayonnaise

Spices:

- 1 tsp salt
- ¼ tsp dried rosemary
- ¼ tsp dried thyme
- ¼ tsp garlic powder
- ½ tsp black pepper, freshly ground

How to Cook:

1. Put lobster tails in the steam basket and move to the pot. Pour in one cup of water and shut and secure the lid. Make sure the steam release handle is on the "Sealing" position and switch your Instant Pot to "Steam' mode. Cook for 5 minutes on high pressure.
2. When finished, preform a quick pressure release and open the lid. Remove the lobster tails from the pot and Switch your Instant Pot to "'Sauté" mode.
3. Pour in the stock and bring it to a boil. Stir in butter and mayonnaise and drizzle with apple cider.
4. Sprinkle with salt, pepper, thyme, rosemary, and garlic powder. Cook for 2-3 minutes.

5. Push the "Cancel" button and remove the sauce from the pot. Drizzle over steamed lobster tails and serve instantly.
6. If you want, you can also drizzle with fresh dill.

Nutritional Info:(Calories 347| Total Fats 25.3g | Net Carbs: 7.1g | Protein: 22.3g |Fiber: 0g)

Mackerel Salad

Aggregate Time to Prepare: 25 Minutes

Yield: 6 Servings

Ingredients:

- 1 ½ cups chopped Tomatoes
- 1 cup Fish Stock
- 1 Garlic Clove, minced
- 1 Large Cucumber, sliced
- 1 Red Onion, sliced
- 1 tbsp. Lemon Juice
- 1 tbsp. Olive Oil
- 1 tsp Oregano
- 2 cups chopped Lettuce
- 8 ounces Mackerel
- ¼ tsp Pepper
- ¼ tsp Salt

How to Cook:

1. Sprinkle the mackerel with salt and pepper and place it in the Instant Pot in the steamer basket.
2. Pour the stock into the Instant Pot and lower the basket.

3. Shut and secure the lid and cook on HIGH for 5 minutes.
4. Release the pressure using the quick release method.
5. Chop and let cool.
6. Mix all of the veggies in a large container and spread on top the mackerel pieces.
7. Drizzle with olive oil and lemon juice.
8. Your dish is ready! Have fun!

Nutritional Info: (Calories 140| Total Fats 7g | Net Carbs 4g | Protein 12g |Fiber: 1g)

Mackerel with Cherry Tomatoes

Aggregate Time to Prepare: **15Minutes**

Yield: 15 Servings

Ingredients:

- 1 ½ cups Water
- 2 cups Cherry Tomatoes
- 2 tbsp. Butter, melted
- 4 Mackerel Fillets
- ¼ tsp Garlic Salt
- ¼ tsp Onion Powder
- ¼ tsp Pepper

How to Cook:

1. Put the tomatoes in a baking dish that can fit inside the Instant Pot.
2. Position the mackerel over.
3. Drizzle with the spices and drizzle with butter.
4. Pour the water into the Instant Pot and put the trivet into the Instant Pot.

5. Put the baking dish inside and shut and secure the lid.
6. Switch the Instant Pot to "High" and cook for 5 minutes.
7. Release the pressure using the quick release method.
8. Your dish is ready! Have fun!

Nutritional Info: (Calories 400| Total Fats: 17 | Net Carbs 3.5g | Protein 40g |Fiber: 0.5g)

Mayo Haddock

Aggregate Time to Prepare: **15 Minutes**

Yield: **4 Servings**

Ingredients:

- 1 pound Haddock
- 1 tsp chopped Dill
- 1 tsp Olive Oil
- 2 tbsp. Lemon Juice
- 2 tbsp. Mayonnaise
- ¼ tsp Old Bay Seasoning
- ½ cup vegetable Stock

How to Cook:

1. Mix together the stock, lemon juice, dill, oil, seasoning, and mayonnaise, in the Instant Pot.
2. Put in the Haddock and lock the lid.
3. Set the Instant Pot to MANUAL.
4. Switch the Instant Pot to "High" and cook for 7 minutes.
5. Depressurize quickly.
6. Your dish is ready! Have fun!

Nutritional Info: (Calories 165| Total Fats 12g | Net Carbs 4g | Protein 14g |Fiber: 1g)

Mediterranean Salmon

Aggregate Time to Prepare: **10 Minutes**

Yield: **4 Servings**

Ingredients:

- 1 cup halved Cherry Tomatoes
- 1 cup Water
- 1 Rosemary Sprig
- 1 tsp Italian Seasoning
- 15 ounces Asparagus Spears
- 2 tbsp. Olive Oil
- ¼ tsp Garlic Powder
- ¼ tsp Pepper
- ¼ tsp Salt

How to Cook:

1. Pour the water into the Instant Pot.
2. Sprinkle the salmon with salt, pepper, garlic powder, and Italian seasoning.
3. Position on the rack.
4. Put in the rosemary sprig on top.
5. Put the asparagus spears over.
6. Spread on top cherry tomatoes.
7. Shut and secure the lid and cook on HIGH for 3 minutes.
8. Release the pressure using the quick release method and move to a plate.
9. Drizzle with olive oil.

10. Your dish is ready! Have fun!

Nutritional Info: (Calories 470| Total Fats 31g | Net Carbs 4.6g | Protein 43g|Fiber: 2.7g)

Mussel Chowder

Aggregate Time to Prepare: **30 Minutes**

Yield: **4 Servings**

Ingredients:

- 1 cup celery stalk, chopped
- 1 cup heavy cream
- 1 lb fresh mussels, cleaned
- 2 cups cauliflower, chopped into florets
- 2 large onions, thinly sliced
- 2 tbsp fresh parsley, thinly copped
- 5 cups fish stock
- ¼ cup olive oil
- ¼ cup Parmesan cheese, grated

Spices:

- 1 tsp sea salt
- ¼ tsp of chili flakes
- ½ tsp white pepper, freshly ground

How to Cook:

1. Thoroughly wash mussels and drain in a large sieve. Put in a deep pot and drizzle with some olive oil. Drizzle with chili flakes and white pepper. Combine thoroughly and save for later,
2. Turn on your Instant Pot and Switch your Instant Pot to "'Sauté" mode. Heat the rest of the oil in the

instant pot and put in onions and chopped celery stalks. Stir thoroughly and cook for 5-6 minutes.
3. After that put in cauliflower and continue to cook for an additional 2 minutes.
4. Lastly, put in mussels and pour in the fish stock. Turn off the Instant Pot by pressing the "Cancel" button.
5. Shut and secure the lid and set the steam release handle to the "Sealing" position. Switch your Instant Pot to "Manual" mode and turn the timer to 8 minutes on high pressure.
6. When finished, release the pressure using the quick release method and open the lid. Stir in the heavy cream and separate the chowder between serving containers.
7. Drizzle with grated Parmesan and chopped parsley. Serve instantly.

Nutritional Info:(Calories 428| Total Fats 30.3g | Net Carbs: 12.5g | Protein: 25g |Fiber: 3.3g)

Orange Glazed Salmon Fillets

Aggregate Time to Prepare: 20 Minutes

Yield: 3 Servings

Ingredients:

- 1 garlic clove, crushed
- 1 lb salmon fillets, approximately 1-inch thick
- 3 tbsp butter
- 3 tbsp olive oil

Spices:

- 1 tsp chili flakes

- 1 tsp orange extract
- 1 tsp smoked salt
- ¼ tsp dried thyme
- ½ liquid stevia

How to Cook:

1. Wash thoroughly the fillets under cold running water and pat-dry with a kitchen towel. Save for later.
2. Turn on your Instant Pot and Switch your Instant Pot to "'Sauté" mode. Oil-coat the inner pot with butter and heat up. Put in garlic and briefly cook for one minute, stirring continuously.
3. After that put in fillets and brown for 2-3 minutes on each side. Push the "Cancel" button and remove the salmon from the pot.
4. In a small container, whisk together olive oil, stevia, chili flakes, orange extract, salt, and thyme. Slightly coat fillets with this mixture and save for later.
5. After that set the steam basket in the inner pot and place the fillets in it. Pour in 2 cups of water in the pot and shut and secure the lid.
6. Make sure the steam release handle is on the "Sealing" position and switch to "Manual' mode. Turn the timer to 12 minutes on high pressure.
7. When finished, release the pressure using the quick release method and open the lid. Move the fillets to serving plates and optionally drizzle with some more olive oil.

Nutritional Info:(Calories 423| Total Fats 34.9g | Net Carbs: 0.3g | Protein: 29.5g |Fiber: 0g)

Parmesan-Crusted Salmon

Aggregate Time to Prepare: 15 Minutes

Yield: 2 Servings

Ingredients:

- 1 ½ cups Water
- 1 ½ tbsp. Butter
- 1 tbsp. Mayonnaise
- 1 tbsp. Olive Oil
- 2 Salmon Fillets
- ¼ tsp Garlic Powder
- ½ cup grated Parmesan Cheese
- ½ tsp Paprika
- Salt and Pepper, to taste

How to Cook:

1. Pour the water into the Instant Pot.
2. Sprinkle the salmon with salt and pepper and place on the steaming rack.
3. Shut and secure the lid and cook on HIGH for 4 minutes.
4. Release the pressure using the quick release method.
5. Discard the water.
6. Mix the olive oil and mayonnaise and brush over the salmon.
7. Mix the parmesan, paprika, and garlic powder.
8. Line the salmon with the mixture thoroughly.
9. Melt the butter in the Instant Pot using the "Sauté" mode.
10. Put in salmon and cook until golden on all sides.
11. Your dish is ready! Have fun!

Nutritional Info: (Calories 400| Total Fats 38g| Net Carbs 0.9| Protein 33g |Fiber: 0g)

Party Oysters

Aggregate Time to Prepare: 15 Minutes

Yield: 6 Servings

Ingredients:

- 1 cup Water
- 36 Oysters
- 6 tbsp. melted Butter

How to Cook:

1. Clean the oysters thoroughly and pace them in the Instant Pot.
2. Pour the water over and shut and secure the lid.
3. Switch the Instant Pot to "High" and cook for 3 minutes.
4. Do a natural pressure release.
5. Move to a serving platter and drizzle with the melted butter.
6. Your dish is ready! Have fun!

Nutritional Info: (Calories 145| Total Fats 12g| Net Carbs 1g | Protein 13g |Fiber: 0g)

Prawn Curry

Aggregate Time to Prepare: 20 Minutes

Yield: 4 Servings

Ingredients:

- 1 large onion, chopped
- 1 tbsp olive oil
- 2 cups fish stock
- 2 garlic cloves, minced
- 2 lbs prawns, peeled and deveined
- ½ cup coriander leaves, chopped

Spices:

- 1 tbsp fresh ginger, grated
- ¼ tsp cinnamon, ground
- ¼ tsp red chili powder
- ½ tsp salt
- ½ tsp turmeric powder

How to Cook:

1. Turn on the Instant Pot and coat the stainless steel insert with olive oil. Push the "Sauté" button and put in prawns. Cook for 2-3 minutes on each side.
2. Put in onions, garlic, and all the spices. Stir-fry for 2 additional minutes.
3. Pour in the fish stock and put in coriander. Stir thoroughly and securely lock the lid.
4. Close the steam release handle and push the "Manual" button. Turn the timer to 5 minutes and cook on "High" pressure.
5. When finished, release the pressure using the quick release method by moving the valve to the "Venting" position.
6. Open the pot and move the curry to a serving pot.
7. Drizzle with some fresh parsley or green onions prior to serving.
8. Have fun!

Nutritional Info: (Calories 344 | Total Fats 8.5g | Net Carbs: 7.7g | Protein: 55g |Fiber: 1.2g)

Quick and Easy Dijon Halibut

Aggregate Time to Prepare: **7Minutes**

Yield: **4 Servings**

Ingredients:

- 1 ½ cups Water
- 1 ½ tbsp. Dijon Mustard
- 4 Halibut Fillets

How to Cook:

1. Pour the water into the Instant Pot.
2. Slightly coat the halibut with Dijon and place in the steaming basket.
3. Lower the basket and shut and secure the lid.
4. Set the Instant Pot to MANUAL.
5. Switch the Instant Pot to "High" and cook for 3 minutes.
6. Release the pressure using the quick release method.
7. Your dish is ready! Have fun!

Nutritional Info: (Calories 190| Total Fats 2g | Net Carbs 0.1g | Protein 40g |Fiber: 0g)

Salmon Fillet with Dill

Aggregate Time to Prepare: **15 Minutes**

Yield: **4 Servings**

Ingredients:

- 1 cup fresh dill, thinly sliced
- 1 tbsp butter, unsalted
- 4 pieces salmon fillet, approximately 2 lbs
- ¼ cup apple cider vinegar

Spices:

- 1 tsp salt
- ¼ tsp black pepper, freshly ground

How to Cook:

1. Turn on your Instant Pot and set the steam basket in the inner pot. Pour in one cup of water and apple cider in the inner pot and save for later.
2. Thoroughly wash the salmon fillets and drizzle with salt and pepper. Put in the steam basket and spread on top fresh dill.
3. Shut and secure the lid and set the steam release handle to the "Sealing" position. Push the "Steam" button and turn the timer to 9 minutes.
4. When finished, depressurize using the quick release method and open the lid. Remove the salmon and save for later.
5. After that Switch your Instant Pot to "'Sauté" mode and coat the inner pot with butter. Heat up and briefly brown salmon on both sides – for approximately 2 minutes.
6. Spread on top some more fresh dill prior to serving.

Nutritional Info:(Calories 359| Total Fats 17.4g | Net Carbs: 5.2g | Protein: 46.4g |Fiber: 1.6g)

Salmon in Lime Sauce

Aggregate Time to Prepare: **10 Minutes**

Yield: **4 Servings**

Ingredients:

- 1 cup Water
- 1 tbsp. chopped Parsley
- 1 tbsp. Hot Water
- 1 tbsp. Olive Oil
- 1 tbsp. Sweetener
- 1 tsp Paprika
- 4 Salmon Fillets
- ½ tsp Cumin
- Juice of 2 Limes

How to Cook:

1. Pour the water into the Instant Pot.
2. Position the salmon on the rack and shut and secure the lid.
3. Switch the Instant Pot to "High" and cook for minutes.
4. Release the pressure using the quick release method.
5. Discard the cooking liquid and return the salmon to the pot.
6. Mix together the rest of the ingredients and pour over.
7. Cook using the "Sauté" mode for 2 minutes.
8. Your dish is ready! Have fun!

Nutritional Info: (Calories 493 | Total Fats 31.5g | Net Carbs 2g| Protein 46g |Fiber: 0.3g)

Salmon Keto Macaroni

Aggregate Time to Prepare: 20 Minutes

Yield: 4 Servings

Ingredients:

- 1 cup cottage cheese
- 1 cup fresh celery, thinly sliced
- 1 cup heavy cream
- 1 onion, thinly sliced
- 2 cups cauliflower, chopped
- 3 cups chicken stock
- 3 tbsp almond flour
- 3 tbsp butter
- 8oz salmon steak, thinly sliced

Spices:

- 2 tsp salt
- ½ tsp black pepper, freshly ground

How to Cook:

1. Wash thoroughly the steaks and pat-dry with a kitchen towel. Put on a large cutting board and chop into bite-sized pieces.
2. Turn on your Instant Pot and pour in the chicken stock. Put in cauliflower and drizzle with salt and pepper. Make a layer of thinly sliced salmon and shut and secure the lid. Set the steam release handle to the "sealing" position and switch to "Manual' mode. Turn the timer to 5 minutes on high pressure.
3. When finished, release the pressure using the quick release method and open the pot. Remove the salmon and cauliflower and save for later.

4. Switch your Instant Pot to "Sauté' mode and coat the inner pot with butter. Put in onions and cook for 2-3 minutes. After that put in cottage cheese and heavy cream. Stir in celery and almond flour.
5. Briefly cook, for 3-4 minutes, stirring continuously.
6. Take out of the pot and serve with salmon macaroni.

Nutritional Info:(Calories 351| Total Fats 25.7g | Net Carbs: 7.4g | Protein: 21.8g |Fiber: 2.4g)

Salmon on a Veggie Bed

Aggregate Time to Prepare: 30 Minutes

Yield: 4 Servings

Ingredients:

- 1 Bell Pepper, julienned
- 1 Carrot, julienned
- 1 cup of Water
- 1 Tarragon Sprig
- 1 Zucchini, julienned
- 3 tsp Olive Oil
- 4 Salmon Fillets
- ½ Lemon, sliced
- A handful of Basil
- A handful of parsley

How to Cook:

1. Pour the water into the Instant Pot and place the herbs inside.
2. Position the veggies on the rack.
3. Spread on top the salmon fillets (skin side down).
4. Drizzle with oil and spread on top lemon sliced.

5. Shut and secure the lid and cook on HIGH for 5 minutes.
6. Release the pressure using the quick release method.
7. Your dish is ready! Have fun!

Nutritional Info: (Calories 308| Total Fats 13g | Net Carbs 4.3g | Protein 40.6g |Fiber: 2.3g)

Salmon Steaks with Cheese

Aggregate Time to Prepare: **20 Minutes**

Yield: **4 Servings**

Ingredients:

- 1 cup mozzarella, shredded
- 2 cups vegetable stock
- 2 medium-sized salmon steaks, approximately 1 lb
- 2 tbsp butter
- 3 tbsp olive oil
- ¼ cup heavy cream
- ½ cup Feta cheese

Spices:

- 1 tsp smoked paprika
- 2 tbsp fresh parsley, thinly sliced
- ½ tsp red pepper flakes
- ½ tsp salt

How to Cook:

1. Wash thoroughly the steaks and dry with a kitchen towel. Drizzle with red pepper flakes and salt. Save for later.

2. Turn on your Instant Pot and Switch your Instant Pot to "'Sauté" mode. Heat the olive oil and put in salmon steaks. Briefly brown, for 2-3 minutes, on both sides and pour in the stock.
3. Sprinkle with smoked paprika and shut and secure the lid.
4. Make sure the steam release handle is on the "Sealing" position and switch to "Manual' mode.
5. Turn the timer to 4 minutes on high pressure.
6. When finished, release the pressure using the quick release method and open the lid. Remove salmon steaks and the rest of the stock.
7. Switch your Instant Pot to "Sauté' mode again and melt the butter. Put in Feta cheese, mozzarella, and heavy cream. If you want, you can also season with some chili flakes and stir thoroughly.
8. Briefly cook – for about 2 minutes, stirring continuously.
9. Put in salmon and coat thoroughly with the sauce. Serve instantly.

Nutritional Info:(Calories 389| Total Fats 31.3g | Net Carbs: 1.4g | Protein: 27.1g |Fiber: 0.3g)

Salmon with Broccoli

Aggregate Time to Prepare: **10 Minutes**

Yield: **4 Servings**

Ingredients:

- 1 ½ cups Water
- 1 tsp Garlic Powder
- 10 ounces Broccoli Florets

- 4 Salmon Fillets
- Salt and Pepper, to taste

How to Cook:

1. Sprinkle the salmon with some salt, pepper, and garlic powder.
2. Pour the water into the Instant Pot.
3. Put the salmon in the steaming basket and put in the broccoli around the fish.
4. Shut and secure the lid and cook on HIGH for 4 minutes.
5. Release the pressure using the quick release method.
6. Your dish is ready! Have fun!

Nutritional Info: (Calories 119| Total Fats 5g | Net Carbs 4g | Protein 16g |Fiber: 0.3g)

Saucy Trout with Chives

Aggregate Time to Prepare: **15 Minutes**

Yield: **4 Servings**

Ingredients:

- 1 ½ cups Water
- 1 tsp Lemon Zest
- 2 tbsp. Olive Oil
- 2 tsp Lemon Juice
- 3 tbsp. chopped Chives
- 4 Trout Fillets
- 6 tbsp. Butter

How to Cook:

1. Pour the water into the Instant Pot.

2. Put the trout inside the steamer basket.
3. Lower it in the Instant Pot.
4. Shut and secure the lid and cook on HIGH for 3 minutes.
5. Move to a plate and discard the water.
6. Mel the butter in the Instant Pot using the "Sauté" mode.
7. In the mean time, chop the trout.
8. Put in the trout in the pot along with the other ingredients.
9. Cook for 2 minutes.
10. Your dish is ready! Have fun!

Nutritional Info: (Calories 320| Total Fats 6g | Net Carbs 3g | Protein 18g |Fiber: 1g)

Sea Bass in a Tomato Feta Sauce

Aggregate Time to Prepare: 30 Minutes

Yield: 4 Servings

Ingredients:

- 1 ½ cups Water
- 1 cup canned diced Tomatoes
- 1 tbsp. Olive Oil
- 1 tsp chopped Basil
- 1 tsp chopped Parsley
- 1 tsp minced Garlic
- 1/2 cup crumbled Feta Cheese
- 4 Sea Bass Fillets
- ¼ tsp Pepper
- ¼ tsp salt

How to Cook:

1. Sprinkle the sea bass with salt and pepper.
2. Pour the water into the Instant Pot and place the sea bass on the rack.
3. Shut and secure the lid and cook on HIGH for 5 minutes.
4. Move to a plate and discard the water.
5. Heat the oil in the Instant Pot using the "Sauté" mode.
6. Put in garlic and cook for 1 minute.
7. Put in tomatoes and cook for 1 additional minute.
8. Stir in basil and parsley.
9. Put in the sea bass and spread on top feta.
10. Cook for 1 minute.
11. Your dish is ready! Have fun!

Nutritional Info: (Calories 275| Total Fats 8g | Net Carbs 2g | Protein 40g |Fiber: 1g)

Seafood Paella

Aggregate Time to Prepare: 30 Minutes

Yield: 4 Servings

Ingredients:

- 1 cup chopped Fish
- 1 Green Bell Pepper, diced
- 1 Onion, sliced
- 1 Red Bell Pepper, diced
- 1 tbsp. Ghee
- 2 cups Cauliflower Rice
- 2 cups Shellfish (clams, mussels, shrimp)

- 4 cups Fish Stock
- A pinch of Saffron
- Salt and Pepper

How to Cook:

1. Melt the ghee in the Instant Pot.
2. Put in peppers and onion and cook for 3 minutes.
3. Stir in the fish, rice, stock, and saffron.
4. Shut and secure the lid and cook for 2 minutes on HIGH.
5. Depressurize naturally.
6. Put in the shellfish (do NOT stir) and shut and secure the lid.
7. Cook for 3 additional minutes.
8. Allow the pressure to drop naturally.
9. Your dish is ready! Have fun!

Nutritional Info: (Calories 156| Total Fats 4.5g | Net Carbs 5g | Protein 15g |Fiber: 1g)

Seafood Stew

Aggregate Time to Prepare: 20 Minutes

Yield: 5 Servings

Ingredients:

- 1 large onion, thinly sliced
- 2 lbs sea bass fillets, chop into chunks
- 2 small tomatoes, roughly chopped
- 3 celery stalks, thinly sliced
- 3 tbsp soy sauce
- 4 tbsp olive oil, extra-virgin
- 5 cups fish stock

- 7oz shrimps, peeled and deveined

Spices:

- 1 tbsp Creole seasoning
- 1 tsp black pepper, freshly ground
- 2 bay leaves
- 2 tsp sea salt

How to Cook:

1. Clean and rinse fish fillets. Pat dry with some kitchen paper and save for later.
2. In a small container, mix Creole seasoning with salt and pepper. Rub the fish with this mixture ensuring to coat on all sides.
3. Turn on your Instant Pot and Switch your Instant Pot to "'Sauté" mode. Oil-coat the inner pot with olive oil and heat up. Put in the readied fish and cook for 4-5 minutes, stirring intermittently.
4. When the fish has nicely browned, tenderly take out of the pot and save for later.
5. Oil-coat the inner pot with some more oil and put in onions and celery stalk. Sprinkle with some salt and stir thoroughly. Carry on cooking for 2-3 minutes.
6. After that push the "Cancel" button and put in the fish, shrimps, and tomatoes. Drizzle with soy sauce and pour in the stock.
7. Shut and secure the lid and set the steam release handle to the "Sealing" position. Switch your Instant Pot to "Manual" mode and turn the timer to 5 minutes on high pressure.
8. When finished, depressurize using the natural release method and open the lid. If you want, you can also mix in some fresh parsley and serve.

Nutritional Info:(Calories 433 | Total Fats 18.5g | Net Carbs: 4.6g | Protein: 58.5g | Fiber: 1.3g)

Shrimp and Tomato Casserole

Aggregate Time to Prepare: 30 Minutes

Yield: 4 Servings

Ingredients:

- 1 ½ pounds Shrimp, peeled and deveined
- 1 ½ pounds Tomatoes, chopped
- 1 cup shredded Cheddar Cheese
- 1 Jalapeno, diced
- 1 Onion, diced
- 1 tsp minced Garlic
- 2 tbsp. Lime Juice
- 2 tbsp. Olive Oil
- ¼ cup chopped Cilantro
- ½ cup Veggie Broth

How to Cook:

1. Heat the olive oil in the Instant Pot using the "Sauté" mode.
2. Put in onion and cook for 3 minutes.
3. Put in garlic and sauté for additional 30-60 seconds.
4. Stir in the broth, cilantro, and tomatoes.
5. Shut and secure the lid and cook on HIGH for 9 minutes.
6. Do a natural pressure release.
7. Put in shrimp and cook on HIGH for 2 additional minutes.
8. Depressurize quickly and mix in cheddar,

9. Your dish is ready! Have fun!

Nutritional Info: (Calories 300| Total Fats 16g | Net Carbs 8g | Protein 22g |Fiber: 2g)

Shrimp Casserole

Aggregate Time to Prepare: 30 Minutes

Yield: 5 Servings

Ingredients:

- 1 ½ cup almond flour
- 2 tbsp cream cheese
- 3 tsp baking powder
- 4 tbsp butter, melted
- 6 large eggs, separated
- 7 oz shrimps, cleaned
- ¼ cup sun-dried tomatoes

Spices:

- 1 tsp dried thyme
- 2 tsp pink Himalayan salt
- ½ tsp garlic powder

How to Cook:

1. Thoroughly wash the shrimps and drain in a large sieve. Save for later.
2. Separate egg whites from yolks and place egg whites in a large mixing container along with the cream cheese. Whisk for 1 minute or until light and foamy.
3. After that put in egg yolks and baking powder. Continue to beat for an additional minute. Lastly, put

in the rest of the ingredients and mix until fully blended.
4. Line a small loaf pan with some parchment paper and pour the mixture in it. Loosely cover with aluminium foil and save for later.
5. Turn on your Instant Pot and set the trivet. Pour in one cup of water and place the loaf pan on top.
6. Shut and secure the lid and switch to "Manual' mode. Make sure the steam release handle is on the "Sealing" position.
7. Cook for 15 minutes on high pressure.
8. When finished, depressurize using the quick release method and cautiously open the lid. Take the pan out of the instant pot and chill for some time.
9. Slice into 15 slices and serve.

Nutritional Info:(Calories 283| Total Fats 21.3g | Net Carbs: 3.6g | Protein: 18.9g |Fiber: 1.1g)

Shrimp Scampi

Aggregate Time to Prepare: **15 Minutes**

Yield: **4 Servings**

Ingredients:

- 1 ½ pounds Shrimp, peeled and deveined
- 2 tbsp. Coconut Oil
- 2 tsp minced Garlic
- 3 tbsp. chopped Parsley
- ¾ cup Chicken Broth
- Juice of 1 Lemon

How to Cook:

1. Melt the coconut oil in the Instant Pot using the "Sauté" mode.
2. Put in the garlic and cook for one minute.
3. Put in broth and shrimp and shut and secure the lid.
4. Switch the Instant Pot to "High" and cook for 2 minutes.
5. Release the pressure using the quick release method.
6. Move to a plate.
7. Stir in parsley and lemon juice.
8. Your dish is ready! Have fun!

Nutritional Info: (Calories 250| Total Fats 10g | Net Carbs 3.2g | Protein 35g |Fiber: 0.2g)

Shrimp with Asparagus and Cajun Seasoning

Aggregate Time to Prepare: **10 Minutes**

Yield: 4 Servings

Ingredients:

- 1 Bunch of Asparagus, trimmed
- 1 pound Shrimp, peeled and deveined
- 1 tbsp. Cajun Seasoning
- 1 tsp Olive Oil
- Salt and Pepper, to taste

How to Cook:

1. Pour the water into the Instant Pot.
2. Position the asparagus – in a single layer – on the Instant Pot's rack.
3. Spread on top the shrimp.
4. Drizzle with oil and season with salt, pepper, and Cajun.
5. Shut and secure the lid and cook for 2 minutes on STEAM.
6. Release the pressure using the quick release method.
7. Your dish is ready! Have fun!

Nutritional Info: (Calories 330| Total Fats 7g | Net Carbs 7g | Protein 45g |Fiber: 1g)

Shrimps with Tomatoes and Feta

Aggregate Time to Prepare: 5 Minutes

Yield: 6 Servings

Ingredients:

- 1 cup Feta Cheese (crumbled)
- 1 lbs. Frozen Shelled Shrimp
- 1 tbsp. Garlic (minced)

- 1 tsp Oregano
- 1 tsp Salt
- 14 oz. Crushed Tomatoes (canned)
- 1½ cups Onion (diced)
- 2 tbsp. Butter
- ¼ cup Parsley (chopped)
- ½ cup Black Olives (pitted and chop into 1-inch slices)
- ½ tsp Paprika Flakes

How to Cook:

1. Switch your Instant Pot to "Sauté" mode and put into it butter. When butter has melted put in garlic and paprika flakes. Stir thoroughly.
2. Put in the onions, tomatoes, oregano and salt, and cook for 2 minutes.
3. Put in the shrimps and stir to mix.
4. Shut and secure the lid and turn the timer and cook for 1 minute at low pressure.
5. When finished depressurize using the quick release method.
6. Separate to plates and garnish with feta, olives and parsley.
7. Serve with riced cauliflower.

Nutritional Info: (Calories: 211 | Total Fats: 11g | Net Carbs: 5g | Proteins: 19g | Fibers: 1g)

Shrimpy Zoodles

Aggregate Time to Prepare: **15 Minutes**

Yield: **4 Servings**

Ingredients:

- 1 cup Veggie Stock
- 1 pound Shrimp, peeled and deveined
- 1 tbsp. chopped Basil
- 2 tbsp. Ghee
- 2 tbsp. Olive Oil
- 3 tsp minced Garlic
- 4 cups zoodles
- ½ tsp Paprika
- Juice of ½ Lemon

How to Cook:

1. Melt the ghee along with the olive oil in the Instant Pot using the "Sauté" mode.
2. Put in garlic and cook for 1 minute.
3. Put in shrimp and lemon juice.
4. Cook for 1 minute.
5. Put in zoodles, paprika, and stock.
6. Switch the Instant Pot to "High" and cook for 3 minutes.
7. Serve topped with basil.
8. Have fun!

Nutritional Info: (Calories 300| Total Fats 20g | Net Carbs 3g | Protein 30g |Fiber: 3g)

Simple Squid Stew

Aggregate Time to Prepare: **40 Minutes**

Yield: **4 Servings**

Ingredients:

- 1 cup cabbage, shredded
- 1 medium-sized yellow bell pepper, sliced

- 1 small onion, thinly sliced
- 2 cups cherry tomatoes, diced
- 3 cups fish stock
- 7 oz shrimps, cleaned
- 7 oz squid rings, defrosted
- ¼ cup olive oil

Spices:

- 1 tsp rosemary powder
- 1 tsp stevia powder
- 2 tsp pink Himalayan salt
- ½ tsp dried oregano

How to Cook:

1. Oil-coat the inner pot with some olive oil and heat up on the "Sauté" mode. Put in onions and stir-fry until translucent. After that put in bell pepper and season with salt. Stir thoroughly and continue to cook for an additional 2 minutes.
2. Stir in tomatoes and put in approximately ¼ cup of the stock. Simmer until the liquid evaporates and push the "Cancel" button.
3. Lastly, put in the rest of the ingredients and season with oregano, rosemary, and stevia powder. Stir thoroughly and shut and secure the lid.
4. Make sure the steam release handle is on the "Sealing" position and switch to "Manual' mode turn the timer to 20 minutes on high pressure.
5. When finished, release the pressure using the quick release method and open the lid. Separate between serving plates and optionally drizzle with some Parmesan.
6. Serve instantly.

Nutritional Info: (Calories 279| Total Fats 15.8g | Net Carbs: 8.4g | Protein: 24.5g |Fiber: 2.3g)

Sockeye Salmon

Aggregate Time to Prepare: 10 Minutes

Yield: 4 Servings

Ingredients:

- 1 ½ cups Water
- 1 Garlic Clove, minced
- 1 tbsp. Lemon Juice
- 1 tsp Dijon Mustard
- 1 tsp Garlic Powder
  ¼ tsp Onion Powder
- 4 Salmon Fillets
- Salt and Pepper, to taste

How to Cook:

1. In a small container, mix the mustard, onion powder, garlic powder, minced garlic, and lemon juice.
2. Slightly coat the mixture over the salmon.
3. Pour the water into the Instant Pot and put the rack into the Instant Pot.
4. Position the salmon on the rack and shut and secure the lid.
5. Switch the Instant Pot to "High" and cook for 4 minutes.
6. Release the pressure using the quick release method.
7. Your dish is ready! Have fun!

Nutritional Info: (Calories 195| Total Fats 10g | Net Carbs 1g | Protein 24g |Fiber: 0g)

Sour King Scallops

Aggregate Time to Prepare: 20 Minutes

Yield: 4 Servings

Ingredients:

- 1 cup fish stock
- 1 medium-sized onion, thinly sliced
- 1 tbsp fresh lemon juice
- 2 tbsp olive oil
- 3 tbsp butter
- 5 king scallops, fresh
- ¼ cup apple cider vinegar

Spices:

- 1 tsp salt
- ½ tsp garlic powder
- ½ tsp white pepper, freshly ground

How to Cook:

1. Turn on your Instant Pot and coat the inner pot with olive oil. Heat up and put in onions. Cook for 3-4 minutes, or until translucent.
2. Pour in the stock and apple cider vinegar. Put in scallops and tenderly simmer for 5 minutes.
3. Sprinkle with salt, garlic powder, and white pepper. Stir thoroughly and push the "Cancel" button.
4. Shut and secure the lid and set the steam release handle. Switch your Instant Pot to "Manual" mode and turn the timer to 8 minutes.
5. When finished, depressurize using the quick release method and open the lid.

6. Stir in the butter and drizzle with lemon juice.
7. Serve instantly.

Nutritional Info:(Calories 389| Total Fats 31.3g | Net Carbs: 1.4g | Protein: 27.1g |Fiber: 0.3g)

Spaghetti Squash with Shrimp and Asparagus

Aggregate Time to Prepare: 30 Minutes

Yield: 4 Servings

Ingredients:

- 1 Asparagus bunch, chopped
- 1 cup Coconut Cream
- 1 cup grated Parmesan Cheese
- 1 Onion, chopped
- 1 pound Shrimp, peeled and deveined
- 1 Spaghetti Squash. Halved
- 1 tsp Red Pepper Flakes
- 2 cups Water
- 2 tbsp. Olive oil
- 2 tsp minced Garlic
- 2 tsp Oregano
- 8 ounces Mushrooms, sliced
- ¼ cup Ghee

How to Cook:

1. Pour the water into the Instant Pot and put in the spaghetti squash in the steamer basket.
2. Lower the basket and shut and secure the lid.
3. Cook for 10 minutes on HIGH.

4. Allow it to cool and scrape the flash with the fork to make spaghetti.
5. Discard the cooking liquid and melt the ghee along with the oil in the Instant Pot.
6. Put in asparagus, squash, seasonings and cook for about 2 minutes.
7. Put in the shrimp, garlic, parmesan, and coconut cream.
8. Stir to mix and shut and secure the lid.
9. Switch the Instant Pot to "High" and cook for 4 minutes.
10. Depressurize quickly.
11. Your dish is ready! Have fun!

Nutritional Info: (Calories 465| Total Fats 7g | Net Carbs 5g | Protein 30g |Fiber: 2g)

Spiced Jamaican Jerk Fish

Aggregate Time to Prepare: **35Minutes**

Yield: 4 Servings

Ingredients:

- 2 cups cherry tomatoes, chopped
- 2 lbs cod fillets, chop into 1-inch slices
- 2 tbsp butter
- 2 tbsp swerve
- 3 tbsp soy sauce
- ¼ cup fish stock

Spices:

- 1 tbsp Jamaican Jerk seasoning
- 2 tsp chili powder

How to Cook:

1. Thoroughly wash the fillets under cold running water and pat dry with a kitchen paper. Save for later.
2. Turn on your Instant Pot and coat the inner pot with butter. Put in fish fillets and cook for 4-5 minutes on each side. You will probably have to do this in several batches.
3. Take out of the pot and move to a plate. Save for later.
4. After that put in cherry tomatoes and pour in the stock. Bring it to a boil and drizzle with soy sauce. Sprinkle with Jamaican Jerk seasoning and chili powder. Put in swerve and cook until tomatoes soften.
5. Put in fish fillets and coat thoroughly with the sauce.
6. Push the "Cancel" button and take out of the pot. Serve instantly.

Nutritional Info:(Calories 507 | Total Fats 25.3g | Net Carbs: 3.2g | Protein: 62.3g |Fiber: 1.2g)

Spicy Pepper Salmon

Aggregate Time to Prepare: 20

Yield: 4 Servings

Ingredients:

- 1 cup fish stock
- 1 medium-sized red bell pepper, thinly sliced
- 1 small chili pepper, thinly sliced
- 1 tbsp olive oil

- 3 tbsp butter
- 4 salmon fillets, approximately 1 lb
- ¼ zucchini, cubed

Spices:

- 1 tsp dried parsley
- 1 tsp sea salt
- 2 tsp black pepper, freshly ground

How to Cook:

1. Thoroughly wash the salmon fillet under cold running water and pat dry with a kitchen paper. Put on a large cutting board and cut in 4 equivalent pieces. Save for later.
2. In a small container, whisk together olive oil, salt, pepper, and dried parsley. Liberally brush fillets with this mixture and place in the steam basket.
3. Pour in 2 cups of water in the inner pot and shut and secure the lid. Make sure the steam release handle is on the "Sealing" position and switch your Instant Pot to "Steam' mode. Turn the timer to 4 minutes on high pressure.
4. When finished, release the pressure using the quick release method and open the lid. Using oven mitts remove the steam basket and save for later.
5. After that Switch your Instant Pot to "'Sauté" mode and melt the butter in the inner pot. Put in red bell pepper, chili pepper, and zucchini. Stir thoroughly and cook for 3-4 minutes.
6. Pour in the stock and stir thoroughly. Shut and secure the lid and set the steam release handle. Switch your Instant Pot to "Manual" mode and turn the timer to 4 minutes on high pressure.

7. When finished, depressurize using the natural release method and open the lid. Put in the previously readied salmon and coat thoroughly with the sauce.
8. If you want, you can also drizzle with few drops of Tabasco sauce and serve instantly.

Nutritional Info:(Calories 364| Total Fats 23.7g | Net Carbs: 2.2g | Protein: 36.4g |Fiber: 0.6g)

Spicy Shrimp Keto Pasta

Aggregate Time to Prepare: 15 Minutes

Yield: 4 Servings

Ingredients:

- 1 cup cream cheese
- 1 tsp apple cider vinegar
- 2 cups cauliflower, chopped into florets
- 2 garlic cloves, crushed
- 2 tbsp olive oil
- 3 cups chicken stock
- 7 oz shrimps, cleaned
- ¼ cup mayonnaise

Spices:

- 1 tsp smoked salt
- ½ tsp onion powder
- ½ tsp red pepper flakes

How to Cook:

1. Put shrimps and cauliflower in the pot. Put in garlic and pour in the stock. Drizzle with olive oil and apple cider and stir thoroughly.

2. Shut and secure the lid and set the steam release handle to the "Sealing" position. Switch your Instant Pot to "Manual" mode and cook for 9 minutes on high pressure.
3. When finished, release the pressure using the quick release method and open the lid. Remove the shrimp mixture and drain the rest of the liquid in the pot. Move to a deep container and save for later.
4. After that Switch your Instant Pot to "'Sauté" mode and heat up the inner pot. put in cream cheese and mayonnaise. Sprinkle with smoked salt, onion powder, and red pepper flakes.
5. Briefly cook, for approximately a minute and mix in the shrimp mixture. Combine thoroughly and push the "Cancel" button.
6. Serve instantly and optionally drizzle with some shredded mozzarella or grated parmesan.

Nutritional Info:(Calories 401 | Total Fats 33.5g | Net Carbs: 8.2g | Protein: 17.4g |Fiber: 1.3g)

Spicy Trout with Broccoli

Aggregate Time to Prepare: **50 Minutes**

Yield: **5 Servings**

Ingredients:

- 1 small onion, thinly sliced
- 2 lbs trout fillets, skin-on
- 2 tbsp apple cider vinegar
- 2 tbsp butter
- 3 cups broccoli, chopped
- 4 cups fish stock

- ¼ cup olive oil

Spices:

- 1 tsp chili powder
- ¼ tsp garlic powder
- ½ tsp chili flakes
- ½ tsp dried celery
- ½ tsp salt

How to Cook:

1. Remove the fish from the fridge approximately an hour before using. Rub with olive oil and drizzle with salt, dried celery, chili powder, chili flakes, and garlic powder. Put in a deep container and cover with a lid. Save for later.
2. Turn on your Instant Pot and pour in the fish stock. Put in broccoli and stir thoroughly. Shut and secure the lid and set the steam release handle to the "Sealing" position. Turn the timer to 20 minutes.
3. When finished, depressurize using the quick release method and open the lid. Remove the cauliflower from the pot and drain. Put in a deep container and mash with a potato masher. If you want, you can also move to a food processor and process until smooth. Save for later.
4. Put the steam insert in the pot and place the fish in it. Pour in 2 cups of water and shut and secure the lid. Set the steam release handle again and push the "Fish" button.
5. When finished, depressurize using the quick release method and open the lid. Remove the fish from the pot and Switch your Instant Pot to "'Sauté" mode.

6. Put in mashed broccoli and mix in the butter. If you want, you can also drizzle with some salt and garlic powder. Heat up and take out of the pot.
7. Serve with steamed fish.

Nutritional Info:(Calories 488| Total Fats 27.2g | Net Carbs: 3.3g | Protein: 54.2g |Fiber: 1.7g)

Spring Fish Stew

Aggregate Time to Prepare: 25 Minutes

Yield: 4 Servings

Ingredients:

- 1 ½ cups tomatoes, chopped
- 1 small green bell pepper, chopped
- 2 cups fish stock
- 2 cups shrimps, cleaned and deveined
- 2 spring onions, thinly sliced
- 3 garlic cloves, crushed
- 3 tbsp extra virgin olive oil
- 7 oz cod fillets, chopped into bite-sized pieces
- 7 oz trout fillets, chopped into bite-sized pieces

Spices:

- 1 tsp sea salt
- 2 bay leaves
- ½ tsp black pepper, freshly ground

How to Cook:

1. Turn on your Instant Pot and Switch your Instant Pot to "'Sauté" mode. Oil-coat the inner pot with olive oil

and put in onions, chopped pepper, garlic, and bay leaves. Stir thoroughly and cook for 5 minutes.
2. After that put in chopped fish fillets and shrimps. Stir thoroughly and continue to cook for an additional 5 minutes. Pour in approximately ¼ cup of the fish stock and put in tomatoes. Bring it to a boil and simmer until softened.
3. Sprinkle with salt and pepper. If you want, you can also put in some dried herbs to taste. Stir thoroughly and shut and secure the lid.
4. Make sure the steam release handle is on the "Sealing" position. Switch your Instant Pot to "Manual" mode and turn the timer to 10 minutes on high pressure.
5. When finished, push the "Cancel" button and depressurize using the natural release method.
6. Carefully, open the lid and serve instantly.

Nutritional Info:(Calories 403| Total Fats 22g | Net Carbs: 5.3g | Protein: 43.7g |Fiber: 1.5g)

Spring Onion Prawn Stew

Aggregate Time to Prepare: **45 Minutes**

Yield: **6 Servings**

Ingredients:

- 1 cup cherry tomatoes, chopped
- 1 cup onions, chopped
- 1 small green bell pepper, thinly sliced
- 1 spring onion, chopped
- 2 celery stalks, chopped
- 20 king prawn tails, peeled

- 3 garlic cloves, crushed
- 3 tbsp fresh parsley, chopped
- 5 cups fish stock
- 7oz chicken breast, chopped into bite-sized pieces
- ½ cup olive oil

Spices:

- 1 tbsp dried celery
- 1 tsp chili powder
- 1 tsp sea salt
- 1 tsp stevia powder
- 1 tsp white pepper, freshly ground
- 2 tsp cayenne pepper, ground
- ½ tsp black pepper, freshly ground

How to Cook:

1. Wash thoroughly and clean prawns. Put in a deep container and season with salt and pepper. Save for later.
2. Thoroughly wash the meat and pat-dry with some kitchen paper. Put on a large cutting board and chop into bite-sized pieces. Sprinkle with the rest of the salt and pepper and save for later.
3. Turn on your Instant Pot and coat the inner pot with some oil. Put in onions, spring onions, celery stalk, and green pepper. Stir thoroughly and cook for 5-6 minutes, stirring continuously.
4. After that put in the meat and prawns. Stir thoroughly and season with the rest of the spices.
5. Carry on cooking for an additional 5-6 minutes. Pour in the fish stock and the rest of the olive oil. Push the "Cancel" button.
6. Shut and secure the lid and set the steam release handle to the "Sealing" position. Switch your Instant

Pot to "Manual" mode and turn the timer to 20 minutes on high pressure.
7. When finished, depressurize using the quick release method and open the lid. Stir in garlic and parsley. Allow it to sit for 5 minutes and serve.

Nutritional Info:(Calories 418 | Total Fats 21.9g | Net Carbs: 6.4g | Protein: 46.8g |Fiber: 1.3g)

Squid Rings with Potato and Spinach

Aggregate Time to Prepare: **35 Minutes**

Yield: **3 Servings**

Ingredients:

- 1 lb fresh spinach, torn
- 1 lb squid rings, frozen
- 2 cups cauliflower, roughly chopped
- 2 tbsp lemon juice
- 4 tbsp extra virgin olive oil

Spices:

- 1 tsp dried rosemary, crushed
- 1 tsp garlic paste
- 1 tsp sea salt
- 2 thyme sprigs, fresh

How to Cook:

1. Put squid rings in a deep container and pour in enough warm water to cover. Allow it to sit for some time. Move to a large colander and drain. Save for later.

2. Turn on your Instant Pot and coat the inner pot with two tablespoons of olive oil. Switch your Instant Pot to "Sauté' mode and put in garlic paste and rosemary. Stir-fry for one minute and then put in the spinach. Sprinkle with salt and cook for 3-4 minutes or until wilted. Remove the spinach from the pot and save for later.
3. Put in the rest of the oil to the pot and heat up on the "Sauté" mode. Put in chopped cauliflower making an even layer. Spread on top squid rings and drizzle with lemon juice and optionally some more olive oil to taste. Drizzle with salt, put in thyme sprigs, and pour in one cup of water (or fish stock).
4. Shut and secure the lid and set the steam release handle to the "Sealing" position. Push the "Fish" button and turn the timer to 9 minutes.
5. When your instant pot sounds the end signal, cautiously move the pressure valve to the "Venting" position to release the pressure.
6. Open the pot and mix in the spinach. If you want, you can also season with some more garlic powder or dried thyme.
7. Serve instantly.

Nutritional Info:(Calories 353| Total Fats 21.5g | Net Carbs: 8.9g | Protein: 29.3g |Fiber: 5g)

Steamed Mussels with Thyme

Aggregate Time to Prepare: **20 Minutes**

Yield: **4 Servings**

Ingredients:

- 1 lb mussels, cleaned
- 2 cups fish stock
- 2 tbsp lemon juice, freshly squeezed
- 3 tbsp butter
- 5 garlic cloves, crushed
- ¼ cup Parmesan cheese, grated

Spices:

- 1 tsp dried thyme
- 2 tbsp fresh parsley, thinly sliced
- ½ tsp chili flakes

How to Cook:

1. Wash thoroughly the mussels under running water and remove any dirt. Drain and save for later.
2. Turn on your Instant Pot and Switch your Instant Pot to "'Sauté" mode. Oil-coat the inner pot with butter and put in garlic. Sauté for 2-3 minutes and then pour in the stock. Drizzle with lemon juice and season with thyme, chili flakes, and parsley.
3. Put mussels in a steam basket and move to the pot. Shut and secure the lid and set the steam release handle to the "Sealing" position.
4. Switch your Instant Pot to "Manual" mode and turn the timer to 5 minutes on high pressure.
5. When finished, release the pressure using the quick release method and open the lid. Remove any mussels that didn't open and move to serving containers. Drizzle with the sauce from the pot and serve instantly.

Nutritional Info:(Calories 207| Total Fats17.1g | Net Carbs: 5.6g | Protein: 17.1g |Fiber: 0.1g)

Stewed Scallops and Mussels

Aggregate Time to Prepare: 20 Minutes

Yield: 4 Servings

Ingredients:

- 1 cup Scallops
- 1 Onion, diced
- 1 tbsp. Coconut Oil
- 2 Bell Peppers, diced
- 2 cups Fish Stock
- 2 cups ground Cauliflower
- 2 cups Mussels
- A pinch of Saffron

How to Cook:

1. Melt the coconut oil in the Instant Pot using the "Sauté" mode.
2. Put in peppers and onions and cook for 3 minutes.
3. Put in scallops and saffron. Cook for 2 minutes.
4. Put in the rest of the ingredients and stir to mix.
5. Switch the Instant Pot to "High" and cook for 6 minutes.
6. Depressurize naturally.
7. Your dish is ready! Have fun!

Nutritional Info: (Calories 195| Total Fats 4.5g | Net Carbs 7.6g | Protein 20g |Fiber: 3.7g)

Sweet and Spicy Trout

Aggregate Time to Prepare: 15 Minutes

Yield: 2 Servings

Ingredients:

- 1 lb trout fillet, chopped
- 1 tbsp fish sauce
- 2 chili peppers, thinly sliced
- 2 tbsp swerve
- 3 garlic cloves, crushed
- 3 tbsp butter
- ¼ cup fish stock

Spices:

- 1 tbsp ginger, freshly grated
- 1 tsp black pepper, freshly ground
- 1 tsp salt
- ½ tsp cumin powder

How to Cook:

1. Liberally rub fillets with salt and pepper. Put on a large plate and cover with aluminium foil. Save for later.
2. In a small container, whisk together fish stock, swerve, and fish sauce. Put in grated ginger and cumin powder and stir thoroughly again.
3. Turn on your Instant Pot and set the steam basket. Put the fish fillets in the basket and liberally brush with the previously readied mixture on all sides.
4. Pour in one cup of water and shut and secure the lid. Make sure the steam release handle is on the "Sealing" position and switch to "Manual' mode. Turn the timer to 5 minutes on high heat.
5. When finished, release the pressure using the quick release method and cautiously open the lid. Remove the fish and save for later.

6. Melt the butter over medium heat and drizzle over fish. Serve instantly.

Nutritional Info:(Calories 600 | Total Fats 36.8g | Net Carbs: 2g | Protein: 62g |Fiber: 0.2g)

Sweet Broccoli Fish Stew

Aggregate Time to Prepare: 25 Minutes

Yield: 3 Servings

Ingredients:

- 1 cup broccoli, chopped
- 1 cup fish stock
- 1 lb trout fillets, defrosted and thinly sliced
- 1 tbsp arrowroot starch
- 1 tbsp garlic paste
- 2 tbsp butter
- 3 tbsp apple cider vinegar
- ¼ cup soy sauce
- ¼ cup spring onions, thinly sliced

Spices:

- 1 tsp marjoram, dried
- ½ tsp stevia extract

How to Cook:

1. Thoroughly wash the broccoli under cold running water and drain in a large colander. Cut into florets and save for later.
2. Turn on your Instant Pot and pour in 1 cup of water. Set the steam basket and place broccoli in it.

3. Shut and secure the lid and switch your Instant Pot to "Steam' mode. Cook on high pressure.
4. When you hear the end signal, depressurize using the quick release method and open the lid. Cautiously remove the steam basket and chill for some time.
5. After that Switch your Instant Pot to "'Sauté" mode and coat the inner pot with butter. Put in trout and cook for 4-5 minutes. Tenderly turn over and continue to cook for an additional 3-4 minutes. Remove from the pot.
6. After that, pour in the stock, soy sauce, and apple cider vinegar. Bring it to a boil and mix in the garlic paste. Drizzle with stevia and marjoram and cook for 30 seconds.
7. Put in trout fillets and broccoli and toss thoroughly to coat with the sauce.
8. Lastly, put in the arrowroot starch and cook for 1 minute.
9. Push the "Cancel" button and serve instantly.

Nutritional Info:(Calories 404| Total Fats 21.3g | Net Carbs: 5g | Protein: 44.6g |Fiber: 1.3g)

Sweet Rosemary Cod Fillet

Aggregate Time to Prepare: 20 Minutes

Yield: 6 Servings

Ingredients:

- 1 cup fish stock
- 2 lbs cod fillets, skinless
- 4 garlic cloves, crushed
- 4 tbsp butter

- ½ cup soy sauce
- ½ cup swerve

Spices:

- 1 tsp sea salt
- 2 rosemary sprigs
- ¼ tsp dried rosemary
- ½ tsp white pepper, freshly ground

How to Cook:

1. Rub the fillets with salt, pepper, and dried rosemary. Put in the pot and put in garlic, swerve, rosemary sprigs, and butter. Pour in the stock and drizzle with soy sauce. Switch your Instant Pot to "Sauté' mode. Heat up and stir thoroughly to mix. Briefly cook for 2-3 minutes and push the "Cancel" button.
2. Shut and secure the lid and set the steam release handle to the "Sealing" position. Switch your Instant Pot to "Manual" mode and turn the timer to 12 minutes.
3. When your instant pot sounds the end signal, depressurize using the quick release method and open the lid.
4. After that Switch your Instant Pot to "'Sauté" mode again and tenderly simmer until half of the liquid evaporates and the sauce thickens.
5. If you want, you can also move the fillets along with the sauce in a small baking dish and bake for 10-15 minutes at 400 degrees F.

Nutritional Info:(Calories 376| Total Fats 20.8g | Net Carbs: 2.3g | Protein: 42.7g |Fiber: 0.2g)

Sweet Teriyaki Shrimps

Aggregate Time to Prepare: 20 Minutes

Yield: 2 Servings

Ingredients:

- 1 cup fish stock
- 1 tbsp rice vinegar
- 2 cups shrimps, peeled and deveined
- 2 tbsp avocado oil
- ¼ cup soy sauce

Spices:

- 1 tbsp fresh ginger, grated
- 1 tsp garlic powder
- 1 tsp sea salt
- 2 tsp stevia powder

How to Cook:

1. Turn on your Instant Pot and put in shrimps. Pour in the fish stock and stir thoroughly. Shut and secure the lid and set the steam release handle to the "Sealing" position. Switch your Instant Pot to "Manual" mode and turn the timer to 4 minutes on high pressure.
2. When finished, release the pressure using the quick release method and open the lid. Switch your Instant Pot to "Sauté' mode and bring the stock to a boil. Stir in the soy sauce, avocado oil, and rice vinegar.
3. Drizzle with salt, stevia, garlic, and ginger. Carry on cooking for 10 minutes.
4. Serve instantly.

Nutritional Info: (Calories 262 | Total Fats 5.6g | Net Carbs: 4.9g | Protein: 43.5g | Fiber: 0.9g)

Thai Seafood Cauliflower Rice

Aggregate Time to Prepare: 25 Minutes

Yield: 4 Servings

Ingredients:

- 1 cup bean sprouts
- 1 cup Thai basil, thinly sliced
- 1 jalapeno pepper, thinly sliced
- 1 medium-sized onion, thinly sliced
- 2 cups cauliflower florets, thinly sliced
- 2 cups seafood mix, frozen
- 3 garlic cloves, crushed
- 3 tbsp coconut oil
- 4 tbsp fish sauce
- ½ cup chicken stock

Spices:

- 1 tsp sea salt
- 2 tsp fresh ginger, grated
- 2 tsp stevia powder

How to Cook:

1. Turn on your Instant Pot and coat the inner pot with coconut oil. Switch your Instant Pot to "Sauté' mode and put in jalapeno pepper and garlic. Briefly cook for 2-3 minutes, stirring continuously.
2. After that put in seafood and continue to cook for 5 minutes. Drizzle with salt, ginger, and stevia. Put in

bean sprouts, cauliflower, and onions. Pour in the stock and shut and secure the lid.
3. Make sure the steam release handle is on the "Sealing" position and switch to "Manual' mode. Turn the timer to 5 minutes on high pressure.
4. When finished, depressurize using the natural release method and open the lid. Stir in chopped Thai basil and drizzle with fish sauce.
5. Stir thoroughly and serve instantly.

Nutritional Info:(Calories 188| Total Fats 11.2g | Net Carbs: 8.1g | Protein: 12.6g |Fiber: 2.1g)

Tiger Prawn Paella

Aggregate Time to Prepare: **25 Minutes**

Yield: **4 Servings**

Ingredients:

- 1 lb tiger prawns, whole
- 1 small red bell pepper, thinly sliced
- 1 tsp apple cider vinegar
- 2 cups cauliflower, chopped into florets
- 2 small onion, thinly sliced
- 3 garlic cloves, crushed
- 3 tbsp butter
- 4 cups fish stock
- 5 bacon slices, chopped

Spices:

- 1 tsp sea salt
- 2 tsp turmeric powder
- 4 tbsp fresh parsley, thinly sliced

- ½ tsp black pepper, freshly ground
- ½ tsp saffron threads

How to Cook:

1. Turn on your Instant Pot and put in cauliflower. Pour in the fish stock and drizzle with salt. Shut and secure the lid and set the steam release handle to the "Sealing" position. Switch your Instant Pot to "Manual" mode and turn the timer to 5 minutes on high pressure.
2. When finished, release the pressure using the quick release method and open the lid. Remove the cauliflower from the pot and drain. Make sure to reserve the stock. Save for later.
3. Switch your Instant Pot to "Sauté' mode and coat the inner pot with butter. Heat up and put in onions and garlic. Stir-fry for 4-5 minutes.
4. After that put in bell pepper and bacon. Carry on cooking for an additional 3-4 minutes, stirring continuously. Sprinkle with some more salt, pepper, and turmeric powder.
5. Stir thoroughly and put in prawns and cauliflower. Pour in the rest of the stock and shut and secure the lid.
6. Set the steam release handle again and switch to "Manual' mode. Turn the timer to 8 minutes on high pressure.
7. When finished, depressurize using the natural release method and open the lid. Stir thoroughly and drizzle with saffron and fresh parsley. Allow it to sit for some time prior to serving.
8. If you want, you can also Switch your Instant Pot to "'Sauté" mode again and tenderly simmer until all the liquid evaporates.

Nutritional Info: (Calories 419| Total Fats 22.6g | Net Carbs: 8.5g | Protein: 41.8g |Fiber: 2.5g)

Tilapia Bites

Aggregate Time to Prepare: 20 Minutes

Yield: 8 Servings

Ingredients:

- 1 pound Tilapia Fillets
- 1 tsp Coriander
- 1 tsp Lemon Zest
- 1 tsp Red Pepper Flakes
- 2 tbsp. ground Almonds
- 3 Eggs
- 3 tbsp. Olive Oil
- ¼ tsp Pepper
- ½ cup Half and Half
- Juice of 1 Lemon

How to Cook:

1. Mix together the eggs, spices, zest, and almond flour.
2. Heat the oil in the Instant Pot using the "Sauté" mode.
3. Chop the tilapia and dip into the egg mixture.
4. Cook using the "Sauté" mode until golden.
5. Pour the lemon juice and half and half over and shut and secure the lid.
6. Switch the Instant Pot to "High" and cook for 2 minutes.
7. Release the pressure using the quick release method.
8. Your dish is ready! Have fun!

Nutritional Info: (Calories 160| Total Fats 10g | Net Carbs 2.3g | Protein 15g |Fiber: 0g)

Tilapia Curry

Aggregate Time to Prepare: **15 Minutes**

Yield: **4 Servings**

Ingredients:

- 1 small chili pepper, chopped
- 1 small onion, thinly sliced
- 1 tsp lemon juice
- 10 oz tilapia fillets, chopped
- 2 cups coconut milk, full-fat
- 3 garlic cloves, crushed
- 3 tbsp olive oil
- ½ cup cherry tomatoes, chopped
- ½ cup Thai basil, chopped

Spices:

- 1 tsp coriander powder
- 1 tsp cumin powder
- 1 tsp sea salt
- 2 tsp chili powder
- 2 tsp fresh ginger, grated
- ½ tsp turmeric powder

How to Cook:

1. Turn on your Instant Pot and coat the inner pot with oil. Switch your Instant Pot to "Sauté' mode and put in onions, garlic, ginger, coriander, chili, cumin

powder, turmeric, and salt. Stir thoroughly and cook for 3-4 minutes or until translucent.
2. After that, pour in the coconut milk and stir thoroughly. Put in cherry tomatoes, tilapia fillets, and chopped chili pepper.
3. Shut and secure the lid and set the steam release handle to the "Sealing" position. Switch your Instant Pot to "Manual" mode and turn the timer to 4 minutes on high pressure.
4. When you hear the end signal, depressurize using the quick release method and open the pot. Drizzle with Thai basil and serve instantly.

Nutritional Info: (Calories 440 | Total Fats 39.9g | Net Carbs: 6.7g | Protein: 16.6g | Fiber: 3.4g)

Tomato Shrimp Stew

Aggregate Time to Prepare: **35 Minutes**

Yield: **4 Servings**

Ingredients:

- 1 cup broccoli, chopped
- 1 cup collard greens, chopped
- 1 large onion, thinly sliced
- 1 lb shrimps, cleaned
- 2 large tomatoes, peeled and chopped
- 3 cups fish stock
- 3 garlic cloves, crushed
- 4 tbsp butter

Spices:

- 1 tsp salt

- 2 tbsp fresh parsley, thinly sliced
- ¼ tsp dried oregano
- ¼ tsp garlic powder
- ¼ tsp onion powder

How to Cook:

1. Put greens in a large colander and rinse under cold running water. Drain thoroughly and save for later.
2. Chop broccoli and onions. Save for later.
3. Turn on your Instant Pot and coat the inner pot with butter. Heat up and put in onions and garlic. Cook for 2-3 minutes and then put in tomatoes. Carry on cooking for an additional 3-4 minutes.
4. After that put in broccoli and season with salt, garlic powder, onion powder, and oregano. Stir thoroughly and pour in approximately ¼ cup of the stock. Bring it to a boil and simmer for 4-5 minutes. Stir intermittently.
5. Push the "Cancel" button and put in the rest of the ingredients. Stir thoroughly and shut and secure the lid.
6. Make sure the steam release handle is on the "Sealing" position and switch to "Manual' mode.
7. Turn the timer to 15 minutes on high pressure.
8. When finished, depressurize using the natural release method and open the lid. Move the stew to serving containers and optionally drizzle with grated Parmesan cheese or some more fresh parsley.

Nutritional Info:(Calories 312| Total Fats 15.3g | Net Carbs: 8.7g | Protein: 32.1g |Fiber: 2.9g)

Tomato Tuna Pasta

Aggregate Time to Prepare: 20 Minutes

Yield: 2 Servings

Ingredients:

- 1 cup canned diced Tomatoes
- 1 tbsp. Butter
- 1 tbsp. chopped Parsley
- 1 tbsp. diced Onions
- 1 tsp minced Garlic
- 1 Tuna Can, drained
- 2 cups Zucchini Noodles
- 3 tbsp. grated Parmesan Cheese
- ¼ cup Tomato Sauce

How to Cook:

1. Melt the butter in the Instant Pot using the "Sauté" mode.
2. Put in onions and garlic and cook for 2 minutes.
3. Put in tomatoes and tomato sauce and cook for 2 additional minutes.
4. Stir in the rest of the ingredients, except the cheese.
5. Shut and secure the lid and cook on HIGH for 3 minutes.
6. Release the pressure using the quick release method.
7. Drizzle with parmesan cheese.
8. Your dish is ready! Have fun!

Nutritional Info: (Calories 310| Total Fats 8g | Net Carbs 3g | Protein 14g |Fiber: 1g)

Trout Casserole

Aggregate Time to Prepare: **40 Minutes**

Yield: **4 Servings**

Ingredients:

- 1 cup cauliflower, chopped into florets
- 1 cup cherry tomatoes, halved
- 1 lb trout fillets, without skin
- 1 small onion, sliced
- 4 tbsp olive oil
- ½ zucchini, sliced

Spices:

- 1 tsp dried rosemary
- 1 tsp dried thyme
- 2 tsp sea salt
- ½ tsp garlic powder

How to Cook:

1. Line a small square pan with some parchment paper and drizzle with two tablespoons of olive oil.
2. Position onions at the bottom of the pan and make a layer with sliced zucchini. Spread on top cherry tomatoes and onions. Drizzle with some salt and drizzle with the rest of the olive oil.
3. Spread on top trout fillets and season with some more salt, rosemary, thyme, and garlic powder.
4. Tightly cover with aluminium foil and save for later.
5. Turn on your Instant Pot and pour in 2 cups of water. Set the trivet at the bottom of the inner pot and place the pan on top.

6. Shut and secure the lid and set the steam release handle to the "Sealing" position. Switch your Instant Pot to "Manual" mode and turn the timer to 20 minutes on high pressure.
7. When finished, release the pressure using the quick release method and open the lid. Cautiously remove the pan and chill for some time.
8. Remove the aluminium foil and if you want, bake for 15 minutes at 450 degrees F.
9. Serve instantly.

Nutritional Info:(Calories 361 | Total Fats 23.8g | Net Carbs: 3.7g | Protein: 31.6g |Fiber: 1.8g)

Tuna Steak with Mushrooms

Aggregate Time to Prepare: 50 Minutes

Yield: 4 Servings

Ingredients:

- 1 large onion, thinly sliced
- 2 cups fish stock
- 2 cups mushrooms
- 2 large tuna steaks, approximately 8 oz each
- 2 tbsp olive oil
- 4 tbsp butter
- ¼ cup Parmesan cheese
- ½ cup heavy cream

Spices:

- 1 tsp dried marjoram
- 1 tsp sea salt
- 1 tsp white pepper, freshly ground

How to Cook:

1. Turn on your Instant Pot and Switch your Instant Pot to "'Sauté" mode. Oil-coat the inner pot with butter and heat up.
2. Put in onions and stir-fry for 3-4 minutes, or until translucent. After that, put in tuna steaks and continue to cook for 2-3 minutes on each side.
3. Pour in the stock and season with salt. Shut and secure the lid and set the steam release handle to the "Sealing" position. Switch your Instant Pot to "Manual" mode and turn the timer to 5 minutes.
4. When finished, depressurize using the quick release method and open the lid. Remove the steaks and place them to a container. Cover and save for later.
5. After that, Switch your Instant Pot to "'Sauté" mode and simmer the stock until the liquid has reduced in half. Put in mushrooms and cook for 7-8 minutes, stirring intermittently.
6. Sprinkle with salt, pepper, and marjoram and mix in the heavy cream and Parmesan cheese.
7. Stir thoroughly and put in tuna steaks. Drizzle with olive oil.
8. Turn off the Instant Pot by pressing the "Cancel" button and serve instantly.

Nutritional Info:(Calories 470| Total Fats 32.6g | Net Carbs: 3.9g | Protein: 39.1g |Fiber: 1.2g)

White Fish in Ginger Orange Sauce

Aggregate Time to Prepare: **20 Minutes**

Yield: **4 Servings**

Ingredients:

- 1 1-inch piece of Ginger, sliced
- 1 cup White Wine
- 1 tbsp. Olive Oil
- 3 Spring Onions, chopped
- 4 White Fish Fillets
- Juice and Zest of 1 Orange
- Salt and Pepper, to taste

How to Cook:

1. Mix the juice, zest, wine, ginger, and spring onions in the Instant Pot.
2. Drizzle the fish with olive oil and drizzle with some salt and pepper.
3. Rub to coat thoroughly.
4. Put in the steamer basket.
5. Lower the basket into the pot and shut and secure the lid.
6. Switch the Instant Pot to "High" and cook for 6 minutes.
7. Release the pressure using the quick release method.
8. Your dish is ready! Have fun!

Nutritional Info: (Calories 240| Total Fats 2g | Net Carbs 2g | Protein 35g |Fiber: 1.8g)

White Fish Stew

Aggregate Time to Prepare: 20 Minutes

Yield: 6 Servings

Ingredients:

- 1 Carrot, sliced
- 1 cup chopped Broccoli

- 1 cup chopped Cauliflower
- 1 cup chopped Kale
- 1 cup Heavy Cream
- 1 Onion, diced
- 1 pound White Fish Fillets
- 2 Celery Stalks, diced
- 2 tbsp. Butter
- 3 cups Fish Broth
- Salt and Pepper, to taste

How to Cook:

1. Melt the butter in the Instant Pot using the "Sauté" mode.
2. Sauté the onions for 3 minutes.
3. Stir all of the ingredients, except for the cream.
4. Shut and secure the lid and select MANUAL.
5. Switch the Instant Pot to "High" and cook for 5 minutes.
6. Do a natural pressure release.
7. Stir in the heavy cream.
8. Discard the bay leaf and serve.
9. Have fun!

Nutritional Info: (Calories 165| Total Fats 13g | Net Carbs 5g | Protein 24g |Fiber: 1g)

Wild Alaskan Cod with Cherry Tomatoes

Aggregate Time to Prepare: **20 Minutes**

Yield: **4 Servings**

Ingredients:

- 1 cup cherry tomatoes
- 2 garlic cloves, crushed
- 2 lbs wild Alaskan cod fillets
- 2 tbsp butter
- 3 tbsp olive oil

Spices:

- 1 tsp salt
- ½ tsp black pepper, freshly ground
- ½ tsp dried thyme
- ½ tsp rosemary powder

How to Cook:

1. Thoroughly wash the fillets under cold running water and pat-dry with a kitchen towel. Put on a cutting board and chop into 4 equivalent pieces.
2. In a large mixing container, mix tomatoes, garlic, salt, pepper, rosemary, and thyme. Stir until thoroughly mixed and save for later.
3. Turn on your Instant Pot and pour two cups of water in the inner pot. Place your trivet in the bottom of your instant pot of the pot and save for later.
4. Line a round 7-inch baking dish with some parchment paper and place the fillets in it. Liberally brush with olive oil and pour in the tomato mixture. Put the dish in the pot and shut and secure the lid.
5. Make sure the steam release handle is on the "Sealing" position and switch to "Manual' mode. Cook for 10 minutes on high pressure.
6. When finished, push the "Cancel" button and release the pressure using the quick release method. Open the pot and cautiously remove the baking dish.
7. Chill for some time and serve. If you want, you can also drizzle with some more salt or pepper to taste.

Nutritional Info: (Calories 354| Total Fats 17.5g | Net Carbs: 1.7g | Protein: 45.6g |Fiber: 0.6g)

Wild Alaskan Salmon

Aggregate Time to Prepare: **25 Minutes**

Yield: **4 Servings**

Ingredients:

- 1 lb fresh asparagus, chopped into bite-sized pieces
- 1 lb wild Alaskan salmon, defrosted
- 1 tbsp butter
- 1 tbsp freshly squeezed lemon juice
- 1 tsp rice vinegar
- 3 garlic cloves, thinly sliced
- 4 tbsp olive oil

Spices:

- 1 tbsp fresh rosemary, thinly sliced
- 1 tsp smoked salt
- ¼ tsp white pepper, freshly ground

How to Cook:

1. Thoroughly wash the fillets and chop into bite-sized pieces. Put in a deep container and drizzle with salt, white pepper, and rosemary. If you want, you can also put in some garlic powder. Combine thoroughly and save for later.
2. Turn on your Instant Pot and put in the olive oil in the stainless steel insert. Switch your Instant Pot to "Sauté' mode and heat up. Put in chopped salmon and cook for 5-6 minutes.

3. After that put in garlic and drizzle with rice vinegar and lemon juice. Carry on cooking for an additional 2-3 minutes.
4. Lastly, put in chopped asparagus and mix in the butter. Cook for 3 minutes more.
5. Push the "Cancel" button and serve instantly.

Nutritional Info:(Calories 323| Total Fats 24.1g | Net Carbs: 2.7g | Protein: 24.7g |Fiber: 2.5g)

Wrapped Zesty and Herbed Fish

Aggregate Time to Prepare: 15 Minutes

Yield: 1 Serving

Ingredients:

- 1 4-ounce Fish Fillet
- 1 ½ cups Water
- 1 Rosemary Sprig
- 1 Thyme Sprig
- 1 tbsp. chopped Basil
- 1 tbsp. Lime Juice
- 1 tbsp. Olive Oil
- 1 tsp Dijon Mustard
- 2 tsp Lime Zest
- ¼ tsp Garlic Powder
- Pinch of Pepper
- Pinch of Salt

How to Cook:

1. Pour the water into the Instant Pot.
2. Sprinkle the fish with salt and paper.

3. Put on a piece of parchment paper and drizzle with zest.
4. Mix together the oil, juice, and mustard, and brush over.
5. Spread on top the herbs.
6. Cover the fish with the parchment paper.
7. Then, cover the wrapped fish in aluminium foil.
8. Put the fish packet inside the basket.
9. Shut and secure the lid and cook for 5 minutes on HIGH.
10. Release the pressure using the quick release method.
11. Your dish is ready! Have fun!

Nutritional Info: (Calories 250| Total Fats 10g | Net Carbs 1g | Protein 30g |Fiber: 0g)

Poultry Recipes

Aromatic Turkey

Aggregate Time to Prepare: **50 Minutes**

Yield: **8 Servings**

Ingredients:

- 1 ½ cups Chicken Broth
- 1 Bay Leaf
- 1 tsp Basil
- 1 tsp Garlic Powder
- 1 tsp Onion Powder
- 2 pounds Turkey Breasts, cubed
- 2 Thyme Sprigs
- 2 tsp Sage

How to Cook:

1. Line the Instant Pot with cooking spray and cook the turkey using the "Sauté" mode until browned.
2. Stir in the rest of the ingredients.
3. Shut and secure the lid and switch your Instant pot to "Manual" mode.
4. Switch the Instant Pot to "High" and cook for 25 minutes.
5. Allow the pressure to drop on its own.
6. Serve the turkey with veggies and drizzle everything with the cooking liquid.
7. Have fun!

Nutritional Info: (Calories 250| Total Fats 18g | Net Carbs 4g | Protein 31g |Fiber: 0g)

Asian Chicken Thighs

Aggregate Time to Prepare: 20 Minutes

Yield: 6 Servings

Ingredients:

- 1 ½ cups Water
- 1 ½ tsp minced Ginger
- 1 tbsp. Olive Oil
- 1 tbsp. Sriracha
- 1 tbsp. Sweetener
- 1 tsp Sesame Seeds
- 1/3 cup White Wine
- 3 tbsp. chopped Scallions
- 3 tbsp. Scallions
- 5 Garlic Cloves, minced
- 6 Chicken Thighs
- ½ cup Soy Sauce

How to Cook:

1. Put in the chicken and cook until browned on all sides.
2. Bring the sauce to a boil and let it cook for 10 minutes.
3. Switch the Instant Pot to "High" and cook for 5 minutes.
4. Release the pressure using the quick release method and set the Instant Pot to "Sauté" mode.
5. Switch the Instant Pot to "Sauté" mode and heat the oil.
6. In the mean time, whisk together the rest of the ingredients in a container.
7. Pour over the chicken and shut and secure the lid.

8. Your dish is ready! Have fun!
9. Set the cooking mode to MANUAL.

Nutritional Info: (Calories 285| Total Fats 11g | Net Carbs 7g | Protein 33g |Fiber: 0g)

Baby Spinach Chicken Wings

Aggregate Time to Prepare: **40 Minutes**

Yield: **5 Servings**

Ingredients:

- 1 celery stalk, thinly sliced
- 1 lb chicken wings, whole
- 1 small onion, thinly sliced
- 3 cups chicken stock
- 3 tbsp oil
- 2 cups cottage cheese (or paneer)
- 2 garlic cloves, crushed
- 2 tbsp ghee
- cups spinach, chopped

Spices:

- ½ tsp cinnamon powder
- 1 tbsp chili powder
- 1 tsp cumin powder
- 1 tsp salt
- 2 tbsp mustard seeds
- 4 cloves
- tsp turmeric powder

How to Cook:

1. Thoroughly wash the meat under running water using a large colander. Drain and save for later.
2. Clean and rinse spinach. Drain and chop with a sharp knife. Put in a deep container and save for later.
3. Turn on your Instant Pot and grease the bottom of the inner pot with oil. Switch your Instant Pot to "Sauté' mode and put in onions, celery stalks, garlic, and mustard seeds.
4. Stir thoroughly and cook for 3-4 minutes.
5. After that put in spinach and stir thoroughly.
6. Lastly, put in the meat and drizzle with spices. Briefly brown on both sides and pour in the stock. Stir thoroughly and put in ghee.
7. Shut and secure the lid and set the steam release handle. Push the "Stew" button.
8. When you hear the end signal, depressurize using the natural release method and mix in the cottage cheese.
9. Stir all thoroughly and serve instantly.

Nutritional Info:(Calories 387 | Total Fats: 22.1g | Net Carbs: 5.4g | Protein: 39.7g |Fiber: 0.6g)

Balsamic Chicken Breast with Basil

Aggregate Time to Prepare: **45Minutes**

Yield: 2 Servings

Ingredients:

- 1 cup cherry tomatoes
- 1 lb chicken breast, chopped into bite-sized pieces
- 2 cups chicken stock
- 2 garlic cloves, whole

- 3 tbsp butter
- ½ cup balsamic vinegar
- ½ cup fresh basil, thinly sliced

Spices:

- 1 tsp sea salt

How to Cook:

1. Thoroughly wash the meat under cold running water and pat dry with some kitchen paper. Put on a cutting board and chop into bite-sized pieces and move to a deep container. Pour in the balsamic vinegar and refrigerate for 20 minutes.
2. In the mean time, plug in the instant pot and Switch your Instant Pot to "'Sauté'' mode. Melt the butter in the inner pot and put in garlic. Briefly cook – for one minute and then put in cherry tomatoes and basil. Stir thoroughly and cook until tomatoes completely soften. Take out of the pot and move to a food processor. Process until smooth. Save for later.
3. Remove the chicken from the fridge and place in the pot. Pour in the stock and shut and secure the lid. Set the steam release handle and push the 'Manual'' button.
4. Turn the timer to 10 minutes on high pressure.
5. When finished, depressurize using the natural release method and open the lid. Stir in the tomato mixture and season with salt.
6. If you want, you can also put in some pepper prior to serving.

Nutritional Info:(Calories 456 | Total Fats: 23.8g | Net Carbs: 4.8g | Protein: 50.1g |Fiber: 1.2g)

Barbecue Chicken

Aggregate Time to Prepare: 30 Minutes

Yield: 6 Servings

Ingredients:

- ½ cup Low-Carb Barbecue Sauce
- ½ cup plus 2 tbsp. Water
- 1 ½ tbsp. Arrowroot
- 1 Onion, chopped
- 1 tbsp. Olive Oil
- 1 tsp minced Garlic
- 6 Chicken Thighs
- Salt and Pepper, to taste

How to Cook:

1. Switch your Instant Pot to "Sauté" mode.
2. Heat the oil in it and sauté the onions for a few minutes.
3. Put in garlic and cook for an additional minute.
4. Stir in the barbecue sauce and ½ cup of water.
5. Put the thighs upside down.
6. Cover and cook on HIGH for 10 minutes.
7. Depressurize quickly.
8. Move the chicken to a plate.
9. Switch your Instant Pot to "Sauté" mode and bring to a boil.
10. Mix the rest of the water and arrowroot and stir the mixture into the sauce.
11. Cook until thickened.
12. Put in the chicken and cook for an additional minute.
13. Your dish is ready! Have fun!

Nutritional Info: (Calories 449| Total Fats 12g | Net Carbs 7g | Protein 27g |Fiber: 0.5g)

Buffalo Chicken Meatballs

Aggregate Time to Prepare: 30 Minutes

Yield: 6 Servings

Ingredients:

- 1 ½ pounds ground Chicken
- 1 tsp minced Garlic
- 1/3 cup Hot Sauce
- 2 tbsp. Ghee
- 2/3 tsp Salt
- 4 tbsp. Butter
- ¼ tsp Pepper
- ¾ cup Almond Meal
- Pinch of Paprika

How to Cook:

1. Mix chicken, garlic, almond meal, salt, pepper, and paprika, in a large container.
2. Make meatballs out of the mixture.
3. Melt the ghee in the Instant Pot using the "Sauté" mode.
4. Working in batches, brown all of the meatballs.
5. Put all of the meatballs in the Instant Pot.
6. Mix together the hot sauce and butter (to make the buffalo sauce).
7. Pour the sauce over the meatballs and shut and secure the lid.
8. Switch the Instant Pot to "Manual" mode and cook for 15 minutes.

9. Release the pressure using the quick release method and have fun!

Nutritional Info: (Calories 240| Total Fats 19g | Net Carbs 3.5g | Protein 28g |Fiber: 1g)

Buffalo Chicken Stew

Aggregate Time to Prepare: 20 Minutes

Yield: 4 Servings

Ingredients:

- ¼ cup diced Onion
- ½ cup diced Celery
- 1 ½ cups Chicken Stock
- 1 cup Heavy Cream
- 1 tbsp. Ranch Dressing Combine
- 1 tsp minced Garlic
- 1/3 cup Red Hot Sauce
- 2 Chicken Breasts
- 2 cups grated Cheddar Cheese
- 2 tbsp. Butter

How to Cook:

1. Put all of the ingredients, except the cheese and heavy cream, in the Instant Pot.
2. Stir to mix and lock the lid.
3. Switch the Instant Pot to "Manual" mode and cook for 15 minutes.
4. Allow the pressure to drop naturally.
5. Stir in the cheese and cream prior to serving.
6. Have fun!

Nutritional Info: (Calories 528| Total Fats 41g | Net Carbs 3.9 g | Protein 33g |Fiber: 0.2g)

Butter Chicken Legs

Aggregate Time to Prepare: 60 Minutes

Yield: 6 Servings

Ingredients:

- 1 cup Greek yogurt
- 1 large tomato, roughly chopped
- 1 tbsp. almond flour
- 2 lbs. chicken legs, skin on
- 3 tbsp. butter

Spices:

- 1 tbsp. cayenne pepper
- 1 tbsp. parsley, thinly sliced
- 1 tsp salt

How to Cook:

1. Turn on the Instant Pot and coat the stainless steel insert with one tablespoon of butter. Make a layer with chicken legs and pour in enough water to cover. Sprinkle with salt and shut and secure the lid.
2. Push the 'Manual' button and turn the timer to 45 minutes.
3. When finished, release the pressure using the quick release method and open the lid.
4. In the mean time, melt the rest of the butter in a small skillet. Put in one tablespoon of cayenne pepper and almond flour. Briefly stir-fry for 2-3 minutes and remove from the heat.

5. Put the legs on a serving plate and drizzle with the cayenne mixture.

Nutritional Info: (Calories 338 | Total Fats 13.3g | Net Carbs: 2.6g | Protein 48.5g | Fiber: 0.9g)

Cajun Chicken Breast

Aggregate Time to Prepare: 35 Minutes

Yield: 4 Servings

Ingredients:

- 1 lb boneless and skinless chicken breast, thinly sliced
- 1 red bell pepper, sliced
- 1 small onion, thinly sliced
- 2 cups cauliflower, chopped into florets
- 2 cups chicken broth
- 3 garlic cloves, crushed
- 3 tbsp olive oil
- ¼ cup cherry tomatoes

Spices:

- 1 tsp onion powder
- 2 tsp paprika
- 2 tsp pink Himalayan salt
- 2 tsp red pepper, freshly ground
- ¼ tsp dried thyme
- ½ tsp dried rosemary
- ¾ tsp garlic powder

How to Cook:

1. Mix spices in a small jar and shut and secure the lid. Shake thoroughly until completely mixed and save for later.
2. Wash thoroughly the chicken and place on a large cutting board. Using a sharp knife, thinly cut each piece and place in a deep container. Liberally drizzle with the Cajun mixture.
3. Turn on your Instant Pot and Switch your Instant Pot to "'Sauté" mode. Oil-coat the inner pot with olive oil and heat up.
4. Put in onions and cook until translucent. After that put in bell peppers, garlic, cherry tomatoes, and cauliflower. Stir thoroughly and continue to cook for 5 minutes.
5. Pour in the chicken broth and put in the seasoned meat. Shut and secure the lid and set the steam release handle.
6. Switch your Instant Pot to "Manual" mode and turn the timer to 10 minutes.
7. When finished, release the pressure using the quick release method and cautiously open the lid.
8. Serve instantly.

Nutritional Info:(Calories 315 | Total Fats: 14.8g | Net Carbs: 6g | Protein: 37g | Fiber: 2.2g)

Cajun Rotisserie Chicken

Aggregate Time to Prepare: 50 Minutes

Yield: 6 Servings

Ingredients:

- 1 ½ cups Chicken Broth

- 1 Lemon, halved
- 1 medium Chicken
- 1 tbsp. Coconut Oil
- 1 tsp Garlic Salt
- 1 Yellow Onion, quartered
- 2 Rosemary Sprigs
- 2 tsp Cajun Seasoning
- ¼ tsp Pepper

How to Cook:

1. Melt the coconut oil in your Instant Pot using the "Sauté" mode.
2. Sprinkle the chicken with garlic salt, pepper, and Cajun.
3. Put the lemon, onion, and rosemary, in the chicken's cavity.
4. Put the chicken in the Instant Pot and brown on all sides.
5. Pour the chicken broth around the chicken (not over) and lock the lid.
6. switch your Instant pot to "Manual" mode and cook on HIGH for 25 minutes.
7. Depressurize naturally.
8. Your dish is ready! Have fun!

Nutritional Info: (Calories 260| Total Fats 27g | Net Carbs 1.2g | Protein 31g |Fiber: 0.5g)

Cajun Turkey in Marsala Sauce

Aggregate Time to Prepare: 25 Minutes

Yield: 4 Servings

Ingredients:

- 1 ½ pounds Turkey Breasts, cubed
- 1 tbsp. Arrowroot
- 1 tbsp. Cajun Seasoning
- 1 tbsp. Olive Oil
- 1 tsp dried Parsley
- 1/3 cup Marsala Wine
- 2/3 cup Chicken Stock
- ¼ cup Heavy Cream
- ¼ Onion, diced

How to Cook:

1. Switch your Instant Pot to "Sauté" mode.
2. Heat the olive oil and put in the onions.
3. Cook for a few minutes, until soft.
4. Put in turkey and cook until no longer pink.
5. Stir in the parsley, Cajun, marsala, and stock.
6. Shut and secure the lid and cook for 10 minutes on HIGH.
7. Release the pressure using the quick release method.
8. Mix together the cream and arrowroot and stir it into the mixture.
9. Bring to a boil using the "Sauté" mode and cook until thickened.
10. Your dish is ready! Have fun!

Nutritional Info: (Calories 300| Total Fats 18g | Net Carbs 5g | Protein 30g |Fiber: 0.2g)

Cauliflower Turkey Risotto

Aggregate Time to Prepare: 30 Minutes

Yield: 3 Servings

Ingredients:

- 1 cup cauliflower florets, thinly sliced
- 1 lb turkey breast, chopped into bite-sized pieces
- 3 cups chicken stock
- 3 tbsp butter
- 3 tbsp Parmesan, freshly grated
- ½ cup feta cheese

Spices:

- 1 tsp salt
- ½ tsp black pepper, freshly ground

How to Cook:

1. Using a sharp cutting knife, chop the meat into smaller pieces and remove the skin (if any). Rub with salt and pepper. Put in your instant pot and pour in the stock.
2. Shut and secure the lid and set the steam release handle. Switch your Instant Pot to "Meat" mode and cook for 12 minutes.
3. When finished, release the pressure using the quick release method and open the lid. Take the meat out of the pot and place in a deep container. Save for later.
4. Remove the rest of the stock and Switch your Instant Pot to "'Sauté" mode. Oil-coat the inner pot with butter and heat up.
5. After that put in thinly sliced cauliflower and drizzle with some more salt and pepper. Pour in approximately ¼ cup of the stock and simmer for 10 minutes.
6. After that put in the meat and stir thoroughly. Carry on cooking for an additional 5 minutes.

7. Lastly, mix in feta cheese and separate the mixture among serving plates. Drizzle with grated Parmesan and serve instantly.

Nutritional Info:(Calories 465 | Total Fats: 27g | Net Carbs: 2.1g | Protein: 51.6g |Fiber: 0g)

Cheesy Chicken with Jalapenos

Aggregate Time to Prepare: 20 Minutes

Yield: 4 Servings

Ingredients:

- ½ cup Water
- ¾ cup Sour Cream
- 1 pound Chicken Breasts
- 3 Jalapenos, seeded and sliced
- 8 ounces Cheddar Cheese, grated
- 8 ounces Cream Cheese
- Salt and Pepper, to taste

How to Cook:

1. Mix together the water, sour cream, and cheeses in the Instant Pot.
2. Stir in the jalapenos and place the chicken inside.
3. Sprinkle with some salt and pepper.
4. Shut and secure the lid and switch your instant pot to "Manual" mode and cook for 12 minutes.
5. Depressurize quickly.
6. Your dish is ready! Have fun!

Nutritional Info: (Calories 310| Total Fats 26g | Net Carbs: 4g | Protein 20g |Fiber: 1.4g)

Cheesy Turkey

Aggregate Time to Prepare: **35Minutes**

Yield: **4 Servings**

Ingredients:

- 1 cup tomatoes, diced
- 2 lbs turkey breasts
- 2 tbsp olive oil
- ½ cup cheddar cheese, grated
- ½ cup chicken stock
- ½ cup cream cheese

Spices:

- 1 tbsp Italian seasoning
- ¼ tsp black pepper, ground
- ½ tsp dried thyme, ground
- ½ tsp salt

How to Cook:

1. Thoroughly wash the meat under cold running water and pat dry with a kitchen towel. Liberally drizzle with Italian seasoning, salt, pepper, and thyme.
2. Turn on the Instant Pot and coat the stainless steel insert with olive oil. Switch your Instant Pot to "Sauté" mode and put in meat. Pour in the chicken stock and tomatoes. Securely shut and secure the lid and set the steam release handle to the "Sealing" position.
3. Push the "Poultry" button. The cooking time will depend on the type of the meat you're using. For the

frozen breasts, add approximately 10 minutes to your cooking time.
4. When finished, depressurize using the quick release method and open the lid.
5. Move the meat to a clean work surface and chop into bite-sized pieces.
6. Preheat the oven to 400 degrees. Line some baking paper over a baking pan and save for later.
7. Put the meat onto a baking sheet and spread the cream cheese and cheddar cheese on top. If you want, you can also drizzle with some red pepper flakes and parsley.
8. Put it in the oven and bake for 10 minutes.

Nutritional Info:(Calories 378 | Total Fats: 24g | Net Carbs: 10.9g | Protein: 27.6g | Fiber: 1.3g)

Chicken Alfredo Pasta

Aggregate Time to Prepare: **10 Minutes**

Yield: **3 Servings**

Ingredients:

- 1 cup cooked and shredded Chicken
- 1 tsp Italian Seasoning
- 15 ounces low-carb Alfredo Sauce
- 3 cupsspiralized Low-Carb Veggies (Zucchini or Spaghetti Squash)
- 3 tbsp. grated Parmesan Cheese
- Salt and Pepper, to taste

How to Cook:

1. Mix all of the ingredients, except the cheese, in your Instant Pot.
2. Sprinkle with some salt and pepper.
3. Shut and secure the lid and choose MANUAL.
4. Switch the Instant Pot to "High" and cook for 3 minutes.
5. Release the pressure using the quick release method.
6. Serve topped with Parmesan.
7. Have fun!

Nutritional Info: (Calories 190| Total Fats 10g | Net Carbs 3g | Protein 14g |Fiber: 0g)

Chicken and Portabella Mushrooms

Aggregate Time to Prepare: 35 Minutes

Yield: 4 Servings

Ingredients:

- 1 can Coconut Cream
- 1 pound Portabella Mushrooms, sliced
- 1 tsp Parsley
- 1 tsp Thyme
- 2 tbsp. Arrowroot
- 2/3 cup plus 1 tbsp. Water
- 4 Chicken Thighs

How to Cook:

1. Mix together the coconut cream and 2/3 cup water in the Instant Pot.
2. Stir in the thyme and parsley and season with some salt and pepper.
3. Put in the chicken and mushrooms.

4. Shut and secure the lid and cook on HIGH for 10 minutes.
5. Release the pressure using the quick release method.
6. Mix together the arrowroot and water and stir this mixture into the pot.
7. Cook using the "Sauté" mode until thickened.
8. Your dish is ready! Have fun!

Nutritional Info: (Calories 420| Total Fats 40g | Net Carbs 9g | Protein 40g |Fiber: 3.5g)

Chicken and Spinach Salad

Aggregate Time to Prepare: **35 Minutes**

Yield: **6 Servings**

Ingredients:

- 1 Avocado, sliced
- 1 cup Sour Cream
- 1 cup Water
- 1 pound Chicken Breasts
- 1 tsp Garlic Powder
- 3 cups Baby Spinach
- 3 Tomatoes, chopped
- ¼ tsp Pepper
- ¼ tsp Salt

How to Cook:

1. Mix the chicken and water in your Instant Pot.
2. Close and cook for 20 minutes on HIGH.
3. Move to a plate and cut the chicken.
4. Discard the water from the pot.

5. Mix together the sour cream and spices in the Instant Pot.
6. Put in chicken slices and stir to mix.
7. Cook for 1 minutes.
8. In the mean time, mix the rest of the ingredients in a serving container.
9. Put in the chicken mixture and toss to coat.
10. Your dish is ready! Have fun!

Nutritional Info: (Calories 360| Total Fats 31g | Net Carbs 2.55g | Protein 28g |Fiber: 0.5g)

Chicken Biryani

Aggregate Time to Prepare: **55 Minutes**

Yield: **4 Servings**

Ingredients:

- 1 ½ cup heavy cream
- 1 lb chicken thighs, skin-on
- 2 cups cauliflower, chopped into florets
- 2 cups chicken stock
- 2 small onions, thinly sliced
- 2 tbsp apple cider vinegar
- 3 tbsp ghee

Spices:

- 1 tbsp cloves
- 1 tsp cloves
- 1 tsp ground mace
- 2 bay leaves
- 2 cinnamon sticks
- 2 tsp coriander powder

- 2 tsp turmeric powder
- ¼ tsp chili flakes
- ½ tsp chili powder

How to Cook:

1. In a medium-sized container, mix together heavy cream, apple cider, and spices. Mix together and put in chicken drumsticks. Coat thoroughly with the marinade and move to large Ziploc bag. Seal the bag and refrigerate overnight.
2. Oil-coat a small baking dish with ghee and put in cauliflower. Remove the chicken from the fridge and place in the container along with spices. Stir thoroughly and tightly cover with aluminium foil.
3. Turn on your Instant Pot and set the trivet at the bottom of inner pot. Pour in 2 cups of water and place the pan on top.
4. Shut and secure the lid and set the steam release handle to the "Sealing" position. Switch your Instant Pot to "Manual" mode and turn the timer to 25 minutes on high pressure.
5. When finished, release the pressure using the quick release method and open the lid. Serve instantly.

Nutritional Info: (Calories 444| Total Fats 30g | Net Carbs: 5.6g | Protein: 35.5g |Fiber: 2g)

Chicken Breast with Spinach

Aggregate Time to Prepare: 40 Minutes

Yield: 2 Servings

Ingredients:

- 1 cup spinach, chopped
- 2 pieces of chicken breast, chop in half
- 2 tbsp cottage cheese
- 3 tbsp heavy cream
- 4 tbsp butter, melted
- ¼ cup mozzarella, shredded

Spices:

- 1 tsp dried celery
- ½ tsp garlic powder
- ½ tsp salt

How to Cook:

1. Put the spinach in a small sieve and rinse thoroughly. Drain and save for later.
2. In a medium-sized container, mix together cottage cheese, mozzarella, heavy cream, and butter. Stir thoroughly and put in spinach. Sprinkle with salt, garlic powder, and celery. Save for later
3. Thoroughly wash the meat and place on a cutting board. Make incisions into breast, approximately 1-inch apart. Fill each with the cheese mixture and save for later.
4. Line a small baking pan with some parchment paper and tenderly place the fillets in it. Loosely cover with aluminium foil and save for later.
5. Turn on your Instant Pot and set the trivet. Put the pan on top and shut and secure the lid.
6. Set the steam release handle and switch to "Manual' mode. Turn the timer to 20 minutes on high pressure.
7. When finished, release the pressure using the quick release method and open the lid. Cautiously remove the pan from the instant pot and chill for some time.
8. Serve.

Nutritional Info: (Calories 566 | Total Fats: 38g | Net Carbs: 1.5g | Protein: 52.2g | Fiber: 0.3g)

Chicken Cacciatore

Aggregate Time to Prepare: **35 Minutes**

Yield: **4 Servings**

Ingredients:

- ¼ cup Red Bell Pepper (diced)
- ½ cup Green Bell Pepper (diced)
- ½ cup Onion (diced)
- ½ tsp Dried Oregano
- ½ tsp Ground Black Pepper
- ½ tsp Salt
- 1 Bay Leaf
- 2 tbsp. Fresh Basil (chopped)
- 2 tbsp. Olive Oil
- 4 Chicken Thighs (skinless)
- 7 oz. Crushed Tomatoes

How to Cook:

1. Slightly coat the chicken thighs with a tablespoon of olive oil and season with salt and pepper.
2. Switch your Instant Pot to "Sauté" mode and place thighs in it. Brown them on both sides for 3 minutes. Take out of the pot and save for later.
3. Put in to the pot the onions, peppers and one tablespoon of olive oil and sauté for 5 minutes while stirring intermittently.
4. Return the chicken thighs to pot, pour over with tomatoes and put in oregano and bay leaf, and stir to mix.

5. Put the lid and lock it, and manually turn the timer and cook for 25 minutes at high pressure.
6. When finished allow the pressure to be released naturally.
7. Discard the bay leaf and serve with spaghetti squash drizzled with chopped basil.

Nutritional Info: (Calories: 133 | Total Fats: 3g | Net Carbs: 9.5g | Proteins: 14g | Fibers: 1g)

Chicken Casserole

Aggregate Time to Prepare: **30 Minutes**

Yield: 2 Servings

Ingredients:

- 1 large onion, thinly sliced
- 1 large tomato, pureed
- 1 lb. chicken breast, boneless and skinless
- 2 cups chicken stock

Spices:

- 1 tsp dried oregano
- 1 tsp salt
- ½ tsp black pepper

How to Cook:

1. Thoroughly wash the meat under cold running water and pat dry with a kitchen towel chop into bite-sized pieces and save for later.
2. Wash the tomato and place in the food processor. Put in oregano, salt, and pepper. Process until pureed and save for later.

3. Turn on the Instant Pot and mix all ingredients in the stainless steel insert. Shut and secure the lid and close the steam release handle. Push the 'Manual' mode and turn the timer to 30 minutes.
4. When finished, release the steam naturally and let it sit covered for 10 minutes before opening the lid.

Nutritional Info: (Calories 315 | Total Fats 6.5g | Net Carbs: 8.6g | Protein 50.4g | Fiber: 2.7g)

Chicken Curry

Aggregate Time to Prepare: **40 Minutes**

Yield: **2 Servings**

Ingredients:

- ¼ cup soy sauce
- 1 cup cauliflower
- 1 cup cherry tomatoes, chopped
- 2 garlic cloves, crushed
- 3 cups chicken stock
- 7 oz chicken breast, chopped into bite-sized pieces

Spices:

- ½ tsp garlic powder
- 2 tbsp chili powder
- 2 tsp coriander powder
- 2 tsp onion powder
- 3 tsp turmeric powder

How to Cook:

1. Turn on your Instant Pot and mix all ingredients in the inner pot. Shut and secure the lid and set the steam

release handle to the "Sealing" position. Switch your Instant Pot to "Manual" mode and turn the timer to 20 minutes on high pressure.
2. When finished, push the "Cancel" button and depressurize using the natural release method. Cautiously, open the lid and chill for some time prior to serving.

Nutritional Info:(Calories 178| Total Fats 3.6g | Net Carbs: 8g | Protein: 26g |Fiber: 2.7g)

Chicken Drumsticks with Mushrooms

Aggregate Time to Prepare: **45Minutes**

Yield: **4 Servings**

Ingredients:

- 1 cup button mushrooms, sliced
- 1 lb chicken drumsticks, skin-on
- 1 medium-sized tomato, chopped
- 1 tbsp Dijon mustard
- 1 tsp freshly squeezed lemon juice
- 2 tbsp apple cider vinegar
- 2 tbsp butter
- 3 cups chicken stock
- 3 tbsp olive oil

Spices:

- 1 tbsp dried rosemary
- 1 tsp pink Himalayan salt

How to Cook:

1. Put drumsticks in the pot and pour in the stock. Shut and secure the lid and set the steam release handle to the "Sealing" position. Push the "Poultry" button.
2. In the mean time, whisk together olive oil, mustard, lemon juice, apple cider, rosemary, and salt. Save for later.
3. When your instant pot sounds the end signal, depressurize using the quick release method and open the lid. Remove the chicken from the pot along with the stock.
4. Switch your Instant Pot to "Sauté' mode and grease the bottom of the inner pot with butter. Put in tomatoes and cook for 2-3 minutes.
5. After that put in mushrooms and continue to cook for an additional 5-6 minutes, stirring intermittently.
6. Slightly coat each thigh with the mustard mixture and place in the pot. Carry on cooking for about 2 minutes more and push the "Cancel" button.
7. Take out of the pot and serve instantly.

Nutritional Info: (Calories 354 | Total Fats: 23.4g | Net Carbs: 1.9g | Protein: 32.8g |Fiber: 0.7g)

Chicken Fajitas

Aggregate Time to Prepare: 45 Minutes

Yield: 4 Servings

Ingredients:

- 1 bell pepper, chop into strips
- 1 cup cherry tomatoes, chopped
- 1 lb chicken breast, chopped into bite-sized pieces
- 1 onion, thinly sliced
- 1 tbsp lime juice

- 2 tbsp homemade taco seasoning
- 3 garlic cloves, minced
- 6 large leaves Iceberg lettuce

For homemade taco seasoning:

- 1 tbsp smoked paprika
- 1 tsp onion powder
- 2 tbsp pink Himalayan salt
- 2 tsp garlic powder
- 2 tsp oregano
- 3 tbsp chili powder
- ½ tsp black pepper, freshly ground
- ½ tsp coriander powder

How to Cook:

1. Mix all ingredients for taco seasoning in a jar and shake thoroughly. Save for later.
2. Wash thoroughly the meat and place in a deep container. Liberally drizzle with taco seasoning. Put in the pot and put in tomatoes, garlic, sliced peppers, onions, and lime juice.
3. Shut and secure the lid and push the "Poultry" button. Turn the timer to 8 minutes on high pressure.
4. When finished, release the pressure using the quick release method and open the lid. Remove the mixture from the pot and place in a container. Cool completely.
5. Spread approximately 2-3 tablespoons of the mixture at the center of each lettuce leaf and cover tightly. Secure each cover with a toothpick and serve instantly.

Nutritional Info:(Calories 322 | Total Fats: 6.1g | Net Carbs: 11.4g | Protein: 50.4g |Fiber: 3.2g)

Chicken Legs the Hungarian Way

Aggregate Time to Prepare: **45 Minutes**

Yield: **4 Servings**

Ingredients:

- 1 tbsp. Olive Oil
- 1 Tomato, chopped
- 2 tsp Hot Paprika
- 4 Chicken Legs
- ½ cup Chicken Stock
- ½ cup Sour Cream
- ½ Onion, diced
- Salt and Pepper, to taste

How to Cook:

1. Heat the oil in your Instant Pot and put in the chicken to it.
2. Cook until golden on all sides. Move to a plate.
3. Put in onions to the pot and sauté for a few minutes, until soft.
4. Stir in the hot paprika and chicken stock.
5. Return the chicken to the pot and place the tomatoes on top.
6. Shut and secure the lid and switch your instant pot to "Manual" mode and cook for 10 minutes.
7. Push CANCEL and release the pressure.
8. Move the chicken to a plate and stir the sour cream into the sauce.
9. Sprinkle with salt and pepper, to taste.
10. Pour the sauce over the chicken and serve.
11. Have fun!

Nutritional Info: (Calories 420| Total Fats 10g | Net Carbs 6g | Protein 30g |Fiber: 1.3g)

Chicken Lettuce Wraps

Aggregate Time to Prepare: 20-25 Minutes

Yield: 6 Servings

Ingredients:

For chicken:

- 1 clove Garlic (crushed)
- 1 cup Chicken Broth
- 1 stalk Celery
- 24 oz. Chicken Breast (boneless and skinless)
- 4 oz. Onion (diced)
- ½ cup Hot Cayenne Pepper Sauce

For wraps:

- 1½ cup Carrots (grated)
- 2 stalks Celery (julienned)
- 6 large leaves Lettuce (bibb or butter)

How to Cook:

1. Put all ingredients for chicken in the Instant Pot.
2. Shut and secure the lid and turn the timer and cook for 15 minutes at high pressure.
3. When finished allow the pressure to be released naturally.
4. Take the chicken out of the pot and save half a cup of cooking juices. Shred the chicken using a fork, and return to pot with reserved cooking juices.

5. Switch your Instant Pot to "Sauté" mode and cook for 2-3 minutes while intermittently stirring.
6. Put equivalent amounts of julienned celery on each lettuce leaf, then top it with the shredded chicken and carrots. Fold all four sides and flip over on serving platters.
7. Serve instantly.

Nutritional Info: (Calories: 147.5 | Total Fats: 0.1g | Net Carbs: 3.7g | Proteins: 25g | Fibers: 1.5g)

Chicken Liver Pate

Aggregate Time to Prepare: 15 Minutes

Yield: 16 Servings

Ingredients:

- 1 cup chopped Leek
- 1 pound Chicken Livers
- 1 tbsp. Sage
- 1 tsp Basil
- 1 tsp Salt
- 1/3 cup Rum
- 2 tbsp. Butter
- 2 tsp Olive Oil
- 2 tsp Thyme
- 3 Anchovies in oil

How to Cook:

1. Switch your Instant Pot to "Sauté" mode and heat the oil in it.
2. Sauté the leeks until soft.

3. Put in the livers and cook for a few minutes, until seared.
4. Pour the rum over and shut and secure the lid.
5. Cook on POULTRY for 10 minutes.
6. Depressurize quickly.
7. Move to a food processor and put in the rest of the ingredients.
8. Process until smooth.
9. Your dish is ready! Have fun!

Nutritional Info: (Calories 82| Total Fats 4g | Net Carbs 6g | Protein 6g |Fiber: 1g)

Chicken Makhani

Aggregate Time to Prepare: 25 Minutes

Yield: 6 Servings

Ingredients:

- 1 tbsp lime juice, freshly squeezed
- 2 cups tomatoes, diced
- 3 lbs chicken thighs, skinless
- 4 tbsp butter
- 5 garlic cloves, minced
- ½ cup plain yogurt, full-fat

Spices:

- 1 tbsp black peppercorns, whole
- 1 tsp salt
- 1 tsp white pepper, ground
- 2 cloves, whole
- 2-3 cardamom pods

How to Cook:

1. Turn on the Instant Pot and put in butter to the stainless steel insert. When melted, put in garlic and all spices. Cook for 3-4 minutes, stirring continuously.
2. Put in chicken thighs and tomatoes. Stir thoroughly and securely lock the lid.
3. Close the steam release handle and push the "Manual" button. Turn the timer to 10 minutes and cook on "High" pressure.
4. When you hear the cooker's end signal, release the pressure using the quick release method by moving the valve to the "Venting" position.
5. Open the pot and mix in the yogurt and lime juice. Push the "Sauté" button and continue to cook for 5 additional minutes. Stir intermittently.
6. When finished, move to a serving dish and serve instantly.

Nutritional Info:(Calories 533 | Total Fats 25g | Net Carbs: 4.4g | Protein: 67.7g |Fiber: 1.3g)

Chicken Paprikash

Aggregate Time to Prepare: **40 Minutes**

Yield: **4 Servings**

Ingredients:

- 1 ½ pounds Chicken Wings
- 1 cup Coconut Milk
- 1 cup Onions, diced
- 1 tbsp. Smoked Paprika
- 2 Bell Peppers, diced
- 2 cups Chicken Stock
- 2 tsp Arrowroot

- 2 tsp Garlic Cloves, minced
- 3 tsp Olive Oil
- ½ cup Tomato Puree
- Salt and Pepper, to taste

How to Cook:

1. Switch the Instant Pot to "Sauté" mode and heat the oil.
2. Put in the onions and peppers and cook for 3 minutes.
3. Put in garlic and cook for an additional minute.
4. Put in the chicken wings (in batches), and cook until browned.
5. In a container, whisk together the paprika, stock, tomato puree and some salt and pepper.
6. Pour over and shut and secure the lid.
7. Switch the Instant Pot to "High" and cook for 15 minutes.
8. Depressurize and mix in the coconut milk and arrowroot.
9. Cook for 7 minutes more.
10. Your dish is ready! Have fun!

Nutritional Info: (Calories 552| Total Fats 18g | Net Carbs 8g | Protein 24g |Fiber: 1.6g)

Chicken Pot Roast

Aggregate Time to Prepare: **60 Minutes**

Yield: **6 Servings**

Ingredients:

- 1 cup chicken stock

- 1 onion, chopped
- 1 whole chicken, approximately 4 lbs
- 3 tbsp lemon zest
- 4 tbsp olive oil
- 5 cherry tomatoes, whole
- 5 garlic cloves, whole

Spices:

- 1 tsp black pepper
- 2 fresh sage sprigs
- 2 tsp salt
- 3 fresh rosemary sprigs

How to Cook:

1. Put the chicken in a large colander and rinse thoroughly under cold running water ensuring to wash the cavity. Rub with salt and pepper and save for later.
2. Turn on your Instant Pot and Switch your Instant Pot to "'Sauté" mode. Oil-coat the inner pot with olive oil and heat up. Put in chicken and brown on all sides for 5-6 minutes.
3. Take out of the pot and place on a large platter. Stuff with rosemary sprigs, sage sprigs, and lemon zest.
4. Put in some more oil in the pot and heat up. Put in onions and garlic. Cook until translucent. Pour in approximately ¼ cup of the stock and bring it to a boil. Simmer for 10 minutes.
5. After that put in the chicken and cherry tomatoes. Shut and secure the lid and set the steam release handle.
6. Switch your Instant Pot to "Manual" mode and turn the timer to 30 minutes.

7. In the mean time, preheat the oven to 450 degrees F. Like a baking sheet with some parchment paper and save for later.
8. When your instant pot sounds the end signal, release the pressure using the quick release method and open the lid. Chill for some time and move the chicken to a large platter.
9. Remove the sprigs from the cavity and stuff with cherry tomatoes.
10. Bake for 15-20 minutes.

Nutritional Info:(Calories 570 | Total Fats: 18.8g | Net Carbs: 5.4g | Protein: 89.1g |Fiber: 1.9g)

Chicken Ranch Immerse

Aggregate Time to Prepare: **20 Minutes**

Yield: 8 Servings

Ingredients:

- 1 cup Hot Sauce
- 1 pound Chicken Breasts, skinless and boneless
- 1 Stick of Butter
- 16 ounces Cheddar Cheese
- 1 packet Ranch Seasoning
- 8 ounces Cream Cheese
- Pinch of Pepper

How to Cook:

1. Put the chicken, hot sauce, pepper, cream cheese, ranch seasoning, and butter, in the Instant Pot.
2. Shut and secure the lid and cook on HIGH for 15 minutes.

3. Release the pressure using the quick release method.
4. Shred the chicken with two forms inside the pot.
5. Stir in the cheddar instantly.
6. Your dish is ready! Have fun!

Nutritional Info: (Calories 220| Total Fats 32g | Net Carbs 3g | Protein 23g |Fiber: 0.3g)

Chicken Sausage and Kale Soup

Aggregate Time to Prepare: **30 Minutes**

Yield: **6 Servings**

Ingredients:

- 1 medium Cauliflower, broken into florets
- 1 Onion, chopped
- 1 pound Chicken Sausage
- 1 tbsp. Red Pepper Flakes
- 1 tsp dried Fennel
- 2 cups chopped Kale
- 2 tbsp. Olive Oil
- 3 Garlic Cloves, minced
- 5 cups Chicken Broth
- ½ cup Heavy Cream
- Salt and Pepper, to taste

How to Cook:

1. Heat the oil in the Instant Pot using the "Sauté" mode.
2. Put in the onions and cook for 3 minutes.
3. Put in garlic, sausage, and fennel, and cook for approximately 5 minutes.

4. Stir in the rest of the ingredients, except kale and cream, and shut and secure the lid.
5. Switch the Instant Pot to "Manual" mode and cook for 12 minutes.
6. Depressurize and mix in the kale and heavy cream.
7. Sprinkle with salt and pepper and serve instantly.
8. Have fun!

Nutritional Info: (Calories 400| Total Fats 30g | Net Carbs 6g | Protein 22g |Fiber: 1.2g)

Chicken Tagine

Aggregate Time to Prepare: **30 Minutes**

Yield: **5 Servings**

Ingredients:

- 1 bell pepper, sliced
- 1 cup cherry tomatoes, chopped
- 1 onion, sliced
- 2 cups chicken stock
- 2 lbs chicken thighs, boneless and skinless
- 3 garlic cloves, crushed
- 4 tbsp olive oil
- ½ cup sun-dried tomatoes

Spices:

- 1 cinnamon stick
- 1 tsp ginger powder
- 1 tsp turmeric powder
- ¼ tsp black pepper, ground
- ½ tsp red pepper flakes
- ½ tsp salt

How to Cook:

1. Mix the spices in a small container. Combine thoroughly and save for later.
2. Thoroughly wash the meat under cold running water and pat dry with a kitchen paper. Rub with spices on all sides and save for later.
3. Turn on your Instant Pot and Switch your Instant Pot to "'Sauté" mode. Oil-coat the inner pot with olive oil and heat up.
4. Put in the meat and briefly brown for about 2 minutes, turning intermittently.
5. Push the "Cancel" button and put in the rest of the ingredients.
6. Shut and secure the lid and set the steam release handle to the "Sealing" position. Switch your Instant Pot to "Manual" mode and cook for 15 minutes on high pressure.
7. When finished, depressurize using the natural release method for 10 minutes and then move the pressure valve to the "Venting" position to release the rest of the pressure
8. Carefully, open the lid and optionally drizzle with some fresh parsley prior to serving.

Nutritional Info: (Calories 473 | Total Fats: 25.1g | Net Carbs: 5.3g | Protein: 53.8g | Fiber: 1.5g)

Chicken Teriyaki

Aggregate Time to Prepare: **30Minutes**

Yield: 2 Servings

Ingredients:

- 1 medium-sized onion, thinly sliced
- 2 medium-sized chicken breast, chop in half lengthwise
- 2 tbsp balsamic vinegar
- 3 tbsp olive oil
- ¼ cup rice vinegar
- ¼ cup soy sauce

Spices:

- 1 tbsp ginger, freshly grated
- 1 tsp black pepper, freshly ground
- 1 tsp garlic powder
- 1 tsp pink Himalayan salt
- 2 tsp red pepper flakes

How to Cook:

1. Wash thoroughly the meat and pat dry with a kitchen paper. Cut each piece in half, lengthwise and save for later.
2. In a large container, mix soy sauce, rice vinegar, balsamic vinegar, ginger, garlic, onions, pepper, red pepper flakes, and olive oil. Combine thoroughly and save for later.
3. Turn on your Instant Pot and put in chicken. Pour in the soy mixture and approximately one cup of water. Shut and secure the lid and set the steam release handle.
4. Switch your Instant Pot to "Manual" mode and turn the timer to 15 minutes on high pressure.
5. When finished, depressurize using the natural release method and open the lid. Sprinkle with salt and stir thoroughly.
6. Optionally put in some more pepper or red chili flakes. Stir thoroughly and serve.

7. For a thicker mixture, Switch your Instant Pot to "'Sauté" mode again and simmer until a favoured thickness.

Nutritional Info:(Calories 370 | Total Fats: 23.9g | Net Carbs: 6.3g | Protein: 26.4g |Fiber: 1.4g)

Chicken Thighs in a Balsamic Sauce

Aggregate Time to Prepare: 30 Minutes

Yield: 4 Servings

Ingredients:

- ¼ tsp Pepper
- ½ cup Balsamic Vinegar
- ½ tsp Salt
- 1 pound Chicken Thighs
- 1 tsp Garlic Powder
- 1 tsp Worcestershire Sauce
- 1/3 cup Sherry (substitute with Chicken Stock for fewer carbs)
- 2 tbsp. chopped Cilantro
- 2 tbsp. minced Onion
- 2 tbsp. Olive Oil

How to Cook:

1. Put everything, except the chicken, in the Instant Pot.
2. Stir to mix thoroughly.
3. Put in the chicken and shut and secure the lid.
4. Cook on POULTRY for 15 minutes.
5. Depressurize quickly.
6. Serve drizzled with the sauce.
7. Have fun!

Nutritional Info: (Calories 210| Total Fats 12g | Net Carbs 9g | Protein 14g |Fiber: 1g)

Chicken Tikka Masala

Aggregate Time to Prepare: **15 Minutes**

Yield: **4 Servings**

Ingredients:

- ¼ tsp Cayenne Pepper
- ¼ tsp Ground Ginger
- ½ tsp Paprika
- ½ tsp Salt
- ½ tsp Turmeric
- 1 cup Greek Yogurt
- 1 cup Whipping Cream
- 1 lbs. Chicken Breasts (chop into 1½ inch chunks)
- 1 tbsp. Lime Juice
- 1 tsp Ground Black Pepper
- 15 oz. Tomato Sauce
- 2 tbsp. Garam Masala
- 5 cloves Garlic (minced)

How to Cook:

1. Put in a container the chicken, yogurt, garam masala, lime juice, pepper and ginger. Combine thoroughly and refrigerate for an hour.
2. Switch your Instant Pot to "Sauté" mode and put in marinated chicken and marinade, and cook for 5 minutes stirring intermittently.
3. Put in all other ingredients, except cream, and stir to mix.

4. Shut and secure the lid, and manually turn the timer and cook for 10 minutes at high pressure.
5. When finished depressurize using the quick release method and mix in the cream.
6. If the thickness of the sauce needs to be adjusted set the Instant Pot to "Sauté" and cook until favoured consistency.
7. Serve with rice and cauliflower.

Nutritional Info: (Calories: 460 | Total Fats: 27g | Net Carbs: 12.5g | Proteins: 32g | Fibers: 6.5g)

Chicken Tostadas

Aggregate Time to Prepare: **20Minutes**

Yield: 2 Servings

Ingredients:

- 1 cup chicken stock
- 1 cup tomatoes, roughly chopped
- 2 large chicken breast, skinless and boneless

Spices:

- 1 tsp salt
- 1 tsp smoked paprika
- 2 tsp chili powder
- ¼ tsp cayenne pepper
- ½ tsp cumin powder
- ½ tsp garlic powder
- ½ tsp white pepper, freshly ground
- ¾ tsp onion powder

How to Cook:

1. Thoroughly wash the chicken under cold running water and pat dry with a kitchen paper. Save for later.
2. Turn on your Instant Pot and put in the chicken. Pour in the chicken stock and shut and secure the lid. Make sure the steam release handle is on the "Sealing" position and switch to "Manual' mode. Cook for 10 minutes on high pressure.
3. When you hear the end signal, depressurize using the natural release method and open the lid. Cautiously move the chicken to a serving plate and cool to a room temperature.
4. Using two forks shred the chicken and place back to the pot. Put in tomatoes and all spices.
5. Stir thoroughly and Switch your Instant Pot to "'Sauté" mode. Cook for 3-4 minutes, stirring continuously.
6. When finished, push the "Cancel" button and remove the meat from the pot. Serve instantly with your favorite toasted keto bread.

Nutritional Info:(Calories 474 | Total Fats: 9.6g | Net Carbs: 2.8g | Protein: 88.1g |Fiber: 1.1g)

Chicken with Capers and Parsley

Aggregate Time to Prepare: **45 Minutes**

Yield: **4 Servings**

Ingredients:

- 1 Onion, diced
- 1 tbsp. Arrowroot Powder
- 1 tbsp. Water
- 1/3 cup Capers

- 1/3 cup White Wine Vinegar
- 2 tbsp. Olive Oil
- 4 Chicken Breasts
- ¼ tsp Pepper
- ½ cup Parsley

How to Cook:

1. Switch your Instant Pot to "Sauté" mode and heat 1 tbsp. o oil.
2. Cook the chicken until no longer pink on all sides. Move to a plate.
3. Heat the rest of the oil and sauté the onions for 5 minutes.
4. Put in parsley and capers and cook for 1 minute.
5. Stir in the vinegar and return the chicken to the pot.
6. Shut and secure the lid and cook for 13 minutes on HIGH.
7. Mix together the water and arrowroot.
8. Release the pressure using the quick release method and mix in the arrowroot mixture.
9. Cook using the "Sauté" mode until thickened.
10. Your dish is ready! Have fun!

Nutritional Info: (Calories 276| Total Fats 12g | Net Carbs 5.8g | Protein 35g |Fiber: 1.2g)

Chicken with Spaghetti Squash

Aggregate Time to Prepare: 40 Minutes

Yield: 6 Servings

Ingredients:

- 1 cup Marsala

- 1 cup Shutake Mushrooms, sliced
- 1 cup Water
- 1 Spaghetti Squash
- 1 tbsp. Coconut Oil
- 2 pounds Chicken Breasts, chopped
- 3 tbsp. Arrowroot
- ½ cup Chicken Broth
- Salt and Pepper, to taste

How to Cook:

1. Pour the water into the Instant Pot. Put the squash inside the steaming basket and close.
2. Switch the Instant Pot to "Manual" mode and cook for 20 minutes.
3. Depressurize quickly. Set the squash aside to cool.
4. Discard the water and wipe the Instant Pot dry.
5. Melt the coconut oil and put in the chicken.
6. Cook until no longer pink.
7. Sprinkle with salt and pepper and pour the marsala and broth over.
8. Shut and secure the lid and cook on HIGH for 8 minutes.
9. In the mean time, scrape out the squash flesh using a fork, making long spaghetti-like strips.
10. Depressurize quickly and move the chicken to a container.
11. Reserve ½ cup of the liquid and discard the rest.
12. Mix in the arrowroot and cook until thickened.
13. Stir in the spaghetti and chicken and stir to coat.
14. Your dish is ready! Have fun!

Nutritional Info: (Calories 260| Total Fats 12g | Net Carbs 4g | Protein 22g |Fiber: 0g)

Chili Turkey Casserole

Aggregate Time to Prepare: 40 Minutes

Yield: 4 Servings

Ingredients:

- 1 celery stalk, chopped
- 1 chili pepper, sliced
- 1 cup broccoli, chopped
- 1 cup cauliflower, chopped
- 1 cup cherry tomatoes, chopped
- 1 lb turkey breast, sliced into half-inch thick slices
- 1 medium-sized onion, sliced
- 3 tbsp olive oil

Spices:

- 1 tsp black pepper, ground
- 1 tsp salt

How to Cook:

1. Sprinkle the meat with salt and pepper. Save for later.
2. Oil-coat the bottom of a round baking pan with some oil. Put in onions to create the first layer. Then put in a layer of cauliflower and meat.
3. Put in cherry tomatoes and finish with chili pepper and broccoli. Drizzle with chopped celery and tightly cover with aluminium foil.
4. Turn on your Instant Pot and set the trivet at the bottom of the inner pot. Pour in two cups of water and place the pan on top.
5. Shut and secure the lid and set the steam release handle to the "Sealing" position and switch to "Manual' mode.

6. Turn the timer to 20 minutes.
7. When finished, release the pressure using the quick release method and open the lid.
8. Remove the aluminium foil and chill for some time.
9. Serve instantly

Nutritional Info: (Calories 242 | Total Fats: 12.6g | Net Carbs: 9.2g | Protein: 21.2g | Fiber: 3g).

Chinese Simmered Chicken

Aggregate Time to Prepare: **45 Minutes**

Yield: **5 Servings**

Ingredients:

- 2 tbsp olive oil
- 3 lbs chicken thighs, boneless and chopped into bite-size pieces

For the sauce:

- ¼ cup apple cider vinegar
- ¼ cup water
- ½ tsp red chili flakes
- 1 small onion, thinly sliced
- 1 tbsp tomato paste, sugar-free
- 1 tsp toasted sesame seeds
- 1/3 cup soy sauce
- 1/3 cup swerve
- 2 garlic cloves, crushed

How to Cook:

1. In a small container, whisk together all sauce ingredients. Save for later.

2. Thoroughly wash the meat and chop into smaller pieces.
3. Turn on your Instant Pot and coat the inner pot with oil. Push the "Sauté' button and heat the oil. Put in chicken in several batches and brown on all sides for 3-4 minutes. Take out of the pot and move to a deep container. Save for later.
4. Pour in the sauce mixture and stir thoroughly. Cook for 2-3 minutes and then put in the meat. Stir thoroughly and continue to cook for an additional 10-12 minutes.
5. Push the "Cancel" button and take out of the pot.
6. Serve instantly.

Nutritional Info:(Calories 590 | Total Fats: 26.1g | Net Carbs: 3.2g | Protein: 80.3g |Fiber: 0.7g)

Cider Partridge with Apples

Aggregate Time to Prepare: 55 Minutes

Yield: 4 Servings

Ingredients:

- 1 Alcmene apple, chopped
- 1 cup apple cider vinegar
- 1 small onion, thinly sliced
- 2 cups chicken broth
- 2 partridges, cleaned and readied
- ¼ cup celery leaves, chopped
- ¼ cup olive oil

Spices:

- 1 tsp salt
- ½ tsp dried sage
- ½ tsp dried thyme

How to Cook:

1. Oil-coat the bottom of your stainless steel insert with some oil and push the 'Sauté' button Put in onions and stir-fry for 2-3 minutes. After that put in celery and apples. Carry on cooking for 5 minutes.
2. In the mean time, rinse the meat under cold running water and rub with thyme and sage. Put in the pot along with apple cider and chicken broth. Shut and secure the lid and set the steam release handle.
3. Turn the timer to 35 minutes.
4. When your instant pot sounds the end signal, release the pressure using the quick release method and open the lid.
5. Serve warm.

Nutritional Info: (Calories 313 | Total Fats 20.3g | Net Carbs: 8.7g | Protein 20.3g | Fiber: 1.8g)

Citrus Chicken Thighs

Aggregate Time to Prepare: **60Minutes**

Yield: **4 Servings**

Ingredients:

- 1 cup chicken stock
- 4 chicken thighs, skin on
- ¼ cup apple cider vinegar

For the marinade:

- 1 lemon, sliced
- 1 tsp salt
- 2 garlic cloves, crushed
- 2 sage sprigs
- 3 rosemary sprigs
- 4 tbsp olive oil
- ¼ cup lemon juice, freshly squeezed
- ½ cup fresh parsley leaves, thinly sliced

How to Cook:

1. Combine together all marinade ingredients and save for later.
2. Wash thoroughly the meat and liberally brush with the marinade. Put in a large Ziploc bag and refrigerate for 30 minutes.
3. Turn on your Instant Pot and put in chicken and approximately 2 tablespoons of the marinade. Pour in the chicken stock and apple cider vinegar.

4. Shut and secure the lid and set the steam release handle to the "Sealing" position. Switch your Instant Pot to "Manual" mode and turn the timer to 15 minutes on high pressure.
5. When finished, release the pressure using the quick release method and open the lid. Switch your Instant Pot to "Sauté' mode and continue to cook for an additional 7-8 minutes.
6. Push the "Cancel" button and serve instantly.

Nutritional Info:(Calories 381 | Total Fats: 10.6g | Net Carbs: 0.6g | Protein: 66g |Fiber: 0.1g)

Clear Chicken and Spinach Soup

Aggregate Time to Prepare: **40 Minutes**

Yield: **4 Servings**

Ingredients:

- ¼ tsp Pepper
- ¼ tsp Salt
- ½ Onion, chopped
- 1 Bulb Fennel, chopped
- 1 cup Spinach
- 1 pound Chicken, chop into chunks
- 1 tsp minced Garlic
- 2 cups Chicken Broth
- 4 Green Onions, chopped

How to Cook:

1. Put all of the ingredients in the Instant Pot.
2. Stir to mix thoroughly.

3. Shut and secure the lid and switch your instant pot to "Soup" mode and cook for 30 minutes.
4. Allow the pressure to release naturally, for approximately 10 minutes.
5. Your dish is ready! Have fun!

Nutritional Info: (Calories 181| Total Fats 2.2g | Net Carbs: 4g | Protein 24g |Fiber: 2g)

Coconut Turkey Curry

Aggregate Time to Prepare: **45 Minutes**

Yield: **5 Servings**

Ingredients:

- 1 cup broccoli, chopped
- 1 lb turkey breast, chopped into bite-sized pieces
- 1 medium-sized onion, thinly sliced
- 3 cups chicken stock
- 3 tbsp ghee
- cups coconut milk

Spices:

- 1 tbsp chili powder
- 1 tsp black pepper, freshly ground
- 1 tsp salt
- 2 tbsp curry powder
- tsp garlic powder

How to Cook:

1. Turn on your Instant Pot and put in onions in the inner pot. Switch your Instant Pot to "Sauté' mode and cook for 3-4 minutes, or until translucent.

2. After that put in broccoli and season with spices. Stir thoroughly and continue to cook for 5 minutes.
3. Pour in the coconut milk and chicken stock. Put in ghee and shut and secure the lid.
4. Set the steam release handle and switch to "Manual' mode. Turn the timer to 20 minutes on high pressure.
5. When finished, release the pressure using the quick release method by moving the pressure valve to the "Venting" position.
6. Cautiously open the lid and serve instantly.

Nutritional Info: (Calories 403 | Total Fats: 32.5g | Net Carbs: 9.3g | Protein: 18.9g | Fiber: 3.5g)

Confit Duck Legs with Thyme

Aggregate Time to Prepare: **8-10 HOURS**

Yield: **4 Servings**

Ingredients:

- 2 celery stalks, chopped
- 2 lbs duck legs, 2-3 pieces
- 3 tbsp duck fat
- 5 cups chicken stock
- ¼ cup fresh parsley, thinly sliced

Spices:

- 1 tbsp fresh thyme, thinly sliced
- 1 tbsp peppercorn
- 2 bay leaves
- 2 tsp salt
- 3 thyme sprigs

How to Cook:

1. Thoroughly wash the meat under cold running water and pat dry with a kitchen towel. Save for later.
2. In a small container, mix all spices and rub the meat with this mixture. Put in the pot along with the rest of the ingredients.
3. Shut and secure the lid and set the steam release handle. Push the "Slow Cook" button and turn the timer to 8-10 hours on low pressure.
4. When finished, depressurize using the natural release method and open the lid.
5. Serve instantly with some mashed cauliflower or roasted asparagus.

Nutritional Info: (Calories 503 | Total Fats: 23.8g | Net Carbs: 1.1g | Protein: 67g | Fiber: 0.3g)

Cream Cheese Chicken with Bacon

Aggregate Time to Prepare: **40 Minutes**

Yield: **4 Servings**

Ingredients:

- 1 cup Water
- 1 packet Ranch Seasoning
- 2 pounds Chicken Breasts
- 2 tbsp. Arrowroot
- 4 ounces Cheddar Cheese, shredded
- 8 Bacon Slices, cooked and crumbled
- 8 ounces Cream Cheese

How to Cook:

1. Mix together the cream cheese, water, and seasoning, in the Instant Pot.

2. Put in the chicken breasts inside.
3. Shut and secure the lid and cook on HIGH for 25 minutes.
4. Push CANCEL, release the pressure using the quick release method, and move the chicken to a cutting board.
5. Shred using two forks.
6. Switch your Instant Pot to "Sauté" mode and mix in the arrowroot.
7. Put in shredded chicken, bacon, and cheddar, and cook for 3-4 minutes, or until thickened.
8. Your dish is ready! Have fun!

Nutritional Info: (Calories 620| Total Fats 38g | Net Carbs: 6g | Protein 48g |Fiber: 2.3g)

Creamy Cauliflower Chicken

Aggregate Time to Prepare: 35 Minutes

Yield: 4 Servings

Ingredients:

- 1 cup cauliflower, chopped
- 1 medium-sized onion, thinly sliced
- 1 small green chili pepper, seeds removed and chopped
- 1 tbsp olive oil
- 2 cups chicken broth
- 2 lbs chicken breasts, boneless and skin-on
- 2 tbsp butter
- 5 garlic cloves, thinly sliced
- ½ cup heavy cream

Spices:

- 1 tsp chili powder
- 1 tsp cumin seeds
- 1 tsp fresh ginger, grated
- 1 tsp salt
- 1 tsp smoked paprika, ground
- ½ fenugreek seeds

How to Cook:

1. Thoroughly wash the chicken under running water. Pat dry with a kitchen paper and chop into bite-sized pieces. Save for later.
2. In a food processor, mix garlic, ginger, olive oil, heavy cream, chili powder, and salt. Process until smooth and creamy.
3. Turn on the Instant Pot and place butter in the stainless steel insert. Push the "Sauté" button and put in chicken. Drizzle with cumin seeds, fenugreek seeds, and some salt to taste. Cook for 5 minutes, or until somewhat browned. Remove the chicken to a plate and save for later.
4. After that, put in onion and green chili pepper. Stir-fry for 3 minutes and put in cauliflower. Cook for 2 minutes and return the chicken to the pot.
5. Pour in the broth and drizzle with smoked paprika. Stir thoroughly and securely lock the lid. Push the "Manual" button and turn the timer to 5 minutes. Cook on "High" pressure.
6. When you hear the cooker's end signal, release the pressure using the quick release method and open the pot. Stir in the heavy cream mixture and push the "Sauté" button. Bring it to a simmer and cook for 5 additional minutes, stirring intermittently.
7. Serve warm.

Nutritional Info:(Calories 615 | Total Fats 32.8g | Net Carbs: 5.6g | Protein: 69.9g |Fiber: 2g)

Creamy Chicken Wings with Peppers

Aggregate Time to Prepare: 50Minutes

Yield: 5 Servings

Ingredients:

- 1 cup Brussels sprouts
- 1 cup heavy cream
- 1 green bell pepper
- 1 red bell pepper
- 2 lbs chicken wings, whole
- 3 tbsp sour cream
- 4 cups chicken stock
- 7 oz Portobello mushrooms, sliced
- ¼ cup olive oil

Spices:

- 1 tsp black pepper, freshly ground
- 1 tsp dried rosemary
- 2 tsp salt

How to Cook:

1. Turn on your Instant Pot and put in sprouts in the stainless steel insert. Pour in three cups of water and put in two tablespoons of olive oil. Drizzle with some salt and shut and secure the lid. Make sure the steam release handle is on the "Sealing" position and switch to "Manual' mode. Turn the timer to 10 minutes on high pressure.

2. When finished, release the pressure by moving the pressure handle to the "Venting" position. Cautiously open the lid and remove the sprouts from the pot. Drain and save for later.
3. After that rinse and clean each pepper. Cut in half and remove the seeds. Thinly cut and save for later.
4. Clean the mushrooms and cut each in half. Save for later.
5. Remove the stock from the pot and Switch your Instant Pot to "'Sauté" mode. Oil-coat the inner pot with the rest of the olive oil and put in the wings. Briefly brown each piece for 3-4 minutes on each side and take out of the pot.
6. After that put in peppers and cook for 3 minutes stirring continuously. Sprinkle with some salt and put in mushrooms. Carry on cooking until the liquid evaporates.
7. After that put in the meat and sprouts. Pour in the reserved stock as thoroughly as he rest of the one cup. Sprinkle with salt, pepper, rosemary, and stir thoroughly.
8. Shut and secure the lid and set the steam release handle to the "Sealing" position. Switch your Instant Pot to "Manual" mode and turn the timer to 15 minutes.
9. When finished, depressurize using the quick release method and open the lid.
10. Chill for some time and then mix in sour cream and heavy cream. Stir thoroughly and optionally season with some more salt or pepper.
11. Serve instantly.

Nutritional Info:(Calories 568 | Total Fats: 34.7g | Net Carbs: 6.4g | Protein: 56.1g |Fiber: 1.7g)

Creamy Turkey with Broccoli

Aggregate Time to Prepare: 50

Yield: 3 Servings

Ingredients:

- 1 cup broccoli, chopped
- 1 cup shredded mozzarella
- 1 spring onion, thinly sliced
- 10 oz ground turkey
- 2 tbsp olive oil
- 3 tbsp sour cream
- ¼ cup chicken stock
- ¼ cup Parmesan cheese, grated

Spices:

- ¼ tsp dried oregano
- ¼ tsp white pepper, freshly ground
- ½ tsp dried thyme
- ½ tsp salt

How to Cook:

1. Turn on your Instant Pot and Switch your Instant Pot to "'Sauté" mode. Put in olive oil and heat up.
2. After that put in spring onions and cook for 1 minute, stirring continuously.
3. Put in turkey and broccoli. Pour in the stock and cook for 12-15 minutes, stirring intermittently.
4. Sprinkle with salt, pepper, thyme, and oregano and mix in the cheese.
5. Push the "Cancel" button and take out of the pot. Move the mixture to a small baking dish and save for later.

6. Preheat the oven to 350 degrees F and bake for 15-20 minutes, or until lightly charred.
7. Remove from the oven and chill for some time. Spread on top sour cream and serve.

Nutritional Info: (Calories 327 | Total Fats: 24.5g | Net Carbs: 1.3g | Protein: 29.8g | Fiber: 0.1g)

Curried Chicken with Tomatoes, Spinach and Yogurt

Aggregate Time to Prepare: 60 Minutes

Yield: 8 Servings

Ingredients:

- 1 ½ cups Yogurt
- 1 Onion, sliced
- 1 tbsp. chopped Coriander
- 1 tbsp. Olive Oil
- 1/3 pound Curry Paste
- 2 Tomatoes, chopped
- 4 ounces Spinach
- 4 pounds Chicken, cubed

How to Cook:

1. Mix the chicken, curry paste, and yogurt, in a container.
2. Cover, and let marinate in the fridge for 30 minutes.
3. Heat the oil in the Instant Pot using the "Sauté" mode.
4. Cook the onions until soft.
5. Put in tomatoes and cook for an additional minute.
6. Pour the chicken mixture over.
7. Stir in spinach and coriander.
8. Shut and secure the lid and cook on HIGH for 15 minutes.
9. Release the pressure using the quick release method.
10. Your dish is ready! Have fun!

Nutritional Info: (Calories 423| Total Fats 18g | Net Carbs 6.8g | Protein 40g |Fiber: 6g)

Duck Breast with Prosciutto

Aggregate Time to Prepare: **50 Minutes**

Yield: **4 Servings**

Ingredients:

- 1 cup cremini mushrooms
- 1 lb duck breasts
- 1 shallot, thinly sliced
- 1 tbsp orange zest
- 2 garlic cloves, crushed
- 2 tbsp fresh parsley, thinly sliced
- 3 tbsp apple cider vinegar
- 4 cups chicken broth
- 7 oz prosciutto, chopped
- ½ cup duck fat

Spices:

- 1 tsp sea salt
- ½ tsp white pepper, freshly ground

How to Cook:

1. Turn on your Instant Pot and Switch your Instant Pot to "'Sauté" mode. Put in duck fat and gradually melt, stirring continuously.
2. After that put in shallots and garlic. Stir thoroughly and cook for 2-3 minutes. Put in mushrooms and continue to cook until the liquid has evaporated.
3. Lastly, put in prosciutto and stir thoroughly. Briefly brown on all sides and push the "Cancel" button.

4. Put in the meat in the pot and pour in the broth. Drizzle with spices and orange zest. Pour in the cider and shut and secure the lid.
5. Make sure the steam release handle is on the "Sealing" position and switch to "Manual' mode.
6. Turn the timer to 20 minutes on high pressure.
7. When finished, depressurize using the natural release method and cautiously open the lid. Drizzle with parsley and let it sit covered for approximately 10 minutes prior to serving.

Nutritional Info: (Calories 496 | Total Fats: 34.3g | Net Carbs: 3.5g | Protein: 40.9g | Fiber: 0.4g)

Duck Breast with Prosciutto

Aggregate Time to Prepare: **50 Minutes**

Yield: **4 Servings**

Ingredients:

- 1 cup cremini mushrooms
- 1 lb duck breasts
- 1 shallot, thinly sliced
- 1 tbsp orange zest
- 2 garlic cloves, crushed
- 2 tbsp fresh parsley, thinly sliced
- 3 tbsp apple cider vinegar
- 4 cups chicken broth
- 7 oz prosciutto, chopped
- ½ cup duck fat

Spices:

- 1 tsp sea salt
- ½ tsp white pepper, freshly ground

How to Cook:

1. Turn on your Instant Pot and Switch your Instant Pot to "'Sauté" mode. Put in duck fat and gradually melt, stirring continuously.
2. After that put in shallots and garlic. Stir thoroughly and cook for 2-3 minutes. Put in mushrooms and continue to cook until the liquid has evaporated.
3. Lastly, put in prosciutto and stir thoroughly. Briefly brown on all sides and push the "Cancel" button.
4. Put in the meat in the pot and pour in the broth. Drizzle with spices and orange zest. Pour in the cider and shut and secure the lid.

5. Make sure the steam release handle is on the "Sealing" position and switch to "Manual' mode.
6. Turn the timer to 20 minutes on high pressure.
7. When finished, depressurize using the natural release method and cautiously open the lid. Drizzle with parsley and let it sit covered for approximately 10 minutes prior to serving.

Nutritional Info: (Calories 496 | Total Fats: 34.3g | Net Carbs: 3.5g | Protein: 40.9g |Fiber: 0.4g)

Duck Breasts with Mushrooms

Aggregate Time to Prepare: **35 Minutes**

Yield: 3 Servings

Ingredients:

- 1 cup button mushrooms, thinly sliced
- 1 lb. duck breasts, sliced into 1-inch thick slices
- 3 tbsp. olive oil

Spices:

- 1 bay leaf
- 1 tsp salt
- ½ tsp freshly ground black pepper

How to Cook:

1. Thoroughly wash the meat under cold running water and rub with salt, pepper, and thyme.
2. Turn on the Instant Pot and put in the meat. Pour in 3 cups of water, put in bay leaf, and shut and secure the lid. Switch the Instant pot to "Manual" mode and

close the steam release handle. Turn the timer to 13 minutes.
3. When finished, push "Cancel" button and release the pressure using the quick release method. Open the lid and remove the steaks. Save for later.
4. After that, grease the bottom of your stainless steel insert with olive oil. Switch your Instant pot to "Sauté" mode and put in mushrooms. Stir-fry for 5 minutes and put in the meat. Tenderly brown on both sides and take out of the pot.
5. Serve instantly.

Nutritional Info: (Calories 391 | Total Fats 24.6g | Net Carbs: 0.6g | Protein 40.6g |Fiber: 0.4g)

Easy Chicken Thighs

Aggregate Time to Prepare: 30 Minutes

Yield: 4 Servings

Ingredients:

- ¼ cup feta cheese
- ¼ cup milk
- 1 cup cream cheese
- 2 cups button mushrooms, sliced
- 2 large chicken thighs, whole
- 2 tbsp olive oil
- 3 garlic cloves, crushed
- 4 tbsp butter

Spices:

- 1 tsp sea salt
- ½ tsp white pepper, freshly ground

- ¼ tsp chili flakes

How to Cook:

1. Wash thoroughly the meat under running water and rub with salt. Save for later,
2. Turn on your Instant Pot and put in butter in the inner pot. Put in chicken thighs and pour in three cups of water (or chicken stock).
3. Shut and secure the lid and set the steam release handle to the "Sealing" position. Push the "Meat" button and cook for 15 minutes.
4. When you hear the end single, release the pressure using the quick release method and open the lid. Remove the thighs and drain.
5. Oil-coat the inner pot with olive oil and put in mushrooms. Drizzle with some salt, white pepper, and chili flakes.
6. Switch your Instant Pot to "Sauté' mode and cook for 5 minutes, stirring continuously.
7. Put in chicken thighs and brown them for 3-4 minutes on each side.
8. Lastly, mix in the cream cheese, Feta cheese, and pour in the milk. Bring it to a boil and tenderly simmer for 4-5 minutes.
9. When finished, push the "Cancel" button and serve thighs with the creamy mushroom sauce.

Nutritional Info:(Calories 579 | Total Fats: 44.6g | Net Carbs: 4.2g | Protein: 40.4g |Fiber: 0.4g)

Easy Poussin

Aggregate Time to Prepare: **60 Minutes**

Yield: **4 Servings**

Ingredients:

- 1 cup cherry tomatoes, sliced
- 1 medium-sized poussin
- 2 cups chicken stock
- 3 tbsp. butter
- 7 oz. bacon

Spices:

- 1 tsp salt
- ½ tsp white pepper

How to Cook:

1. Thoroughly wash the meat and rub with pepper. Put in your instant pot along with chicken sauce and cherry tomatoes.
2. Shut and secure the lid and set the steam release handle. Push the 'Manual' button and turn the timer to 40 minutes.
3. In a large skillet, melt the butter and put in bacon. Stir thoroughly and fry for 1-2 minutes. Remove from the heat.
4. After you hear the cooker's end signal, depressurize using the natural release method and remove the meat. Serve with bacon.

Nutritional Info: (Calories 501 | Total Fats 32.6g | Net Carbs: 2.3g | Protein 46.7g | Fiber: 0.5g)

Easy Turkey Roast

Aggregate Time to Prepare: **60Minutes**

Yield: **5 Servings**

Ingredients:

- 2 lbs turkey breast, boneless and skinless
- 3 tbsp Dijon mustard
- 3 tbsp garlic infused oil
- 4 cups chicken stock
- ¼ cup olive oil

Spices:

- 1 tsp white pepper, freshly ground
- 2 tsp sea salt

How to Cook:

1. Put the meat in the pot and put in chicken stock. Shut and secure the lid and set the steam release handle.
2. Switch your Instant Pot to "Manual" mode and cook for 25 minutes. When finished, depressurize using the quick release method and open the lid. Take the meat out of the pot and save for later.
3. Preheat the oven to 425 degrees F. Line some parchment paper over a baking sheet and save for later.
4. In a small container, whisk together garlic infused oil, olive oil, Dijon, salt, and pepper. Slightly coat the meat with this mixture and place on a baking sheet.
5. Roast for 15 minutes on each side.
6. Remove from the oven and serve instantly.

Nutritional Info: (Calories 458 | Total Fats: 25.4g | Net Carbs: 0.9g | Protein: 54.1g | Fiber: 0.3g).

Fall-Off-Bone Chicken Drumsticks

Aggregate Time to Prepare: **45 Minutes**

Yield: 3 Servings

Ingredients:

- 1 tbsp. Olive Oil
- 2 cups Water
- 2 tbsp. Tomato Paste
- 2 tsp minced Garlic
- 6 Chicken Drumsticks
- ½ Bell Pepper, diced
- ½ Onion, diced
- Salt and Pepper, to taste

How to Cook:

1. Heat the oil in the Instant Pot using the "Sauté" mode.
2. Put in pepper and onion and cook for a few minutes, until soft.
3. Stir in the garlic and cook for 1 additional minute.
4. Position the drumsticks over.
5. Mix together the water and tomato paste.
6. Pour the mixture over the drumsticks.
7. Shut and secure the lid and cook on HIGH for 15 minutes.
8. Do a natural pressure release.
9. Your dish is ready! Have fun!

Nutritional Info: (Calories 450| Total Fats 27g | Net Carbs 5.3g | Protein 42g |Fiber: 1.4g)

Garam Masala Chicken

Aggregate Time to Prepare: 25 Minutes

Yield: 4 Servings

Ingredients:

- ½ cup cherry tomatoes, diced
- 1 cup heavy cream
- 1 small onion, diced
- 2 tbsp vegetable oil
- 3 cups chicken broth
- lbs chicken breasts, skinless and boneless

Spices:

- ½ tsp black pepper, ground
- ½ tsp salt
- 1 tsp cayenne pepper, ground
- 1 tsp coriander powder
- 1 tsp cumin powder
- 1 tsp garam masala powder

How to Cook:

1. Thoroughly wash the chicken breasts under cold running water and pat dry with a kitchen paper. Cut into bite-sized pieces and save for later.
2. Turn on the Instant Pot and coat the stainless steel insert with vegetable oil. Put in chicken pieces and drizzle with salt and pepper. Cook for 5 minutes, or until lightly browned. Remove the chicken to a plate and save for later.
3. Put in onions and cherry tomatoes. Put in all the rest of the spices and stir-fry for 5 minutes. Pour in the heavy cream and broth. Stir thoroughly and finally put in the chicken.
4. Shut and secure the lid . Close the steam release handle and push the "Manual" button. Turn the timer to 10 minutes and cook on "High" pressure.

5. When your instant pot sounds the end signal, release the pressure using the quick release method and open the pot.
6. Move to serving containers and drizzle with some fresh parsley prior to serving.

Nutritional Info: (Calories 638 | Total Fats 36g | Net Carbs: 3.8g | Protein: 70.4g | Fiber: 0.9g)

Garlic and Paprika Whole Chicken

Aggregate Time to Prepare: 45 Minutes

Yield: 6 Servings

Ingredients:

- 1 ½ cup Chicken Stock
- 1 ½ tsp Smoked Paprika
- 1 medium Whole Chicken
- 1 tsp Garlic Powder
- 2 tbsp. Butter, softened
- 6 Garlic Cloves, smashed
- ¼ tsp Pepper
- ¼ tsp Salt
- ½ tsp Onion Powder

How to Cook:

1. In a container, whisk together the butter, salt, pepper, paprika, onion powder, and garlic powder.
2. Wash and pat dry the chicken and rub this mixture into the meat.
3. Put in the Instant Pot upside down and cook for a few minutes, or until golden.
4. Pour the chicken broth around (not over) the chicken.

5. Put the smashed garlic cloves inside and shut and secure the lid.
6. Switch the Instant Pot to "Manual" mode and cook for 25 minutes.
7. Depressurize naturally.
8. Your dish is ready! Have fun!

Nutritional Info: (Calories 250| Total Fats 30.2g | Net Carbs 1.7g | Protein 32.6g |Fiber: 1g)

Garlic Meatballs

Aggregate Time to Prepare: **40 Minutes**

Yield: **4 Servings**

Ingredients:

- 1 lb. ground turkey
- 2 eggs, beaten
- 2 garlic cloves, minced
- 2 small onions, thinly sliced
- ¼ cup almond flour

Spices:

- 1 tsp salt
- 3 tbsp. olive oil
- ¼ cup parsley

How to Cook:

1. In a large container, mix ground turkey, almond flour, chopped onions, minced garlic, eggs, salt, and parsley. Mould the mixture into 15-20 meatballs, depending on the size.

2. Turn on the Instant Pot and grease the bottom of the stainless steel insert with one tablespoon of olive oil. Switch your Instant Pot to "Sauté" mode and fry for 3-4 minutes, or until golden color.
3. After that put in the rest of the oil and shut and secure the lid. Close the steam release handle.
4. Push the 'Meat' button and cook for 15 minutes.
5. Push the 'Cancel' button and depressurize using the natural release method. Serve instantly.

Nutritional Info: (Calories 251 | Total Fats 8.7g | Net Carbs: 3.3g | Protein 36.9g | Fiber: 1g)

Garlicky and Lemony Turkey

Aggregate Time to Prepare: **25 Minutes**

Yield: **4 Servings**

Ingredients:

- ¼ cup Cooking Wine
- ¼ tsp Paprika
- ½ cup Chicken Broth
- 1 ¼ pounds Turkey Breasts, cubed
- 1 Onion, diced
- 1 tbsp. Arrowroot Powder
- 1 tbsp. Ghee
- 1 tsp Salt
- 5 Garlic Cloves, minced
- Juice and Zest of 1 Lemon

How to Cook:

1. Melt the ghee in your Instant Pot using the "Sauté" mode.

2. Cook the onions until soft.
3. Put in the broth, wine, lemon juice and zest, paprika, and salt.
4. Stir to mix and put in the turkey cubes.
5. Close and lock the lid.
6. Switch your instant pot to "Poultry" mode and allow to cook on DEFAULT.
7. Release the pressure using the quick release method.
8. Stir in the arrowroot and cook using the "Sauté" mode until thickened.
9. Your dish is ready! Have fun!

Nutritional Info: (Calories 539| Total Fats 24g | Net Carbs 4.5g | Protein 50g |Fiber: 0g)

Ginger Chicken with Vegetables

Aggregate Time to Prepare: 30 Minutes

Yield: 4 Servings

Ingredients:

- 1 cup broccoli, chopped
- 1 cup shiitake mushrooms, chopped
- 1 cup spinach, torn
- 1 large tomato, roughly chopped
- 1 small onion, thinly sliced
- 3 cups chicken stock
- 4 garlic cloves, crushed
- 4 large chicken thighs, skin on
- 4 tbsp butter
- ¼ cup Dijon mustard
- ¼ cup olive oil

Spices:

- 1 tbsp cayenne pepper
- 1 tbsp fresh mint, thinly sliced
- 2 tbsp fresh ginger, grated
- 2 tsp sea salt

How to Cook:

1. In a small container, whisk together olive oil, Dijon mustard, garlic, salt, min, ginger, and cayenne pepper. Save for later.
2. Thoroughly wash each piece of chicken under cold running water and pat dry with some kitchen paper. Liberally brush with the marinade and place in a container. Allow it to sit for some time.

3. After that plug in the instant pot and Switch your Instant Pot to "'Sauté" mode. Oil-coat the inner pot with butter and heat up. Put in onion and cook for 2 minutes.
4. After that put in tomatoes and mushrooms. Carry on cooking for an additional 3 minutes. Lastly, put in the rest of the vegetables and stir thoroughly.
5. Put in the chicken thighs and pour in the stock. Shut and secure the lid and set the steam release handle to the "Sealing" position.
6. Push the "Meat" button.
7. When finished, depressurize using the natural release method and open the lid. Serve instantly.

Nutritional Info:(Calories 578 | Total Fats 31.6g | Net Carbs: 9.6g | Protein: 61.5g |Fiber: 3g)

Glazed Duck Breast

Aggregate Time to Prepare: **50 Minutes**

Yield: 2 Servings

Ingredients:

- 1 lb. duck breast, chopped into bite-sized pieces
- 1 tbsp. Dijon mustard
- 1 tbsp. olive oil
- 1 tsp honey
- 3 cups chicken broth
- ¼ cup apple cider vinegar

Spices:

- 1 tsp garlic powder
- 1 tsp salt

- ½ tsp pepper

How to Cook:

1. Take the meat out of the fridge approximately one hour before cooking.
2. Rub the meat with onion powder and place in your instant pot along with the chicken broth. Shut and secure the lid and push the 'Meat' button. When your instant pot sounds the end signal, release the pressure using the quick release method and open the lid. Take the meat out of the pot along with the broth.
3. Switch your Instant Pot to "Sauté" mode and coat the stainless steel insert with oil. Put in apple cider, Dijon, and honey. Drizzle with salt and pepper and cook for 3-4 minutes.
4. Put in the meat and coat thoroughly. Serve instantly.

Nutritional Info: (Calories 398 | Total Fats 15g | Net Carbs: 4.7g | Protein 55.7g | Fiber: 0.3g)

Habanero Chicken

Aggregate Time to Prepare: 30 Minutes

Yield: 6 Servings

Ingredients:

- 1 ½ cups Water
- 1 tbsp. Sweetener by choice
- 1 tsp Basil
- 1 tsp Salt
- 1 tsp smoked Paprika
- 6 Chicken Breasts

- 6 tbsp. Habanero Sauce
- ½ cup Tomato Puree
- ½ tsp Cumin

How to Cook:

1. Pour the water into the Instant Pot and put the rack into the Instant Pot.
2. Mix the rest of the ingredients in a baking dish and place on the rack.
3. Close and lock the lid.
4. Switch the Instant Pot to "High" and cook for 15 minutes.
5. Allow the pressure to release naturally, for 10 minutes.
6. Your dish is ready! Have fun!

Nutritional Info: (Calories 280| Total Fats 15g | Net Carbs 8g | Protein 28g |Fiber: 2g)

Hearty Duck Stew

Aggregate Time to Prepare: **30Minutes**

Yield: 7 Servings

Ingredients:

- 2 garlic cloves, minced
- 3 celery stalks, chopped
- 3 large Pekin duck legs
- 5 slices bacon, chopped
- 6 cups chicken stock
- ½ cup canned tomatoes, sugar-free
- ½ cup duck fat

Spices:

- 1 bay leaf
- 1 tsp salt
- 2 thyme sprigs

How to Cook:

1. Mix the ingredients in the pot and season with salt. Put in one bay leaf and thyme sprigs.
2. Shut and secure the lid and set the steam release handle to the "Sealing" position.
3. Switch your Instant Pot to "Manual" mode and turn the timer to 25 minutes on high heat.
4. When finished, depressurize using the quick release method.
5. Cautiously open the lid. The meat should be tender enough to fall off the bone. Remove the bones and stir thoroughly.
6. If you want, you can also drizzle with some grated Parmesan cheese and serve instantly.

Nutritional Info: (Calories 536 | Total Fats: 38.6g | Net Carbs: 1.1g | Protein: 43.5g | Fiber: 0.3g)

Herb Marinated Chicken Fillets

Aggregate Time to Prepare: 80Minutes

Yield: 4 Servings

Ingredients:

- 1 cup olive oil
- 1 lemon, sliced
- 1 tbsp Dijon mustard
- 10 oz chicken fillets, sliced into half-inch thick slices
- 2 garlic cloves, crushed

- 3 tbsp apple cider vinegar

Spices:

- 1 fresh rosemary sprig
- 1 tbsp fresh oregano leaves
- 1 tsp dried marjoram
- 1 tsp dried thyme
- 1 tsp sea salt
- ½ tsp dried rosemary

How to Cook:

1. In a small container, mix together olive oil, garlic cloves, mustard, apple cider, and spices. Put in sliced lemon and mix thoroughly.
2. Thoroughly wash the meat and pat dry with a kitchen paper. Submerge each piece into the marinade and move to large Ziploc bag. Seal the bag and refrigerate for an hour.
3. When finished, remove the meat from the fridge and let it sit for 10 minutes.
4. In the mean time, plug in the instant pot and set the trivet at the bottom of the stainless steel insert. Pour in 1 cup of water and place the steam basket on top.
5. Put in fillets and drizzle with some of the marinade – approximately 3 tablespoons.
6. Position the lemon slices on top and shut and secure the lid.
7. Make sure the steam release handle is on the "Sealing" position and switch to "Manual' mode. Turn the timer to 13 minutes on high pressure.
8. When finished, release the pressure using the quick release method and open the lid. Serve instantly.

9. If you want, you can also brown the fillets for 2-3 minutes in a large non-stick pan over medium-high heat.

Nutritional Info: (Calories 574 | Total Fats: 55.8g | Net Carbs: 0.6g | Protein: 20.8g | Fiber: 0.2g).

Hot Artichoke Stew

Aggregate Time to Prepare: 20 Minutes

Yield: 5 Servings

Ingredients:

- 1 tbsp sesame seeds
- 2 cups chicken stock
- 2 green onions, thinly sliced
- 2 tbsp light soy sauce
- 2 tbsp rice vinegar
- 3 garlic cloves, crushed
- 4 tbsp canola oil
- 5 chicken thighs, whole
- 7 oz artichoke hearts, chopped

Spices:

- 1 tbsp fresh ginger, grated
- ½ tsp black pepper

How to Cook:

1. Put chicken thighs in the pot and pour in the stock. Shut and secure the lid and set the steam release handle to the "Sealing" position. Switch your Instant Pot to "Manual" mode and turn the timer to 10 minutes on high pressure.

2. When done, release the pressure using the quick release method and open the lid. Put in green onions, artichoke, and sesame seeds. Drizzle with rice vinegar, soy sauce, and canola oil.
3. Stir thoroughly and season with ginger and pepper.
4. Shut and secure the lid again and set the steam release handle.
5. Carry on cooking for an additional 5 minutes on the "Manual" mode.
6. When finished, release the pressure using the quick release method and cautiously open the lid.
7. Serve instantly.

Nutritional Info: (Calories 489 | Total Fats: 25.8g | Net Carbs: 3.8g | Protein: 55g | Fiber: 2.6g)

Hot Chicken Wings

Aggregate Time to Prepare: **50 Minutes**

Yield: 3 Servings

Ingredients:

- 1 cup cherry tomatoes, diced
- 2 jalapeno pepper, thinly sliced
- 2 tbsp. olive oil
- 4 cups chicken broth
- 4 tbsp. butter
- 6 chicken wings

Spices:

- ½ tsp chili powder
- ½ tsp salt

How to Cook:

1. Oil-coat the stainless steel insert with some oil and place the chicken wings. Pour in the chicken broth and jalapeno peppers. Shut and secure the lid. Set the steam release handle and push the 'Meat' button.
2. When your instant pot sounds the end signal, release the pressure using the quick release method and open the lid. Remove the wings from the broth and save for later.
3. In a large, non-stick skillet, melt the butter over medium-high heat. Put in wings and brown for 3-4 minutes, turning once. Lastly, put in the cherry tomatoes, salt, and chili powder. Stir thoroughly and remove from the heat.
4. Serve instantly.

Nutritional Info: (Calories 478 | Total Fats 39.9g | Net Carbs: 3.1g | Protein 25.5g | Fiber: 1g)

Italian Chicken Thighs

Aggregate Time to Prepare: 25 Minutes

Yield: 6 Servings

Ingredients:

- 1 cup Chicken Broth
- 1 Onion, chopped
- 1 tbsp. Olive Oil
- 1 tbsp. Tomato Paste
- 3 Garlic Cloves, minced
- 6 Chicken Thighs
- ¼ cup Parsley
- ½ cup Basil

- ½ cup Olives
- ½ pound Cremini Mushrooms, sliced
- cups Cherry Tomatoes

How to Cook:

1. Heat the olive oil in your Instant Pot using the "Sauté" mode.
2. Sear the chicken until golden. Save for later.
3. Put in mushrooms and onions and cook for a few minutes.
4. Put in garlic and cook for 30 seconds.
5. Stir in the rest of the ingredients including the chicken, and shut and secure the lid.
6. Switch the Instant Pot to "High" and cook for 10 minutes.
7. Release the pressure using the quick release method.
8. Your dish is ready! Have fun!

Nutritional Info: (Calories 245| Total Fats 25g | Net Carbs 7g | Protein 35g |Fiber: 3g)

Italian Duck with Spinach

Aggregate Time to Prepare: **40 Minutes**

Yield: **6 Servings**

Ingredients:

- 1 cup Spinach, chopped
- 2 pound Duck Breasts, halved
- 2 tsp minced Garlic
- ½ cup Chicken Stock
- ½ cup chopped Sun-Dried Tomatoes
- ½ cup grated Parmesan Cheese

- ½ tbsp. Italian Seasoning
- ¾ cup Heavy Cream
- Salt and Pepper, to taste

How to Cook:

1. Mix together the oil, garlic, Italian seasoning, and some salt and pepper.
2. Rub this mixture into the meat.
3. Put the duck in the Instant Pot and cook using the "Sauté" mode until golden on all sides.
4. Put in the stock, shut and secure the lid, and switch your instant pot to "Manual" mode and cook for 4 minutes.
5. Push CANCEL and release the pressure using the quick release method.
6. Stir in the rest of the ingredients, lock the lid once again, and cook on HIGH for 5 additional minutes.
7. Depressurize quickly and serve
8. Have fun!

Nutritional Info: (Calories 455| Total Fats 26g | Net Carbs 1g | Protein 57g |Fiber: 2g)

Jalapeno Chicken

Aggregate Time to Prepare: 30 Minutes

Yield: 5 Servings

Ingredients:

- 1 chili pepper, chopped
- 1 large onion, chopped
- 1 tbsp swerve
- 2 tbsp extra virgin olive oil
- 3 jalapeno peppers, chopped
- 3 tbsp fish sauce
- 5 chicken thighs, skin on
- 5 cups chicken stock
- ¼ cup bean sprouts
- ¾ cup cauliflower, chopped into florets

Spices:

- 1 ½ tsp salt
- 1 tsp dried thyme
- 1 tsp peppercorn
- 3 bay leaves

How to Cook:

1. Mix all ingredients in the instant pot and stir thoroughly. Shut and secure the lid and set the steam release handle to the "Sealing" position.
2. Push the "Poultry" button and turn the timer to 20 minutes on high heat.
3. When finished, depressurize using the natural release method and open the lid. Take the meat out of the bones and stir thoroughly again.
4. Serve with some grated Parmesan cheese.

Nutritional Info: (Calories 358 | Total Fats: 11.9g | Net Carbs: 4.4g | Protein: 55g | Fiber: 1.4g)

Keto Piccata

Aggregate Time to Prepare: 45 Minutes

Yield: 4 Servings

Ingredients:

- 1 cup chicken broth
- 2 cups button mushrooms, sliced
- 2 tbsp brined capers, drained
- 2 tbsp butter
- 4 chicken breast, boneless and skinless
- ¼ cup apple cider vinegar

Spices:

- 2 tbsp flat-leaf parsley, chopped
- ½ tsp black pepper, freshly ground
- ½ tsp salt

How to Cook:

1. Thoroughly wash the meat under cold running water and rub with salt and pepper.
2. Turn on your Instant Pot and Switch your Instant Pot to "'Sauté" mode. Oil-coat the inner pot with butter and heat up. Put in the readied chicken and briefly brown on all sides, for 2-3 minutes.
3. Push the "Cancel" button and pour in the broth. Shut and secure the lid and switch to "Manual' mode. Turn the timer to 15 minutes on high pressure.
4. When finished, depressurize using the quick release method and open the lid.

5. Remove the chicken from the pot and move to a deep container. Cover with the lid and or a large piece of aluminium foil and save for later.
6. Remove the broth from the instant pot and Switch your Instant Pot to "'Sauté" mode. Put in the apple cider vinegar, the rest of the butter, capers, and parsley. Stir thoroughly and put in mushrooms. Cook until mushrooms soften.
7. Lastly, put in chicken and stir thoroughly. Serve instantly.

Nutritional Info:(Calories 414 | Total Fats: 13.1g | Net Carbs: 1.1g | Protein: 68.1g |Fiber: 0.4g)

Leftover Chicken with Broccoli and Parmesan

Aggregate Time to Prepare: 10 Minutes

Yield: 4 Servings

Ingredients:

- ½ cup Heavy Cream
- 1 cup Chicken Broth
- 1/3 cup grated Parmesan Cheese
- 2 cups Broccoli Florets
- 3 cups cooked and shredded Chicken
- Salt and Pepper, to taste

How to Cook:

1. Mix the broth, broccoli, and chicken, in the Instant Pot.
2. Shut and secure the lid and cook on HIGH for 2 minutes.

3. Release the pressure using the quick release method and mix in the rest of the ingredients.
4. Set the Instant Pot to sauté and cook for 2 additional minutes.
5. Your dish is ready! Have fun!

Nutritional Info: (Calories 354| Total Fats 24g | Net Carbs: 4g | Protein 33g |Fiber: 1.6g)

Lemon Herb Wings

Aggregate Time to Prepare: **30Minutes**

Yield: 2 Servings

Ingredients:

- 1 cup chicken broth
- 2 garlic cloves, minced
- 3 tbsp olive oil
- 4 chicken wings, whole
- ½ lemon, sliced
- ½ onion, chopped

Spices:

- 1 tsp pink Himalayan salt
- 2 rosemary sprigs, whole
- ½ black pepper, freshly ground

How to Cook:

1. Rub the wings with olive oil and drizzle with salt and pepper. Save for later.
2. Turn on your Instant Pot and Switch your Instant Pot to "'Sauté" mode. Heat the inner pot and put in

wings. Brown on both sides for 3-4 minutes. Take out of the pot and save for later.
3. After that put in onions and garlic. Stir thoroughly and cook until translucent. Pour in the broth and put in wings along with lemon slices and rosemary sprigs.
4. Shut and secure the lid and set the steam release handle. Cook for 15 minutes on high pressure.
5. When finished, release the pressure using the quick release method and open the lid. Remove the wings from the pot and serve with fresh vegetables.

Nutritional Info:(Calories 495 | Total Fats: 33.7g | Net Carbs: 3.3g | Protein: 46.9g |Fiber:0.7g)

Lemongrass and Spinach Turkey Soup

Aggregate Time to Prepare: 30 Minutes

Yield: 2 Servings

Ingredients:

- 1 cup Spinach, chopped
- 1 Garlic Clove, minced
- 1 Lemongrass, chopped
- 1 Red Onion, diced
- 1 tsp Coconut Oil
- 1 tsp ground Ginger
- 2 tbsp. chopped Coriander
- 2 tbsp. Lime Juice
- 8 ounces cooked and shredded Turkey Meat
- ¼ cup Coconut Milk
- ½ cup Chicken Stock
- Salt and Pepper, to taste

How to Cook:

1. Melt the coconut oil in your Instant Pot using the "Sauté" mode.
2. Put in onions and cook for 3 minutes.
3. Put in garlic and ginger and cook for one additional minute.
4. Put in stock, coconut milk, and lemongrass.
5. Shut and secure the lid and switch your instant pot to "Soup" mode and cook for 10 minutes.
6. Release the pressure using the quick release method and put in mix in the rest of the ingredients, except the lime juice.
7. Shut and secure the lid and cook on HIGH for 3 additional minutes.
8. Allow the pressure to drop on its own.
9. Serve drizzled with lime juice and have fun!

Nutritional Info: (Calories 327| Total Fats 15.4g | Net Carbs 6.8g | Protein 35.8g |Fiber: 3.4g)

Lime and Salsa Chicken with Cauliflower Rice

Aggregate Time to Prepare: **35 Minutes**

Yield: 4 Servings

Ingredients:

- 2 Chicken Breasts
- 2 cups riced Cauliflower
- 3 tbsp. Olive Oil
- ¼ cup Lime Juice
- ½ cup Mexican Cheese Blend
- ½ cup Salsa
- ½ cup Tomato Sauce

- ½ tsp Garlic Powder
- Salt and Pepper, to taste

How to Cook:

1. Mix all of the ingredients, except the cauliflower and cheese, in your Instant Pot.
2. Shut and secure the lid and set the MANUAL cooking mode.
3. Switch the Instant Pot to "High" and cook for 12 minutes.
4. Release the pressure using the quick release method and put in mix in the rice and cheese.
5. Cook for 5 additional minutes.
6. Release the pressure using the quick release method.
7. Your dish is ready! Have fun!

Nutritional Info: (Calories 280| Total Fats 16g | Net Carbs 5g | Protein 19g |Fiber: 0.8g)

Marinara and Cheese Stewed Chicken

Aggregate Time to Prepare: 25 Minutes

Yield: 6 Servings

Ingredients:

- 1 ½ pounds Chicken Meat (boneless thighs or breasts), cubed
- 15 ounces Chicken Broth
- 15 ounces Keto Marinara Sauce
- 8 ounces Cheese (Monterey Jack or Cheddar), shredded
- Salt and Pepper, to taste

How to Cook:

1. Combine everything in the Instant Pot.
2. Cover and lock the lid.
3. switch your Instant pot to "Manual" mode and cook on HIGH for 15 minutes.
4. Release the pressure using the quick release method.
5. Your dish is ready! Have fun!

Nutritional Info: (Calories 270| Total Fats 17g | Net Carbs 2g | Protein 21.5g |Fiber: 3g)

Masala Chicken Curry

Aggregate Time to Prepare: **60 Minutes**

Yield: **5 Servings**

Ingredients:

- 1 cup cauliflower, chopped into florets
- 1 large onion, thinly sliced
- 1 large tomato, roughly chopped
- 2 garlic cloves, crushed
- 2 lbs chicken wings
- 4 tbsp butter (can be replaced with ghee)
- 5 cups chicken stock

Spices:

- 1 tbsp cayenne pepper
- 1 tsp white pepper, freshly ground
- 2 tbsp coriander powder
- 2 tsp garam masala
- 2 tsp ginger powder
- 2 tsp salt
- 2 tsp turmeric powder
- 4 tbsp fresh parsley, thinly sliced

How to Cook:

1. Oil-coat the inner pot with butter and Switch your Instant Pot to "'Sauté" mode. Heat up and put in onions and garlic. Stir-fry for 3-4 minutes and then put in tomato. Carry on cooking until tomato has completely softened.
2. Put in chicken wings and season with spices. Cook for an additional 5 minutes, turning the wings several times.
3. Lastly, pour in the stock and put in the rest of the ingredients. Shut and secure the lid and set the steam release handle.
4. Switch your Instant Pot to "Manual" mode and turn the timer to 40 minutes on high pressure.
5. When finished, depressurize using the natural release method and open the lid. Stir thoroughly again and serve.

Nutritional Info:(Calories 391| Total Fats 15.4g | Net Carbs: 4.8g | Protein: 54.5g |Fiber: 1.6g)

Mexican Chicken Soup

Aggregate Time to Prepare: **15 Minutes**

Yield: 8 Servings

Ingredients:

- 1 cup Celery Root, diced
- 1 tbsp. Cumin
- 1 tsp Garlic Powder
- 1 tsp Onion Powder
- 1/3 cup Salsa
- 2 cups cooked and shredded Chicken

- 4 ounces canned and chopped Green Chilies
- 8 cups Chicken Broth
- ½ cup chopped Cilantro
- ½ cup chopped Scallions
- ½ tsp minced Habanero
- Salt and Pepper, to taste

How to Cook:

1. Put all of the ingredients in the Instant Pot.
2. Stir to mix and season with some salt and pepper.
3. Shut and secure the lid and choose the SOUP mode.
4. Cook for 10 minutes.
5. Allow the pressure to drop on its own.
6. Your dish is ready! Have fun!

Nutritional Info: (Calories 100| Total Fats 4g | Net Carbs 3g | Protein 11g |Fiber: 0.5g)

Moroccan Risotto

Aggregate Time to Prepare: **35Minutes**

Yield: 2 Servings

Ingredients:

- 1 lb chicken breast, boneless and skinless, chop into bite-sized pieces
- 1 spring onion, thinly sliced
- 2 cups cauliflower, chopped into florets
- 2 cups chicken stock
- 3 tbsp olive oil

Spices:

- 1 pinch saffron

- 1 tsp fresh oregano
- 1 tsp turmeric powder
- 2 tsp salt
- ½ tsp white pepper

How to Cook:

1. Wash thoroughly the meat and pat dry with a kitchen paper. Save for later.
2. Turn on your Instant Pot and Switch your Instant Pot to "'Sauté" mode. Heat the inner pot and put in olive oil and onions. Briefly cook, for 3-4 minutes.
3. After that put in the rest of the ingredients and stir thoroughly. Shut and secure the lid and close the steam release handle. Switch your Instant Pot to "Manual" mode. Turn the timer to 15 minutes.
4. When you hear the end signal, depressurize using the natural release method and open the lid.
5. Move the mixture to a large platter and chop the cauliflower into small piece.
6. Drizzle with some more saffron and serve instantly.

Nutritional Info:(Calories 476 | Total Fats: 27.3g | Net Carbs: 3.9g | Protein: 50.9g |Fiber: 2.7g)

Mozzarella and Tomato Chicken

Aggregate Time to Prepare: 35 Minutes

Yield: 4 Servings

Ingredients:

- ¼ Salt
- ¼ tsp Pepper
- 1 cup grated Mozzarella Cheese

- 1 cup Water
- 1 tbsp. Olive Oil
- 1 tsp minced Garlic
- 14 ounces canned crushed Tomatoes
- 4 Chicken Breasts, skinless and boneless

How to Cook:

1. Sprinkle the chicken with some salt and pepper.
2. Switch the Instant Pot to "Sauté" mode and heat the oil.
3. Cook the chicken for a few minutes, or until it becomes golden brown.
4. Move to a plate.
5. Put in garlic to the pot and cook for a minute.
6. Stir in the tomatoes and water.
7. Return the chicken to the pot and shut and secure the lid.
8. Switch the Instant Pot to "High" and cook for 5 minutes.
9. Release the pressure using the quick release method.
10. Set to "Sauté" mode and put in the mozzarella.
11. Cook for a few additional minutes.
12. Your dish is ready! Have fun!

Nutritional Info: (Calories 415| Total Fats 26g | Net Carbs 5.6g | Protein 42g |Fiber: 3.2g)

Mughlai Almond Chicken

Aggregate Time to Prepare: 25 Minutes

Yield: 6 Servings

Ingredients:

- 1 cup heavy cream

- 1 medium-sized onion, chopped
- 1 tbsp olive oil
- 2 lbs chicken breasts, skinless and boneless
- 3 garlic cloves, peeled
- ½ cup toasted almonds

Spices:

- 1 bay leaf
- 1 small cinnamon stick
- 1 tbsp fresh ginger, grated
- 1 tsp coriander powder
- 1 tsp garam masala powder
- 1 tsp red pepper flakes
- 2 cardamom pods

How to Cook:

1. Mix garlic, almonds, and ginger in a food processor. Put in 2 tablespoons of water and pulse until mixed and creamy. Save for later,
2. Turn on the Instant Pot and coat the stainless steel insert with olive oil. Put in chicken breasts and cook for 3-4 minutes on each side, or until lightly browned.
3. After that, put in all the rest of the spice and cook for 2-3 minutes more, stirring continuously.
4. Put in onions and heavy cream. Stir thoroughly and securely lock the lid.
5. Close the steam release handle and push the "Manual" button. Turn the timer to 8 minues and cook on "High" pressure.
6. When you hear the cooker's end signal. Depressurize naturally.
7. Open the pot and move all to a serving dish.
8. Have fun!

Nutritional Info:(Calories 439 | Total Fats 25.1g | Net Carbs: 4.1g | Protein: 48.4g | Fiber: 2g)

Orange-Flavored Duck

Aggregate Time to Prepare: 75 Minutes

Yield: 4 Servings

Ingredients:

- ½ cup Fresh Orange Juice
- ½ tbsp. diced Lemongrass
- 1 ½ cups Water
- 1 tsp Orange Zest
- 2 Chilies, chopped
- 2 Duck Breasts, halved
- 2 Duck Legs, halved
- 2 tbsp. Fish Sauce
- 2 tsp ground Ginger
- 8 Spring Onions, chopped

How to Cook:

1. Coat your IO with cooking spray and set it to "Sauté" mode.
2. Put in the duck and cook until brown on all sides.
3. Put in garlic and ginger and cook for 1 minute.
4. Stir in the rest of the ingredients and shut and secure the lid.
5. Switch the Instant Pot to "High" and cook for 10 minutes.
6. Release the pressure using the quick release method.
7. Serve the duck drizzled with the sauce.

Nutritional Info: (Calories 400| Total Fats 25g | Net Carbs 4.5g | Protein 45g |Fiber: 0.7g)

Parmesan Chicken Wings

Aggregate Time to Prepare: 45 Minutes

Yield: 4 Servings

Ingredients:

- 1 cup chicken broth
- 1 cup heavy cream
- 1 red bell pepper, sliced
- 1 yellow bell pepper, sliced
- 2 tbsp butter
- 2 tbsp olive oil
- 3 garlic cloves, crushed
- 4 chicken wings, whole
- ½ cup parmesan cheese
- ½ onion, thinly sliced

Spices:

- 1 ½ tsp Italian seasoning
- 1 tsp salt
- ½ tsp garlic powder
- ½ tsp pepper, ground

How to Cook:

1. Turn on your Instant Pot and Switch your Instant Pot to "'Sauté" mode. Oil-coat the inner pot with oil and heat up.

2. Put in the wings and brown for 4 minutes on both sides. Take out of the pot and save for later.
3. After that the bell peppers, onions, and garlic. Stir thoroughly and continue to cook for 5 minutes, stirring intermittently.
4. Put in the wings and stir thoroughly. Pour in the broth and drizzle with salt, pepper, Italian seasoning, and garlic powder.
5. Shut and secure the lid and set the steam release handle to the "Sealing" position.
6. Switch your Instant Pot to "Manual" mode and turn the timer to 12 minutes on high pressure.
7. When finished, depressurize using the natural release method for 10 minutes and then move the pressure valve to the "Venting" position.
8. Cautiously open the lid and Switch your Instant Pot to "'Sauté" mode again.
9. Stir in the butter and allow it to melt. After that put in heavy cream and Parmesan.
10. Stir thoroughly and cook for 3-4 minutes.
11. When finished, push the "Cancel" button and serve instantly.

Nutritional Info: (Calories 434 | Total Fats: 28.6g | Net Carbs: 6.6g | Protein: 36.8g | Fiber: 1.1g)

Pina Colada Chicken

Aggregate Time to Prepare: **35 Minutes**

Yield: **4 Servings**

Ingredients:

- 1 cup Pineapple Chunks
- ½ cup chopped Green Onion

- ½ cup Coconut Cream
- 2 tbsp. Coconut Aminos
- Pinch of Cinnamon
- Pinch of Sea Salt
- pounds Chicken, cubed

How to Cook:

1. Put everything, except the green onions, in the Instant Pot.
2. Shut and secure the lid and switch your instant pot to "Poultry" mode.
3. Cook for 15 minutes.
4. Depressurize quickly.
5. Serve garnished with green onions.
6. Have fun!

Nutritional Info: (Calories 530| Total Fats 24g | Net Carbs 7g | Protein 60g |Fiber: 2g)

Pollo en Salsa Roja

Aggregate Time to Prepare: 20 Minutes

Yield: 8 Servings

Ingredients:

- 1 small Onion (diced)
- 1 tbsp. Salt
- 14 oz. Diced Tomatoes (can)
- 1½ tbsp. Chili Powder
- 1½ tbsp. Cumin
- 2 lbs. Chicken Thighs (boneless, skinless, chop into 1-inch chunks)
- 2 oz. Pickled Jalapenos

- 2 tbsp. Olive Oil
- 3 cloves Garlic (minced)
- 5 oz. Tomato Paste

How to Cook:

1. In a container place cumin, chili and salt, and mix. Put in chicken and mix thoroughly to coat.
2. Switch your Instant Pot to "Sauté" mode and pour in olive oil. Put in chicken and cook for 5 minutes while intermittently stirring.
3. Put in all other ingredients and stir to mix.
4. Shut and secure the lid, and turn the timer and cook for 15 minutes at high pressure.
5. When finished allow the pressure to be released naturally for 10 minutes and then quick release it.
6. Serve warm.

Nutritional Info: (Calories: 299 | Total Fats: 22g | Net Carbs: 3g | Proteins: 19g | Fibers: 1g)

Roast Goose

Aggregate Time to Prepare: **40 Minutes**

Yield: **5 Servings**

Ingredients:

- 1 cup onions, thinly sliced
- 2 cups chicken stock
- 2 garlic cloves, crushed
- 2 lbs. goose fillets, sliced into one-inch thick slices
- 4 tbsp. butter

Spices:

- 1 tsp dried thyme
- 1 tsp sea salt
- 2 bay leaves
- ¼ tsp white pepper

How to Cook:

1. Thoroughly wash the meat under cold running water and liberally drizzle with salt and white pepper. Put at the bottom of your instant pot and put in bay leaves, and dried thyme. Pour in two cups of water and shut and secure the lid. Set the steam release handle and push the 'Meat' button.
2. When your instant pot sounds the end signal, release the pressure using the quick release method and open the lid. Take the meat out of the pot along with the liquid.
3. Put in butter and push the 'Sauté' button. Allow it to melt and put in onions and garlic. Stir-fry for 3-4 minutes. Put in fillets, one at the time and brown on both sides for 2 minutes.
4. Take out of the pot and serve.

Nutritional Info: (Calories 441 | Total Fats 22.9g | Net Carbs: 2.4g | Protein 53.2g | Fiber: 0.5g)

Roasted Chicken

Aggregate Time to Prepare: 40-45 Minutes

Yield: 6 Servings

Ingredients:

- 1 tbsp. Coconut Oil
- 1 tsp Dried Thyme

- 1 tsp Paprika
- 1 whole Chicken (cca 4 lbs.)
- 1½ cup Chicken Bone Broth
- 2 tbsp. Lemon Juice
- 6 cloves Garlic (peeled)
- ¼ tsp Ground Black Pepper
- ½ tsp Sea Salt

How to Cook:

1. In a container mix together the paprika, thyme, salt and pepper.
2. Coat the outside and inside of the bird with seasonings mixture.
3. Set the Instant Pot on "Sauté" and put into it coconut oil. Leave it to warm up for about 2 minutes.
4. Put the bird in with breast side down, and cook with the lid removed for 6 minutes, until nicely browned.
5. Turn over the bird and put into Instant Pot broth, lemon juice and garlic.
6. Shut and secure the lid and turn the timer and cook for 25 minutes at high pressure.
7. When finished allow the Instant Pot to naturally release the pressure.
8. Remove the chicken and allow it to rest covered with a kitchen towel for 5-10 minutes before carving.

Nutritional Info: (Calories: 688 | Total Fats: 50g | Net Carbs: 3g | Proteins: 54g | Fibers: 0.23g)

Rosemary Chicken with Bacon

Aggregate Time to Prepare: 60 Minutes

Yield: 6 Servings

Ingredients:

- 2 lbs. chicken breast, boneless and skinless, sliced into 1-inch thick slices
- 6 bacon slices
- 8 garlic cloves

Spices:

- 1 teaspoon rosemary
- 2 tbsp. oil
- 3 cups chicken broth
- ¼ tsp freshly ground black pepper
- ½ tsp Himalayan salt

How to Cook:

1. Oil-coat the bottom of your stainless steel insert with oil. Put in bacon and season with salt. Push "Sautée" button. Cook for 3 minutes.
2. In the mean time, place the meat in a separate dish. Using a sharp knife, make 8 incisions into the meat and place a garlic clove in each. Rub the meat with spices and move to the pot.
3. Push "Cancel" button and pour in the chicken broth. Shut and secure the lid and set the steam release handle. Set the "Manual" mode for 25 minutes.
4. When finished, push "Cancel" button and perform a natural pressure release.
5. Serve warm.

Nutritional Info: (Calories 441 | Total Fats 23.3g | Net Carbs: 2g | Protein 52.3g | Fiber: 0.2g)

Salsa Verde Chicken

Aggregate Time to Prepare: 30 Minutes

Yield: 6 Servings

Ingredients:

- ¼ tsp Garlic Powder
- ¼ tsp Pepper
- 1 tsp Cumin
- 1 tsp Salt
- 16 ounces Salsa Verde
- 2 ½ pounds Chicken Breasts
- Pinch of Paprika

How to Cook:

1. Mix together the salsa and spices in the Instant Pot.
2. Put in the chicken.
3. Close the Instant Pot's lid and switch your Instant pot to "Manual" mode.
4. Cook for 25 minutes on HIGH.
5. Release the pressure using the quick release method.
6. Your dish is ready! Have fun!

Nutritional Info: (Calories 340| Total Fats 6.8g | Net Carbs: 5g | Protein 55g |Fiber: 1g)

Savory Turkey Breast

Aggregate Time to Prepare: 60 Minutes

Yield: 4 Servings

Ingredients:

- 1 ½ cup chicken stock

- 1 red bell pepper, thinly sliced
- 1 small onion, thinly sliced
- 2 garlic cloves, crushed
- 2 lbs turkey breast, chopped into bite-sized pieces
- 3 tbsp olive oil
- 4 tbsp apple cider vinegar
- 4 tbsp soy sauce

Spices:

- 1 tsp red pepper flakes
- 2 tsp pink Himalayan salt
- ½ tsp white pepper, ground

How to Cook:

1. Thoroughly wash the meat under cold running water and place on a cutting board. Using a sharp knife, chop into bite-sized pieces and move to a container.
2. In a medium-sized container, mix together chicken stock, soy sauce, and olive oil. Mix until completely mixed and drizzle the meat with this mixture. Allow it to sit in the fridge for 15-20 minutes.
3. Turn on your Instant Pot and Switch your Instant Pot to "'Sauté" mode. Oil-coat the inner pot with some oil and heat up. Put in onions, bell peppers, and garlic. Stir thoroughly and cook for 4-5 minutes, stirring intermittently.
4. After that remove the meat from the fridge and move to the pot. Stir thoroughly and continue to cook for 7-8 minutes.
5. Lastly, put in the rest of the ingredients and stir thoroughly. Push the "Cancel" button and shut and secure the lid.

6. Make sure the steam release handle is on the "Sealing" position and switch to "Manual' mode. Turn the timer to 15 minutes on high pressure.
7. When finished, release the pressure using the quick release method and open the lid. Stir thoroughly and serve instantly.

Nutritional Info: (Calories 360 | Total Fats: 14.6g | Net Carbs: 13.5g | Protein: 40.6g | Fiber: 2.1g)

Sesame Ginger Chicken

Aggregate Time to Prepare: **15 Minutes**

Yield: **6 Servings**

Ingredients:

- 1 tbsp. Agave
- 1 tbsp. Garlic (minced)
- 1 tbsp. Ginger (minced)
- 1 tbsp. Rice Vinegar
- 1 tbsp. Sesame Oil
- 1½ lbs. Chicken Thighs (boneless, skinless and chop into 2-inch chunks)
- 2 tbsp. Soy Sauce

How to Cook:

1. Combine all ingredients in an oven-safe container with a lid, which fits into the Instant Pot, and then close it.
2. Pour 2 cups of water in the Instant Pot then put in a steamer insert and the container on it.
3. Shut and secure the lid, and turn the timer and cook for 10 minutes at high pressure.

4. When finished allow the pressure to be released naturally and then quick release it.
5. Remove the container and remove the lid it.
6. Shred the chicken and mix thoroughly. Serve warm.

Nutritional Info: (Calories: 286 | Total Fats: 21g | Net Carbs: 3g | Proteins: 19g | Fibers: 0g)

Shredded Chicken Breasts

Aggregate Time to Prepare: 10 Minutes

Yield: 20 Servings

Ingredients:

- 1 cup Chicken Broth
- 1 tbsp. Italian seasoning
- 4 lbs. Chicken breasts
- ½ tsp Ground Black pepper
- ½ tsp Sea Salt

How to Cook:

1. Put the chicken breast in a container and put in the seasoning to it. Toss to coat thoroughly.
2. Move the chicken in the Instant Pot and pour chicken broth around it.
3. Shut and secure the lid, and set manually cooking time to 8 minutes at high pressure if each breast is 8 oz. or smaller. If breast are larger than 8 oz. put in 1 minute for each 2 oz. extra.
4. When finished allow the pressure to naturally release.
5. Open the Instant Pot and shred the breasts using a fork. Stir the shreds to reabsorb released juices and serve.

Nutritional Info: (Calories: 176 | Total Fats: 7g | Net Carbs: 0g | Proteins: 27g | Fibers: 03g)

Shredded Chicken with Shiitake

Aggregate Time to Prepare: 30Minutes

Yield: 5 Servings

Ingredients:

- 1 ½ cup chicken stock
- 1 lb chicken breast, boneless and skinless
- 1 spring onion, thinly sliced
- 1 tbsp light soy sauce
- 2 tbsp butter
- 2 tbsp dark soy sauce
- 2 tsp rice vinegar
- 4 tbsp sesame oil
- 6 shiitake mushrooms
- ½ tsp stevia powder

Spices:

- 1 tbsp fresh ginger, grated
- ½ tsp chili flakes
- ½ tsp pepper, freshly ground

How to Cook:

1. In a small container, whisk together oil, dark soy sauce, light soy sauce, stevia powder, rice vinegar, ginger, chili flakes, and pepper. If you want, you can also put in some salt and save for later.
2. Thoroughly wash the meat and place on a cutting board. Chop into smaller pieces and place at the

bottom of your instant pot. Put in spring onions and pour in the stock.
3. Shut and secure the lid and set the steam release handle to the "Sealing" position. Push the "Poultry" button and cook for 10 minutes.
4. When your instant pot sounds the end signal, depressurize using the quick release method and open the lid. Remove the chicken from the pot and place in a deep container. Drizzle with the readied soy mixture and Shred using two forks. Save for later.
5. Remove the rest of the stock from the pot and Switch your Instant Pot to "'Sauté" mode. Oil-coat the inner pot with butter and heat up.
6. Put in shiitake and briefly cook – for 3-4 minutes, stirring continuously.
7. After that put in the meat and stir thoroughly. Cook for an additional 5 minutes.
8. When finished, take out of the pot and serve instantly.

Nutritional Info:(Calories 299 | Total Fats: 18.1g | Net Carbs: 11.3g | Protein: 21.7g | Fiber: 2g)

Simple Chicken Vindaloo

Aggregate Time to Prepare: 20 Minutes

Yield: 4 Servings

Ingredients:

- 1 cup chicken broth
- 1 tbsp apple cider vinegar
- 2 medium-sized onions, chopped
- 2 tbsp butter
- 3 lbs chicken thighs, skinless

- 3 small green chili peppers, chopped
- 4 garlic cloves, minced

Spices:

- 1 tsp black peppercorns, whole
- 1 tsp mustard seeds
- 1 tsp salt
- ½ tsp coriander seeds
- ½ tsp cumin seeds
- ½ tsp turmeric powder

How to Cook:

1. Turn on the Instant Pot and push the "Sauté" button. Melt the butter in the stainless steel insert and put in all spices. Fry for 3 minutes, stirring continuously.
2. Remove the seeds from the pot and move to a food processor. Put in garlic and apple cider vinegar. Pulse until thoroughly mixed. Line the chicken thighs with this paste and save for later.
3. After that, put in onions and green chili peppers to the pot. Cook for 3-4 minutes, or until the onions translucent. Put in chicken thighs and cook for 2 minutes on each side.
4. Pour in the chicken broth and securely lock the lid.
5. Close the steam release handle and push the "Manual" button. Turn the timer to 5 minutes and cook on "High" pressure.
6. When you hear the cooker's end signal, release the pressure using the quick release method and turn off the pot.
7. Move the chicken to a serving plate and serve instantly.

Nutritional Info:(Calories 528 | Total Fats 21.7g | Net Carbs: 6.1g | Protein: 70.8g |Fiber: 0.5g)

Simple Frozen Chicken Breasts

Aggregate Time to Prepare: 35 Minutes

Yield: 6 Servings

Ingredients:

- 1 cup Chicken Broth
- 1 cup Water
- 4 Chicken Breasts, frozen
- Salt and Pepper, to taste

How to Cook:

1. Put everything in the Instant Pot and season with some salt and pepper.
2. Close and lock the lid.
3. Switch the Instant Pot to "Manual" mode and cook for 25 minutes.
4. Release the pressure using the quick release method.
5. Your dish is ready! Have fun!

Nutritional Info: (Calories 270| Total Fats 11g | Net Carbs 6g | Protein 28g |Fiber: 0g)

Simple Turkey Stew

Aggregate Time to Prepare: 30 Minutes

Yield: 5 Servings

Ingredients:

- ¾ cup heavy cream
- 1 onion, thinly sliced
- 2 celery stalks, chopped

- 2 cups cherry tomatoes, chopped
- 2 lbs turkey breast, chopped into smaller pieces
- 4 cups chicken broth
- 4 tbsp butter

Spices:

- 1 tsp dried thyme
- 1 tsp peppercorn
- 2 tsp salt

How to Cook:

1. Mix the ingredients in the instant pot and shut and secure the lid.
2. Make sure the steam release handle is on the "Sealing" position and push the "Stew" button. Turn the timer to 20 minutes on high heat.
3. When finished, depressurize using the natural release method and open the lid. Chill for some time and mix in some sour cream.
4. Serve instantly.

Nutritional Info: (Calories 386 | Total Fats: 20.1g | Net Carbs: 11.5g | Protein: 36.2g | Fiber: 2.4g).

Smoked Slow-Cooked Turkey

Aggregate Time to Prepare: **4 hours and 15 minutes** | *Yield:* 4 Servings

Ingredients:

- 1 ½ pounds Turkey Breast
- 1 cup Chicken Stock
- 1 tbsp. Dijon Mustard
- 1 tsp Liquid Smoke

- 1 tsp minced Garlic
- 2 tbsp. Sweetener
- 2 tsp Smoked Paprika
- 4 tbsp. Olive Oil
- Salt and Pepper, to taste

How to Cook:

1. Switch the Instant Pot to "Sauté" mode and heat the oil.
2. Put in turkey and cook it on all sides, until brown.
3. Mix half of the stock with the rest of the ingredients and pour this mixture over the turkey.
4. Shut and secure the lid and switch your Instant Pot to "Slow Cook" mode.
5. Cook for 2 hours.
6. Release the pressure using the quick release method and pour the rest of the broth over.
7. Shut and secure the lid and slow cook for additional 2 hours.
8. Depressurize quickly.
9. Let sit for a few minutes prior to serving.
10. Have fun!

Nutritional Info: (Calories 400| Total Fats 30g | Net Carbs 2g | Protein 39g |Fiber: 0.5g)

Soft and Juicy Chicken

Aggregate Time to Prepare: 50 Minutes

Yield: 10 Servings

Ingredients:

- ¼ tsp Pepper

- ½ tsp Salt
- 1 ½ cups Chicken Stock
- 1 3-4 pound Chicken
- 1 tbsp. Coconut Oil
- 1 tsp Onion Powder
- 1 tsp Paprika
- 2 Garlic Cloves, peeled
- 2 tbsp. Lemon Juice

How to Cook:

1. Mix all of the spices in a small container.
2. Massage the mixture onto the chicken.
3. Melt the coconut oil in your Instant Pot using the "Sauté" mode.
4. Put in the chicken and cook until browned on all sides.
5. Pour the stock and lemon juice over.
6. Put in the garlic cloves.
7. Close and switch your instant pot to "Manual" mode and cook for 25 minutes.
8. Allow the pressure to drop naturally.
9. Your dish is ready! Have fun!

Nutritional Info: (Calories 270| Total Fats 20g | Net Carbs: 3g | Protein 22g |Fiber: 1.3g)

Spiced Turkey

Aggregate Time to Prepare: 70 Minutes

Yield: 4 Servings

Ingredients:

- 2 garlic cloves, crushed

- 2 lbs. turkey breast, boneless
- 3 cups chicken broth
- ¼ cup oil

Spices:

- 1 tsp dried basil
- 3 whole cloves
- ½ tsp stevia powder

How to Cook:

1. Thoroughly wash the meat under cold running water and pat dry with a kitchen towel. Put in a large Ziploc bag and put in basil, cloves, and oil. Pour in one cup of chicken broth and seal the bag. Shake thoroughly and refrigerate for 20 minutes.
2. Oil-coat the stainless steel insert with some oil and put in garlic. Stir-fry for 2 minutes. Take the turkey out of the fridge and place in the pot along with 2 tablespoons of the marinade and the rest of the chicken broth.
3. Shut and secure the lid and set the steam release handle. Push the 'Manual' button and turn the timer to 25 minutes.
4. When finished, depressurize using the natural release method.

Nutritional Info: (Calories 313 | Total Fats 20.3g | Net Carbs: 8.7g | Protein 20.3g | Fiber: 1.8g)

Spicy Chicken Stew

Aggregate Time to Prepare: **35Minutes**

Yield: **4 Servings**

Ingredients:

- 1 cup cabbage, shredded
- 1 cup Greek yogurt, plain
- 1 onion, thinly sliced
- 10 oz chicken breast, chopped into bite-sized pieces
- 2 celery stalks, thinly sliced
- 2 garlic cloves, whole
- 4 cups chicken stock
- 4 tbsp olive oil

Spices:

- 1 tbsp cayenne pepper
- 1 tsp cumin powder
- 1 tsp garlic powder
- 1 tsp salt
- 2 tbsp chili powder
- ½ tsp coriander powder

How to Cook:

1. Thoroughly wash the meat and place on a large cutting board. Cut into bite-sized pieces and place in a deep container. Sprinkle with spices coat thoroughly. Save for later.
2. Turn on your Instant Pot and Switch your Instant Pot to "'Sauté" mode. Heat up the olive oil and put in onions, garlic, and celery stalk. Stir thoroughly and cook for 5-6 minutes, stirring continuously.
3. After that put in the meat and continue to cook for 3-4 minutes.
4. Lastly, put in shredded cabbage and stir thoroughly. Pour in the stock and shut and secure the lid.
5. Make sure the steam release handle is on the "Sealing" position and switch to "Manual' mode.
6. Turn the timer to 13 minutes on high pressure.

7. When finished, depressurize using the natural release method for 10-15 minutes and then open the lid. Chill for some time and mix in Greek yogurt prior to serving.

Nutritional Info: (Calories 293 | Total Fats: 17.8g | Net Carbs: 5.9g | Protein: 26.9g | Fiber: 1.2g).

Spicy Chicken with Lime

Aggregate Time to Prepare: 25 Minutes

Yield: 4 Servings

Ingredients:

- 1 cup plain yogurt, full-fat
- 1 medium-sized tomato
- 2 lbs chicken fillets, chop into bite-sized pieces
- 2 small onions, chopped
- 2 tbsp olive oil
- 3 tsp lime juice, freshly squeezed

Spices:

- 1 tsp chili powder
- 1 tsp mustard seeds, ground
- 1 tsp salt
- ¼ tsp nutmeg, ground
- ½ tsp garam masala powder

How to Cook:

1. Thoroughly wash the fillets under running water and pat dry with a kitchen paper. Cut into bite-sized pieces and save for later.

2. Turn on the Instant Pot and coat the stainless steel insert with olive oil. Push the "Sauté" button and put in onions. Drizzle with chili powder, garam masala, mustard seeds, salt, and nutmeg. Stir-fry for 5 minutes, or until onions translucent.
3. Put in diced tomato and cook for 2 additional minutes.
4. After that put in, chicken and pour in 1 cup of water. Shut and secure the lid and close the steam release handle.
5. Push the "Manual" button and turn the timer to 10 minutes. Cook on "High" pressure.
6. When finished, depressurize using the natural release method and open the lid. Stir in the yogurt instantly and push the "Sauté" button. Cook for 4-5 minutes more and turn off the pot.
7. Move to a serving dish and drizzle with lime juice.
8. If you want, you can also drizzle with some thinly sliced green onions and garnish with lime slices prior to serving.

Nutritional Info:(Calories 561 | Total Fats 25.1g | Net Carbs: 8.2g | Protein: 70.1g |Fiber: 1.5g)

Spicy Keto Pasta

Aggregate Time to Prepare: 40Minutes

Yield: 5 Servings

Ingredients:

- 1 ½ cups cottage cheese
- 1 chili pepper, thinly sliced
- 1 cup canned tomatoes, sugar-free
- 1 lb cauliflower, chopped into florets
- 2 cups chicken broth
- 3 tbsp butter
- 7 oz ground turkey
- ¼ cup sour cream
- ½ cup onions, thinly sliced

Spices:

- 1 tsp chili powder
- 1 tsp salt
- 2 tbsp fresh parsley, thinly sliced
- ½ tsp chili flakes

How to Cook:

1. Thoroughly wash the cauliflower and drain in a large sieve. Put in the instant pot and pour in the broth. Drizzle with salt and shut and secure the lid.
2. Make sure the steam release handle is on the "Sealing" position and switch to "Manual' mode. Turn the timer to 6 minutes on high pressure.
3. When finished, depressurize using the quick release method and open the lid. Remove the cauliflower from the pot and drain. Chill for some time and then chop into smaller florets. Save for later.

4. After that remove the broth from the pot and Switch your Instant Pot to "'Sauté" mode. Oil-coat the stainless steel insert with butter and heat up. Put in onions and briefly cook, for two minutes.
5. Then put in ground beef and season with salt, chili flakes, and chili pepper. Cook for 10 minutes, stirring continuously.
6. After that put in the chili pepper and continue to cook for an additional 2-3 minutes.
7. Lastly, put in tomatoes and stir thoroughly. Cook until most of the liquid from tomatoes evaporates.
8. Stir in the cheese and cauliflower. Push the "Cancel" button and take out of the pot.
9. Move to serving containers and spread on top sour cream prior to serving. Drizzle with parsley and have fun!

Nutritional Info: (Calories 274 | Total Fats: 15.7g | Net Carbs: 7.7g | Protein: 24.8g | Fiber: 3g)

Spicy Shredded Chicken with Asparagus

Aggregate Time to Prepare: **50 Minutes**

Yield: 2 Servings

Ingredients:

- 1 lb chicken breast, chopped into bite-sized pieces
- 1 tbsp lime juice
- 2 cups vegetable stock
- 2 green chili peppers, chopped
- 3 large asparagus, chopped
- 3 tbsp butter
- 4 garlic cloves, crushed
- ½ cup fresh parsley, thinly sliced
- ½ onion, thinly sliced

Spices:

- 1 tsp chili powder
- 1 tsp salt
- 2 tsp smoked paprika

How to Cook:

1. Turn on your Instant Pot and Switch your Instant Pot to "'Sauté" mode. Oil-coat the inner pot with butter and put in chicken in several batches. Cook for 4-5 minutes, stirring continuously.
2. Take out of the pot and save for later.
3. After that put in onions and cook until translucent. Then, put in garlic and continue to cook for an additional minute.
4. Lastly, put in chili peppers and asparagus. Carry on cooking for 2 minutes.

5. Put in the meat and season with salt, chili, and smoked paprika. Drizzle with lime juice and pour in the broth. Stir thoroughly and shut and secure the lid.
6. Make sure the steam release handle is on the "Sealing" position and switch to "Manual' mode. Cook for 17 minutes on high pressure.
7. When finished, depressurize using the quick release method and open the lid. Take the meat out of the pot and place on a large cutting board.
8. Using two forks shred the meat and place back in the pot.
9. Drizzle with parsley and serve.

Nutritional Info: (Calories 449 | Total Fats: 23.3g | Net Carbs: 5.3g | Protein: 50.4g | Fiber: 2.4g)

Summer Chicken Cacciatore

Aggregate Time to Prepare: **15Minutes**

Yield: **6 Servings**

Ingredients:

- 1 ½ tbsp. Olive Oil
- 1 Bell Pepper, diced
- 1 can pitted Black Olives
- 2 cans crushed Tomatoes
- 2 Shallots, chopped
- 2 tbsp. Tomato Paste
- 2 tsp minced Garlic
- 6 Chicken Breasts
- 8 ounces Mushrooms, sliced
- ½ cup Chicken Broth
- Salt and Pepper, to taste

How to Cook:

1. Heat the oil in you Instant Pot using the "Sauté" mode.
2. Put in the shallots and bell pepper and cook for a few minutes, until soft.
3. Put in mushrooms and cook for 2 minutes.
4. Stir in the garlic and cook for 30 more seconds.
5. Pour the broth and tomato paste over and arrange the chicken inside.
6. Spread on top the tomatoes and olives.
7. Sprinkle with some salt and pepper and shut and secure the lid.
8. Switch the Instant Pot to "Manual" mode and cook for 10 minutes.
9. Depressurize quickly.
10. Your dish is ready! Have fun!

Nutritional Info: (Calories 320| Total Fats 30g | Net Carbs 5g | Protein 29g |Fiber: 2g)

Sweet Chicken Leg Stew

Aggregate Time to Prepare: **35 Minutes**

Yield: **4 Servings**

Ingredients:

- 1 cup diced canned tomatoes, sugar-free
- 1 onion, thinly sliced
- 1 red bell pepper, chopped
- 2 cups mushrooms, sliced
- 2 garlic cloves, whole
- 2 tbsp balsamic vinegar
- 3 celery stalks, chopped

- 3 tbsp avocado oil
- 3 tbsp fresh parsley
- 4 cups chicken broth
- 4 medium-sized chicken legs

Spices:

- 1 tsp black pepper
- 1 tsp dried oregano
- 1 tsp fresh thyme, thinly sliced
- 1 tsp salt
- 2 tbsp fresh basil, thinly sliced
- ¼ tsp red pepper flakes

How to Cook:

1. Put the meat in a large colander and rinse thoroughly under cold running water. Dry with a kitchen paper and rub each piece with salt and pepper.
2. Turn on your Instant Pot and Switch your Instant Pot to "'Sauté" mode. Heat the oil and put in chicken thighs in a couple of batches. Brown on all sides, for 3-4 minutes. Take out of the pot and save for later.
3. In a deep container, mix onions, peppers, celery stalks, and mushrooms. Sprinkle with some salt and mix thoroughly. Move the mixture to the pot and cook for 4-5 minutes, stirring continuously.
4. After that put in garlic and season with oregano and red pepper flakes. Toss thoroughly to mix and continue to cook for an additional 2 minutes.
5. Lastly, put in the rest of the ingredients and shut and secure the lid.
6. Make sure the steam release handle is on the "Sealing" position and switch to "Manual' mode. Turn the timer to 15 minutes on high pressure.

7. When finished, release the pressure using the quick release method and open the lid.
8. Serve instantly.

Nutritional Info: (Calories 267 | Total Fats: 6.5g | Net Carbs: 7.7g | Protein: 40.2g | Fiber: 2.7g)

Sweet Chicken Salad with Cheese

Aggregate Time to Prepare: 20 Minutes

Yield: 4 Servings

Ingredients:

- 1 large piece of chicken breast, whole
- 2 cups arugula, torn
- 2 tbsp rice vinegar
- 2 tsp apple cider vinegar
- 4 cherry tomatoes
- 4 tbsp butter
- ¼ cup chicken stock
- ¼ cup cottage cheese
- ½ cup soy sauce

Spices:

- 1 tbsp dried thyme
- 1 tsp salt

How to Cook:

1. Turn on your Instant Pot and set the trivet at the bottom of the stainless steel insert. Pour in 1 cup of water and place the meat on top.

2. Shut and secure the lid and set the steam release handle and switch to "Manual' mode. Turn the timer to 15 minutes.
3. When finished, release the pressure using the quick release method and open the lid. Take the meat out of the pot along with the rest of the liquid. Switch your Instant Pot to "Sauté' mode and coat the inner pot with butter. Heat up.
4. In the mean time, chop the chicken into bite-sized pieces and put into the pot. Pour in the soy sauce, rice vinegar, and chicken stock. Stir thoroughly and simmer for 10-12 minutes.
5. When finished, take out of the pot ensuring to reserve the liquid.
6. Put arugula in a deep container. Put in tomato and cottage cheese and toss to mix. Drizzle with salt and dried thyme. Drizzle with apple cider vinegar.
7. Spread on top the meat and drizzle with some of the reserved liquid.

Nutritional Info: (Calories 275 | Total Fats: 14.4g | Net Carbs: 6.3g | Protein: 27.2g | Fiber: 1.9g).

Sweet Chicken Thighs

Aggregate Time to Prepare: 50 Minutes

Yield: 5 Servings

Ingredients:

- 2 chili peppers, chopped
- 2 cups beef broth
- 2 cups cherry tomatoes, chopped
- 3 tbsp soy sauce
- 5 tbsp ghee

- lbs chicken thighs, whole

Spices:

- 1 salt
- 1 tbsp fresh ginger, grated
- 3 tsp stevia powder
- ½ tsp cinnamon

How to Cook:

1. Turn on your Instant Pot and Switch your Instant Pot to "'Sauté" mode. Oil-coat the inner pot with ghee and put in cherry tomatoes. Drizzle with salt, stevia, cinnamon, and ginger. Stir thoroughly and cook for 10-12 minutes, or until tomatoes soften.
2. Stir in the soy sauce and chili peppers. Carry on cooking for an additional 5 minutes.
3. After that put in chicken thighs and pour in the broth.
4. Shut and secure the lid and set the steam release handle to the "Sealing" position and switch to "Manual' mode.
5. Turn the timer to 20 minutes.
6. When finished, depressurize using the quick release method and open the lid. Stir thoroughly and serve instantly.

Nutritional Info:(Calories 491| Total Fats: 26.9g | Net Carbs: 3g | Protein: 55.7g |Fiber: 1g)

Sweet Chicken Wings

Aggregate Time to Prepare: **75 Minutes**

Yield: **3 Servings**

Ingredients:

- 1 cup chicken broth
- 1 tbsp. butter
- 2 tbsp. oil
- 6 chicken wings, whole

Spices:

- 1 tsp salt
- 1 tsp stevia powder
- ¼ tsp cinnamon
- ½ tsp black pepper, ground

How to Cook:

1. Thoroughly wash the meat and pat dry with some kitchen paper.
2. Turn on the Instant Pot and heat up the oil in the stainless steel insert. Briefly brown for 3 minutes on each side. Take the meat out of the pot and put in butter.
3. When butter melts, put in chicken broth, stevia, and cinnamon. Cook for one minute and then push "Cancel" button.
4. Put in the meat and shut and secure the lid. Set the steam release handle and push the "Meat" mode. Turn the timer to 40 minutes.
5. When your instant pot sounds the end signal, push "Cancel" button and open the lid.
6. Serve warm.

Nutritional Info: (Calories 309 | Total Fats 23.4g | Net Carbs: 1.7g | Protein 23g | Fiber: 0.2g)

Sweet Chili Thighs with Cloves

Aggregate Time to Prepare: **70 Minutes**

Yield: 6 Servings

Ingredients:

- 1 cup coconut milk, unsweetened
- 2 green chilies, whole
- 2 large onions, sliced
- 2 lbs chicken thighs, whole
- 3 cups chicken broth
- 3 tbsp butter
- cups cauliflower, chop into florets

Spices:

- 1 tbsp chili powder
- 1 tsp curry powder
- 2 tbsp cloves
- 2 tbsp cumin seeds
- 2 tsp stevia powder
- tbsp lime juice

How to Cook:

1. Wash thoroughly the meat and place in the instant pot along with chilies and onions. Pour in the broth and drizzle with spices.
2. Shut and secure the lid and set the stem release handle to the "Sealing" position. Switch your Instant Pot to "Manual" mode and turn the timer to 35 minutes on high pressure.
3. When finished, release the pressure using the quick release method and open the lid. Remove the meat along with the liquid and move to a large container.
4. After that, pour in one cup of water in the stainless steel insert and set the steam basket. Put the cauliflower in the basket and shut and secure the lid.

Switch your Instant Pot to "Manual" mode and cook for 15 minutes on high pressure.

5. When finished release the pressure using the quick release method and open the lid. Cautiously remove the cauliflower and move to a food processor. Process until smooth.
6. Pour the meat and the stock back in the pot and Switch your Instant Pot to "'Sauté" mode. Pour in the coconut milk and mix in the cauliflower puree.
7. Tenderly simmer for 10 minutes.
8. When finished, mix in butter and serve instantly.

Nutritional Info:(Calories 478 | Total Fats: 27.3g | Net Carbs: 6.4g | Protein: 48.4g |Fiber: 2.8g)

Sweet Orange Turkey Legs

Aggregate Time to Prepare: 35 Minutes

Yield: 4 Servings

Ingredients:

- 1 cup chicken stock
- 1 small green chili, chopped
- 2 green onions, thinly sliced
- 2 tbsp chili sauce, sugar-free
- 2 tbsp orange zest
- 2 tbsp stevia powder
- 2 turkey legs, whole
- ½ cup soy sauce

Spices:

- 1 tsp sea salt
- ½ tsp white pepper, freshly ground

How to Cook:

1. Put turkey legs in a colander and rinse thoroughly. Drain and move to a clean work surface. Drizzle with salt and pepper and move to the pot. Pour in the stock and shut and secure the lid.
2. Make sure the steam release handle is on the "Sealing" position and switch to "Manual' mode. Turn the timer to 15 minutes on high pressure.
3. When finished, release the pressure using the quick release method and open the lid.
4. After that Switch your Instant Pot to "'Sauté" mode and pour in the soy sauce and chili sauce. Stir thoroughly and put in onions, green chili, stevia, and orange zest.
5. Carry on cooking for 10 minutes, stirring intermittently and turning the meat once.
6. Push the "Cancel" button and serve.

Nutritional Info: (Calories 325 | Total Fats: 9g | Net Carbs: 3.7g | Protein: 53.7g | Fiber: 0.8g)

Sweet Turkey Drumsticks

Aggregate Time to Prepare: **40 Minutes**

Yield: 5 Servings

Ingredients:

- ½ cup Soy Sauce
- ½ cup Water
- ½ tsp Garlic Powder
- 1 tsp Pepper
- 1 tsp Salt
- 2 tsp Sweetener
- 6 Turkey Drumsticks

How to Cook:

1. Mix the spices in a small container.
2. Massage the mixture onto the turkey.
3. Mix the water and soy sauce in the Instant Pot.
4. Put in the drumsticks and shut and secure the lid.
5. Switch the Instant Pot to "Manual" mode and cook for 25 minutes.
6. Depressurize for 10 minutes.
7. Your dish is ready! Have fun!

Nutritional Info: (Calories 209| Total Fats 15g | Net Carbs 3g | Protein 34g |Fiber: 0g)

Taco Chicken

Aggregate Time to Prepare: 35 Minutes

Yield: 16 Servings

Ingredients:

- 1 ½ pounds Chicken Breasts
- 1 ounce Taco Seasoning
- ½ cup mild Salsa Verde
- ½ cup Red Salsa

How to Cook:

1. Mix all of the ingredients in the Instant Pot.
2. Shut and secure the lid and cook on HIGH for 25 minutes.
3. Release the pressure using the quick release method.
4. Grab two forks and shred the chicken inside the pot.
5. Stir to coat thoroughly.
6. Your dish is ready! Have fun!

Nutritional Info: (Calories 240| Total Fats 9g | Net Carbs 5g | Protein 33g |Fiber: 0g)

Tandoori Chicken

Aggregate Time to Prepare: **20 Minutes**

Yield: **4 Servings**

Ingredients:

- 1 cup chicken broth
- 1 cup plain yogurt, full-fat
- 1 tbsp olive oil
- 2 garlic cloves, minced
- 2 lbs chicken breasts, skinless and boneless
- 2 tbsp lime juice, freshly squeezed

Spices:

- 1 tsp coriander powder
- 1 tsp cumin seeds
- 1 tsp garam masala powder
- 1 tsp onion powder
- 1 tsp salt
- 1 tsp smoked paprika, ground
- 2 tsp fresh ginger, grated

How to Cook:

1. Thoroughly wash the meat under cold running water and pat dry with a kitchen paper. Cut into thin slices and save for later.
2. In a large container, mix yogurt, lime juice, crushed garlic, and all spices. Combine until thoroughly mixed and put in chicken breasts. Coat thoroughly with marinade and refrigerate for 20 minutes.
3. Turn on the Instant Pot and push the "Sauté" button. Melt the butter in th stainless steel insert and put in

chicken. Cook for 3 minutes on each side, or until lightly browned.
4. After that, pour in the broth and securely lock the lid.
5. Set the steam release handle and push the "Manual" button. Turn the timer to 8 minutes and cook on "High" pressure.
6. When you hear the cooker's end signal, perform a quick release of the pressure by moving the valve to the "Venting" position.
7. Open the pot and move the chicken to a serving plate.
8. If you want, you can also serve with mashed cauliflower and drizzle with some thinly sliced green onions prior to serving.
9. Have fun!

Nutritional Info:(Calories 528 | Total Fats 21.7g | Net Carbs: 6.1g | Protein: 70.8g |Fiber: 0.5g)

Tarragon Chicken with Mushrooms

Aggregate Time to Prepare: 25 Minutes

Yield: 4 Servings

Ingredients:

- 1 tbsp. chopped Tarragon
- 1 tsp Dijon Mustard
- 2 cups Button Mushrooms, sliced
- 2/2 cup Water
- 4 Chicken Thighs
- ¼ cup Ghee
- ½ tsp Garlic Powder
- Salt and Pepper, to taste

How to Cook:

1. Sprinkle the chicken with salt, pepper, and garlic powder.
2. Melt the ghee in your Instant Pot using the "Sauté" mode.
3. Put in chicken and cook until browned on all sides. Move to a plate.
4. Put in the mushrooms, tarragon, and Dijon and cook for 2 minutes.
5. Return the thighs to the pot and pour the water over.
6. Shut and secure the lid and cook on HIGH for 10 minutes.
7. Release the pressure using the quick release method.
8. Your dish is ready! Have fun!

Nutritional Info: (Calories 263| Total Fats 17g | Net Carbs 2.2g | Protein 18g |Fiber: 3.7g)

Teriyaki Chicken Thighs with Peppers

Aggregate Time to Prepare: 70 Minutes

Yield: 5 Servings

Ingredients:

- 1 cup chicken stock
- 2 lbs chicken thighs, skin on
- 2 red bell peppers, sliced
- 2 tbsp sesame oil
- 2 tbsp swerve
- 5 garlic cloves, crushed
- 5 tbsp soy sauce
- ¼ cup rice vinegar

Spices:

- 1 tsp chili flakes
- 1 tsp salt
- ½ tsp white pepper, freshly ground

How to Cook:

1. First, you will have to prepare the teriyaki mixture. In a small container, whisk together sesame oil, rice vinegar, swerve, soy sauce, chili flakes, pepper, and salt. Save for later.
2. Thoroughly wash the thighs and pat dry with a kitchen towel. Liberally brush with the teriyaki mixture and place in a large Ziploc bag. Seal the bag and refrigerate for 20 minutes.
3. In the mean time, plug in the instant pot and Switch your Instant Pot to "'Sauté" mode. Oil-coat the inner pot with some oil and put in garlic. Briefly cook, for

one minute, and then put in sliced pepper. Carry on cooking for an additional couple of minutes.
4. After that put in the meat along with teriyaki and briefly brown – for 2-3 minutes on each side. You will probably have to do this in several batches.
5. After that pour in the stock and shut and secure the lid. Set the steam release handle and switch to "Manual' mode. Turn the timer to 15 minutes on high pressure.
6. When finished, depressurize using the natural release method and open the lid.
7. In the mean time, preheat the oven to 400 degrees. Line a large baking sheet with some parchment paper and put in the thighs.
8. Cook for 15 minutes, turning once.

Nutritional Info:(Calories 431 | Total Fats: 19.1g | Net Carbs: 5.2g | Protein: 54.3g |Fiber: 0.8g)

Thai Basil Goose Cubes

Aggregate Time to Prepare: 40 Minutes

Yield: 4 Servings

Ingredients:

- 1 ½ cup Water
- 1 tsp granulated Sweetener
- 1 tsp minced Ginger
- 2 cups cubed Goose Breasts
- 2 tbsp. Avocado Oil
- 2 tbsp. Fish Sauce
- 2 tbsp. minced Chilies
- 2 tsp minced Garlic

- ¼ cup chopped Basil Leaves
- Salt and Pepper, to taste

How to Cook:

1. Heat half of oil in the Instant Pot using the "Sauté" mode.
2. Put in goose and cook until golden.
3. Move to a baking dish.
4. Mix together the fish sauce, rest of the oil, ginger, chilies, garlic, and sweetener.
5. Pour over the goose.
6. Put in basil and season with some salt and pepper.
7. Pour the water into your Instant Pot and put the rack into the Instant Pot.
8. Lace the baking dish inside the Instant Pot and shut and secure the lid.
9. Switch the Instant Pot to "Manual" mode and cook for 10 minutes.
10. Release the pressure using the quick release method.
11. Your dish is ready! Have fun!

Nutritional Info: (Calories 192| Total Fats 9g | Net Carbs 1g | Protein 27g |Fiber: 1g)

Thyme Roasted Chicken with Dill

Aggregate Time to Prepare: **55 Minutes**

Yield: **8 Servings**

Ingredients:

- 1 cup apple cider vinegar
- 1 cup cranberries
- 1 whole chicken (approximately 4 lbs.)
- 3 cups chicken broth

- ¼ cup olive oil

Spices:

- 1 tbsp. fresh dill
- 1 tsp garlic powder
- 2 tbsp. fresh thyme, minced
- ¼ tsp red pepper flakes
- ¼ tsp stevia powder

How to Cook:

1. Thoroughly wash the chicken under cold running water and pat dry with some kitchen towel. Liberally brush with oil and drizzle with thyme, garlic powder, and pepper flakes. Put the butter in the stainless steel insert and push the 'Sauté' button to melt it. Tenderly place the chicken in the pot and briefly brown for 4-5 minutes.
2. After that, pour in the 2 cups of chicken broth and apple cider. Shut and secure the lid and set the steam release handle. Push the 'Manual' button and cook for 25 minutes on high pressure.
3. Depressurize naturally and open the lid. Remove the chicken from the pot and save for later.
4. In a small, heavy-bottomed pot, mix the rest of the broth with cranberries and stevia powder. Pour in 1 cup of the broth from the instant pot and bring it to a boil.
5. Cook for 10-15 minutes, stirring intermittently.
6. Fill the chicken's cavity with the sauce, fresh dill, and cool to room temperature prior to serving.

Nutritional Info: (Calories 433 | Total Fats 13.7g | Net Carbs: 4.7g | Protein 67.6g | Fiber: 0.5g)

Tikka Masala

Aggregate Time to Prepare: 25Minutes

Yield: 4 Servings

Ingredients:

- 1 cup tomatoes, roughly chopped
- 1 lb chicken breast, boneless and skinless
- 1 small onion, thinly sliced
- 3 tbsp butter
- 4 garlic cloves, crushed
- ½ cup coconut cream
- ½ cup yellow bell peppers, thinly sliced

Spices:

- 1 tbsp cayenne pepper
- 1 tsp cumin powder
- 1 tsp garam masala
- 1 tsp salt
- 2 tsp coriander powder
- 2 tsp fresh ginger, grated
- ½ tsp turmeric powder

How to Cook:

1. Turn on your Instant Pot and Switch your Instant Pot to "'Sauté" mode. Oil-coat the inner pot with butter and heat up.
2. Put in onions and peppers. Cook for 3-4 minutes, stirring continuously. After that put in garlic and season with all spices. Stir thoroughly and continue to cook for an additional minute.
3. Push the "Cancel" button and put in the chicken and tomatoes. Pour in the stock and shut and secure the

lid. Make sure the steam release handle is on the "Sealing" position and push the "Poultry" button. When finished, depressurize using the natural release method and open the lid.
4. Stir in the coconut cream and cool for some time. Separate the mixture among serving containers and serve.

Nutritional Info: (Calories 299 | Total Fats: 18.8g | Net Carbs: 5.4g | Protein: 25.8g | Fiber: 1.8g?

Turkey and Cauliflower Enchilada Casserole

Aggregate Time to Prepare: 25 Minutes

Yield: 6 Servings

Ingredients:

- 1 ½ cups Water
- 1 cup shredded Cheddar Cheese
- 2 cups cooked and shredded Turkey
- 20 ounces Cauliflower Florets, chopped
- 4 ounces Cream Cheese
- ¼ cup Sour Cream
- ½ cup Salsa Verde
- Salt and Pepper, to taste

How to Cook:

1. Pour the water into the Instant Pot and put the rack into the Instant Pot.
2. Mix all of the ingredients in an oil-coated baking dish.
3. Put the dish in the Instant Pot and shut and secure the lid.

4. Switch the Instant Pot to "High" and cook for 15 minutes.
5. Release the pressure using the quick release method.
6. Your dish is ready! Have fun!

Nutritional Info: (Calories 311| Total Fats 18g | Net Carbs 4g | Protein 33g |Fiber: 1.2g)

Turkey and Mushrooms in a Creamy Wine Sauce

Aggregate Time to Prepare: **45 Minutes**

Yield: 10 Servings

Ingredients:

- 1 ¼ pounds Turkey Breast
- 6 ounces White Button Mushrooms, sliced
- 1 tbsp. Arrowroot
- 1 Garlic Clove, minced
- 3 tbsp. minced Shallots
- 2 tbsp. Olive Oil
- ½ tsp Parsley
- 3 tbsp. Heavy Cream
- 1/3 cup White Wine
- 2/3 cup Chicken Stock

How to Cook:

1. Tie your Turkey every 2 inches, crosswise.
2. Switch the Instant Pot. to "Sauté" mode and heat the oil in it.
3. Put in the turkey and brown on all sides. Save for later.
4. Put in the shallots, mushrooms, garlic, and parsley, and cook for a few additional minutes.
5. Pour the broth over and return the turkey to the pot.
6. Switch the Instant Pot to "High" and cook for 15 minutes.
7. Release the pressure using the quick release method.
8. Move the turkey to a plate. Untie and cut it.
9. Mix the arrowroot and cram in the Instant Pot and cook until thickened.

10. Drizzle the sauce over the turkey.
11. Your dish is ready! Have fun!

Nutritional Info: (Calories 192| Total Fats 15g | Net Carbs: 4.5g | Protein 25g |Fiber: 1.5g)

Turkey Breast with Cranberries

Aggregate Time to Prepare: **55 Minutes**

Yield: **4 Servings**

Ingredients:

- 1 lb. turkey breast, boneless and skinless, sliced into half-inch thick slices
- 2 cups fresh cranberries
- 2 tbsp. olive oil
- 3 tbsp. butter
- ¼ cup apple cider vinegar

Spices:

- 1 tbsp. fresh rosemary, thinly sliced
- 1 tsp orange extract
- 1 tsp salt
- ¼ cup fresh parsley, chopped

How to Cook:

1. Thoroughly wash the breast and pat dry with a kitchen towel. Rub with oil, orange extract, and rosemary.
2. Oil-coat the bottom of your instant pot with butter and put in chicken breast. Pour in cider and put in cranberries and parsley. Pour in 1 cup of water (or chicken broth) and shut and secure the lid.

3. Push the 'Manual' button and turn the timer to 17 minutes.
4. In the mean time, preheat the oven to 400 degrees.
5. When your Instant Pot sounds the end signal, depressurize using the natural release method and open the lid. Move the chicken breast along with its sauce to an 8-inch baking pan and bake for 15-20 minutes, or until golden.
6. Serve instantly.

Nutritional Info: (Calories 287 | Total Fats 17.5g | Net Carbs: 7.3g | Protein 19.5g |Fiber: 2.6g)

Turkey Breast with Garlic Gravy

Aggregate Time to Prepare: 40 Minutes

Yield: 6 Servings

Ingredients:

- 1 celery stalk, thinly sliced
- 1 large onion, thinly sliced
- 2 cups chicken stock
- 3 garlic cloves, crushed
- 3 lbs turkey breast, boneless and skinless
- 4 tbsp butter

Spices:

- 1 sea salt
- 1 thyme sprig, whole
- 1 tsp onion powder
- ¼ smoked paprika
- ½ tsp garlic powder

How to Cook:

1. In a small container, mix salt, garlic powder, onion powder, and smoked paprika. Save for later.
2. Thoroughly wash the meat and place on a clean work surface. Using a sharp knife, cut each piece lengthwise to create a pocket. Stuff each with celery, garlic, and onions. Liberally run with spices and move to the pot.
3. Pour in the stock and put in thyme sprig. Shut and secure the lid and set the steam release handle to the "Sealing" position.
4. Switch your Instant Pot to "Manual" mode and turn the timer to 20 minutes on high pressure.

5. When finished, depressurize using the natural release method and open the lid. Stir in the butter and let it sit, covered, for some time prior to serving.

Nutritional Info: (Calories 320 | Total Fats: 11.7g | Net Carbs: 10.9g | Protein: 39.3g | Fiber: 1.8g).

Turkey Breast with Gorgonzola Sauce

Aggregate Time to Prepare: **45 Minutes**

Yield: 5 Servings

Ingredients:

- 1 ½ cup chicken broth
- 1 lb turkey breast, chopped into bite-sized pieces
- 2 cups heavy cream
- 2 tbsp butter
- 2 tbsp oil
- ¼ cup fresh parsley, thinly sliced
- ½ cup gorgonzola, chopped

Spices:

- 1 tsp dried thyme
- 1 tsp garlic powder
- ¼ tsp dried oregano
- ½ tsp onion powder

How to Cook:

1. Wash thoroughly the meat and pat dry with a kitchen towel. Put on a large cutting board and chop into bite-sized pieces. Move to a large container. Coat thoroughly with spices and save for later.

2. Turn on your Instant Pot and Switch your Instant Pot to "'Sauté'' mode. Oil-coat the inner pot with oil and put in the meat. Briefly cook for 4-5 minutes, stirring continuously and pour in the broth. Push the "Cancel" button and shut and secure the lid.
3. Make sure the steam release handle is on the "Sealing" position and switch to "Manual' mode. Cook for 13 minutes on high pressure.
4. When finished, depressurize using the natural release method for 10-15 minutes and then move the pressure valve to the "Venting" position to release any rest of the pressure.
5. Open the lid and remove any rest of the broth. Switch your Instant Pot to "Sauté' mode and put in butter.
6. Stir in heavy cream and gorgonzola. Sauté for about 2 minutes or until the cheese melts.
7. Drizzle with parsley and serve instantly.

Nutritional Info:(Calories 480 | Total Fats: 37.6g | Net Carbs: 2.3g | Protein: 32.9g |Fiber:0.6g)

Turkey Breast with Salsa Verde

Aggregate Time to Prepare: **35Minutes**

Yield: **4 Servings**

Ingredients:

- 1 onion, sliced
- 2 medium-sized turkey breast, chop in half
- 3 cups chicken broth

For the salsa verde:

- 1 cup tomatillos, chopped
- 1 green chili, thinly sliced

- 1 tsp onion powder
- 1 tsp salt
- 2 garlic cloves, crushed
- 3 tbsp olive oil
- ¼ cup fresh parsley, thinly sliced
- ¼ tsp chili powder

For the rub:

- 1 tsp chili powder
- 1 tsp onion powder
- 1 tsp salt
- 2 tsp garlic powder
- ½ tsp cumin powder

How to Cook:

1. In a small container, mix together chili powder, garlic powder, onion powder, salt, and cumin powder. Combine thoroughly and save for later.
2. Thoroughly wash the meat under cold running water and rub thoroughly with spices. Put at the bottom of the pot and pour in the chicken broth. Put in onions and shut and secure the lid.
3. Make sure the steam release handle is on the "Sealing" position and push the "Poultry" button. Turn the timer to 15 minutes on high pressure. When finished, depressurize using the natural release method and cautiously open the lid. Take the meat out of the pot and save for later.
4. Remove broth and Switch your Instant Pot to "'Sauté" mode. Oil-coat the inner pot with olive oil and heat up.
5. Put in green chili and garlic. Cook for 2-3 minutes and then put in tomatillos along with the rest of the ingredients for the salsa.

6. Pour in approximately 3 tablespoons of the broth and simmer for 10-12 minutes, stirring intermittently.
7. Push the "Cancel" button and remove the mixture from the pot. Move to a food processor and process until smooth.
8. Drizzle over the meat and serve.

Nutritional Info: (Calories 342 | Total Fats: 17.7g | Net Carbs: 5.5g | Protein: 37.8g | Fiber: 1.5g)

Turkey Burgers

Aggregate Time to Prepare: 20 Minutes

Yield: 4 Servings

Ingredients:

- 1 cup almond flour
- 1 cup sour cream
- 1 lb. ground turkey
- 1 small onion, thinly sliced
- 2 large eggs

Spices:

- 1 tbsp. dill, chopped
- ½ tsp black pepper
- ½ tsp salt

How to Cook:

1. In a large mixing container, mix all ingredients and mix thoroughly with your hands. Save for later.
2. Turn on the Instant Pot and pour in 1 cup of water. Save for later.

3. For the patties with the previously readied mixture. Line some parchment paper over an oven-safe dish and place the patties in it. Put the steamer rack in your instant pot and put the patties on top.
4. Shut and secure the lid and close the steam release handle.
5. Push the 'Manual' button and set the timer to 10 minutes on high pressure.
6. When finished, depressurize using the natural release method and serve.

Nutritional Info: (Calories 401 | Total Fats 23.6g | Net Carbs: 4.7g | Protein 39.9g | Fiber: 1.1g)

Turkey Cauliflower Curry

Aggregate Time to Prepare: 15 Minutes

Yield: 4 Servings

Ingredients:

- 1 cup cauliflower, chopped
- 1 cup tomatoes, diced
- 1 medium-sized green bell pepper, chopped
- 1 small red onion, diced
- 1 tbsp butter
- 2 cups chicken broth
- 2 garlic cloves, minced
- 2 lbs chicken fillets, chop into bite-sized pieces

Spices:

- 1 bay leaf
- 1 tsp curry powder
- 1 tsp salt

- 1 tsp smoked paprika, ground

How to Cook:

1. Turn on the Instant Pot and push the "Sauté" button. Melt the butter in the stainless steel insert and put in onions, garlic, bell pepper, and all the spices. Stir-fry for 3-4 minutes, or until the onions translucent.
2. Put in turkey pieces and cook for 5 minutes more, stirring intermittently.
3. After that, put in tomatoes and pour in the broth. Stir all thoroughly and shut and secure the lid.
4. Close the steam release handle and push the "Manual" button. Turn the timer to 8 minutes and cook on "High" pressure.
5. When finished, depressurize using the natural release method and open the pot.
6. Remove the bay leaf and move all to serving dish.
7. Have fun!

Nutritional Info:(Calories 512 | Total Fats 20.7g | Net Carbs: 6.1g | Protein: 69.7g |Fiber: 2.4g)

Turkey Keto Lasagna

Aggregate Time to Prepare: **25 Minutes**

Yield: 4 Servings

Ingredients:

- 1 ½ cups mozzarella
- 1 cup cherry tomatoes, chopped
- 1 cup heavy cream
- 1 lb ground turkey
- 1 small eggplant, chop lengthwise

- 2 cups cottage cheese
- 2 cups fresh spinach, thinly sliced
- 3 tbsp butter

Spices:

- 1 tsp Italian seasoning
- 1 tsp salt

How to Cook:

1. In a deep container, mix together spinach, cottage cheese, and mozzarella. Combine thoroughly and save for later.
2. Turn on your Instant Pot and Switch your Instant Pot to "'Sauté" mode. Oil-coat the inner pot with butter and put in cherry tomatoes. Sprinkle with salt and cook until completely tender. Push the "Cancel" button and remove tomatoes from the pot. Move to a container and save for later.
3. After that take a small, fitting baking pan and grease with some oil. Make a first layer with eggplants and then put in ground turkey meat. Spread on top the spinach mixture and make another layer of eggplants.
4. Sprinkle with Italian seasoning and then put in a layer of sautéed tomatoes. Drizzle with some more salt and loosely cover with aluminium foil.
5. After that, set the trivet at the bottom of the inner pot and pour in 1 cup of water.
6. Put the pan on top and shut and secure the lid. Make sure the steam release handle is on the "Sealing" position and switch to "Manual' mode.
7. Turn the timer to 15 minutes on high pressure.
8. When finished, depressurize using the quick release method and open the lid. Remove the pan from the instant pot and cool for some time.

9   Spread on top heavy cream and serve instantly.

Nutritional Info: (Calories 436 | Total Fats: 23.9g | Net Carbs: 7.6g | Protein: 43.5g | Fiber: 3.9g)

Turkey Leg with Garlic

Aggregate Time to Prepare: 55 Minutes

Yield: 1 Serving

Ingredients:

- 1 turkey leg
- 2 tbsp olive oil
- 3 cups chicken stock
- 3 tbsp light soy sauce
- 4 garlic cloves, crushed

Spices:

- 1 tbsp garlic paste
- 1 tsp salt
- 2 tsp dried thyme
- 2 tsp oregano, dried
- ¾ tsp white pepper, ground

How to Cook:

1. Mix together crushed garlic, garlic paste, oregano, thyme, salt, and pepper. Combine thoroughly and liberally rub over turkey leg. Tightly cover in a large piece of plastic foil and refrigerate for 30 minutes (up to an hour).
2. Remove from the fridge and place in the pot. Pour in the stock and shut and secure the lid. Make sure the steam release handle is on the "Sealing" position and switch to "Manual' mode.
3. Turn the timer to 15 minutes on high pressure.
4. When finished, depressurize using the quick release method and open the lid. Remove the leg along with the stock from the pot and save for later.

5. After that coat the inner pot with olive oil and Switch your Instant Pot to "'Sauté" mode. Put the leg back to the pot and pour in the soy sauce. Briefly brown for about 2 minutes on each side. Take out of the pot and serve.

Nutritional Info: (Calories 629 | Total Fats: 39.7g | Net Carbs: 9.6g | Protein: 62.2g | Fiber: 0.3g).

Turkey Meatballs in Sweet Sauce

Aggregate Time to Prepare: 35Minutes

Yield: 4 Servings

Ingredients:

- 1 lb ground turkey meat
- 5 tbsp almond flour
- 3 tbsp butter
- 3 large eggs
- 2 tbsp olive oil
- ¼ cup soy sauce
- ¼ tsp rice vinegar
- ½ cup chicken stock
- 1 tbsp sesame seeds

Spices:

- 1 tsp salt
- ½ tsp black pepper
- 2 tsp stevia powder
- ¼ tsp garlic powder

How to Cook:

1. In a large container, mix ground turkey with almond flour, olive oil, and eggs. Sprinkle with some salt and pepper. Combine thoroughly until completely mixed and shape balls –about 1-inch in diameter.
2. Turn on your Instant Pot and pour in 1 cup of water. Set the steam basket and place meatballs in it. Shut and secure the lid and set the steam release handle to the "Sealing" position. Switch your Instant Pot to "Manual" mode and cook for 10 minutes.
3. When you hear the end signal, depressurize using the quick release method and open the lid. Remove the basket from the pot and save for later.
4. Remove the rest of the water and Switch your Instant Pot to "'Sauté" mode. Put in butter and pour in the soy sauce, chicken stock and rice vinegar. Drizzle with sesame seeds and the rest of the spices. Stir thoroughly and put in meatballs. Cook for 3-4 minutes.
5. Take out of the pot and serve instantly.

Nutritional Info:(Calories 448 | Total Fats: 29.6g | Net Carbs: 2.4g | Protein: 41g |Fiber: 1.2g).

Turkey Meatballs in Tomato Sauce

Aggregate Time to Prepare: 20 Minutes

Yield: 4 Servings

Ingredients:

- 1 pound Ground Turkey
- ¼ cup Chicken Stock
- 1/3 cup Almond Flour
- 28 ounces canned and diced Tomatoes, undrained
- 1 tsp Basil

- ¼ Onion, diced
- 1 tsp minced Garlic
- 1 tsp Italian Seasoning
- Salt and Pepper, to taste

How to Cook:

1. Put the turkey, basil, onion, and almond flour in a container.
2. Sprinkle with some salt and pepper.
3. Combine with your hands and make meatballs out of the mixture.
4. Mix the rest of the ingredients in the Instant Pot.
5. Put the meatballs inside.
6. Switch the Instant Pot to "High" and cook for 10 minutes.
7. Release the pressure using the quick release method and serve.
8. Have fun!

Nutritional Info: (Calories 320| Total Fats 14g | Net Carbs: 4g | Protein 27g |Fiber: 1g)

Turkey Roast

Aggregate Time to Prepare: **45Minutes**

Yield: **4 Servings**

Ingredients:

- 1 small onion, thinly sliced
- 2 lbs turkey breast, chop into smaller pieces
- 2 tbsp swerve
- 3 cups chicken stock
- ¼ cup chili sauce, sugar-free

- ¼ cup soy sauce

Spices:

- 1 tsp salt
- ½ tsp black pepper, freshly ground

How to Cook:

1. In a large container, mix onions, swerve, stock, salt, pepper, soy sauce, and chili sauce. Combine until thoroughly mixed and save for later.
2. Thoroughly wash the turkey and pat dry using a kitchen paper. Save for later.
3. Turn on your Instant Pot and place the meat in the inner pot. our in the sauce mixture and securely lock the lid.
4. Adjust he steam release handle and push the "Manual' button. Turn the timer to 15 minutes and cook on high pressure.
5. When finished, depressurize using the natural release method for approximately 15 minutes.
6. In the mean time, preheat the oven to 425 degrees F. Line some parchment paper over a large baking sheet and save for later.
7. Cautiously open the cooker's lid and move the meat to the baking sheet. Slightly coat with the sauce from the pot and drizzle over the sheet.
8. Bake for 10-15 minutes.

Nutritional Info:(Calories 410 | Total Fats: 11.8g | Net Carbs: 3g | Protein: 68.2g |Fiber: 0.6g)

Turkey with Mushrooms

Aggregate Time to Prepare: **60 Minutes**

Yield: 3 Servings

Ingredients:

- 1 cup button mushrooms, chopped
- 1 medium-sized onion, chopped
- 1 tbsp balsamic vinegar
- 1 tbsp butter
- 2 lbs turkey breasts, skinless and boneless
- 3 cups chicken broth
- 3 garlic cloves, minced
- ½ cup olive oil

Spices:

- 1 bay leaf
- 1 tsp dried parsley, ground
- 1 tsp salt
- ½ tsp black pepper, ground
- ½ tsp dried rosemary, ground
- ½ tsp dried thyme, ground

How to Cook:

1. In a small container, mix olive oil, balsamic vinegar, salt, pepper, rosemary, thyme, and parsley. Combine until thoroughly mixed and save for later.
2. Thoroughly wash the meat under cold running water and pat dry with a kitchen paper. Cut into bite-sized pieces and place in a large Ziploc bag. Put in previously readied mixture and shake thoroughly to coat all the meat. Refrigerate for 20 minutes.
3. Turn on the Instant Pot and Switch your Instant Pot to "'Sauté" mode. Melt the butter in the stainless steel insert and put in mushrooms. Cook for 5 minutes, stirring intermittently.

4. After that, put in onions and garlic. Cook for 3-4 minutes, or until the onions translucent.
5. Lastly, put in meat and pour in the broth. Throw in the bay leaf and stir thoroughly. Shut and secure the lid.
6. Set the steam release handle and switch to "Manual' mode. Turn the timer to 40 minutes. Cook on "High" pressure.
7. When your instant pot sounds the end signal, release the pressure using the quick release method the pressure by moving the valve to the "Venting" position. Open the lid and move to a serving dish.
8. If you want, you can also drizzle with some fresh thyme prior to serving.

Nutritional Info:(Calories 297 | Total Fats 11.8g | Net Carbs: 9.9g | Protein: 34.7g |Fiber: 1.7g)

Turmeric Chicken

Aggregate Time to Prepare: **40 Minutes**

Yield: **4 Servings**

Ingredients:

- ¼ cup almonds, raw
- ¼ cup Greek yogurt
- 1 cup beef broth
- 1 cup cherry tomatoes
- 1 large onion, thinly sliced
- 3 tbsp ghee
- 4 garlic cloves, whole
- pieces of chicken breast, approximately 1 lb

Spices:

- ¼ cup coriander, thinly sliced
- ½ tsp ginger powder
- 3 tsp chili powder
- 5 cloves, whole
- tsp turmeric powder

How to Cook:

1. Turn on your Instant Pot and Switch your Instant Pot to "'Sauté" mode. Melt the ghee and put in onions and garlic. Stir thoroughly and cook for 3-4 minutes. After that put in cherry tomatoes and cloves. Carry on cooking for an additional 5 minutes.
2. In the mean time, rinse the meat and chop into bite-sized pieces. Drizzle with turmeric and put into the pot.
3. Briefly brows, stirring continuously and season with the rest of the spices. Cook for one minute. Take out of the pot and put in almonds. Cook until lightly toasted. If needed, put in some more ghee.
4. Put the chicken back to the pot and stir thoroughly. Pour in the broth and shut and secure the lid.
5. Make sure the steam release handle is on the "Sealing" position and switch to "Manual' mode.
6. Turn the timer to 15 minutes on high pressure.
7. When finished, depressurize using the quick release method and open the lid. Remove the chicken from the pot and chill for some time.
8. Spread on top Greek yogurt and serve.

Nutritional Info:(Calories 336| Total Fats: 16.7g | Net Carbs: 6.1g | Protein: 37.6g |Fiber: 2.1g)

White Chicken with Cauliflower

Aggregate Time to Prepare: 30 Minutes

Yield: 4 Servings

Ingredients:

- 1 Butter Stick
- 1 tbsp. chopped Basil
- 1 tsp minced Garlic
- 2 cups Cauliflower Florets
- 2 cups Heavy Cream
- 4 Chicken Breasts, cubed
- 8 ounces Cream Cheese

How to Cook:

1. Preheat the Instant Pot using the "Sauté" mode.
2. Melt the butter inside.
3. Mix together the cream cheese and heavy cream inside.
4. Stir in the rest of the ingredients and shut and secure the lid.
5. Switch the Instant Pot to "High" and cook for 15 minutes.
6. Release the pressure using the quick release method.
7. Your dish is ready! Have fun!

Nutritional Info: (Calories 700| Total Fats 40g | Net Carbs: 5g | Protein 70g |Fiber: 0.9g)

Worcestershire Belizean Chicken

Aggregate Time to Prepare: 95 Minutes

Yield: 8 Servings

Ingredients:

- 1 cup sliced Onions
- 1 tbsp. Coconut Oil
- 1 tbsp. Sweetener
- 1 tsp Cumin
- 1 tsp Oregano
- 2 cups Chicken Broth
- 2 tbsp. Recado Rojo
- 2 tbsp. White Vinegar
- 2 tsp minced Garlic
- 3 tbsp. Worcestershire Sauce
- 4 Whole Chicken Legs
- ½ tsp Pepper

How to Cook:

1. In a container, whisk together the Worcestershire, recado rojo, vinegar, pepper, oregano, sweetener, and cumin.
2. Put in the chicken legs, and rub to coat them thoroughly.
3. Cover the container and let marinate in the fridge for 60 minutes.
4. Melt the coconut oil in your Instant Pot using the "Sauté" mode.
5. Put in onions and cook for 2 minutes
6. Stir in the garlic and sauté for an additional minute.
7. Put in chicken and cook until browned on all sides.

8. Stir in the rest of the ingredients and shut and secure the lid.
9. Switch the Instant Pot to "High" and cook for 20 minutes.
10. Depressurize and serve.
11. Have fun!

Nutritional Info: (Calories 320| Total Fats 20g | Net Carbs 3g | Protein 28g |Fiber: 1g)

BONUS: Breakfast Recipes

It is said that Breakfast is the most important meal of the day. According to science, the jury is still undecided on that. What is a fact, however, that a breakfast rich in simple or fast digesting carbohydrates can increase the risk of metabolic syndrome.

Don't worry though. If you are following the ketogenic diet, you will never be eating enough simple carbohydrates to do any damage.

So, what are we waiting for? Let's dive right into the recipes!

Almond Bread in a Mug

Aggregate Time to Prepare: 25 Minutes

Yield: 3 Servings

Ingredients:

- ½ cup minced almonds
- 1 cup almond flour
- 1 tsp baking powder
- 2 large eggs, beaten
- 3 tbsp coconut oil, melted

Spices:

- ¼ tsp cinnamon, ground
- ½ tsp powdered stevia
- ½ tsp salt

How to Cook:

1. In a large mixing container, mix almond flour, baking powder, minced almonds, salt, cinnamon, and stevia. Stir with a kitchen spatula until thoroughly blended. Put in eggs and coconut oil. With a paddle attachment on, beat until all thoroughly mixed.
2. Pour the mixture into the oven-safe mugs, approximately 1/3 of a mug. Save for later.
3. Turn on the Instant Pot and pour 1 cup of water in the stainless steel insert. Place your trivet in the bottom of your instant pot and place the mugs on top. Cover with lid and close the steam release handle. Switch the Instant pot to "Manual" mode and turn the timer to 4 minutes. Cook on "High" pressure.
4. When finished, depressurize using the natural release method. Open the pot and let it chill for some time.
5. Using oven mitts cautiously move the mugs to a wire rack. Allow it to cool to room temperature before serving.

Nutritional Info: (Calories 362 | Total Fats 31.9g | Net Carbs: 4.8g | Protein 11.7g | Fiber: 4.6g)

Almond Flour Breakfast Bread

Aggregate Time to Prepare: **40 Minutes**

Yield: **15 Servings**

Ingredients:

- ¼ cup Whey Protein Powder
- ½ cup Oat Fiber
- ½ tsp Baking Soda
- 1 ½ cups Water
- 1 tbsp. Erythritol

- 1 tsp Xanthan Gum
- 2 ½ cups Almond Flour
- 2 tsp Baking Powder
- 4 Eggs
- 6 ounces Yogurt
- Pinch of Salt
- 6 tbsp. Butter, softened
- 6 tbsp. Milk

How to Cook:

1. Pour the water into the Instant Pot and put the trivet into the Instant Pot.
2. Mix the dry ingredients in one bow, and whisk the wet ones in another.
3. Tenderly mix the two mixtures.
4. Oil-coat loaf pan that can fit into the Instant Pot, with cooking spray.
5. Pour the batter into the loaf pan.
6. Put the pan inside the Instant Pot and shut and secure the lid.
7. Switch the Instant Pot to "High" and cook for 30 minutes.
8. Depressurize quickly.
9. Your dish is ready! Have fun!

Nutritional Info: (Calories 180| Total Fats 11 g | Net Carbs: 2.9 g | Protein 12 g |Fiber: 5.5g)

Almond Porridge

Aggregate Time to Prepare: **10 Minutes**

Yield: 2 Servings

Ingredients:

- 1 cup unsweetened almond milk
- 2 tbsp chia seeds
- 3 tbsp coconut oil
- 3 tbsp hemp seeds
- Fresh raspberries, optional for topping

Spices:

- ¼ tsp salt
- 1 tsp swerve
- 1 tsp vanilla extract

How to Cook:

1. Turn on your Instant Pot and coat the inner pot with coconut oil. Put in hemp seeds and chia seeds. Pour in ½ cup of water and Switch your Instant Pot to "'Sauté" mode. Cook for 5 minutes, stirring continuously.
2. After that pour in the almond milk and drizzle with salt, vanilla extract, and swerve. If you want, you can also put in a few drops of stevia extract. Stir thoroughly and cook for an additional 5 minutes.
3. When finished, push the "Cancel" button and move the porridge to a serving container. If you want, you can also place on top a couple of fresh raspberries and serve.

Nutritional Info: (Calories 380| Total Fats 37.4g | Net Carbs: 2.3g | Protein 11g |Fiber: 6.2g)

Asparagus with Cottage Cheese

Aggregate Time to Prepare: 25 Minutes

Yield: 2 Servings

Ingredients:

- 1 cup asparagus, trimmed and chopped
- 1 tbsp olive oil
- 4 large eggs, beaten
- ½ cup cottage cheese, crumbled
- 2 garlic cloves, thinly sliced
- 2 tbsp Greek yogurt, full-cream

Spices:

- 1 tsp salt
- ¼ tsp black pepper, ground
- ¼ tsp chili pepper, ground
- 2 tsp balsamic vinegar

How to Cook:

1. Thoroughly wash the asparagus under cold running water and trim off the woody ends. Cut into bite-sized pieces and save for later.
2. Turn on the Instant Pot and pour one cup of water in the stainless steel insert. Place your trivet in the bottom of your instant pot and place a steam basket on top. Put in the asparagus and drizzle with some salt. Shut and secure the lid and close the steam release handle.
3. Switch your instant pot to "Steam" mode and turn the timer to 10 minutes.
4. When finished, release the pressure using the quick release method and open the pot. Remove the steam

basket and water from the pot and wipe with a kitchen paper.

5. After that, put olive oil into the stainless steel insert and switch your instant pot to "Sauté" mode. Put in garlic and cook for 1 minute. Put in eggs, cheese, and yogurt. Drizzle with chili, salt, and pepper. Cook for 3-4 minutes, or until eggs are set. Turn off your Instant pot.
6. Move the asparagus to a serving plate and spread on top cheesy mixture.
7. Serve instantly.

Nutritional Info: (Calories 289 | Total Fats 18.6g | Net Carbs: 5.9g | Protein 24.1g |Fiber: 1.6g)

Avo Bacon Muffins

Aggregate Time to Prepare: **40 Minutes**

Yield: **16 Servings**

Ingredients:

- ¼ cup Flaxseed Meal
- ½ cup Almond Flour
- 1 ½ cups Coconut Milk
- 1 ½ cups Water
- 1 ½ tbsp. Lemon Juice
- 1 ½ tbsp. Phylum Husk Powder
- 1 tsp Baking Powder
- 1 tsp minced Garlic
- 1 tsp Onion Powder
- 1 tsp Oregano

- 1 tsp Salt
- 2 Avocados, diced
- 2 tbsp. Butter
- 3 Spring Onions, diced
- 4 ½ ounces grated Cheese
- 5 Bacon Slices, cooked and crumbled
- 5 Eggs, beaten
- Pinch of Pepper

How to Cook:

1. Pour the water into the Instant Pot and put the trivet into the Instant Pot.
2. Mix together the wet ingredients.
3. Gradually and tenderly, mix in the dry ingredients until smooth.
4. Stir in the avocado, bacon, onions, and cheese.
5. Separate the mixture into 16 small or medium muffin cups.
6. Put half of them inside your Instant Pot. Shut and secure the lid and cook on HIGH for 12 minutes.
7. Release the pressure using the quick release method.
8. Repeat the process one more time.
9. Your dish is ready! Have fun!

Nutritional Info: (Calories 144| Total Fats 11g | Net Carbs: 1.7g | Protein 6.2g |Fiber: 2.6g)

Avocado Chicken with Spinach

Aggregate Time to Prepare: 50 Minutes

Yield: 3 Servings

Ingredients:

- 1 cup avocado chunks
- 1 cup cottage cheese
- 1 cup fresh spinach, chopped
- 1 garlic clove, crushed
- 1 large leek, thinly sliced
- 1 small onion, thinly sliced
- 3 tbsp butter
- 7 oz boneless and skinless chicken breast, chopped into bite-sized pieces

Spices:

- ½ tsp dried rosemary
- 1 tsp salt

How to Cook:

1. Turn on your Instant Pot and Switch your Instant Pot to "'Sauté" mode. Oil-coat the inner pot with butter and heat up. Put in chicken and drizzle with salt. Cook for 12-15 minutes, stirring intermittently.
2. After that put in avocado and continue to cook for 5 minutes. If necessary, put in more olive oil.
3. Lastly, put in onions, garlic, and chopped leeks. Stir thoroughly and cook until completely soft.
4. Put in spinach and drizzle with rosemary. Press the "Cancel" button and cover with the lid. Allow it to sit for 10 minutes.
5. Take out of the pot and move to a deep container. Stir in the cottage cheese and serve instantly.

Nutritional Info:(Calories 382g | Total Fats 24.5g | Net Carbs: 5.8g | Protein 31.2g |Fiber: 4g)

Avocado Eggs Stir-Fry

Aggregate Time to Prepare: 15 Minutes

Yield: 2 Servings

Ingredients:

- 1 medium-sized avocado, pitted and cubed
- 1 tbsp butter
- 1 tsp olive oil
- 2 large eggs, beaten
- 2 tbsp green onions, thinly sliced

Spices:

- ¼ tsp black pepper, ground
- ¼ tsp red chili flakes
- ½ tsp sea salt

How to Cook:

1. Remove the rind of the avocado and chop in half. Remove the pit and chop into bite-sized cubes. Save for later.
2. Turn on the Instant Pot and melt the butter using the stainless steel insert. Switch the Instant Pot to "Sauté" mode and put in avocado cubes. Drizzle with salt and pepper and cook for 3-4 minutes, stirring intermittently.
3. After that, put in eggs, green onions, and olive oil to taste. If you want, you can also put in 2 tablespoons of milk for a creamier texture.
4. Cook for 3 additional minutes, or until the eggs are set. Turn off your instant pot by pressing the "cancel" button. Move all to serving plate and if you want,

spread on top some heavy cream or plain Greek yogurt.
5. Have fun!

Nutritional Info:(Calories 350 | Total Fats 32.7g | Net Carbs: 2.6g | Protein 8.4g |Fiber: 7g)

Baby Spinach Egg Cups

Aggregate Time to Prepare: 10 Minutes

Yield: 4 Servings

Ingredients:

- ¼ tsp Garlic Powder
- ½ cup shredded Mozzarella Cheese
- ½ tsp salt
- 1 ½ cups Water
- 1 cup chopped Baby Spinach
- 1 Tomato, chopped
- 1 tsp Pepper
- 14/4 cup crumbled Feta Cheese
- 6 Eggs

How to Cook:

1. Pour the water into your Instant Pot and put the trivet into the Instant Pot.
2. Whisk the eggs along with the spices.
3. Stir in the tomato and cheeses.
4. Oil-coat 4 ramekins and distribute the spinach among them.
5. Pour the egg mixture over.

6. Position the ramekins inside the Instant Pot and shut and secure the lid.
7. Switch the Instant Pot to "High" and cook for 8 minutes.
8. Your dish is ready! Have fun!

Nutritional Info: (Calories 114 | Total Fats 7g | Net Carbs: 2g | Protein 11g | Fiber: 3g)

Bacon and Cheese Egg Bake

Aggregate Time to Prepare: 15 Minutes

Yield: 4 Servings

Ingredients:

- ¼ cup green onions, chopped
- ½ cup milk
- 1 cup mozzarella cheese, shredded
- 2 cups cauliflower, chopped
- 8 eggs
- 8 pieces of bacon, chopped

Spices:

- ½ tsp salt

How to Cook:

1. Turn on your Instant Pot and coat the inner pot with oil. Switch your Instant Pot to "Sauté' mode and heat up.

2. Put in chopped bacon and briefly cook for about 2 minutes or until lightly brown on all sides.
3. Using a wooden spatula spread the bacon uniformly over the bottom of the pot creating the first layer.
4. Put in chopped cauliflower creating the second layer in your pot. Save for later.
5. In another container, crack the eggs and season with salt. Pour in the milk and whisk together until foamy. Pour the mixture over cauliflower and spread on top mozzarella cheese.
6. Shut and secure the lid and switch to "Manual' mode. Turn the timer to 7 minutes on high pressure.
7. When finished, depressurize using the quick release method and open the lid. Drizzle with green onions and serve instantly.

Nutritional Info:(Calories 381g | Total Fats 26.6g | Net Carbs: 4.7g | Protein 29.3g | Fiber: 1.4g)

Bacon Brussels Sprouts

Aggregate Time to Prepare: **15 Minutes**

Yield: 3 Servings

Ingredients:

- 1 cup Brussels sprouts, chopped
- 1 tbsp balsamic vinegar
- 1 tbsp green onions, thinly sliced
- 1 tbsp olive oil
- 3 oz bacon, chop into bite-sized pieces
- 4 large eggs, beaten

Spices:

- ½ tsp smoked paprika, ground
- 1 tsp garlic powder
- 1 tsp sea salt

How to Cook:

1. Turn on the Instant Pot and coat the stainless steel insert with olive oil. Switch the Instant Pot to "Sauté" mode and put in Brussels sprouts. Drizzle with garlic powder, paprika and salt. Stir thoroughly and cook for 5 minutes.
2. After that, put in beaten eggs, onions, and balsamic vinegar. Stir thoroughly and cook for 2-3 additional minutes. Turn off your Instant pot and mix in the bacon instantly. Allow it to stand for 10 minutes before serving.
3. Have fun!

Nutritional Info:(Calories 307 | Total Fats 23.3g | Net Carbs: 3.3g | Protein 20.1g | Fiber: 1.4g)

Bacon Cheese Rolls

Aggregate Time to Prepare: **10 Minutes**

Yield: **3 Servings**

Ingredients:

- ½ cup cheddar cheese
- 2 tbsp green onions, thinly sliced
- 6 bacon slices
- 6 large eggs

Spices:

- ½ tsp black pepper, ground
- ½ tsp dried oregano, ground
- 1 tsp salt

How to Cook:

1. In a large mixing container, mix eggs, cheddar cheese, green onions, salt, pepper, and oregano. Mix until thoroughly mixed and foamy. Save for later.
2. Oil-coat 6 silicone muffin molds with some cooking spray. Line the walls of each cup with bacon and pour in the previously readied mixture. Save for later.
3. Turn on the Instant Pot and pour 1 cup of water in the stainless steel insert. Place your trivet in the bottom of your instant pot and place molds on top.
4. Shut and secure the lid and close the steam release handle. Switch the Instant pot to "Manual" mode and turn the timer to 3 minutes. Cook on "High" pressure.
5. When your instant pot sounds the end signal, release the pressure using the quick release method of the pressure. Open the pot and move molds to wire rack using oven mitts.
6. Allow it to cool to room temperature before serving.

Nutritional Info:(Calories 427 | Total Fats 32.1g | Net Carbs: 0.9g | Protein 31.5g | Fiber: 0.3g)

Baked Avocado with Eggs

Aggregate Time to Prepare: 30 Minutes

Yield: 2 Servings

Ingredients:

- 1 avocado, sliced in half
- 2 eggs, whole
- tbsp butter

Spices:

- 1 tsp dried oregano
- ½ tsp pink Himalayan salt

How to Cook:

1. Slice the avocado in half and liberally brush with butter. Save for later,
2. Turn on your Instant Pot and set the steamer insert. Put in avocados and tenderly crack eggs in each avocado and drizzle with salt and oregano.
3. Pour in approximately one cup of water in the inner pot and shut and secure the lid.
4. Make sure the steam release handle is on the "Sealing" position and switch your Instant Pot to "Steam' mode.
5. Turn the timer to 20 minutes and cook on low pressure.
6. When finished, push the "Cancel" button and turn off the pot. Depressurize using the quick release method.
7. Open the lid and chill for some time. Move avocado to serving plates and serve instantly.

Nutritional Info:(Calories 421| Total Fats 41.3g | Net Carbs: 2.3g | Protein 7.6g |Fiber: 6.7g)

Beef Kale Patties

Aggregate Time to Prepare: 25 Minutes

Yield: 4 Servings

Ingredients:

- 1 cup fresh kale, thinly sliced
- 1 large egg, beaten
- 1 lb ground beef
- 1 tbsp almond flour
- 1 tbsp olive oil

Spices:

- ½ tsp black pepper, ground
- ½ tsp dried oregano, ground
- ½ tsp dried rosemary, ground
- 1 tsp sea salt

How to Cook:

1. Wash thoroughly the kale under cold running water using a large colander. Drain and thinly slice. Save for later.
2. In a large mixing container, mix ground beef, kale, egg, and flour. Combine with your hands until thoroughly blended. Put in flour and all spices. Stir again until a smooth mixture is achieved. Mould approximately 8 patties, about 2-inch in diameter.
3. Oil-coat a fitting springform pan with some olive oil. Put in the patties and save for later.

4. Turn on the Instant Pot and pour 1 cup of water in the stainless steel insert. Place your trivet in the bottom of your instant pot and place the pan on top. Shut and secure the lid and close the steam release handle. Switch the Instant pot to "Manual" mode and turn the timer to 15 minutes. Cook on "High" pressure.
5. When finished, release the pressure using the quick release method and open the pot. Take the pan out of the instant pot using oven mitts. Put on a wire rack and cool to room temperature.
6. If you want, you can also brown the patties on "Sauté" mode for 1 minute on both sides.

Nutritional Info:(Calories 279 | Total Fats 12.7g | Net Carbs: 1.9g | Protein 36.9g | Fiber: 0.7g)

Beef Shiitake Bowl

Aggregate Time to Prepare: **20 Minutes**

Yield: **4 Servings**

Ingredients:

- ¼ cup olives, pitted
- ½ medium-sized avocado, sliced
- 1 cup Shiitake mushrooms, sliced
- 1 small onion, chopped
- 1 tbsp extra virgin olive oil
- 4 large eggs, beaten
- 8 oz ground beef

Spices:

- 1 tsp black pepper

- 1 tsp salt
- 1 tsp smoked paprika, ground

How to Cook:

1. Turn on the Instant Pot and coat the stainless steel insert with olive oil. Switch the Instant Pot to "Sauté" mode and put in onions and beef. Cook for 5 minutes, stirring intermittently.
2. Put in mushrooms and avocado. Drizzle with smoked paprika, salt, and pepper. Stir thoroughly and put in ½ cup of water. Shut and secure the lid and close the steam release handle. Switch the Instant pot to "Manual" mode and turn the timer to 5 minutes. Cook on "High" pressure.
3. When finished, release the pressure using the quick release method by turning the valve to the "Venting" position. Open the lid and mix in the eggs and olives. Switch the Instant Pot to "Sauté" mode and cook for 2-3 minutes more.
4. Turn off your Instant pot and move all to serving containers.
5. Serve instantly.

Nutritional Info: (Calories 297 | Total Fats 18g | Net Carbs: 7g | Protein 24.9g | Fiber: 3.4g)

Blackberry Cobbler

Aggregate Time to Prepare: **40 Minutes**

Yield: 2 Servings

Ingredients:

- ¼ cup Blackberries

- ¼ cup Coconut Flour
- ¼ tsp Baking Powder
- ½ tsp Lemon Zest
- 1 ½ cups Water
- 2 tbsp. Coconut Oil
- 2 tbsp. Erythritol
- 2 tbsp. Heavy Cream
- 2 tsp Lemon Juice
- 10 drops of Liquid Stevia
- 5 Egg Yolks
- Pinch of Sea Salt

How to Cook:

1. Pour the water into the Instant Pot and put the trivet into the Instant Pot.
2. Mix together the yolks, coconut oil, butter, stevia, lemon juice, heavy cream, erythritol, and salt.
3. Stir in the wet ingredients, slowly, until smooth.
4. Separate the mixture among 2 oil-coated ramekins.
5. Push the blackberries into the batter.
6. Put the ramekins inside the Instant Pot.
7. Switch the Instant Pot to "High" and cook for 10 minutes.
8. Depressurize quickly.
9. Your dish is ready! Have fun!

Nutritional Info: (Calories 459| Total Fats 44g | Net Carbs: 4.9g | Protein 9g |Fiber: 5.7g)

Blueberry Cinnamon Scones

Aggregate Time to Prepare: 25 Minutes

Yield: 7 Servings

Ingredients:

For dough:

- ¼ tsp salt
- ½ cup heavy cream
- ½ tsp baking powder
- 1 cup almond flour
- 1 egg
- 1 tsp cinnamon, ground
- 1 tsp lemon zest, freshly grated
- 1 tsp powdered stevia
- 1 tsp vanilla extract
- 4 tbsp butter, melted

For icing:

- 1 tsp blueberry extract
- 1 tsp liquid stevia
- 4 tbsp coconut butter, melted

How to Cook:

1. In a large mixing container, mix almond flour, baking powder, stevia, cinnamon, and salt. Stir until thoroughly mixed. Put in heavy cream, butter, egg, vanilla extract, and lemon zest. Stir until thoroughly blended. Save for later.
2. Line a fitting springform pan with some parchment paper and grease the sides with some cooking spray. Save for later.
3. Dust a clean work surface with some flour and move the dough. Make the dough into balls of favoured

size and move to the pan. Tenderly push with your palm to form scone-shaped cookies.
4. Turn on the Instant Pot and pour one cup of water in the stainless steel insert. Place your trivet in the bottom of your instant pot and place the pan on top.
5. Shut and secure the lid and close the steam release handle. Switch the Instant pot to "Manual" mode and turn the timer to 15 minutes. Cook on "High" pressure.
6. In the mean time, prepare the icing. Mix all ingredients in a large mixing container and beat until smooth and creamy.
7. When finished, depressurize using the natural release method. Open the lid and move to wire rack. Allow it to cool to room temperature.
8. Using a piping bag, spread on top icing and refrigerate for 10 minutes before serving.

Nutritional Info:(Calories 259 | Total Fats 24g | Net Carbs: 3g | Protein 5.1g |Fiber: 3.6g)

Boiled Eggs with Spinach

Aggregate Time to Prepare: 25 Minutes

Yield: 2 Servings

Ingredients:

- 1 lb spinach, chopped
- 1 tbsp butter
- 1 tbsp olives
- 3 tbsp olive oil
- 4 large eggs

Spices:

- ½ tsp chili flakes
- ½ tsp sea salt
- 1 tbsp mustard seeds
- 1 tbsp raw almonds

How to Cook:

1. Thoroughly wash the spinach under cold running water and drain in a large colander. Save for later.
2. Turn on your Instant Pot and pour in three cups of water in the stainless steel insert. Put in eggs and shut and secure the lid. Close the steam release handle and switch to "Manual' mode. Turn the timer to 4 minutes and cook on high pressure.
3. When finished, push the "Cancel" button and depressurize using the quick release method. Cautiously, open the lid and move the eggs into ice cold water.
4. Clean and pat dry the insert with a kitchen towel and place in the pot. Oil-coat with some olive oil and Switch your Instant Pot to "'Sauté" mode. Put in spinach and cook for 2-3 minutes, stirring intermittently.
5. After that, mix in one tablespoon of butter and season with salt and chili flakes. Stir thoroughly and cook for one minute.
6. Turn off your Instant pot and drizzle with nuts.
7. Tenderly peel and cut each egg in half, lengthwise. Move to a serving plate and put in olives.
8. If you want, you can also serve with sliced avocado and drizzle with some more olive oil.

Nutritional Info:(Calories 414| Total Fats 36.8g | Net Carbs: 4.1g | Protein 17.7g |Fiber: 5.1g)

Breakfast Biscuit

Aggregate Time to Prepare: 40 Minutes

Yield: 8 Servings

Ingredients:

- ¼ tsp Xanthan Gum
- ½ cup Butter
- ½ tsp Salt
- ¾ cup Milk
- 1 ½ cups Water
- 1 ½ tsp Baking Powder
- 1 cup Coconut Flour
- 1 tbsp. Sugar-Free Vanilla Protein Powder
- 2 tbsp. Gluten-Free Baking Combine
- 3 Eggs

How to Cook:

1. Pour the water into the Instant Pot and put the trivet into the Instant Pot.
2. Mix the dry ingredients in a container.
3. Put in the butter and rub the mixture using your fingers, until crumbly.
4. Stir in the wet ingredients and knead using your hand.
5. Roll out the dough and chop into 8 equivalent pieces.
6. Put on an oil-coated baking tray and in the Instant Pot (Do NOT overcrowd. Work in batches if you have to).
7. Shut and secure the lid and cook on HIGH for 10 minutes.
8. Release the pressure using the quick release method.
9. Your dish is ready! Have fun!

Nutritional Info: (Calories 198| Total Fats 16g | Net Carbs: 4g | Protein 5g |Fiber: 1.5g)

Breakfast Brownie Muffins

Aggregate Time to Prepare: 30 Minutes

Yield: 6 Servings

Ingredients:

- ¼ cup Cocoa Powder, unsweetened
- ¼ cup Slivered Almonds
- ¼ cup Sugar- Free Caramel Syrup
- ½ cup Pumpkin Puree
- ½ tsp Salt
- 1 ½ cups Water
- 1 cup Flaxseed Meal
- 1 Egg
- 1 tsp Apple Cider Vinegar
- 1 tsp Vanilla
- 2 tbsp. Coconut Oil, melted

How to Cook:

1. Pour the water into the Instant Pot and put the trivet into the Instant Pot.
2. Mix the dry ingredients in one container, and whisk the wet ones in another.
3. Mix the two mixtures tenderly.
4. Separate the mixture among 6 silicone muffin cups.
5. Spread on top the almonds.
6. Put the muffin cups into the Instant Pot.

7. Shut and secure the lid and switch your instant pot to "Manual" mode and cook for 20 minutes.
8. Release the pressure using the quick release method.
9. Allow it to cool before serving.
10. Have fun!

Nutritional Info: (Calories 193| Total Fats 14g | Net Carbs: 4.4g | Protein 7g |Fiber: 7.1g)

Breakfast Caulicheese

Aggregate Time to Prepare: 20 Minutes

Yield: 4 Servings

Ingredients:

- ¼ tsp Salt
- ¼ tsp White Pepper
- ½ cup Half and Half
- ½ cup shredded Cheddar Cheese
- 1 ½ cups Water
- 2 cups Cauliflower Rice (ground in a food processor)
- 2 tbsp. Cream Cheese

How to Cook:

1. Pour the water into the Instant Pot and put the trivet into the Instant Pot.
2. Mix all of the ingredients in an oil-coated baking dish.
3. Cover with a foil and place inside the Instant Pot.
4. Shut and secure the lid and cook for 5 minutes on HIGH.

5. Allow the pressure to drop on its own for approximately 10 minutes.
6. Your dish is ready! Have fun!

Nutritional Info: (Calories 134 | Total Fats 10g | Net Carbs: 4g | Protein 5g | Fiber: 1g)

Breakfast Cauliflower Tots

Aggregate Time to Prepare: 60 Minutes

Yield: 4 Servings

Ingredients:

- 1 Cauliflower Head, chopped
- 1/3 cup shredded Cheddar Cheese
- 2 tbsp. Butter
- 2 tbsp. Heavy Cream
- 4 Egg Whites
- Salt and Pepper, to taste

How to Cook:

1. Put the cauliflower in a microwave-safe container and microwave for 5 minutes.
2. Drain and place in a container.
3. Put in egg whites, heavy cream, cheddar, and season with salt and pepper.
4. Stir to incorporate thoroughly.
5. Put in the refrigerator for 40 minutes.
6. Melt the butter in your Instant Pot using the "Sauté" mode.
7. Make small nuggets out of the cauliflower mixture.

8. Put in the Instant Pot and cook until golden.
9. Your dish is ready! Have fun!

Nutritional Info: (Calories 250 | Total Fats 21g | Net Carbs: 2g | Protein 10g | Fiber: 0.5g)

Breakfast Cinnamon Bars

Aggregate Time to Prepare: **25 Minutes**

Yield: **2 Servings**

Ingredients:

- 1 cup unsweetened almond milk
- 1 tbsp almonds, chopped
- 1/3 cup hemp seeds
- 1/3 cup pumpkin puree
- 2 large eggs
- 2 tbsp coconut oil
- 2 tbsp sesame seeds

Spices:

- 2 tbsp swerve

How to Cook:

1. Cover a small baking dish with some parchment paper. Save for later.
2. Put coconut oil and swerve in a microwave-safe container and microwave for 1 minute. Mix together and move to a deep container along with the rest of the ingredients. Stir thoroughly and move to the

readied dish. Loosely cover with aluminum foil and save for later.
3. Turn on your Instant Pot and pour in 1 cup of water in the inner pot. Position the trivet and place the baking dish on top.
4. Shut and secure the lid and set the steam release handle to the "Sealing" position. Switch your Instant Pot to "Manual" mode and turn the timer to 15 minutes on high pressure.
5. When finished, depressurize using the quick release method. Cautiously open the lid and remove the dish.
6. Chill for some time and chop into 4 bars. Serve instantly.

Nutritional Info:(Calories 417| Total Fats 36.7g | Net Carbs: 5g | Protein 17g |Fiber: 3.9g)

Breakfast Frittata

Aggregate Time to Prepare: 30 Minutes

Yield: 3 Servings

Ingredients:

- ¼ cup red bell pepper
- ½ cup cottage cheese
- ½ cup feta cheese
- 1 cup chopped cauliflower
- 10 oz spinach, chopped
- 2 cherry tomatoes
- 5 large eggs
- 5 tbsp butter

Spices:

- ¼ tsp dried oregano
- ¼ tsp freshly ground black pepper
- ½ cup fresh celery leaves
- ½ tsp salt

How to Cook:

1. Turn on your Instant Pot and coat the stainless steel insert with butter. Switch your Instant Pot to "Sauté' mode and heat up.
2. Put in spinach and stir thoroughly. Cook for 5 minutes, stirring intermittently. After that, put in tomatoes, bell peppers, and cauliflower. Carry on cooking for 3-4 minutes.
3. In a small container, whisk together two eggs, cottage cheese, and feta cheese. Put in the mixture to the pot and cook for 2 additional minutes.
4. Lastly, crack the rest of the three eggs. Cook for an additional 5 minutes.
5. When finished, turn off the pot. Move the frittata to a serving plate and drizzle with freshly chopped celery leaves.

Nutritional Info:(Calories 422| Total Fats 33.1g | Net Carbs: 8.1g | Protein 22.3g |Fiber: 4g)

Breakfast Plum Cake

Aggregate Time to Prepare: 40 Minutes

Yield: 8 Servings

Ingredients:

- ¼ tsp Almond Extract
- ¼ tsp Xanthan Gum
- ½ cup Butter, softened
- ½ cup Coconut Flour
- ½ cup Granulated Sweetener
- ¾ cup Almond Milk
- 1 ½ cups almond Flour
- 1 ½ cups Water
- 1 tbsp. Vanilla
- 2 tsp Baking Powder
- 3 Eggs
- Pinch of Sea Salt
- 4 Plums, pitted and halved

How to Cook:

1. Pour the water into the Instant Pot and put the rack into the Instant Pot.
2. Whisk the butter and sweetener until the mixture becomes smooth.
3. Whisk in the eggs, one at a time.
4. Whisk in the extracts and milk.
5. Mix the dry ingredients in a container, and slowly beat this mixture into the wet one.
6. Coat a baking dish with cooking spray and pour the batter into it.
7. Spread on top the plums (chop side down).

8. Put the dish inside the Instant Pot and shut and secure the lid.
9. Cook for 25 minutes on HIGH.
10. Your dish is ready! Have fun!

Nutritional Info: (Calories 296| Total Fats 25g | Net Carbs: 6.5g | Protein 9g |Fiber: 1g)

Broccoli Ham and Pepper Frittata

Aggregate Time to Prepare: 35 Minutes

Yield: 4 Servings

Ingredients:

- 1 cup Cheddar Cheese (grated)
- 1 cup Green Bell Peppers (sliced)
- 1 cup Half & Half
- 1 tsp Salt
- 2 cups Broccoli (frozen)
- 2 tbsp. Butter
- 2 tsp Ground Black Pepper
- 4 Eggs
- 8 ounces Ham (diced)

How to Cook:

1. Oil-coat a 6x3 inch pan with butter, ensuring that all corners are thoroughly buttered.
2. Layer the green bell peppers, followed by ham, followed by broccoli in the pan.

3. Put eggs and salt in a container and whisk thoroughly. Put in the half & half, pepper and cheddar, and stir thoroughly to mix.
4. Pour the eggs mixture into the pan over other ingredients, and cover with a silicone lid or tin foil.
5. Pour two cups of water in the inner liner of Instant Pot. Put a steamer insert in it followed by the pan.
6. Shut and secure the lid, and turn the timer and cook for 20 minutes.
7. When finished allow the pressure to be released naturally for 10 minutes and then quick release it.
8. Take the pan out of the Instant Pot, remove the lid and allow it to rest for 10 minutes.
9. Tip over on a serving platter and serve.

Nutritional Info: (Calories: 422 | Total Fats: 30g | Net Carbs: 7g | Proteins: 28g | Fibers: 2g)

Carrot and Pecan Muffins

Aggregate Time to Prepare: **40 Minutes**

Yield: **8 Servings**

Ingredients:

- ¼ cup Coconut Oil
- ½ cup chopped Pecans
- ½ cup Heavy Creamy
- 1 ½ cups Water
- 1 cup Almond Flour
- 1 cup shredded Carrots
- 1 tsp Apple Pie Spice

- 1 tsp Baking Powder
- 1/3 cup Truvia
- 3 Eggs

How to Cook:

1. Pour the water into the Instant Pot and put the rack into the Instant Pot.
2. Put all of the ingredients, except the carrots and pecans, in a mixing container.
3. Combine with an electric mixer until fluffy.
4. Fold in the pecans and carrots.
5. Separate the mixture among 8 silicone muffin cups.
6. Position on the rack and shut and secure the lid.
7. Switch the Instant Pot to "Manual" mode and cook for 15-20 minutes.
8. Release the pressure using the quick release method.
9. Your dish is ready! Have fun!

Nutritional Info: (Calories 263 | Total Fats 25g | Net Carbs: 4g | Protein 6g | Fiber: 2g)

Cauliflower and Sausage Egg Pie

Aggregate Time to Prepare: 30 Minutes

Yield: 6 Servings

Ingredients:

- ¼ tsp Pepper
- 1 ½ cups Water
- 1 Onion, diced
- 1 pound Pork Sausage
- 1 tsp Garlic Powder
- 2 cups Cauliflower Rice
- 2 tsp dried Basil

- 8 Eggs, beaten
- Pinch of Cumin
- Pinch of Turmeric

How to Cook:

1. Put the sausage into your Instant Pot and cook using the "Sauté" mode for a few minutes until browned. Make sure to break it up while sautéing.
2. Coat a baking dish with cooking spray and move the sausage to it.
3. Stir in the rest of the ingredients, except the water.
4. Pour the water into the Instant Pot and put the trivet into the Instant Pot.
5. Put the dish inside and shut and secure the lid of the Instant Pot.
6. Switch the Instant Pot to "High" and cook for 15-20 minutes. Depending on the favoured consistency.
7. Depressurize quickly.
8. Your dish is ready! Have fun!

Nutritional Info: (Calories 353| Total Fats 26g | Net Carbs: 5.1g | Protein 22g |Fiber: 1.4g)

Cauliflower Fritters

Aggregate Time to Prepare: 25 Minutes

Yield: 12 Servings

Ingredients:

- ¼ cup grated Parmesan Cheese
- ¼ tsp Pepper

- ½ tsp Garlic Salt
- ½ tsp Italian Seasoning
- 1 ½ cups Water
- 1 Cauliflower Head, chopped
- 1 cup ground Almonds
- 1 cup shredded Cheddar Cheese
- 2 Eggs
- 3 tbsp. Olive Oil

How to Cook:

1. Put the cauliflower in a microwave-safe container and microwave for 5 minutes.
2. Drain thoroughly and pulse using a food processor until ground.
3. Put in the rest of the ingredients (except ¼ cup of cheddar) and mix until thoroughly blended.
4. Make 12 patties out of the mixture.
5. Preheat the Instant Pot on "Sauté" mode and put in 1 tbsp. of the oil.
6. Put in 4 patties and cook for approximately 2 minutes on each side.
7. Repeat the process two more times.
8. Pour the water into the Instant Pot and put the rack into the Instant Pot.
9. Position the patties in an oil-coated baking dish and spread on top the rest of the cheddar.
10. Shut and secure the lid and cook for 3 minutes on MANUAL.
11. Depressurize quickly.
12. Your dish is ready! Have fun!

Nutritional Info: (Calories 100 | Total Fats 7g | Net Carbs: 2.7g | Protein 3g |Fiber: 16g)

Cauliflower Mash

Aggregate Time to Prepare: 35 Minutes

Yield: 3 Servings

Ingredients:

- ¼ cup olive oil
- 1 lb cauliflower, chopped into florets
- 2 cups broccoli, chopped
- 2 garlic cloves, crushed

Spices:

- 1 tsp dried rosemary
- 1 tsp salt

How to Cook:

1. Put vegetables in a large colander and rinse thoroughly under cold running water. Drain and place in the instant pot.
2. Pour in enough water to cover and shut and secure the lid. Make sure the steam release handle is on the "Sealing" position. Switch your Instant Pot to "Manual" mode and turn the timer to 12 minutes.
3. When finished, depressurize using the natural release method and open the lid. Drain vegetables and put back in the pot.
4. Switch your Instant Pot to "Sauté' mode and pour in the olive oil. Put in garlic, salt, and rosemary. Stir thoroughly and cook for 10 minutes, stirring intermittently.
5. Press the "Cancel" button and chill the mixture for some time. Mash with a potato masher and

optionally season with some more salt, pepper, or dried rosemary.
6. Serve warm or cold.

Nutritional Info:(Calories 205| Total Fats 17.2g | Net Carbs: 7.3g | Protein 4.8g |Fiber: 5.4g)

Cauliflower-Crusted Sausage and Avocado Breakfast Pizza

Aggregate Time to Prepare: 45

Yield: 4 Servings

Ingredients:

For the Crust:

- ½ tsp Pepper
- ½ tsp Salt
- 1 cup shredded Mozzarella Cheese
- 1 Egg
- 12 ounces Cauliflower Rice (ground)

For the Pizza:

- ¼ cup chopped Tomato
- 1 ½ cups shredded Cheddar Cheese
- 1 Avocado, sliced
- 1 Jalapeno, diced
- 4 Sausage Links, cooked and sliced
- 4 Eggs
- Salt and Pepper, to taste

How to Cook:

1. Put the cauliflower in a microwave-safe container and microwave for 5 minutes.
2. Drain and move to a container.
3. Stir in the rest of the crust ingredients. Combine thoroughly, until the mixture is blended.
4. Oil-coat the Instant Pot with some cooking spray and preheat using the "Sauté" mode.
5. Press the cauliflower mixture and cook for 6 minutes on each side.
6. Oil-coat a baking dish and place the crust inside (you may need to chop around the edges for the crust to fit).
7. Drizzle with the cheese, crack the eggs on top, and spread on top tomatoes, jalapenos, and sausage.
8. Sprinkle with salt and pepper.
9. Pour 1 ½ cups of water into your Instant Pot and put the trivet into the Instant Pot.
10. Put the baking dish inside and shut and secure the lid.
11. Switch the Instant Pot to "Manual" mode and cook for 8 minutes.
12. Depressurize naturally.
13. Your dish is ready! Have fun!

Nutritional Info: (Calories 432 | Total Fats 29g | Net Carbs: 5.4g | Protein 27g | Fiber: 4.2g)

Cheesy Bacon and Chive Omelet

Aggregate Time to Prepare: 30 Minutes

Yield: 1 Serving

Ingredients:

- 1 ½ cups Water
- 1 ounce Cheddar Cheese, shredded
- 1 tsp chopped Chives
- 2 Eggs
- 2 slices Bacon, chopped

How to Cook:

1. Put the bacon in the Instant Pot and cook using the "Sauté" mode until crunchy.
2. Move to a plate.
3. Oil-coat a baking dish with the bacon fat.
4. Whisk the eggs along with the chives and mix in the bacon and cheddar.
5. Pour the mixture into the baking dish.
6. Pour the water into the Instant Pot and put the trivet into the Instant Pot.
7. Put the baking dish inside, close, and switch your instant pot to "Manual" mode and cook for 17 minutes.
8. Depressurize quickly.
9. Your dish is ready! Have fun!

Nutritional Info: (Calories 386| Total Fats 30g | Net Carbs: 1.8g | Protein 25g |Fiber: 0g)

Cheesy Breakfast Bagels

Aggregate Time to Prepare: **30 Minutes**

Yield: **3 Servings**

Ingredients:

- ¾ cup Almond Flour
- 1 ½ cups grated Mozzarella Cheese, melted

- 1 ½ cups Water
- 1 Egg
- 1 tsp Xanthan Gum
- 1 tbsp. Butter, melted
- 2 tbsp. Cream Cheese
- Pinch of Sea Salt

How to Cook:

1. Pour the water into the Instant Pot.
2. Whisk the egg along with the salt and xanthan gum.
3. Mix in the cheeses.
4. Stir in the flour.
5. Make a log out of the dough and separate into three equivalent pieces.
6. Make three rings shaped like bagels and roll them out.
7. Slightly coat with the butter. You can spread on top seeds if you wish to.
8. Position on a previously oil-coated baking tray and place on the Instant Pot's rack.
9. Shut and secure the lid and switch your instant pot to "Manual" mode and cook or 15 minutes.
10. Depressurize quickly.
11. Your dish is ready! Enjoy with your favorite toppings!.

Nutritional Info: (Calories 367| Total Fats 29g | Net Carbs: 3.5g | Protein 20g |Fiber: 3.2g)

Cheesy Chili Mexican Frittata

Aggregate Time to Prepare: **40 Minutes**

Yield: 4 Servings

Ingredients:

- ¼ cup chopped Cilantro
- ¼ tsp Pepper
- ½ tsp Cumin
- ½ tsp Salt
- 1 cup Half and Half
- 1 cup shredded Mexican Blend Cheese
- 10 ounces canned Green Chilies, chopped
- 2 cups Water
- 4 Eggs

How to Cook:

1. Pour the water into the Instant Pot and put the rack into the Instant Pot.
2. Whisk together the eggs salt, cumin, half and half, and ½ of the cheese, in a container.
3. Stir in the chilies and cilantro.
4. Oil-coat a baking dish and pour the egg mixture into it.
5. Coat the dish with foil and place in the Instant Pot.
6. Cook for 20 minutes at HIGH.
7. Wait 10 minutes before releasing the pressure naturally.
8. Drizzle with the rest of the cheese and cook for 2 additional minutes on HIGH, with the lid removed.
9. Your dish is ready! Have fun!

Nutritional Info: (Calories 257 | Total Fats 19g | Net Carbs: 5g | Protein 14g | Fiber: 1g)

Cheesy Egg Muffins

Aggregate Time to Prepare: **25 Minutes**

Yield: 8 Servings

Ingredients:

- ¼ cup shredded Pepper Jack Cheese
- ¼ tsp Salt
- 1 ½ cups Water
- 1 Green Onion, chopped
- 4 Bacon Slices
- 4 Eggs
- Pinch of Garlic Powder
- Pinch of Pepper

How to Cook:

1. Switch the Instant Pot. to "Sauté" mode.
2. Cook the bacon for a few minutes, until crunchy.
3. Clean off the bacon grease, pour the water inside, and put the rack into the Instant Pot.
4. Whisk the eggs along with the pepper, garlic powder, and salt.
5. Crush the bacon and put into this mixture.
6. Stir in the onion and cheese.
7. Pour this mixture into 4 silicone muffin cups.
8. Position them on the rack and shut and secure the lid.
9. Switch the Instant Pot to "High" and cook for 8 minutes.
10. Allow to sit for two minutes and then release the pressure using the quick release method.
11. Your dish is ready! Have fun!

Nutritional Info: (Calories 282 | Total Fats 12g | Net Carbs: 1g | Protein 24g | Fiber: 16g)

Cheesy Eggs de Provence

Aggregate Time to Prepare: **30 Minutes**

Yield: **3 Servings**

Ingredients:

- ¼ cup heavy cream
- ½ cup bacon slices
- ½ cup cheddar cheese
- ½ cup fresh kale, chopped
- ½ small onion, thinly sliced
- 3 large eggs

Spices:

- ¼ tsp black pepper, ground
- ¼ tsp sea salt
- 1 tsp Herbs de Provence

How to Cook:

1. In a large mixing container, mix eggs and heavy cream. With a paddle attachment, beat on high speed for 2 minutes or until light and fluffy mixture. After that, put in bacon, kale, and cheddar cheese. Sprinkle with salt, pepper, and Herbs de Provence. Combine thoroughly again and move the mixture to the oven-safe baking dish.

2. Turn on the Instant Pot and pour 1 cup of water in the stainless steel insert. Set the trivet and place the baking dish on top.
3. Shut and secure the lid and close the steam release handle. Switch the Instant pot to "Manual" mode and turn the timer to 20 minutes. Cook on "High" pressure.
4. When finished, depressurize using the natural release method and open the lid.
5. Cautiously remove the dish from the pot and chill for some time before serving.

Nutritional Info:(Calories 205 | Total Fats 16.1g | Net Carbs: 0.9g | Protein 12.5g |Fiber: 0.4g)

Cheesy Quesadillas

Aggregate Time to Prepare: 10

Yield: 2 Servings

Ingredients:

- ¼ cup shredded Cheddar
- 1 Butter Stick
- 2 Low Carb Tortillas (Such as Mission Fajita)

How to Cook:

1. Melt half of the butter in the Instant Pot using the "Sauté" mode.
2. Lay one tortilla and spread on top some cheese.
3. Cover with the other tortilla and spread on top more cheese.

4. Put the butter on top and flip over.
5. Sauté until it becomes crunchy on both sides.
6. Your dish is ready! Have fun!

Nutritional Info: (Calories 155 | Total Fats 13g | Net Carbs: 1g | Protein 7g | Fiber: 0g)

Cheesy Tomato Frittata

Aggregate Time to Prepare: 40 Minutes

Yield: 4 Servings

Ingredients:

- 1 cup cottage cheese
- 3 large eggs
- 3 tbsp olive oil
- 4 large tomatoes, peeled and roughly chopped

Spices:

- ¼ cup fresh parsley, thinly sliced
- ¼ tsp stevia powder
- ½ tsp salt
- 2 tsp Italian seasoning mix

How to Cook:

1. Turn on your Instant Pot and coat the inner pot with oil. Switch your Instant Pot to "Sauté' mode and put in tomatoes, stevia, Italian seasoning, parsley, and salt.
2. Stir thoroughly and cook for 15 minutes or until tomatoes soften. Stir intermittently.
3. In the mean time, whisk together eggs and cottage cheese. If you want, you can also put in some more salt.
4. Pour the mixture into the pot and stir thoroughly.
5. Cook for 3 additional minutes.
6. Serve warm.

Nutritional Info:(Calories 217| Total Fats 15.6g | Net Carbs: 5.6g | Protein 13.6g |Fiber: 1.5g)

Cherry Clafoutis

Aggregate Time to Prepare: **45 Minutes**

Yield: 8 Servings

Ingredients:

- ¼ cup Heavy Cream
- ½ tsp Cherry Extract
- ½ tsp Xanthan Gum
- 1 ½ cups pitted and halved Fresh Cherries
- 1 ½ cups Water
- 1 cup Almond Flour
- 1 cup Milk
- 1 tbsp. Butter
- 1 tbsp. Vanilla
- 1/3 cup Swerve
- 6 Eggs
- Pinch of Salt

How to Cook:

1. Pour the water into the Instant Pot and put the trivet into the Instant Pot.
2. Coat a baking dish with the butter.
3. Throw all ingredients except the cherries into a blender.
4. Pulse for 10 seconds, or until smooth.
5. Pour the mixture into the pan and spread on top the cherries (chopped side up).

6. Wrap the dish with a foil and place inside the Instant Pot.
7. Shut and secure the lid and switch your instant pot to "Manual" mode and cook for 25-30 minutes.
8. Depressurize for 5 minutes.
9. Your dish is ready! Have fun!

Nutritional Info: (Calories 194 | Total Fats 15g | Net Carbs: 6g | Protein 8g | Fiber: 2.3g)

Chia Rum Pancakes

Aggregate Time to Prepare: **10 Minutes**

Yield: 3 Servings

Ingredients:

- 1 tbsp butter, melted
- 1 tbsp erythritol
- 2 tbsp almond flour
- 2 tbsp chia seeds
- 2 tbsp shredded coconut, unsweetened
- 4 large eggs, beaten
- 4 oz cream cheese, softened

Spices:

- ¼ tsp powdered stevia
- ¼ tsp salt
- 1 tsp rum extract

How to Cook:

1. In a large mixing container, mix all ingredients except coconut. Combine until smooth and creamy.

2. Turn on the Instant Pot and coat the stainless steel insert with melted butter. Pour approximately 1/3 of the mixture in the pot and shut and secure the lid. Close the steam release handle and switch your Instant Pot to "Manual" mode. Turn the timer to 2 minutes and switch your instant pot to "high pressure" setting and cook.
3. When your instant pot sounds the end signal, release the pressure using the quick release method and open the pot. With a large kitchen spatula, remove the pancake from the pot. Repeat the process with the rest of the batter.
4. Drizzle the pancakes with shredded coconut and serve instantly.

Nutritional Info:(Calories 350 | Total Fats 29.9g | Net Carbs: 8g | Protein 14g |Fiber: 4g)

Chicken and Greens Frittata

Aggregate Time to Prepare: 45 Minutes

Yield: 4 Servings

Ingredients:

- ¼ cup fresh parsley leaves, chopped
- 1 cup collard greens, chopped
- 1 cup kale, chopped
- 1 cup spinach, chopped
- 1 cup Swiss chard, chopped
- 2 cups cauliflower, chopped
- 2 tbsp butter

- 3 cups chicken stock
- 4 tbsp olive oil
- 7 oz boneless and skinless chicken breast, chopped into bite-sized pieces

Spices:

- 1 tsp sea salt
- ¼ tsp black pepper, freshly ground

How to Cook:

1. Thoroughly wash the greens under cold running water and drain in a large colander. Using a sharp knife, chop the vegetables and save for later.
2. Turn on your Instant Pot and place the cauliflower at the bottom of the stainless steel insert. Pour in enough water to cover and shut and secure the lid. Set the steam release handle and switch to "Manual' mode. Turn the timer to 9 minutes on high pressure.
3. When finished, release the pressure using the quick release method and open the lid. Drain the cauliflower and chill for some time. Move to a food processor and process until smooth. Save for later.
4. After that, Switch your Instant Pot to "'Sauté" mode and coat the inner pot with olive oil. Put in chicken breast and drizzle with some salt and pepper. Briefly brown, for 4-5 minutes, stirring continuously. Pour in the stock and put in vegetables. Shut and secure the lid again and set the steam release handle to the 'Sealing' position.
5. Switch your Instant Pot to "Manual" mode and turn the timer to 8 minutes on high pressure. When finished, release the pressure using the quick release method and open the lid. Chill for some time.

6. In the mean time, preheat the oven to 400 degrees. Oil-coat a 7-inch round ban with butter and save for later.
7. Remove the meat and greens from the pot and move to a food processor. Process until smooth. Stir in the cauliflower and move to the readied pan.
8. Bake for 15 minutes, or until lightly golden and crunchy on top. Serve instantly.

Nutritional Info:(Calories 282 | Total Fats 21.9g | Net Carbs: 4.1g | Protein 17.2g | Fiber: 2.3g)

Chorizo Shakshuka

Aggregate Time to Prepare: 25 Minutes

Yield: 6 Servings

Ingredients:

- ¼ tsp Pepper
- ½ cup diced Onion
- ½ tsp Salt
- ½ tbsp. Cumin
- 1 ½ cup Water
- 1 pound Ground Chorizo
- 1 Red Bell Pepper, diced
- 1 tsp minced Garlic
- 1 tbsp. Coconut Oil
- 28 ounces canned diced Tomatoes
- 6 Eggs

How to Cook:

1. Switch your Instant Pot to "Sauté" mode and melt the coconut oil in it.
2. Put in the onions and peppers and sauté for 3 minutes.
3. Put in garlic and cook for 30 additional seconds.
4. Put in the chorizo and cook until browned.
5. Stir in the tomatoes and spices.
6. Move the mixture to a baking dish.
7. Pour the water into the Instant Pot and put the rack into the Instant Pot.
8. Crack the eggs into the baking dish and put it on the rack.
9. Shut and secure the lid and cook on HIGH for 10 minutes.

10. Release the pressure using the quick release method.
11. Your dish is ready! Have fun!

Nutritional Info: (Calories 504| Total Fats 39g | Net Carbs: 7g | Protein 29g |Fiber: 3.6g)

Cinnamon Pancakes

Aggregate Time to Prepare: 20 Minutes

Yield: 3 Servings

Ingredients:

- ½ tsp baking powder
- 1 cup almond flour
- 1 tbsp coconut butter, melted
- 2 large eggs
- 2 tbsp milk

Spices:

- ½ tsp powdered stevia
- ½ tsp vanilla extract
- 1 tsp cinnamon, ground

How to Cook:

1. In a large mixing container, mix almond flour, baking powder, cinnamon, and stevia. Using a kitchen spatula, mix until blended.
2. After that, put in eggs, vanilla extract, and milk. With a whisking attachment on, beat until smooth batter.
3. Turn on the Instant Pot and coat the stainless steel insert with coconut butter. Pour approximately 1/3 of

the mixture into the pot and securely lock the lid. Close the steam release handle and switch your Instant Pot to "Manual" mode. Turn the timer to 5 minutes and switch your instant pot to "high pressure" setting and cook.
4. When finished, release the pressure using the quick release method and open the pot. Cautiously remove the pancake to a serving plate. Repeat the process with the rest of the batter.
5. Serve pancakes with some fresh raspberries.

Nutritional Info:(Calories 312 | Total Fats 24.3g | Net Carbs: 5.7g | Protein 12.9g | Fiber: 5.3g)

Coconut Cherry Pancakes

Aggregate Time to Prepare: **20 Minutes**

Yield: 3 Servings

Ingredients:

- ½ cup cream cheese, softened
- 1 cup almond flour
- 1 tbsp coconut butter, melted
- 1 tsp baking powder
- 2 tbsp coconut milk
- 3 large eggs, beaten

Spices:

- ¼ tsp nutmeg, ground
- 1 tsp cherry extract

- 1 tsp powdered stevia

How to Cook:

1. In a large mixing container, mix coconut flour, baking powder, stevia, and nutmeg. Stir thoroughly using a kitchen spatula. After that, put in eggs, cream cheese, coconut milk, nutmeg and cherry extract. With a whisking attachment on, beat until smooth and creamy.
2. Turn on the Instant Pot and coat the stainless steel insert with coconut butter. Pour approximately 1/3 of the mixture and securely lock the lid. Close the steam release handle and switch your Instant Pot to "Manual" mode. Turn the timer to 5 minutes and switch your instant pot to "high pressure" setting and cook.
3. When your instant pot sounds the end signal, release the pressure using the quick release method by moving the valve to the "Venting" position. Open the pot and repeat the process with the rest of the batter.
4. Spread on top some plain yogurt and drizzle with some shredded coconut
5. Serve instantly.

Nutritional Info:(Calories 350 | Total Fats 31.3g | Net Carbs: 4.2g | Protein 12.1g |Fiber: 3g)

Cottage Cheese and Pine Nut Egg Pie

Aggregate Time to Prepare: **40 Minutes**

Yield: **6 Servings**

Ingredients:

- ¼ cup grated Parmesan Cheese
- ¼ cup Heavy Cream
- 1 ½ cups Water
- 1 cup Cottage Cheese
- 1 Tomato, diced
- 2 tbsp. chopped Basil
- 2 tbsp. chopped Pine Nuts
- 6 Eggs, beaten
- Pinch of Pepper
- Pinch of Salt

How to Cook:

1. Pour the water into the Instant Pot and put the trivet into the Instant Pot.
2. Mix all of the ingredients in a large container.
3. Oil-coat a baking dish and pour the mixture inside.
4. Put the dish inside the Instant Pot and shut and secure the lid.
5. Cook for 30 minutes on MANUAL.
6. Depressurize quickly.
7. Your dish is ready! Have fun!

Nutritional Info: (Calories 182| Total Fats 13g | Net Carbs: 3g | Protein 13g |Fiber: 0.9g)

Cream Cheese Pancakes

Aggregate Time to Prepare: 15 Minutes

Yield: 1 Serving

Ingredients:

- ½ tsp Cinnamon
- 1 tsp Swerve
- 2 Eggs
- 2 ounces Cream Cheese
- 2 tsp Butter

How to Cook:

1. Put the eggs, cream cheese, swerve, and cinnamon, in a blender.
2. Pulse until smooth.
3. Melt half of the butter in the Instant Pot using the "Sauté" mode.
4. Put in half of the batter and cook for approximately 3 minutes.
5. Turn over and cook for 1-2 minutes on the other side.
6. Repeat with the other pancake.
7. Your dish is ready! Have fun!

Nutritional Info: (Calories 344 | Total Fats 29g | Net Carbs: 3g | Protein 17g | Fiber: 1.5g)

Creamy Avocado Muffins

Aggregate Time to Prepare: 15 Minutes

Yield: 5 Servings

Ingredients:

- ¼ cup almond flour

- ¼ cup milk, full-fat
- ½ cup cream cheese, softened
- ½ cup heavy cream
- 1 ripe avocado, chop into-bite sized pieces
- 1 tbsp green onions, thinly sliced
- 1 tsp lime juice, freshly squeezed
- 4 large eggs

Spices:

- ¼ tsp smoked paprika, ground
- ½ tsp garlic powder
- 1 tsp husk powder
- 1 tsp salt

How to Cook:

1. Remove the rind of the avocado and chop in half. Remove the pit and chop into small cubes. Save for later.
2. In a food processor, mix avocado, cream cheese, heavy cream, eggs, and green onions. Pulse until smooth and creamy. Put in flour, milk, husk powder, salt, smoked paprika, garlic, and lime juice. Pulse again until all thoroughly blended. Pour the batter in silicone muffin molds and save for later.
3. Turn on the Instant Pot and pour 1 cup of water in the stainless steel insert. Place your trivet in the bottom of your instant pot and place silicone molds on the top.
4. Shut and secure the lid and close the steam release handle. Switch the Instant pot to "Manual" mode and turn the timer to 8 minutes. Cook on "High" pressure.
5. When your instant pot sounds the end signal, release the pressure using the quick release method and open the pot. Allow it to chill for some time.

6. Cautiously move muffins to a wire rack and let it cool to room temperature.
7. If you want, you can also spread on top plain yogurt and serve instantly.

Nutritional Info:(Calories 307 | Total Fats 27.3g | Net Carbs: 4.2g | Protein 9.5g | Fiber: 3.9g)

Creamy Mushrooms with Thyme

Aggregate Time to Prepare: 25 Minutes

Yield: 3 Servings

Ingredients:

For mushrooms:

- ¼ cup milk
- ½ cup feta cheese, crumbled
- 1 cup button mushrooms, sliced
- 1 large onion, thinly sliced
- 2 tbsp olive oil
- 3 eggs

Spices:

- ¼ tsp dried oregano
- ¼ tsp sea salt
- 1 tsp dried thyme

How to Cook:

1. Turn on the Instant Pot and coat the stainless steel insert with some oil. Switch your Instant Pot to "Sauté' mode. Put in onions and stir-fry until

translucent. Sprinkle with oregano and put in button mushrooms.
2. Carry on cooking for 5-7 minutes, stirring intermittently.
3. Crack the eggs into a mixing container and season with oregano. Put in crumbled feta and milk. Mix together and save for later.
4. Take the mushrooms out of the pot and save for later. Pour the egg mixture into the inner pot and cook for 2 minutes, stirring intermittently.
5. Serve with button mushrooms.

Nutritional Info: (Calories 244| Total Fats 19.6g | Net Carbs: 6.5g | Protein 11g |Fiber: 1.3g)

Creamy Raspberry Mug Cake

Aggregate Time to Prepare: **10 Minutes**

Yield: **3 Servings**

Ingredients:

- 4 large eggs
- ¼ cup fresh raspberries
- ½ cup almond flour
- ½ cup cream cheese
- ½ cup heavy whipping cream
- ½ tsp baking powder

Spices:

- ¼ tsp powdered stevia
- ¼ tsp vanilla extract

How to Cook:

1. In a large mixing container, mix eggs, cream cheese, almond flour, and baking powder. With a whisking attachment on, beat until thoroughly mixed and smooth.
2. Pour the mixture into oven-safe mugs and save for later.
3. Turn on the Instant Pot and pour 1 cup of water in the stainless steel insert. Position a trivet and place mugs on top.
4. Shut and secure the lid and close the steam release handle. Switch the Instant pot to "Manual" mode and turn the timer to 3 minutes. Cook on "High" pressure.
5. In the mean time, mix heavy whipping cream with powdered stevia and vanilla extract. Whisk until mixed and save for later.
6. When your instant pot sounds the end signal, release the pressure using the quick release method by moving the valve to the "Venting" position. Open the pot and move the mugs to a wire rack using oven mitts.
7. Top each mug with raspberry cream and serve instantly.
8. Have fun!

Nutritional Info:(Calories 418 | Total Fats 36.5g | Net Carbs: 5.1g | Protein 15.8g |Fiber: 2.7g)

Creamy Smoked Salmon

Aggregate Time to Prepare: **15 Minutes**

Yield: **2 Servings**

Ingredients:

- ¼ tsp dried thyme
- 1 tsp olive oil
- 2 large eggs, beaten
- 2 oz smoked salmon, chop into bite-sized pieces

For the creamy sauce:

- ¼ cup walnuts, chopped
- ½ cup almond milk, unsweetened
- ½ cup spinach, chopped
- ½ tsp black pepper, ground
- 1 tbsp lemon juice, freshly squeezed
- 1 tsp sea salt

How to Cook:

1. Mix almond milk, walnuts, and spinach in food processor. Blend until thoroughly mixed and put in salt, pepper, and lemon juice. Blend again for 1 minute and save for later.
2. Turn on the Instant Pot and coat the stainless steel insert with some olive oil. Put in salmon pieces and eggs. Drizzle with thyme and cook for 3 minutes. Using a large spatula, remove the omelet from the pot. Save for later covered.
3. After that, put in the previously blended sauce mixture to the pot. Shut and secure the lid and close the steam release handle. Switch the Instant pot to "Manual" mode and turn the timer to 3 minutes. When finished, release the pressure using the quick release method and open the pot.
4. Move the omelet to a serving plate and drizzle with hot sauce.
5. Serve instantly.

Nutritional Info:(Calories 365 | Total Fats 32.2g | Net Carbs: 3.3g | Protein 16.9g | Fiber: 2.8g)

Creamy Vanilla Chia Seeds

Aggregate Time to Prepare: 15 Minutes

Yield: 2 Servings

Ingredients:

- 2 tbsp coconut oil
- 2 tbsp Greek yogurt
- 2/3 cup unsweetened almond milk
- 3 tbsp chia seeds

Spices:

- ¼ tsp salt
- 1 tsp swerve
- 1 tsp vanilla extract

How to Cook:

1. Turn on your Instant Pot and Switch your Instant Pot to "'Sauté" mode. Pour in the milk and put in chia seeds. Cook for 5 minutes, stirring continuously.
2. After that put in coconut oil and drizzle with swerve, vanilla extract, and salt. Stir thoroughly and pour in approximately ¼ cup of water.
3. Carry on cooking for an additional 3-4 minutes.
4. When finished, push the "Cancel" button and mix in Greek yogurt.

5. If you want, you can also spread on top some fresh strawberries or seeds. Move to serving containers and chill thoroughly before serving.

Nutritional Info:(Calories 227| Total Fats 22.5g | Net Carbs: 2.4g | Protein 6.1g |Fiber: 7.8g)

Crustless Meat-Loaded Quiche

Aggregate Time to Prepare: 45 Minutes

Yield: 4 Servings

Ingredients:

- ¼ tsp Salt
- ½ cup diced Ham
- ½ cup Milk
- 1 ½ cups Water
- 1 cup ground Sausage, cooked
- 1 cup shredded Cheddar Cheese
- 2 Green Onions, chopped
- 4 Bacon Slices, cooked and crumbled
- 6 Eggs, beaten
- Pinch of Pepper

How to Cook:

1. Pour the water into your Instant Pot and put the trivet into the Instant Pot.
2. Coat a baking dish with cooking spray.
3. Put all of the ingredients in a container, and stir to mix thoroughly.
4. Pour this mixture into the readied dish.

5. Put the dish on the rack in your Instant Pot and shut and secure the lid.
6. Switch the Instant Pot to "High" and cook for 30 minutes.
7. Depressurize naturally, for 10 minutes.
8. Your dish is ready! Have fun!

Nutritional Info: (Calories 419 | Total Fats 32g | Net Carbs: 4g | Protein 29g | Fiber: 0.6g)

Crustless Quiche

Aggregate Time to Prepare: **45 Minutes**

Yield: **4 Servings**

Ingredients:

- ½ cup almond flour
- ½ cup milk
- 1 ½ cup cottage cheese
- 1 cup tomatoes, chopped
- 1 large red bell pepper, chopped
- 2 green onions, chopped
- 8 large eggs

Spices:

- ¼ tsp black pepper
- ¼ tsp salt
- ½ tsp oregano

How to Cook:

1. Plug in the Instant Pot and place the trivet at the bottom of the stainless steel insert. Put aluminum foil over the trivet creating sling and pour in 1 cup of water. Save for later.
2. In a large mixing container, mix flour, salt, and black pepper. Optionally put in some herbs of choice. Combine until completely blended. Gradually put in eggs, one at the time beating continuously with a paddle mixing attachment. Pour in the milk and continue to beat for 2 minutes on moderate speed.
3. Lastly put in vegetables and shredded vegan cheese. Combine again and move the mixture to oven-safe dish.
4. Tenderly place the dish in the Instant Pot and shut and secure the lid. Make sure the steam release handle is on the "Sealing" position and select the MANUAL mode. Turn the timer to 30 minutes on HIGH pressure.
5. When finished, depressurize using the natural release method for 10 minutes and move the pressure valve to the VENTING position to release any rest of the steam.
6. Cautiously open the lid and remove the dish using an aluminum sling. Chill for some time and serve.

Nutritional Info:(Calories 276 | Total Fats 14g | Net Carbs: 9.2g | Protein 26.8g |Fiber: 1.5g)

Delicious Pumpkin Bread

Aggregate Time to Prepare: 30 Minutes

Yield: 4 Servings

Ingredients:

- ¼ cup almond milk
- ½ cup pumpkin puree
- 1 cup almond flour
- 1 tbsp almond butter, melted
- 2 large eggs, beaten

Spices:

- ¼ tsp nutmeg, ground
- ¼ tsp turmeric powder
- ½ tsp pumpkin pie spice
- ½ tsp salt

How to Cook:

1. In a large mixing container, mix flour, baking powder, salt, nutmeg, turmeric, and pumpkin pie spice. Stir until mixed and put in eggs, pumpkin puree, and milk. Stir until all thoroughly blended and save for later.
2. Oil-coat a fitting springform pan with melted butter. Put in the dough and cover with aluminium foil.
3. Turn on the Instant Pot and pour 1 cup of water in the stainless steel insert. Place your trivet in the bottom of your instant pot and place the pan on top. Cover with a lid and switch your Instant Pot to "Manual" mode. Turn the timer to 25 minutes and cook on "Low" pressure.
4. When finished, depressurize using the natural release method. Open the pot and move the springform pan to a wire rack using oven mitts. Allow it to cool to room temperature.
5. Cut the bread into slices and serve.

Nutritional Info:(Calories 275 | Total Fats 21.8g | Net Carbs: 5.8g | Protein 10.7g | Fiber: 4.7g)

Easy Deviled Eggs

Aggregate Time to Prepare: 30 Minutes

Yield: 4 Servings

Ingredients:

- ¼ cup sour cream
- 1 tbsp Dijon mustard
- 12 eggs
- 2 tbsp butter
- 2 tbsp parsley, thinly sliced
- 2 tsp lemon juice

Spices:

- 1 tsp sea salt

How to Cook:

1. Plug in the Instant Pot and pour in 1 cup of water. Set the steaming insert and tenderly place egg in it. Securely shut and secure the lid and set the steam release handle to SEALING position. Press the MANUAL button and set the timer to 7 minutes.
2. After that prepare the deviled eggs stuffing. In a medium-sized container, mix sour cream, butter, cilantro, Dijon, and lime juice. Sprinkle with salt and mix thoroughly using a hand mixer. You wish to get a nice and creamy mixture.
3. When you hear the end signal, set the steam valve to VENTING position to depressurize using the quick

release method. Open the lid and tenderly remove the eggs. Chill for some time.
4. In the mean time, prepare the ice bath. Take a large container and pour in 4 cups of ice cold water. If you want, you can also put in 2 cups of ice cubes to speed up the cooling process. Put eggs in it and cool them completely. This will stop the cooking process and prevent the eggs of being overcooked.
5. Tenderly peel the eggs and cut them in half, lengthwise. Remove the yolks and place them in the cream mixture. Stir thoroughly to mix avoiding any large pieces. Put the cream mixture in a large piping pastry bag with a star tip. Pipe approximately 1 tbsp of the mixture at the center of each egg and move to a serving plate.

Nutritional Info:(Calories 274 | Total Fats 22.1g | Net Carbs: 1.8g | Protein 17.4g |Fiber: 0.2g)

Eggs and Cream

Aggregate Time to Prepare: **15 Minutes**

Yield: **4 Servings**

Ingredients:

- 1 ½ cups Water
- 1 ½ tbsp. Chives
- 4 Eggs
- 4 tbsp. Cream
- Salt and Pepper, to taste

How to Cook:

1. Pour the water into the Instant Pot.

2. Oil-coat 4 ramekins with some cooking spray.
3. Pour a tablespoon of cream inside each ramekin.
4. Crack an egg into each of the ramekins, making sure not to break the yolk.
5. Sprinkle with salt and pepper.
6. Drizzle with chives.
7. Position the ramekins on the rack inside the Instant Pot, and shut and secure the lid.
8. Switch the Instant Pot to "Manual" mode and cook for 2 minutes.
9. Depressurize quickly.
10. Your dish is ready! Have fun!

Nutritional Info: (Calories 173 | Total Fats 16.6g | Net Carbs: 0.8g | Protein 5.8g | Fiber: 0g)

Eggs with Spicy Marinara Sauce

Aggregate Time to Prepare: 20 Minutes

Yield: 3 Servings

Ingredients:

- ½ onion, thinly sliced
- 1 red bell pepper, diced
- 2 cup cherry tomatoes
- 2 garlic cloves, minced
- 2 tbsp olive oil
- 5 large eggs

Spices:

- ¼ tsp freshly ground black pepper

- ½ tsp cumin powder
- ½ tsp smoked paprika
- 1 tbsp dried parsley
- 1 tsp chili powder
- 1 tsp salt

How to Cook:

1. Oil-coat the bottom of the stainless steel insert and switch your Instant Pot to "SAUTÉ" mode. Heat the oil and put in diced onion, garlic cloves, and diced red bell pepper. Sprinkle with chili powder, paprika, salt, pepper, and cumin. Stir thoroughly and cook for 5 minutes, or until translucent and soft.
2. Put in tomatoes and stir thoroughly. Press the CANCEL button and chill for an additional 5 minutes.
3. In a medium-sized container, separate egg whites from yolks. Pour the egg whites into the pot and stir tenderly with a wooden spoon or a spatula.
4. Shut and secure the lid and make sure the steam release handle is on "Sealing" position. Press the Manual button and turn the timer to 1 minute on LOW pressure.
5. When you hear the end signal, push the CANCEL button release the pressure using the quick release method. Open the lid and move the mixture to a serving plate.
6. If you want, you can also drizzle with some chopped parsley or season with some smoked paprika.

Nutritional Info:(Calories 244 | Total Fats 18g | Net Carbs: 8.3g | Protein 12.3g |Fiber: 2.4g)

Giant Ricotta and Blueberry Pancake

Aggregate Time to Prepare: **60 Minutes**

Yield: 5 Servings

Ingredients:

- ¼ cup Blueberries
- ¼ cup Milk
- ½ cup Flaxseed Meal
- ½ tsp Stevia Powder
- ½ tsp Vanilla
- ¾ cup Ricotta Cheese
- 1 cup Almond Flour
- 1 cup Water
- 1 tsp Baking Powder
- 3 Eggs
- Pinch of Salt

How to Cook:

1. Pour the water into the Instant Pot and put the trivet into the Instant Pot.
2. Blend all of the wet ingredients in a blender.
3. Put in the flour, flaxseed, salt, baking powder, and stevia, and blend until mixed.
4. Stir in the blueberries.
5. Coat a baking dish with cooking spray.
6. Pour the batter into the dish.
7. Put inside the Instant Pot and shut and secure the lid.
8. Cook on LOW for 45 minutes.
9. Your dish is ready! Have fun!

Nutritional Info: (Calories 311| Total Fats 22g | Net Carbs: 5.8g | Protein 15.2g |Fiber: 5g)

Green Beans with Bacon

Aggregate Time to Prepare: 10 Minutes

Yield: 6 Servings

Ingredients:

- ¼ cup Water
- 1 cup Onion (diced)
- 1 tsp Ground Black Pepper
- 1 tsp Salt
- 6 cups Green Beans (chop in half)
- 5 rashers Bacon (diced)

How to Cook:

1. Set the Instant Pot to "Sauté" and put in the bacon. Cook until the grease melts, some 2-3 minutes, intermittently stirring.
2. Put in the onions, and cook for an additional 2 minutes while intermittently stirring.
3. Put in the green beans, salt, pepper and water and stir to mix.
4. Shut and secure the lid, and turn the timer and cook for 4 minutes at high pressure.
5. When finished depressurize using the quick release method and adjust salt and pepper if you wish.
6. Serve warm.

Nutritional Info: (Calories: 122 | Total Fats: 7g | Net Carbs: 7g | Proteins: 4g | Fibers: 3g)

Ground Beef with Steamed Cauliflower

Aggregate Time to Prepare: 35 Minutes

Yield: 2 Servings

Ingredients:

- 1 cup cauliflower, chopped
- 1 tbsp butter
- 1 tbsp chives, thinly sliced
- 2 medium-sized bell pepper, chopped
- 2 tbsp heavy cream
- 8 oz ground beef

Spices:

- ¼ tsp black pepper, ground
- ¼ tsp red chili flakes
- ¼ tsp smoked paprika, ground
- ½ tsp dried thyme, ground
- ½ tsp sea salt

How to Cook:

1. Turn on the Instant Pot and put the butter into the stainless steel insert. Switch the Instant Pot to "Sauté" mode and put in ground beef. Drizzle with some salt, pepper, and smoked paprika. Cook for 5 minutes, or until golden brown. Stir intermittently.
2. Put in bell peppers and heavy cream. Stir thoroughly and cook for 2 additional minutes.
3. Turn off the heat by pressing the "Cancel" button on the Instant Pot and mix in the chives instantly. Allow

it to stand for 5 minutes and then move to a serving dish.
4. After that, wash the stainless steel insert and pour in 1 cup of water. Place your trivet in the bottom of your instant pot. Put the cauliflower in the steam basket and set the basket on the top of a trivet. Shut and secure the lid and close the steam release handle.
5. Switch your instant pot to "Steam" mode and turn the timer to 10 minutes. Cook on "High" pressure. When finished, release the pressure using the quick release method and open the lid. Drizzle with chili flakes and if you want, with some olive oil for better taste.
6. Your dish is ready! Serve with steamed cauliflower.

Nutritional Info: (Calories 366 | Total Fats 18.8g | Net Carbs: 9.4g | Protein 37.1g | Fiber: 3.1g)

Ham and Dill Pressure-Cooked Eggs

Aggregate Time to Prepare: 15 Minutes

Yield: 4 Servings

Ingredients:

- ¼ cup grated Parmesan Cheese
- ¼ tsp White Pepper
- 1 tbsp.
- 2 tbsp. chopped Dill
- 5 Eggs
- 6 ounces Ham, chopped

How to Cook:

1. Pour 1 ½ cups of water into the Instant Pot and put the rack into the Instant Pot.
2. Whisk the eggs in a container.
3. Stir in the rest of the ingredients.
4. Oil-coat 4 ramekins and separate this mixture among them.
5. Put in the Instant Pot and shut and secure the lid.
6. Switch the Instant Pot to "Manual" mode and cook for 5 minutes.
7. Release the pressure using the quick release method.
8. Your dish is ready! Have fun!

Nutritional Info: (Calories 250 | Total Fats 17 g | Net Carbs: 3g | Protein 14g | Fiber: 1g)

Hollandaise Eggs and Ham

Aggregate Time to Prepare: 10 Minutes

Yield: 2 Servings

Ingredients:

- 1 ½ cups plus 2 tbsp. Water
- 2 Eggs
- 2 Ham Slices, chopped
- 2 tbsp. Hollandaise Sauce

How to Cook:

1. Pour 1 ½ cups water into your Instant Pot and put the rack into the Instant Pot.
2. Crack the eggs into 2 ramekins, keeping the yolks intact.
3. Pour a tablespoon of water on top.
4. Put the ramekins in the Instant Pot and shut and secure the lid.
5. Switch your Instant Pot to "Steam" mode and cook for 2-3 minutes.
6. Spread on top chopped ham and Hollandaise sauce.
7. Your dish is ready! Have fun!

Nutritional Info: (Calories 271 | Total Fats 16.2g | Net Carbs: 5.2g | Protein 25.3g | Fiber: 1.1g)

Indian Zucchini Kheer

Aggregate Time to Prepare: 10 Minutes

Yield: 4 Servings

Ingredients:

- ¼ cup Splenda
- ½ tsp Ground Cardamom
- 2 cups Zucchini (grated)
- 5 oz. Evaporated Milk
- 5 oz. Half & Half

How to Cook:

1. Put all ingredients, except cardamom, into the Instant Pot.
2. Shut and secure the lid, and turn the timer and cook for 10 minutes.
3. When finished allow the pressure to be released naturally for 10 minutes and then quick release it.
4. Put in cardamom and stir thoroughly.
5. Serve warm.

Nutritional Info: (Calories: 105 | Total Fats: 6g | Net Carbs: 7g | Proteins: 4g | Fibers: 2g)

Italian Omelet with Herbs

Aggregate Time to Prepare: 20 Minutes

Yield: 2 Servings

Ingredients:

For omelet:

- ½ medium-sized tomato, chopped
- 2 garlic cloves, crushed
- 3 large eggs

Spices:

- ½ tsp sea salt
- 1 tsp Italian seasoning mix
- 2 tbsp olive oil

How to Cook:

1. Oil-coat the inner pot with two tablespoons of olive oil and Switch your Instant Pot to "'Sauté" mode. Heat up and put in tomatoes. Cook for 2-3 minutes, stirring continuously.
2. After that put in garlic and season with Italian seasoning mix. Carry on cooking for an additional 1-2 minute. Take out of the pot and move to a container. Save for later.
3. In the mean time, in a small container, whisk the eggs together. Pour the mixture in the pot and continue to cook for 2-3 minutes or until set.
4. Press the "Cancel" button and tenderly remove the inner pot. Using a wooden spatula, loosen the edges and remove the eggs.
5. Put in tomatoes and fold over. Serve instantly.

Nutritional Info:(Calories 235| Total Fats 21.5g | Net Carbs: 1.9g | Protein 9.8g |Fiber: 0.3g)

Jalapeno Egg Poppers

Aggregate Time to Prepare: **25 Minutes**

Yield: **6 Servings**

Ingredients:

- ¼ tsp Garlic Powder
- 1 ½ cups Water
- 1 cup shredded Cheddar Cheese
- 1 tsp Lemon Pepper Seasoning
- 12 Eggs
- 4 Jalapeno Peppers, seeded and chopped

How to Cook:

1. Pour the water into the Instant Pot and put the rack into the Instant Pot.
2. Whisk the eggs with the garlic powder and lemon pepper seasoning.
3. Stir in the cheese and jalapenos.
4. Separate the mixture among 6 jars.
5. Close the jars and place them on the rack.
6. Shut and secure the lid and switch your instant pot to "Manual" mode and cook for 8 minutes.
7. Depressurize naturally, for 10 minutes.
8. Your dish is ready! Have fun!

Nutritional Info: (Calories 219 | Total Fats 16g | Net Carbs: 2g | Protein 18g | Fiber: 4g)

Jalapeno Popper Keto Frittata

Aggregate Time to Prepare: **40 Minutes**

Yield: **8 Servings**

Ingredients:

Cream Cheese Mixture:

- ¼ cup shredded Cheddar Cheese
- 2 tbsp. chopped Jalapeno Peppers

- 2 tbsp. Salsa Verde
- 6 ounces Cream Cheese, softened

Egg Mixture:

- ¼ tsp Salt
- 1/3 cup Milk
- 2 tbsp. Heavy Cream
- 6 Eggs
- Pinch of Pepper

Toppings:

- ½ cup shredded Cheddar Cheese
- 1 tbsp. sliced Jalapeno Peppers
- 6 Bacon Slices, chopped and cooked

How to Cook:

1. Pour some water into the Instant Pot, approximately 1 ½ cups, and put the trivet into the Instant Pot.
2. Oil-coat a baking dish with some cooking spray.
3. Mix together the cream cheese mixture ingredients. Put in a microwave and microwave for a minute, to soften.
4. Drop spoonfuls of that mixture to the bottom of the dish.
5. Mix the egg mixture ingredients and pour over the cream cheese.
6. Put the toppings on top.
7. Wrap the baking dish with a foil, and place in the Instant Pot.
8. Switch the Instant Pot to "High" and cook for 20 minutes.

9. Release the pressure using the quick release method and serve.

Nutritional Info: (Calories 361| Total Fats 40g | Net Carbs: 3g | Protein 24g |Fiber: 2g)

Kale Cheddar Cheese Omelet

Aggregate Time to Prepare: 10 Minutes

Yield: 2 Servings

Ingredients:

For omelet:

- ½ cup cheddar cheese, crumbled
- 1 small onion, thinly sliced
- 2 tbsp heavy cream
- 6 large eggs

Spices:

- ½ tsp black pepper, freshly ground
- ½ tsp Italian seasoning
- 1 tsp sea salt

How to Cook:

1. In a large mixing container, mix eggs, salt, pepper, and heavy cream. Mix together until thoroughly mixed and then put in all the rest of the ingredients. Mix again and save for later.
2. Turn on your Instant Pot and coat the stainless steel insert with some cooking spray or olive oil.
3. Pour in the egg mixture and switch to "Manual' mode. Make sure the steam release handle is on the "Sealing" position and turn the timer to 5 minutes and cook on high pressure.
4. When finished, depressurize using the quick release method. Cautiously open the lid and serve instantly.

Nutritional Info:(Calories 394| Total Fats 29.9g | Net Carbs: 4.4g | Protein 26.6g |Fiber: 0.8g)

Leek Stir-Fry

Aggregate Time to Prepare: 15 Minutes

Yield: 2 Servings

Ingredients:

- 1 cup leeks, chopped into bite-sized pieces
- 1 tbsp butter
- 2 tbsp olive oil
- 3 eggs

Spices:

- ¼ tsp chili flakes
- ¼ tsp salt
- 1 tbsp dried rosemary
- 1 tsp mustard seeds

How to Cook:

1. Thoroughly wash leeks under cold running water. Drain in a large colander and place on a clean work surface. Using a sharp knife, chop into one-inch long pieces. Save for later.
2. Turn on your Instant Pot and coat the stainless steel insert with olive oil. Switch your Instant Pot to "Sauté' mode and put in mustard seeds. Stir-fry for 2-3 minutes.
3. After that put in leeks and butter. Cook for 5 minutes, stirring continuously. Tenderly crack three eggs and season with dried rosemary, chili flakes, and salt.

4. Cook until set, for about 4 minutes. Turn off your Instant pot.
5. Serve instantly.

Nutritional Info: (Calories 292| Total Fats 26.5g | Net Carbs: 6g | Protein 9g |Fiber: 0.8g)

Mushroom and Spinach Omelet Pie

Aggregate Time to Prepare: 25 Minutes

Yield: 12 Servings

Ingredients:

- ¼ cup Butter
- ½ cup Heavy Cream
- ½ tsp Pepper
- 1 cup grated Cheddar Cheese
- 2 Garlic Cloves, minced
- 2 tsp Baking Powder
- 2/3 cup Coconut Flour
- 7 Eggs
- 5 ounces Fresh Spinach, chopped
- 8 ounces Mushrooms, sliced

How to Cook:

1. Melt the butter in your Instant Pot using the "Sauté" mode.
2. Put in mushrooms and cook for 5 minutes.
3. Put in garlic and cook for an additional minute.
4. Move to a container.
5. Mix together the eggs and heavy cream.
6. Stir in the flour and baking powder.

7. Put in the rest of the ingredients, including the garlicky mushrooms, and stir to mix.
8. Oil-coat a baking dish and pour the mixture into it. Cover with a foil.
9. Pout 1 ½ cups water into your Instant Pot and put the rack into the Instant Pot.
10. Insert the baking dish inside and cook for 25 minutes on MANUAL.
11. Release the pressure using the quick release method.
12. Your dish is ready! Have fun!

Nutritional Info: (Calories 148 | Total Fats 10.6g | Net Carbs: 2.5g | Protein 6.2g |Fiber: 2.5g)

Mustard Pork with Mushrooms

Aggregate Time to Prepare: 20 Minutes

Yield: 2 Servings

Ingredients:

- 1 small onion, thinly sliced
- 1 small zucchini, chopped
- 1 tbsp Dijon mustard
- 1 tbsp olive oil
- 6 oz button mushrooms, sliced
- 10 oz pork, minced

Spices:

- ¼ tsp dried basil, ground
- ¼ tsp garlic powder
- ½ tsp black pepper, ground

- ½ tsp salt

How to Cook:

1. Turn on the Instant Pot and put in the olive oil in the stainless steel insert. Switch the Instant Pot to "Sauté" mode and put in onions. Stir-fry for 2-3 minutes and put in minced pork. Drizzle with garlic powder, salt, and pepper. Stir thoroughly and cook for 3-4 minutes, or until browned.
2. Put in zucchini and mushrooms. Pour 1 cup of water and shut and secure the lid. Close the steam release handle and switch your Instant Pot to "Manual" mode. Turn the timer to 6 minutes and switch your instant pot to "high pressure" setting and cook.
3. When your instant pot sounds the end signal, release the pressure using the quick release method.
4. Open the pot and switch your instant pot to "Sauté" mode.
5. Stir in the Dijon mustard and drizzle with dried thyme. Move to a serving plate and have fun!

Nutritional Info:(Calories 312 | Total Fats 12.7g | Net Carbs: 6.4g | Protein 41.3g |Fiber: 2.7g)

No-Crust Tomato & Spinach Quiche

Aggregate Time to Prepare: **35 Minutes**

Yield: **6 Servings**

Ingredients:

- ¼ cup grated Parmesan Cheese
- ¼ tsp Pepper

- ½ cup Milk
- ½ Tomato, sliced
- ½ tsp Garlic Salt
- 1 ½ cups Water
- 1 cup diced Tomatoes
- 12 Eggs
- 3 cups chopped Spinach
- 3 Green Onions, chopped

How to Cook:

1. Pour the water into the Instant Pot.
2. Coat a baking dish with cooking spray.
3. Mix the diced tomatoes, green onions, and spinach, in it.
4. Whisk the eggs along with the milk, salt, and pepper.
5. Pour this mixture over the spinach and tomatoes.
6. Drizzle with parmesan cheese and spread on top tomato slices.
7. Put the baking dish on the rack and shut and secure the lid.
8. Switch the Instant Pot to "High" and cook for 20 minutes.
9. Wait 10 minutes and release the pressure using the quick release method.
10. Your dish is ready! Have fun!

Nutritional Info: (Calories 178 | Total Fats 11.2g | Net Carbs: 3.8g | Protein 15.3g | Fiber: 1.2g)

Onion and Spinach Omelet with Goat Cheese

Aggregate Time to Prepare: 25 Minutes

Yield: 1 Serving

Ingredients:

- ¼ Onion, sliced
- ¼ tsp Garlic Salt
- 1 ½ cups Water
- 1 ounce Goat Cheese
- 1 Spring Onion, chopped
- 2 cups Spinach
- 2 tbsp. Butter
- 3 Eggs, beaten
- Pinch of Pepper

How to Cook:

1. Melt the butter in the Instant Pot using the "Sauté" mode.
2. Put in onions and cook for 3 minutes.
3. Stir in spinach and spices and cook for 1 additional minute.
4. Move the mixture to an oil-coated baking dish.
5. Pour the eggs over and mix in the cheese.
6. Pour the water into the Instant Pot and put the rack into the Instant Pot.
7. Put the baking dish inside and shut and secure the lid.
8. Switch the Instant Pot to "High" and cook for 12 minutes.
9. Your dish is ready! Have fun!

Nutritional Info: (Calories 321| Total Fats 54g | Net Carbs: 4.8g | Protein 36g |Fiber: 2g)

Pizza Frittata

Aggregate Time to Prepare: 40 Minutes

Yield: 8 Servings

Ingredients:

- ½ cup grated Parmesan Cheese
- ½ cup Ricotta Cheese
- 1 ½ cups Water
- 1 Garlic Clove, minced
- 1/3 cup mini Pepperoni
- 12 Eggs
- 4 tbsp. Olive Oil
- 5 ounces Mozzarella Cheese, grated
- 9 ounces Spinach
- Pinch of Pepper
- Pinch of Salt

How to Cook:

1. Pour the water into the Instant Pot.
2. Whisk the eggs along with the oil, salt, and pepper.
3. Stir in the ricotta, parmesan, spinach, and garlic.
4. Oil-coat a baking dish and pour the mixture into it.
5. Spread on top pepperoni and mozzarella.
6. Put the dish on the rack and shut and secure the lid of the Instant Pot.
7. Cook for 15 minutes on HIGH.
8. Depressurize naturally.

9. Your dish is ready! Have fun!

Nutritional Info: (Calories 301| Total Fats 23g | Net Carbs: 2.8g | Protein 18g |Fiber: 1g)

Poached Eggs with Garlic Spinach

Aggregate Time to Prepare: 15 Minutes

Yield: 1 Serving

Ingredients:

- 2 eggs
- 3 tbsp olive oil
- 7 oz spinach, chopped

Spices:

- ¼ tsp dried oregano
- ¼ tsp dried rosemary
- ½ tsp garlic powder
- ½ tsp sea salt

How to Cook:

1. Turn on your Instant Pot and coat the inner pot with olive oil. Switch your Instant Pot to "Sauté' mode and put in chopped spinach. Sprinkle with some salt and garlic powder.
2. Stir thoroughly and cook for 4-5 minutes, stirring continuously.
3. Tenderly crack eggs and season with dried oregano, rosemary, and the rest of the salt. Cook until completely set, approximately 2-3 minutes.
4. When finished, turn off the pot and move to a serving plate.

5. If you want, you can also serve with a couple of kalamata olives or fresh lettuce.

Nutritional Info:(Calories 531| Total Fats 52.5g | Net Carbs: 3.5g | Protein 16.8g |Fiber: 4.4g)

Poached Eggs with Mushrooms

Aggregate Time to Prepare: 25 Minutes

Yield: 1 Serving

Ingredients:

- ½ cup button mushrooms, sliced
- 1 egg
- 2 oz fresh arugula
- 2 tbsp olive oil

Spices:

- 1 tbsp dried thyme
- ¼ tsp chili flakes

How to Cook:

1. Put mushrooms in a large sieve and rinse under cold running water. Pat dry with a kitchen towel ensuring to wipe away any extra debris.
2. Using a sharp paring knife, cut each mushroom in half, lengthwise, but keep the stems on. Save for later.
3. Turn on your Instant Pot and put butter into the stainless steel insert. Switch your Instant Pot to "Sauté' mode and melt it.

4. Put in mushrooms and cook for 4-5 minutes, or until the liquid evaporates.
5. After that, put in arugula and stir thoroughly. If you want, you can also put in one tablespoon of olive oil for some extra taste. Cook for one minute.
6. Lastly, crack the eggs and cook until set – for 2 minutes. Sprinkle with dried thyme and drizzle with chili flakes.
7. Turn off your Instant pot and cautiously move the mixture to a serving plate using a large kitchen spatula.
8. Serve instantly.

Nutritional Info:(Calories 325| Total Fats 32.8g | Net Carbs: 2.3g | Protein 8.1g |Fiber: 1.3g)

Poached Eggs with Tomatoes

Aggregate Time to Prepare: **15 Minutes**

Yield: **4 Servings**

Ingredients:

- 4 Eggs
- 1 Tomato, chopped
- ½ Red Onion, diced
- ½ tsp Salt
- ¼ tsp Pepper
- ½ tsp Paprika
- ½ tsp dried Parsley

How to Cook:

1. Oil-coat 4 ramekins with cooking spray.
2. Whisk the eggs along with the salt, pepper, paprika, and parsley.
3. Stir in the tomatoes and red onion
4. Separate this mixture among the ramekins.
5. Pour 1 ½ cups water into the Instant Pot and put the trivet into the Instant Pot.
6. Put the ramekins inside and shut and secure the lid.
7. Switch your Instant Pot to "Steam" mode and cook for 5 minutes.
8. Depressurize quickly.
9. Your dish is ready! Have fun!

Nutritional Info: (Calories 194 | Total Fats 13.5g | Net Carbs: 5g | Protein 10g | Fiber: 1.5g)

Poppy Seed Lemony Muffins

Aggregate Time to Prepare: **25 Minutes**

Yield: 4 Servings

Ingredients:

- ¼ cup Coconut Milk
- ¼ tsp Lemon Zest
- 1 cup Coconut Flour
- 1 Egg
- 1 tbsp. Coconut Flour
- 1 tbsp. Lemon Juice
- 1 tbsp. Poppy Seeds
- 1 tbsp. Swerve
- 1 tsp Coconut Oil, melted
- Pinch of Baking Soda
- Pinch of Salt

How to Cook:

1. Pour 1 ½ cups of water into the Instant Pot and put the rack into the Instant Pot.
2. Mix the dry ingredients in one container.
3. Mix the wet ones in another.
4. Fold the two mixtures together.
5. Separate the mixture among 4 silicone muffin cups.
6. Put the muffin cups on the rack and shut and secure the lid.
7. Switch the Instant Pot to "High" and cook for 15 minutes.
8. Depressurize quickly.
9. Your dish is ready! Have fun!

Nutritional Info: (Calories 116 | Total Fats 6g | Net Carbs: 3.9g | Protein 4.4g | Fiber: 2g)

Pumpkin Hemp Spread

Aggregate Time to Prepare: **15 Minutes**

Yield: **2 Servings**

Ingredients:

- ¼ cup chia seeds
- ¼ cup swerve
- 1 cup pumpkin puree
- 1 tbsp butter

Spices:

- ¼ tsp salt
- 1 tsp cinnamon
- 1 tsp pumpkin pie spice

How to Cook:

1. Turn on your Instant Pot and Switch your Instant Pot to "'Sauté" mode. Coat the inner pot with butter and put in chia seeds and swerve.
2. Cook for 3 minutes, stirring continuously. After that put in pumpkin puree and drizzle with cinnamon, pumpkin pie spice, and salt.
3. Stir thoroughly and pour in 1 cup of water. Shut and secure the lid and set the steam release handle to the 'Sealing' position.
4. Switch your Instant Pot to "Manual" mode and turn the timer to 6 minutes on high pressure.
5. When finished, release the pressure using the quick release method and open the lid.
6. Move to serving containers and chill for some time.
7. Refrigerate for minimum one hour before serving.

Nutritional Info:(Calories 100| Total Fats 6.7g | Net Carbs: 6.5g | Protein 1.8g |Fiber: 4.2g)

Quick and Easy Paprika Eggs

Aggregate Time to Prepare: 15 Minutes

Yield: 6 Servings

Ingredients:

- ¼ tsp Salt
- ½ tsp Smoked Paprika
- 1 ½ cups Water
- 6 Eggs
- Pinch of Pepper

How to Cook:

1. Pour the water into the Instant Pot.
2. Crack the eggs into a baking dish, without breaking the yolks.
3. Coat the dish with foil and place on the rack.
4. Shut and secure the lid and cook on HIGH for 4 minutes.
5. Depressurize quickly and remove the 'loaf' of eggs.
6. Put on a cutting board and dice the eggs thinly.
7. Stir in the spices.
8. Your dish is ready! Have fun!

Nutritional Info: (Calories 62 | Total Fats 4g | Net Carbs: 0g | Protein 5g |Fiber: 0g)

Raspberry Mousse

Aggregate Time to Prepare: 20 Minutes

Yield: 2 Servings

Ingredients:

- ¼ cup heavy cream
- ¼ cup swerve
- 1 cup unsweetened almond milk
- 2 cups fresh raspberries
- 3 tbsp whipped cream, sugar-free

Spices:

- ¼ tsp ginger powder
- ¼ tsp salt
- 1 tsp vanilla extract

How to Cook:

1. Turn on your Instant Pot and Switch your Instant Pot to "'Sauté" mode. Put raspberries at the bottom of the inner pot and pour in ¼ cup of water. Put in swerve and stir thoroughly. Cook for 10-12 minutes, stirring continuously.
2. When most of the liquid has evaporated, pour in the milk and vanilla extract. Carry on cooking for an additional 3-4 minutes.
3. Stir in the whipped cream and heavy cream. Sprinkle with salt and ginger powder.
4. Press the "Cancel" button and move the mousse to serving containers. Chill thoroughly before serving.

Nutritional Info:(Calories 151| Total Fats 8.9g | Net Carbs: 7.6g | Protein 2.3g |Fiber: 8.5g)

Rich Plantain Bread

Aggregate Time to Prepare: 55 Minutes

Yield: 12 Servings

Ingredients:

- 1 ½ cup Water
- 1 tbsp. Vanilla
- 1 tsp Baking Powder
- 2 cups Almond Flour
- 2 Eggs, beaten
- 3 tbsp. Butter, melted
- 4 Plantains, mashed
- Sweetener, to taste

How to Cook:

1. Pour the water into the Instant Pot and put the trivet into the Instant Pot.
2. Mix the eggs, plantains, butter, and vanilla.
3. Stir in the dry ingredients and mix until smooth.
4. Oil-coat a loaf pan with cooking spray and pour the mixture inside.
5. Put in the Instant Pot and shut and secure the lid.
6. Switch the Instant Pot to "Manual" mode and cook for 40 minutes.
7. Your dish is ready! Have fun!

Nutritional Info: (Calories 102| Total Fats 3.8g | Net Carbs: 8.4g | Protein 1.6g |Fiber: 0.6g)

Ricotta and Sausage-Crusted Pie

Aggregate Time to Prepare: **40 Minutes**

Yield: **8 Servings**

Ingredients:

- ¼ cup grated Parmesan Cheese
- ½ cup diced Onion
- 1 cup shredded Mozzarella Cheese
- 1 Garlic Clove, minced
- 1 pound Mild Sausage
- 2 cups Ricotta Cheese
- 2 cups Water
- 3 Eggs
- 3 tsp Olive Oil
- 8 cups chopped Swiss Chard
- Salt and Pepper, to taste

How to Cook:

1. Switch the Instant Pot to "Sauté" mode and heat the oil.
2. Put in onions and garlic and cook for 3 minutes.
3. Put in chard and cook for about 2 minutes, or until it shrivels up.
4. Sprinkle with some salt and pepper and move to a plate.
5. Whisk the eggs in a container and mix in the cheeses.
6. Roll out the sausage and push it tightly into the bottom of an oil-coated baking dish.
7. Spread on top the chard mixture.

8. Pour the cheesy egg mixture on top.
9. Pour the water into the Instant Pot and put the trivet into the Instant Pot.
10. Line the pie dish with a foil and put it inside the Instant Pot.
11. Shut and secure the lid and cook for 25 minutes.
12. Depressurize naturally and remove the lid.
13. Shut and secure the lid again and cook with the lid removed for an additional 5-10 minutes.
14. Your dish is ready! Have fun!

Nutritional Info: (Calories 344 | Total Fats 27g | Net Carbs: 4g | Protein 23g | Fiber: 3.3g)

Salted Thyme Biscuits

Aggregate Time to Prepare: 25 Minutes

Yield: 4 Servings

Ingredients:

- ½ cup almond flour
- ½ tsp baking soda
- 1 small onion, thinly sliced
- 1 tsp apple cider vinegar
- 2 garlic cloves, crushed
- 2 large eggs
- 4 tbsp butter

Spices:

- ¼ tsp black pepper, ground
- ¼ tsp dried rosemary, ground
- ½ tsp dried thyme, ground
- ½ tsp salt

How to Cook:

1. In a large mixing container, mix almond flour, butter, garlic, eggs, onions, thyme, rosemary, salt, and pepper. Combine until thoroughly mixed.
2. In a separate container, mix apple cider vinegar and baking soda. Stir until soda dissolves in vinegar and pour into the container with previously mixed ingredients. Stir until all thoroughly blended. Save for later.
3. Cover a fitting springform pan with some parchment paper and coat the sides with some cooking spray. Drop a spoonful of the batter onto the pan and make circle-shaped biscuits. Save for later.
4. Turn on the Instant Pot and pour 1 cup of water in the stainless steel insert. Place your trivet in the bottom of your instant pot and place the pan on top. Shut and secure the lid and close the steam release handle. Switch the Instant pot to "Manual" mode and cook for 30 minutes. Cook on "High" pressure.
5. When finished, release the pressure using the quick release method by turning the valve to the "Venting" position. Open the pot and move the pan to a wire rack using oven mitts. Allow it to cool to room temperature before serving.

Nutritional Info:(Calories 232 | Total Fats 20.7g | Net Carbs: 3.6g | Protein 6.6g | Fiber: 2g)

Sausage and Bacon Omelet

Aggregate Time to Prepare: 40 Minutes

Yield: 6 Servings

Ingredients:

- ¼ tsp Pepper
- ¼ tsp Salt
- ½ cup Milk
- 1 ½ cups Water
- 1 Onions, diced
- 1/4 tsp Garlic Powder
- 6 Bacon Slices, cooked and crumbled
- 6 Eggs
- 6 Sausage Links, sliced

How to Cook:

1. Pour the water into the Instant Pot and put the rack into the Instant Pot.
2. Whisk the eggs along with the milk and seasonings.
3. Stir in the rest of the ingredients.
4. Coat a baking dish with cooking spray.
5. Pour the egg mixture into it.
6. Put the dish on the rack and shut and secure the lid.
7. Switch the Instant Pot to "Manual" mode and cook for 25 minutes.
8. Depressurize naturally.
9. Your dish is ready! Have fun!

Nutritional Info: (Calories 222 | Total Fats 15.5g | Net Carbs: 3.5g | Protein 16.8g | Fiber: 0g)

Sausage and Cheddar Frittata

Aggregate Time to Prepare: **45 Minutes**

Yield: **4 Servings**

Ingredients:

- ¼ cup grated Cheddar Cheese
- ¼ tsp Salt
- ½ cup ground Sausage, cooked
- 1 ½ cups Water
- 1 tbsp. Butter
- 2 tbsp. Sour Cream
- 4 Eggs
- Pinch of Pepper

How to Cook:

1. Pour the water into the Instant Pot and put the rack into the Instant Pot.
2. Coat a baking dish that can fit inside the Instant Pot with some cooking spray.
3. Mix together the eggs and sour cream, in a container.
4. Stir in the rest of the ingredients.
5. Pour the mixture into the readied baking dish.
6. Put the dish on the rack and shut and secure the lid.
7. Cook on LOW pressure for 17 minutes.
8. Release the pressure using the quick release method.
9. Your dish is ready! Have fun!

Nutritional Info: (Calories 282 | Total Fats 12g | Net Carbs: 1g | Protein 24g | Fiber: 0g)

Sausage and Eggs Casserole

Aggregate Time to Prepare: 25 Minutes

Yield: 6 Servings

Ingredients:

- ¼ tsp Ground Black Pepper
- ½ tsp Salt
- ¾ cup Whipping Cream
- 1 cup Cheddar Cheese (grated)
- 1 medium head Broccoli (chopped)
- 1 tbsp. Olive Oil
- 10 eggs
- 12 oz. Jones Dairy Farm Little Pork Sausages (cooked and chop into inch slices)
- 2 cloves Garlic (minced)

How to Cook:

1. Slightly coat the inside of the Instant Pot with olive oil.
2. Layer half of the broccoli, then half of the sausages and half of the cheese. Repeat in the same manner with the rest of ingredients.
3. Mix thoroughly in a container eggs and salt. Put in the cream, garlic and pepper, and whisk thoroughly to mix.
4. Pour the eggs mixture over the ingredients in the Instant Pot.
5. Shut and secure the lid, and manually turn the timer and cook for 15 minutes at high pressure.
6. Release the pressure using the "quick release" method and serve warm.

Nutritional Info: (Calories: 484 | Total Fats: 38.9g | Net Carbs: 4.2g | Proteins: 26.1g | Fibers: 1.2g)

Scotch Eggs

Aggregate Time to Prepare: 15 Minutes

Yield: 2 Servings

Ingredients:

- ½ tbsp. Olive Oil
- 1 Egg, beaten
- 1 tbsp. Coconut Oil
- 2 Hardboiled Eggs
- 2 tbsp. Coconut Flour
- 2 tbsp. grated Parmesan Cheese
- 4 Bacon Slices

How to Cook:

1. Remove the shell of your hardboiled eggs.
2. In a shallow container, mix the flour, and parmesan cheese.
3. Cover the eggs in one bacon cut horizontally, and in one cut vertically.
4. Immerse in the beaten egg first and then cover with flour/parmesan mixture.
5. Melt the coconut oil along with the olive oil in your Instant Pot using the "Sauté" mode.
6. Put in the eggs and cook until golden and crunchy.
7. Your dish is ready! Have fun!

Nutritional Info: (Calories 477| Total Fats 42g | Net Carbs: 2.95g | Protein 19g |Fiber: 3g)

Scrambled Eggs with Cranberries

Aggregate Time to Prepare: **15 Minutes**

Yield: 2 Servings

Ingredients:

- 1 tbsp milk
- 2 tbsp butter
- large eggs, beaten

Spices:

- ¼ tsp salt
- ¼ tsp stevia powder
- ½ tsp cranberry extract, sugar-free
- 2 tbsp cranberries

How to Cook:

1. In a medium-sized container, whisk together eggs, stevia, cranberry extract, salt, and milk.
2. Turn on your Instant Pot and put in butter to the stainless steel insert. Switch your Instant Pot to "Sauté' mode and allow it to melt. Pour the egg mixture and tenderly pull the eggs across the pot with a wooden spatula. Don't stir continuously.
3. Cook for approximately 2 minutes or until thickened ad no visible egg liquid remains.
4. When finished, turn off the pot by pressing the "Cancel" button and move the mixture to a serving

plate. Spread on top fresh cranberries and optionally garnish with some mint.
5. Serve warm.

Nutritional Info:(Calories 252| Total Fats 21.6g | Net Carbs: 1.5g | Protein 13g |Fiber: 0.3g)

Scrambled Eggs with Ground Beef

Aggregate Time to Prepare: 25 Minutes

Yield: 2 Servings

Ingredients:

For eggs:

- ¼ cup fresh goat's cheese
- ¼ cup milk
- 1 onion, thinly sliced
- 3 eggs
- 7 oz ground beef

Spices:

- ¼ tsp rosemary powder
- ½ tsp sea salt
- 1 tbsp tomato paste
- 1 tsp garlic powder
- 2 tbsp olive oil

How to Cook:

1. Turn on your Instant Pot and coat the stainless steel insert with olive oil. Switch your Instant Pot to "Sauté' mode and put in onions. Stir-fry until translucent. After that, put in beef and tomato paste. Carry on cooking for 5 additional minutes, stirring intermittently.
2. In the mean time, whisk together eggs, milk, goat's cheese, rosemary powder, garlic powder, and salt. Pour the mixture into the pot and stir gradually with a wooden spatula. Cook until somewhat underdone.
3. Turn off the heat and serve.

Nutritional Info: (Calories 483| Total Fats 31g | Net Carbs: 6.3g | Protein 43.1g |Fiber: 1.2g)

Scrambled Eggs with Tomato and Green Onions

Aggregate Time to Prepare: 35 Minutes

Yield: 2 Servings

Ingredients:

For eggs:

- ¼ cup milk
- ½ cup cottage cheese
- ½ tomato, thinly sliced
- 1 cup button mushrooms, sliced
- 2 spring onions, chopped
- 3 large eggs

Spices:

- 2 tbsp olive oil
- ½ tsp salt

How to Cook:

1. Oil-coat the bottom of your instant pot and switch your Instant Pot to "Steam' mode. Put in onions and cook for 3 minutes.

2. After that put in tomatoes and mushrooms. Carry on cooking until all the liquid evaporates, for 5-6 minutes.
3. In the mean time, whisk the eggs, cottage cheese, and milk. Sprinkle with salt and optionally some freshly ground black pepper.
4. Pour the mixture into the pot and stir thoroughly. Cook for 2 minutes.
5. Serve warm.

Nutritional Info: (Calories 308| Total Fats 23.3g | Net Carbs: 6.1g | Protein 19.7g |Fiber: 0.9g)

Simple Hardboiled Eggs

Aggregate Time to Prepare: **10 Minutes**

Yield: **6 Servings**

Ingredients:

- 1 cup of Water
- 12 Eggs

How to Cook:

1. Pour the water into the Instant Pot.
2. Put the stainless steaming basket inside.
3. Put the eggs in the basket.
4. Shut and secure the lid and cook on HIGH for 7 minutes.
5. Release the pressure using the quick release method.
6. Serve as favoured and have fun!

Nutritional Info: (Calories 140| Total Fats 9g | Net Carbs: 1.8g | Protein 12g |Fiber: 0g)

Simple Spicy Scrambled Eggs

Aggregate Time to Prepare: **15 Minutes**

Yield: **4 Servings**

Ingredients:

- ¼ cup chopped Fresh Parsley
- ¼ tsp Salt
- ½ cup Milk
- ½ tsp dried Basil
- ½ tsp dried Thyme
- 1 tbsp. chopped Cilantro
- 1 tsp Paprika
- 7 Eggs
- 4 ounces Bacon, chopped

How to Cook:

1. Whisk the eggs with the milk, dried herbs, and spices.
2. Switch your Instant Pot to "Sauté" mode and cook the bacon until crunchy.
3. Pour the egg mixture over.
4. Cook for approximately 5 minutes stirring regularly.
5. Stir in the chopped herbs and cook for an additional 5 minutes.
6. Your dish is ready! Have fun!

Nutritional Info: (Calories 290 | Total Fats 23.4g | Net Carbs: 4.5g | Protein 16g | Fiber: 1g)

Slow-Cooked Good-Morning Casserole

Aggregate Time to Prepare: 6 hours and 15 Minutes

Yield: 8 Servings

Ingredients:

- ¼ cup chopped Cilantro
- ¼ tsp Pepper
- ½ tsp Salt
- 1 ½ cups shredded Cheese
- 1 Bell Pepper, chopped
- 1 cup chopped Green Onions
- 1 cup Milk
- 12 Eggs
- 24 ounces Breakfast Sausage
- 4 ounces canned Green Chilies, diced

How to Cook:

1. Line the Instant Pot with some cooking spray and switch it to "sauté" mode and preheat it.
2. Put in onions and pepper and cook for 3 minutes.
3. Put in breakfast and cook for a few minutes, until browned.
4. Whisk the eggs along with the milk, salt, and pepper and pour the mixture over the sausage.
5. Stir in the chilies and cilantro and drizzle the cheese on top.
6. Switch your instant Pot to "Slow Cook" mode and cook for 6 hours.
7. Your dish is ready! Have fun!

Nutritional Info: (Calories 439| Total Fats 31g | Net Carbs: 10.1g | Protein 31g |Fiber: 2.7g)

Smoked Salmon Baked Eggs

Aggregate Time to Prepare: 10 Minutes

Yield: 4 Servings

Ingredients:

- 1 cup of Water
- 1 tbsp. Olive Oil
- 1 tsp chopped Chives
- 4 slices of Smoked Salmon
- 4 Eggs

How to Cook:

1. Pour the water into your Instant Pot and put the trivet into the Instant Pot.
2. Oil-coat 4 ramekins with the olive oil.
3. Put a cut of salmon at the bottom of each ramekin.
4. Crack an egg on top and put in a teaspoon of cream over.
5. Cover the ramekins in foil and arrange them on the rack.
6. Shut and secure the lid and cook for 5 minutes on HIGH.
7. Serve drizzled! with chopped chives.
8. Have fun!

Nutritional Info: (Calories 240 | Total Fats 17g | Net Carbs: 2g | Protein 19g |Fiber: 0g)

Spicy Mushroom Chicken with Eggs

Aggregate Time to Prepare: 40 Minutes

Yield: 2 Servings

Ingredients:

- 1 cup button mushrooms, sliced
- 2 cups chicken stock
- 2 garlic cloves, crushed
- 2 tbsp almond flour
- 3 eggs
- 3 tbsp olive oil
- 7 oz boneless and skinless chicken breast, chop into bite-size pieces

Spices:

- ¼ tsp black pepper
- 1 tsp cayenne pepper
- 1 tsp salt

How to Cook:

1. Thoroughly wash the meat under cold running water and pat dry with a kitchen paper. Cut into bite-sized pieces and save for later.
2. Turn on your Instant Pot and coat the inner pot with some oil. Put in garlic and meat. Sprinkle with salt and cook for 3 minutes.
3. After that put in mushrooms and continue to cook for 5 minutes.
4. Pour in the chicken stock and stir thoroughly. Shut and secure the lid and set the steam release handle to the "Sealing" position. Switch your Instant Pot to

"Manual" mode and turn the timer to 9 minutes on high pressure.

5. When finished, depressurize using the quick release method and open the lid. Switch your Instant Pot to "Sauté' mode and cook until half of the liquid evaporates.
6. After that mix in the almond flour and drizzle with cayenne pepper and black pepper. Cook for 5 minutes, stirring continuously.
7. Lastly, crack the eggs and cook until completely set. Serve instantly.

Nutritional Info:(Calories 456g | Total Fats 32.1g | Net Carbs: 3.2g | Protein 39.4g |Fiber: 0.6g)

Spinach Bacon Frittata

Aggregate Time to Prepare: **10 Minutes**

Yield: **5 Servings**

Ingredients:

- 1 oz ricotta cheese
- 2 oz bacon, chop into bite-sized pieces
- 2 tbsp extra virgin olive oil
- 3 oz cottage cheese, crumbled
- 6 large eggs, beaten
- 6 oz fresh spinach, thinly sliced

Spices:

- ½ tsp garlic powder
- ½ tsp onion powder
- 1 tsp black pepper, ground
- 1 tsp salt

How to Cook:

1. Thoroughly wash the spinach under cold running water. Drain thoroughly and thinly slice. Save for later.
2. In a large mixing container, mix eggs, garlic powder, onion powder, salt, and pepper. With a whisking attachment, beat until foamy. Put in cottage cheese and ricotta cheese and beat again until mixed. After that, mix in the spinach and bacon. Save for later.
3. Turn on the Instant Pot and coat the stainless steel insert with olive oil. Switch your Instant Pot to SAUTÉ mode and pour in the previously readied mixture. Cook for 4-5 minutes, or until eggs are set.
4. Turn off your Instant pot and move the frittata to serving plate. Drizzle with some thinly sliced chives and serve instantly.

Nutritional Info: (Calories 286 | Total Fats 21.5g | Net Carbs: 3.2g | Protein 19.8g |Fiber: 1.1g)

Spinach Omelet

Aggregate Time to Prepare: **20 Minutes**

Yield: **1 Serving**

Ingredients:

For omelet:

- 1 cup spinach, chopped
- 1 cup Swiss chard, chopped
- 2 tbsp olive oil
- 3 eggs

Spices:

- ¼ tsp red pepper flakes
- ½ tsp sea salt
- 1 tsp garlic powder

How to Cook:

1. Thoroughly wash the greens under cold running water and drain in a large colander. Save for later.
2. Turn on your Instant Pot and coat the stainless steel insert with two tablespoons of olive oil. Switch your Instant Pot to "Sauté' mode and put in greens.
3. Stir-fry for 5 minutes and take out of the pot. Save for later.
4. Mix together eggs, garlic powder, salt, and red pepper flakes. Pour the mixture into the stainless steel insert. Spread the eggs uniformly with a wooden spatula and cook for 2-3 minutes.
5. Using a kitchen spatula, ease around the edges and slide to a serving plate. Put in greens and fold over in half.
6. If you want, you can also drizzle with some more sea salt or dried thyme.

Nutritional Info: (Calories 443| Total Fats 41.3g | Net Carbs: 2.2g | Protein 18.1g |Fiber: 1.3g)

Steamed Eggs with Scallions

Aggregate Time to Prepare: 10 Minutes

Yield: 1 Serving

Ingredients:

- ¼ cup scallions, thinly sliced
- 2 eggs
- 3 tbsp butter

Spices:

- ¼ tsp black pepper
- ¼ tsp garlic powder
- ½ tsp sea salt

How to Cook:

1. Turn on your Instant Pot and pour in 1 cup of water. Set the steam basket in the inner pot and save for later.
2. In a small, heat-proof container, crack eggs and season liberally with salt, pepper, and garlic powder. Drizzle with chopped scallions and place in the steam basket.
3. Shut and secure the lid and set the steam release handle to the "Sealing" position. Switch your Instant Pot to "Manual" mode and turn the timer to 5 minutes.
4. When you hear the end signal, depressurize using the quick release method and open the lid.
5. Using oven mitts remove the container and chill for some time before serving.

Nutritional Info: (Calories 439| Total Fats 43.4g | Net Carbs: 1.9g | Protein 11.9g |Fiber: 0.7g)

Steamed Eggs with Scallions

Aggregate Time to Prepare: **15 Minutes**

Yield: 1 Serving

Ingredients:

- ½ cup cold water
- 1 tbsp sesame seeds
- 2 large eggs
- 2 tbsp scallions, chopped

Spices:

- ½ tsp garlic powder
- ½ tsp white pepper, freshly ground
- 1 tsp sea salt

How to Cook:

1. Pour 1 cup of water in your Instant pot and set the steamer insert.
2. In a small container, mix together eggs and water. Move to a small sieve and drain the surplus liquid into an oven-safe container. Stir in chopped scallions and season with salt, pepper, and garlic powder. Drizzle the mixture with some sesame seeds and mix thoroughly.
3. Put the container on the steamer insert and securely shut and secure the lid. Set the steam release handle to the SEALING position. Press the MANUAL button and set the timer to 5 minutes on HIGH pressure.
4. When you hear the end signal, move the steam valve to the VENTING position and tenderly open the lid.
5. Using oven mitts remove the container from the Instant Pot and serve instantly.

Nutritional Info:(Calories 198 | Total Fats 14.4g | Net Carbs: 2.4g | Protein 14.4g |Fiber: 1.4g)

Sunrise Almond and Coconut Cake

Aggregate Time to Prepare: **50 Minutes**

Yield: **8 Servings**

Ingredients:

- ¼ cup Butter, melted
- ½ cup Heavy Cream
- ½ cup shredded Coconut
- 1 cup Almond Flour
- 1 tsp Apple Pie Spice
- 1 tsp Baking Powder
- 1/3 cup Truvia
- 2 cups Water
- 2 Eggs
- Pinch of Sea Salt

How to Cook:

1. Mix the dry ingredients, including the coconut, in one container.
2. Mix together the wet ones in a different container.
3. Fold the two mixtures tenderly.
4. Oil-coat a 6-inch round pan and pour the batter into it and coat using a foil.
5. Pour the water into your Instant Pot and put the rack into the Instant Pot.
6. Put the cake on the rack and shut and secure the lid.
7. Switch the Instant Pot to "High" and cook for 40 minutes.
8. Depressurize for 5 minutes.
9. Your dish is ready! Have fun!

Nutritional Info: (Calories 236 | Total Fats 23g | Net Carbs: 3g | Protein 5g | Fiber: 2g)

Sweet Chia Pudding

Aggregate Time to Prepare: **20 Minutes**

Yield: 3 Servings

Ingredients:

- ½ cup chia seeds
- ½ cup milk
- ½ tsp agar powder
- 1 cup raspberries
- 1 cup water
- 1 tsp vanilla extract
- 2 tbsp swerve

Spices:

- ½ tsp cinnamon powder
- ¼ tsp salt

How to Cook:

1. Turn on your Instant Pot and Switch your Instant Pot to "'Sauté" mode. Put chia in the inner pot and put in swerve, vanilla extract, cinnamon powder, and salt. Pour in one cup of water and stir thoroughly. Cook for 3-4 minutes.
2. After that put in raspberries and continue to cook for 5 minutes.
3. Lastly, pour in the milk and put in agar powder. Cook for 5 minutes, stirring continuously.
4. Turn off the Instant Pot by pressing the "Cancel" button. Move the pudding to serving containers and chill thoroughly before serving.

Nutritional Info: (Calories 123g | Total Fats 7.8g | Net Carbs: 5.7g | Protein 5.8g | Fiber: 9.4g)

Thyme Prosciutto Eggs

Aggregate Time to Prepare: 15 Minutes

Yield: 4 Servings

Ingredients:

- ¼ tsp Pepper
- ¼ tsp Salt
- 1 ½ cups Water
- 3 tbsp. Heavy Cream
- 4 Hardboiled Eggs
- 4 Prosciutto Slices
- 4 Kale Leaves

How to Cook:

1. Remove the shell of the eggs and cover them in kale.
2. Cover them in prosciutto and drizzle with salt and pepper.
3. Pour the water into your Instant Pot and put the trivet into the Instant Pot.
4. Put the eggs inside and shut and secure the lid.
5. Switch the Instant Pot to "Manual" mode and cook for 5 minutes.
6. Your dish is ready! Have fun!

Nutritional Info: (Calories 250 | Total Fats 21g | Net Carbs: 3.2g | Protein 15g | Fiber: 2g)

Veggie Egg Cups

Aggregate Time to Prepare: **15 Minutes**

Yield: **4 Servings**

Ingredients:

- ¼ cup Half and Half
- ½ shredded Cheddar Cheese
- 1 cup diced Vegies (onions, mushrooms, and tomatoes)
- 2 tbsp. chopped Cilantro
- 4 Eggs
- Salt and Pepper, to taste

How to Cook:

1. Whisk the eggs together with the half and half and some salt and pepper.
2. Stir in the rest of the ingredients.
3. Pour some water into your Instant Pot (1-2 cups) and put the trivet into the Instant Pot.
4. Separate the egg mixture among 4 small jars.
5. Seal and place on the rack.
6. Shut and secure the lid and cook on HIGH for 5 minutes.
7. Depressurize quickly.
8. Your dish is ready! Have fun!

Nutritional Info: (Calories 115 | Total Fats 9g | Net Carbs: 2g | Protein 9g | Fiber: 0.6g)

Zucchini Walnut Bread

Aggregate Time to Prepare: **40 Minutes**

Yield: **16 Servings**

Ingredients:

- ¼ tsp Nutmeg
- ½ cup chopped Walnuts
- ½ cup Olive Oil
- ½ tsp Cinnamon
- 1 ½ cups Water
- 1 ½ tsp Baking Powder
- 1 cup grated Zucchini
- 1 tsp Vanilla Extract
- 2 ½ cups Almond Flour
- 3 Eggs
- Pinch of Ginger Powder
- Pinch of Sea Salt

How to Cook:

1. Pour the water into the Instant Pot and put the rack into the Instant Pot.
2. Mix together the wet ingredients in one container.
3. Mix the dry ingredients in another container.
4. Mix the dry and wet mixture together.
5. Stir in the zucchini.
6. Oil-coat a loaf pan and pour the batter inside.
7. Spread on top chopped walnuts.
8. Put the loaf pan on the rack and shut and secure the lid of the Instant Pot.
9. Cook for 40 minutes on MANUAL.
10. Release the pressure using the quick release method.
11. Allow it to cool before serving.

12. Have fun!

Nutritional Info: (Calories 200| Total Fats 19g | Net Carbs: 2.6g | Protein 6g |Fiber: 2.3g)

Endnote

Well, this is all that there is to this book. If you are looking for more, make sure you search for more books in the series "Instant Keto" by "David Maxwell". Also, don't forget to leave a review on amazon so I can make the necessary improvements in this book, and the books to come.

I hope this book helps you take a step towards a healthier you!

Happy cooking!

Made in the USA
Columbia, SC
09 May 2020